The Ailsa Mellon Bruce Studies
in American Art

VOLUME TWO

Copley in England

John Singleton Copley

In England 1774-1815

Jules David Prown

Published for the
NATIONAL GALLERY OF ART · WASHINGTON

1966

HARVARD UNIVERSITY PRESS · CAMBRIDGE · MASSACHUSETTS

Distributed in Great Britain by Oxford University Press, London

Typographer ~ Burton L. Stratton

Library of Congress Catalog Card Number 66–13183

Printed in the United States of America at the Harvard University Printing Office
and the Meriden Gravure Company. Binding by the Stanhope Bindery.

Contents

v

Illustrations

ILLUSTRATIONS

ILLUSTRATIONS

Copley in England

X Interlude: England and the Continent

1774-1775 JOHN SINGLETON COPLEY ARRIVED IN ENGLAND EARLY IN JULY 1774, after an easy passage of twenty-nine days. Going directly to London he located his brother-in-law, Jonathan Clarke, and as soon as possible got in touch with his fellow American artist and long-time correspondent, Benjamin West. With characteristic warmth, West issued a blanket invitation to Copley to dine with him "when not otherwise engaged," and took him to see the collection of pictures at the queen's palace (Kensington). He quickly introduced his young compatriot to Sir Joshua Reynolds, who showed Copley many of his portraits and his "fine collection of Other Masters," and later took him to see the ceiling at Whitehall. Copley visited the Royal Academy, of course, admiring the facade of the building, "as designed by Inogo Jones," as well as the collection housed within.[1]

Now for the first time Copley could see paintings by the old and modern masters, which he had been able to visualize before only on the basis of books and prints. The grand preconceptions that he had formed from the inflated statements in the books on art theory were now whittled down by actuality. In one sense this was reassuring, since "I find the practice of Painting or rather the means by which the composition is attained easier than I thought it had been. the sketches are made from the life, and not only from figures singly, but often from groups. This you remember was [what I] have often talked of, and by this a great difficulty is removed that lay on my mind." Yet it was disappointing, too, since the theory books had led him to expect much more than he found. Later he tried to prepare Henry Pelham for this disillusionment by advising him that, in fact, "the works of the great Masters are but Pictures, and when a man can go but a very little beyond his cotemporarys he becomes a great Man. the differance be-

---

[1] Guernsey Jones, ed., *Letters and Papers of John Singleton Copley and Henry Pelham*, Vol. LXXI of The Massachusetts Historical Society Collections (Boston, 1914), pp. 225–27, Copley to Pelham, July 11, 1774, and p. 239, Copley to Pelham, Aug. 17, 1774; Martha Babcock Amory, *The Domestic and Artistic Life of John Singleton Copley, R.A.* (Boston, 1882), p. 28, letter from Copley to Mrs. Copley, July 21, 1774.

tween Raphael, Titiano, Angelo and the common run of moderately good Artists, is not so great as one would Imagin from the Praises bestow'd on those Great men. but they are the first Artists and they merit the Most elaborate Praises from the World." [2]

In London Copley naturally associated with the Americans who were there. One day he dined with Thomas Hutchinson, the recent governor of Massachusetts, and a party of twelve Bostonians, on "Choice Salt Fish." With Hutchinson and Jonathan Clarke, Copley went in a post chaise to Greenwich Hospital, and also visited the Park, Vauxhall, and the queen's yacht. Busy with seeing and absorbing, he resolved not to accept any painting commissions. [3]

Since Copley's half brother, Henry Pelham, was a neophyte painter and still in Boston, Copley was assiduous in sending him a considerable amount of technical information, reflecting his own thinking and learning as he traveled in England, France, and Italy. [4] From London Copley urged Pelham to continue to practice. He suggested ways to handle chiaroscuro and color, citing as examples available to Pelham in Boston Smibert's copy of Van Dyck's *Cardinal Bentivoglio* and "Mrs. Sidley's Picture at Capt. Phillips's," the face of which Copley now believed to be by Van Dyck. He spelled out for Pelham the necessity of subordinating the peripheral parts of a picture to the center, referring to a *Diana* owned by Pelham as a good instance of what he meant. He particularly recommended Sir Joshua Reynolds' lectures (*Discourses*), and urged industry in study and practice, undoubtedly reflecting his own conviction when he affirmed, "you must be conspecuous in the Croud if you would be happy and great." [5]

After a month and a half in London, Copley set off for Rome on August 26, 1774, in the company of George Carter, a forty-five-year-old English artist also heading for Italy. They went first to Paris and immediately began to sightsee — the church of St. Roch, the Place des Victoires, and the Coliseum. "I have seen the Church of St. Sulpice," he reported to Henry Pelham. "It is rather grand from its quantity than the Eliganc[e] of proportion." Copley was generally interested in architecture, but his comments were brief and superficial. In general he preferred the new buildings in Paris to the old, having been told that "there is a Capital Architect in this place." He did specifically observe that Notre Dame was "a very Beautiful pile of Gothick architecture," that the "Colledge for Surgions" had a "fine Corinthian Portico Wonderfully beautifull" and an interesting

---

[2] *Copley-Pelham Letters*, p. 226, Copley to Pelham, July 15, 1774, and p. 340, June 25, 1775.

[3] *Ibid.*, pp. 236–37, Copley to Pelham, Aug. 5, 1774; "Diary of Elisha Hutchinson, 1744–1788," British Museum, Egerton Ms. 2669, fol. 116, July 20, 1774; Amory, p. 28. Governor Hutchinson had arrived in England to report to the government on June 29, 1774. Copley had been one of the signers in Boston on May 30, 1774, of a testimonial of satisfaction on his administration. George Atkinson Ward, *Journal and Letters of the Late Samuel Curwen* (New York and Boston, 1842), pp. 423ff. Copley had arrived in London with a commission

from "Mr. [probably Gov. John or Mark Hunking] Wentworth" to paint portraits of the king and queen. If permission were granted, he planned to do the heads and finish the pictures after his return from Italy. But nothing took place before he left. *Copley-Pelham Letters*, pp. 236, 253; Amory, p. 37.

[4] This "shop talk" is only summarized here. The interested reader is referred to the letters, printed in their entirety in the *Copley-Pelham Letters*, especially pp. 240–41, 244–52, 295–307, 333–42.

[5] *Copley-Pelham Letters*, pp. 240–41, Aug. 17, 1774.

bas-relief in the pediment, and that the Hospital of the Invalids was "a Most magnificent peace of Architector." [6]

At the Palais Royale Copley admired paintings by Raphael, Correggio, Titian, Veronese, and Guido Reni, among others, but decided to defer writing to Pelham about these artists until he would have a chance to examine their work in Italy. However, he did pass along some general observations and suggestions. Feeling himself handicapped by his lack of French, he urged Pelham to study languages. He had just been to the Opera (*Orpheus in the Underworld*) and could not understand the words, though "the Musick Charmed me." Again he entreated Pelham to be industrious, feeling that he himself was now reaping the fruits of his own application. "I write under a Kind of impu[l]se, and would perswade you from inactivity as I would a near friend from plunging into certain destruction." He urged Pelham to practice, to "Draw Landscapes, Dogs, Cats, Cows, horses, in short I would have you keep in your Pocket a book and Porto Crayon — as I now do — and where ever you see a butifull form Sketch it in your Book." In particular he recommended the study of Raphael, especially the cartoons.

Commenting on Poussin's *Seven Sacraments* at the Palais Royale, he wrote, "the prints you have seen in Mr. [Thomas] Palmer's Vollumn of Italian Masters. they are very Dark, much more so than his Scipeo at Smibert's, and about the same size of that." He noted that, although these were thought to be Poussin's best pictures, he would have preferred them if they were more brilliantly colored. Poussin's outlines were sharp, not blended, he noted, and he praised the expression of the figures, which revealed what went on within their souls. He referred to some bister drawings by Albonius that Pelham had, which demonstrated how far one could go in drawing a figure from the imagination. Beyond that point, a live model should be used for the hands, feet, and head, and the drapery should be worked out on the "Layman."

At Notre Dame Copley was impressed by the 1723 marble *Pieta* group by Coustoux the elder. He observed that the cross behind the figures supports the drapery, aiding the composition by gently dissipating the mass, just as in a picture the eye should be led off both by light and by color. Although he had seen interesting paintings by Coypel and Cheron, it would be pointless, he thought, to list everything; nor would he bother to discuss LeBrun until he had seen his major works at Versailles, where he planned to stop on his return from Italy.

Copley twice visited the Luxembourg Gallery "intirely Painted by Rubens," and, aware that Pelham knew the design from prints, he described Rubens' coloristic effects. Desperately trying to cite examples familiar to Pelham, he drew analogies with a "head of Vandyck at Mrs. Hancocks," a "Pan and Sirinks at Mr. Chardon's," a nymph in Pel-

[6] *Ibid.*, p. 244, Sept. 2, 1774, pp. 253–54, Copley to his mother, Mary Pelham, Sept. 8, 1774; and pp. 247–52, Copley to Pelham, Sept. 2 and 7, 1774. Copley's interest in architecture appears to have been recent, dating from his instructions to Henry Pelham in 1771 in regard to the remodeling of Copley's great house on Beacon Hill (*ibid.*, pp. 122–77). The following year he made plans and elevations for the Brattle Square Church, "with the Steple compleat . . . which was much admired for its Elegance and Grandure" (*ibid.*, pp. 185–87).

ham's *Diana*, and Smibert's copy of Van Dyck's *Cardinal Bentivoglio*. Copley counseled Pelham to try to paint a copy of one of the Rubens prints, following his written description of the coloring, secure in Carter's assurance that "this Account I have given you is so just that it is equal to your seeing the Pictures." [7]

Leaving Paris, the two artists traveled through Lyons and Marseilles. Copley's letters home are full of general descriptions that reflect his enjoyment of the passing scene. Unfortunately the friendly relations between Copley and Carter deteriorated. They bickered about such petty issues as the relative softness of a huckaback towel versus a Barcelona silk towel, the relative heat-yielding power of American and European firewood, the merits of an American wood fire versus a European coal fire (Copley for the huckaback and all things American), and once they stood in a rain shower while debating whether to walk or ride. Although rather a jaundiced reporter, Carter gives us the only description we have of Copley the traveler:

> He had on one of those white French bonnets which, turned on one side, admit of being pulled over the ears: under this was a yellow and red silk handkerchief, with a large Catherine wheel flambeaued upon it, such as may be seen upon the necks of those delicate ladies who cry Malton oysters: this flowed half way down his back. He wore a red-brown, or rather cinnamon, great coat, with a friar's cape, and worsted binding of a yellowish white; it hung near his heels, out of which peeped his boots: under his arm he carried the sword which he bought in Paris, and a hickory stick with an ivory head. Joined to this dress, he was very thin, pale, a little pock-marked, prominent eyebrows, small eyes, which, after fatigue, seemed a day's march in his head.

Copley's opinion of Carter was no more favorable, and considerably more succinct: "He was a sort of snail which crawled over a man in his sleep, and left its slime and no more." [8]

From Marseilles, Copley and Carter went to Toulon and Antibes, and from there in a small coastal boat to Genoa, a town that according to Copley made Boston look like "a collection of wren boxes." He visited the churches to see the paintings and sculpture, and toured the art gallery of the Marquis Maria Francesco Balbi. Seeing the works of the masters made his painting hand itch: "I am impatient to get to work," he wrote his wife, "and to try if my hand and my head cannot do something like what others have done, by which they have astonished the world and immortalized themselves, and for which they will be admired as long as this earth shall continue." [9]

From Genoa the two painters went to Leghorn, Pisa, and Florence, where Copley saw the Grand Duke's gallery and the great collection in the palace, including, he told Sukey, the "sweet picture of the Virgin with Jesus, by Raphael . . . the one that hung over our chimney." [10] He also saw the Medici Venus.

[7] *Ibid.*, pp. 244–52, Sept. 2 and 7, 1774.
[8] Allan Cunningham, *The Lives of the Most Eminent British Painters and Sculptors*, IV (New York, 1834), 143–44.
[9] Amory, pp. 34–36, Oct. 8, 1774.
[10] *Ibid.*, p. 38, Oct. 26, 1774.

Arriving in Rome, Copley found a large colony of English painters, centering on the English Coffee House.[11] Although Copley spent some time with them there, little is known about whatever friends he may have had in this group. Copley apparently knew most of the English artists in Rome, but he seems to have been set apart from them by a certain lack of urbanity and by his seriousness of purpose. It had taken years for him to realize his dream of a visit to Italy to study the old masters, and it had required a long journey and the abandonment of his family at a perilous time to achieve it. It is difficult to imagine Copley's passing long leisurely hours at the English Coffee House, when he felt that his time in Italy was so precious. Obviously Copley was not too close with his erstwhile traveling companion, Carter, and this probably curtailed friendships with the artists who were friendly with Carter.[12] Furthermore, some of the English artists in Rome, such as Allan Ramsay and Henry Tresham, were politically anti-American, and this may have further limited his circle of friends.[13]

The English-speaking artists in Rome were apparently divided into two groups, those patronized by Thomas Jenkins and those patronized by James Byers. Jenkins' group was larger, with Byers' restricted to Scottish artists and a few others.[14] When he arrived in Rome, Copley carried letters of introduction from Thomas Palmer of Boston and Dr. John Morgan of Philadelphia to James Byers. Morgan, along with his friend Samuel Powel, had in 1760 pursued a course of study with Byers on the artistic monuments of Rome while on a grand tour before undertaking medical studies in Edinburgh. Copley also carried a letter from Morgan to another prominent Scot in the Roman art world, L'Abbé Grant. Copley's most intimate artist friend in Rome seems to have been another Scot, Gavin Hamilton, who chose rooms for him opposite his own house and was a frequent source of advice and encouragement, as well as an artistic influence.[15] The links between provincial Britons in the eighteenth century — the Scots, the Irish, and the Americans — were manifold, and the significance of this has not yet been adequately measured. Certainly this bond was a major factor in inducing Copley, son and stepson of Irish immigrants and a provincial American, whose art received early nourishment from the Scot John Smibert, to gravitate naturally into Byers' circle.

Once settled in Rome, Copley visited the important sights — the Vatican, St. Peter's, the Capitol, the Coliseum, and the other Roman ruins. He saw the Farnese Palace and

[11] On leaving London, Copley wrote home that there were about fifty English artists in Rome (Amory, p. 31). The artist Thomas Jones, who came to Rome in November 1776, described the English Coffee House, where he found a large group of artists, as "a filthy vaulted room, the walls of which were painted with Sphinxes, Obelisks and Pyramids, from capricious designs of Piranesi," in which they could "amuse ourselves for an hour or two over a cup of Coffee or glass of Punch." "Memoirs of Thomas Jones," *Walpole Society*, XXXII, 1946–48 (London, 1951), 54.

[12] These include George Romney, who has stylis-

tic affinities with Copley though the two were apparently quite remote personally. Sir Herbert Maxwell, *George Romney* (London and New York, 1902), p. 57.

[13] Alastair Smart, *The Life and Art of Allan Ramsay* (London, 1952), pp. 158ff; Royal Academy, London, "Original Correspondence of Ozias Humphry, R.A.," II, 38, Henry Tresham, Rome, to Ozias Humphry, Florence, n.d. (bound in with late 1775).

[14] "Jones Memoirs," p. 56.

[15] Amory, p. 41, Copley to his wife, Dec. 4, 1774.

the paintings by Annibale Carracci, but was delayed in getting to see the Sistine Chapel because a conclave was in session to choose a pope. Soon he settled into a routine, rising at eight and going to the French Academy or the Capitol to study reliefs and antique statuary. Although most of the studies Copley made in Rome were destroyed in the Boston fire of November 1872,[16] figs. 335 and 336 are surviving examples of the type of work he was doing. By December it began to get too cold to study in the galleries, and Copley contemplated painting an Ascension as a winter project at home. He had made a preliminary drawing, "which has the approbation of all who have seen it. I am encouraged to paint it; Mr. Hamilton also assures me it will please, and advises the same." He now felt ready to try his hand at rivaling the master artists: "I know the extent of the arts, to what length they have been carried, and I feel more confidence in what I do myself than I did before I came." [17]

The Ascension (fig. 337) was Copley's first painting since leaving the American colonies, and it was his first original essay into history painting.[18] Fortunately Copley forwarded a long and full account of his creative procedure for *The Ascension* to Henry Pelham.[19] Copley in this account turns time and again to Raphael, and particularly mentions Raphael's *Transfiguration*, which a month earlier he had told his wife "has always been allowed to be the greatest picture in the world." [20] Copley's method, as he described it, was first to fix upon the idea and then to consider the ways in which figures would react to the central event. After this, his imagination was fired by looking at works of art (in this case by Raphael), reading, or conversing. He made a sketch of the general idea and the disposition of the figures, not only on the surface but in depth as Raphael did in *The School of Athens* with its "kind of ground plan." The individual figures were then refined and improved in pose, gesture, and expression. He found that, by having a good general concept of the grouping of the figures, he could move directly to the specific problems of masses of light and shadow, and thus further refine the placement and pose of the principals. Then he would work out the drapery, with the aid of a lay figure swathed with wet table cloths. After the outline of the figures and the drapery had been decided upon, he put the whole composition into a clean outline, the light and shade washed in with bister and the expression and detail of heads and hands carried forward by posing himself in front of a mirror. He had now arrived at the point at which he could square the drawing, transfer the design to canvas, and call in a model to sit for hands, heads, feet, and so on. A comparison of the finished picture and the drawing for the lower register of *The Ascension* (fig. 339), squared for transfer, reveals the way in

[16] *Ibid.*, p. 41n.
[17] *Ibid.*, pp. 40–41, Copley to his wife, Nov. 5, and Dec. 4, 1774.
[18] The juvenile works such as *Galatea, The Return of Neptune,* or *Mars, Venus and Vulcan* were not original compositions.
[19] *Copley-Pelham Letters*, pp. 295–301, Copley to Pelham, March 14, 1775.
[20] *Ibid.*, p. 39, Nov. 5, 1774. The Raphael

Transfiguration was then in San Pietro in Montorio (Maxwell, *Romney*, p. 53). Copley had a high opinion of this picture even before he saw it (*Copley-Pelham Letters*, p. 249). It is possible that Copley acquired at this time the Morghen engraving of the Raphael *Transfiguration* that was sold with his collection of prints after his death, but he may have obtained it later. See appendix, Copley Print Sale (140).

which Copley used a single model for heads, hands, and feet. Fig. 338 is a sketch on the back of a later drawing that also relates to the development of this picture. Copley noted that throughout the creative process he continued to study the works of Raphael in order to keep his imagination aglow. When necessary he made separate sketches of individual figures to alter their poses and fit them back into the composition, which, he said, also seemed to have been Raphael's method.

Copley was apparently quite pleased with *The Ascension*. Proudly he told Pelham that Gavin Hamilton said "he never saw a finer Composition in his life, and that he knows no one who can equil it; that it is a subject the most dificult I could have ingaged in, that there is no subject but I can compose with less Dificulty." But Copley did not think it worthwhile to paint the picture on a large scale at this time. Although Hamilton told him that it would establish his reputation (Piranesi had also praised the picture), he hesitated to lose time on a repeat performance during this period of learning. Moreover, he felt that at some point a church might commission a life-size version of *The Ascension* as a 24-by-18-foot altarpiece, and there would be little point in painting a second version now.

Copley also wanted sooner or later to follow the religious *Ascension* with another kind of history picture, "a Classick subject" such as the "Reconciliation of Achilles and Agamammon [*sic*]," to demonstrate a second string to his bow. The idea certainly reflects the influence of Gavin Hamilton who, only the year before, had painted *Priam Beseeching Achilles for the Body of Hector*.[21] All of this suggests that Copley did undertake his one classical subject, also *Priam Beseeching Achilles for the Body of Hector*, at this time. It is known today only through a 1799 engraving by A. Fogg (fig. 340) and one preliminary drawing (fig. 341). In style the composition is related to Copley's work of this general period, especially the slightly later *Nativity* (fig. 347), which was exhibited at the Royal Academy in 1777.

At the urging and in the company of Gulian Verplanck, whose portrait he had painted in New York less than four years earlier, Copley left Rome on a side trip to Naples in the middle of January 1775. He visited the collection of the King of Naples and particularly noted Raphael's *Holy Family* and paintings by Correggio, da Vinci, and Titian, including the latter's *Danae*, which "is somewhat damaged, but is a *very* fine work." He visited the catacombs and on January 27 went to Pompeii and Herculaneum, which he found remarkable and worthy of extensive comment in his next letter home.

In Naples Copley struck up a friendship with Mr. and Mrs. Ralph Izard of Charleston, South Carolina, and he accompanied them to Paestum. One scholar has suggested that Copley and the Izards may have been the first Americans to see a Greek temple. Certainly Copley now became particularly interested in classical antiquity. Upon re-

[21] Jean Locquin, "Le Retour à l'antique dans l'école anglaise et dans l'école française avant David," *La Renaissance de l'art français et des industries de luxe*, V (1922), 476.

turning to Rome with the Izards after a month in Naples, he applied himself to a large double portrait of *Mr. and Mrs. Ralph Izard* (fig. 342), posed amidst an assortment of classical material including a vase in the manner of the Niobid Painter, a cast of the Orestes and Electra marble group (which then was in the Villa Ludovisi), and the Coliseum in the background.[22] Copley was again quite pleased with his accomplishment. When he wrote to Pelham in mid-March, the double portrait was within two weeks of completion, and already Gavin Hamilton on seeing it had pronounced Copley "a perfect Master of Composition," apparently unperturbed by the low placement of the figures on the canvas (characteristic of Copley's work in the 1770's and 1780's) or by the clutter of accessories. Copley himself felt that the portrait would "support its merrit in any Cumpany whatever." [23]

In the same letter in which he gave Henry Pelham his account of the composition of *The Ascension*, written on March 14, 1775, Copley also fulfilled his promise to assess the master painters, having had an opportunity to see their work in Italy. As might be expected, he began his account with Raphael, "the greatest of The Modern Painters." Noting without a blush that Raphael painted his *Transfiguration* with the same careful attention that he himself had applied to his double portrait of *Mr. and Mrs. Thomas Mifflin*, he observed that Raphael painted all the parts from nature by means of precise outline and plain areas of color. To give some idea of Raphael's style, Copley directed Pelham's attention to the copy of *The Holy Family* at Smibert's, although stressing that it was very different from the actual painting, particularly in color. Turning to Titian, Copley assumed that on the basis of his reading Pelham probably had a misconception of Titian's style. Before he had seen any of Titian's paintings, Copley himself had thought his style to be precise, smooth, glossy, "something like Enamil wrought up with care," which turned out not to be the case at all. He referred Pelham to Benjamin West's copy of the *Danae*, in Philadelphia, for an approximate idea of the original.[24]

Before leaving Rome for his return journey to England, Copley wrote to a former Boston compatriot, John Greenwood, now a London art dealer and auctioneer, who since 1771 had gone on annual buying trips to Holland, Germany, and France and knew the continent well. Copley asked for advice on a return route and requested letters of introduction that would help him to see as much important art as possible. After ten months on the continent, Copley's visual appetite was still far from sated; as he noted

---

[22] Albert TenEyck Gardner and Stuart P. Feld, *American Paintings: A Catalogue of the Collection of the Metropolitan Museum of Art*, I (New York, 1965), 46; Amory, pp. 43–48; William B. Dinsmoor, "Early American Studies of Mediterranean Archaeology," *Proceedings of the American Philosophical Society*, LXXXVII (1943–44), 75; J. D. Beazley, *Attic Red-Figure Vase Painters* (Oxford, 1942), p. 424; Margaret R. Scherer, *Marvels of Ancient Rome* (New York and London, 1955), plate 27 and accompanying text. For further data on the classical accessories in this picture, see

Adolph Greifenhagen, "Griechische Vasen auf Bildnessen den Zeit Winckelmanns und des Klassizismus," *Nachrichten von den Gesellschaften des Wissenschaften zu Gottingen*, n.s. III, no. 7 (1939), 217ff, or *idem*, "Antiken als Beiwerk auf Porträts des 18 Jahrhunderts," *Pantheon*, XXVI (Dec. 1940), 292–93.

[23] *Copley-Pelham Letters*, p. 300. Copley sent this letter to England with Ralph Izard. So both Mr. and Mrs. Izard probably left Rome before the picture was finished (*ibid.*, pp. 294–95).

[24] *Ibid.*, pp. 301–07.

to Greenwood, "there is a kind of luxury in *seeing*, as in eating and drinking, and the more we indulge our senses in either the less are they to be restrained." Copley's plan was to go to Parma to discharge a commission from an English nobleman to copy Correggio's *Holy Family with St. Jerome*, proceeding then to "Mantua, Venice, Trieste, Innsbruck, Augsburg, Ulm, Stuttgart, Mannheim, Mayence, Coblentz, Cologne, Dusseldorf, Nimeguen, Utrecht, Amsterdam, Haarlem, Leyden, the Hague, Rotterdam, Antwerp, Brussels, Ghent, Bruges, Lille, Paris and London." [25]

For a while Copley had considered remaining in Rome until the following spring, in order to pursue further the study of antique statuary that had increasingly claimed his attention after his trip to Naples and Paestum. But he decided against a delay in returning to England since, by buying good casts, he could "always have the advantage of drawing from them, which will be much superior to spending one or two years in Rome." He had purchased a cast of the Laocoön and a few others and, having these, "I shall possess all I would recommend an artist to study; for it is not the number that he studies, but a thorough understanding of the best and the principles of art, which can alone make him great." Unfortunately for Copley, by the time the casts arrived in England, they were broken to bits, a mishap that Copley, according to his son, "never ceased to regret during the whole course of his after-life." [26]

On June 4, 1775, Copley turned his steps northward toward Parma. He had originally planned to stop on the way to Parma to make copies of "the Madonna" in the collection of the Grand Duke in Florence for Sukey and for Mr. Izard, but he decided not to take the time. He did stop for two days in Bologna, which impressed him beyond his expectations with its churches, palaces, and works by the Carracci. He was particularly struck by Guido Reni, since "the pictures in Rome by him give no idea of his genius," and especially liked Reni's "St. Peter, seated, leaning on his hand, and St. Paul standing by him." He had praise too for Domenichino's *Martyrdom of St. Agnes*. Continuing toward Parma, he also saw some interesting things in Modena.

He arrived in Parma on June 10 and found the city disappointing. However, the Correggio he was to copy was "a wonderful piece of art," and he estimated that the copying would take two months. The English artist William Parry was copying the picture when he arrived, but there was no conflict of scheduling. Parry introduced him to the engraver Simon François Ravenet, who helped him to get settled. [27]

Copley immediately set to work on his copy of *The Holy Family with St. Jerome*. The much-copied picture was hanging in good light at the academy, with a guard in constant attendance. Copley worked on it from 8:00 A.M. until 12:30 P.M.; after dining he returned to work from 3:00 P.M. until sunset. Joseph Wright of Derby was one of the English artists then in Parma, and he reported on July 24, 1775, to his and

[25] Isaac John Greenwood, *The Greenwood Family of Norwich, England, in America*, ed. H. Minot Pitman and Mary M. Greenwood (privately printed, 1934), pp. 63–65; Amory, pp. 51–52, May 7, 1775.

[26] Amory, pp. 52–54, Copley to his wife, June 9, 1775.

[27] Ibid., pp. 55–59, Copley to his wife, June 12 and July 2, 1775.

Copley's mutual friend, Ozias Humphry, in Florence: "Mr. Copley has been hard at it five weeks, says he will spend twice that time more over it, but he will get it like the original. It is with infinite labour that he produces what he does, but that is *entre nous.*" [28]

Copley did not bother to send a full account of his work on *The Holy Famliy with St. Jerome* to Henry Pelham as he had done with *The Ascension,* for there was a good chance that he would see him shortly in London. But he did send some general observations and some technical data.[29] In this letter he concentrated on Titian's *Venus* at Florence, referring Pelham to the print and to West's copy, which he presumed Pelham had seen in Philadelphia. He particularly tried to convey the quality of Titian's handling of flesh color, which he noted matches the color of one's hand if one puts it next to the painting. He told Pelham he might observe something of this effect in "the knee and part of the thigh of the little Jesus in the Madonna's lap at Mr. Chardons." He advised him to mix up some flesh color with turpentine and to compare its effect with some flesh color mixed with poppy oil. The brilliance of the former in contrast with the dark, cold, and greasy quality of the other would parallel the effect of Titian's treatment of flesh in contrast with that of the other masters.

In technical terms Copley described the steps of a painting process that he believed would produce an effect something like Titian's. He suggested that Pelham experiment a little with it and send him a small sample of the result for an opinion. Observing that technique is a means, not an end, he also sent various recipes for varnishes. He compared his varnish with those used by West and others, and noted of *The Holy Family with St. Jerome* that the colors were so rich and clear that "Correggio must have us'd Varnish or something of that sort in his Colours." Copley noted further that Titian's flesh shadows were light and that in some ways the effect of his color harmonies was like a strong pastel. He then discussed the technical means by which this could be simulated. Although he planned to experiment with this, he did not plan to spend much time trying to imitate another painter, especially since Reynolds, West, and others had wisely told him it would be a mistake for him to alter his style.

Copley stressed to Pelham the importance of a knowledge of anatomy, especially for history painting. He enjoined Pelham to get an anatomical figure at Smibert's and also an anatomy book in order to learn where the external muscles are and what they

[28] William Bemrose, *The Life and Works of Joseph Wright* [of Derby] (London, 1885), p. 36. Copley himself sent an account of his progress to Humphry, who apparently was planning to copy the Correggio *St. Jerome* when Copley was finished. Copley had learned that George Carter also intended to copy the picture, and he wished to establish Humphry's prior rights. The letter is dated July 2, 1775, but the contents suggest that it was written in August (Archives of American Art, Detroit Institute of Arts). The letter also included a receipt for varnish, which Humphry later entered in his memo book on March 22, 1779 in reduced proportions: "Mr. Copelys Varnish/ a pint of Spirits of rectified Wine/ ¼ of a p^d of Gum Sandrack/ 4 Spoon — fulls of Canada Balsam [Copley called it Balsam of Fir] put these together in a Bottle & place them either in a Summer Sun or near the fire remembering that the Bottle must not be stop'd close as it w^d certainly burst." British Museum, Add. Ms. 22949.

[29] *Copley-Pelham Letters*, pp. 333–42, June 25, 1775.

do: "The length of the bones you have in the Book of Antique Statues publish'd with their measures." With a knowledge of bones and muscles, Pelham could confidently go on to sketch historical subjects. "I don't mean to draw you from your portraits, for that is the most advantageous at least at present. Only I don't think a Man a perfect Artist who on occation cannot Paint History, and who knows but you may have a talent in history like Raphael till you try; and if you have, your fortune is secure in this Life."

Copley noted that the lay figure Pelham had for arranging and painting drapery, which probably had been Copley's own before he left Boston, was as good a one as any he had seen since. He noted that "the best Drapery for history is Cloath, flaniel or Linnen, Wet and rung out." Citing the essential importance of getting "a breadth of Light and Shadow as one great thing essential in Art," a precept that he assiduously adhered to in his own work, Copley told Pelham not to get discouraged at failure in his initial attempts. After all, West had told him that he had made at least fifty sketches for his *Return of Regulus*. And Gavin Hamilton had had a colored sketch of *The Parting of Hector and his Wife* on his easel since before Copley's arrival in Rome; now and then he would change some part, but he still had not finished it when Copley left Rome. Once the general idea was fairly well fixed and Pelham was ready to shade, he should do it figure by figure. Copley had seen an original drawing in Modena for a figure in Raphael's *Transfiguration* that was shaded and partially blocked out by parts of other figures, and this he felt confirmed his own procedure.

For Pelham's edification, Copley also discussed some of the copies he was familiar with in the colonies:

> The Picture of a Naked Venus and Cupid at Smibert's is Copy'd from one of Titiano's in the possession of the Great Duke of Tuskany, which hangs over the Celebrated Titian Venus, but is by no means equil to it. the little head of St. John that hangs by the side of the window in your little Painting Room is copied from a St. John in an holy Family by Titiano in the same appartment, and in its general effect just what Titianos is. perhaps it may have been an original sketch by Titian for that Picture . . . if at Philadelphia you saw in Mr. Allens house A Picture containing three figures very Dark, one of them playing on a harpsicord with the head much turned to one Shoulder, you will be glad to know it is a Copy of Georgione.[30]

The first part of Copley's stay in Parma was clouded by his deepening concern with the political situation in the new world as reports of events at Lexington and Concord arrived. He was greatly worried about the safety of his family and the fate of his country. Copley had long held to a conviction that all would work out well for America. In March 1775, he had written to Pelham, "poor America! I hope the best but I fear the worst. yet certain I am She will finially Imerge from he[r]

---

[30] *Ibid.*, pp. 340-41.

present Callamity and become a Mighty Empire. and it is a pleasing reflection that I shall stand amongst the first of the Artists that shall have led that Country to the Knowledge and cultivation of the fine Arts, happy in the pleasing reflection that they will one Day shine with a luster not inferior to what they have done in Greece or Rome in my Native Country." [31]

After he learned that fighting had begun, he wrote to his wife:

By a Letter from London I was informed, since I wrote you, that what I greatly feared has at last taken place. The war has begun, and, if I am not mistaken, the country, which was once the happiest on the globe, will be deluged with blood for many years to come. It seems as if no plan of reconciliation could now be formed; as the sword is drawn, all must be finally settled by the sword. I cannot think that the power of Great Britain will subdue the country, if the people are united, as they appear to be at present. I know it may seem strange to some men of great understanding that I should hold such an opinion, but it is very evident to me that America will have the power of resistance until grown strong to conquer, and that victory and independence will go hand in hand.[32]

He later expanded on this theme:

Whoever thinks the Americans can be easily subdued is greatly mistaken; they will keep their enthusiasm alive till they are victorious, if I am not extremely mistaken. You know, years ago, I was right in my opinion that this would be the result of the attempt to tax the colony; it is now my settled conviction that all the power of Great Britain will not reduce them to obedience. Unhappy and miserable people, once the happiest, now the most wretched! How warmly I expostulated with some of the violent "Sons of Liberty" against their proceedings they must remember; and with how little judgment, in their opinion, did I then seem to speak! But all this is past; the day of tribulation is come, and years of sorrow will not dry the orphans' tears nor stop the widows' lamentations; the ground will be deluged with the blood of its inhabitants before peace will again assume its dominion in that country.[33]

Yet Copley was less sure about the welfare of his own family. He had no way of knowing that shortly before he left Rome his wife had sailed from America with the three oldest children — Elizabeth, John Singleton, and Mary [34] — leaving behind the infant Clarke, who was too feeble to undertake the rigors of the passage, in the care of Copley's mother, Mary Pelham. "While I am in ease and quiet," he wrote, "you may want the common necessaries of life. The reflection is too much for me to bear with a tolerable degree of fortitude . . . I should fly to you, but the distance is too great . . . I am all impatience to finish in this city and to hurry to England. I find there is a great deal of work in the picture I am copying; my anxiety almost renders me incapable

---

[31] *Ibid.,* p. 301.
[32] Amory, pp. 57–58, July 2, 1775.
[33] *Ibid.,* p. 62, July 22, 1775.
[34] They had sailed on May 27 from Marblehead aboard the *Minerva* with Captain John Calahan and

enjoyed an "agreeable passage of twenty eight days," arriving in England on June 24, 1775. Martha C. Codman, ed., *The Journal of Mrs. John Amory, 1775–1777* (Boston, 1923), pp. 1–4.

of proceeding with it, but it must be done; it is of too much consequence to throw it up, and If I should it would not bring about the happy moment of our meeting one instant sooner." [35]

By the same mail Copley wrote to Henry Pelham, urging with vigor and insistence that he not take up arms in the struggle: "for God Sake, dont think this a Triffling thing. My reasons are very important. You must follow my directions and be neuter at all events." [36] Although Copley did not present his "important reasons," his warning was consistent with the position he had taken during his last few years in Boston, when he had painted Tories and Whigs alike and had tried to retain the semblance of impartiality as the political split widened. Then his position had been a matter of professional expedience as well as of conviction. Now it was a matter of the safety of his own family that recommended political caution.

Shortly afterward, Copley learned to his joy that his family had arrived safely in England. Now he could finish his work, free from the fears that had plagued him. He planned to return to London, determined now to stay there and confident of his ability to build a new career. Earlier he had observed, "I have no doubt I shall meet with as much to do as in Boston, and on better terms. I might have begun many pictures in London, if I had pleased, and several persons are awaiting my return to employ me." [37]

Copley's work in Parma was finished in September, and he set out for London by way of Venice, the Tyrol, Mannheim, and Cologne, foregoing his earlier plan to return through Paris. [38]

[35] Amory, pp. 60–61, Copley to his wife, July 15, 1775.
[36] *Copley-Pelham Letters*, pp. 343–44, July 15, 1775.
[37] Amory, p. 37, Copley to his wife, Oct. 26, 1774.

[38] *Ibid.*, p. 64, Copley to his wife, [probably Sept., erroneously given as Nov.] 23, 1775; *Copley-Pelham Letters*, pp. 353, 355, 358, Copley to Henry Pelham, Aug. 22, 1775, and Mrs. Copley to Henry Pelham, Sept. 18, 1775.

A New Beginning

1775-1779   C OPLEY WAS REUNITED WITH HIS FAMILY IN LONDON EARLY IN October 1775. At the age of thirty-seven, he stood at the threshold of a new career. If he met with success in England, he intended to remain there, which he knew would please his wife. He felt fortunate that his departure from Boston for the study tour had been so timely. His American property was lost, he thought, and as he looked at his present position he considered himself a poor man who possessed only his health, his family, and his art. This last, he was confident, would enable him to make his way in England. He planned to concentrate on portraits and to paint history pictures only if presented with outright commissions. The dream of achieving success as a history painter certainly was still with him, but for the moment the task of providing for his family was paramount. One reason for his decision to concentrate on portraits and for his general optimism was that Gavin Hamilton had told him before he left Rome that he would be better equipped in London as a painter of portraits than Benjamin West, who could not paint anything as good as the *Izard* portrait. Hamilton had added the practical observation that portraits were always in demand.

Copley also found a waiting circle of friends in London. While he had been in Italy, the city filled with expatriate American loyalists, especially Bostonians. When Mrs. Copley arrived in London with her children in June, she spent the first night at an inn where she was immediately visited by her cousin, Elisha Hutchinson, the governor's son, who sought news of his wife in the colonies. The following day she drove with her children to Islington, outside London, to stay with the family of Thomas Bromfield, the brother of her sister Hannah's husband. Her original plan was to stay with the Bromfields only for about three weeks while her children had their inoculations and some time to recover, but the Bromfields prevailed upon her to remain with them until Copley arrived from the continent. Here, waiting anxiously, she enjoyed the company of other loyalist friends in London, especially the Hutchinsons.[1]

---

[1] The earliest reference to Copley in England after the European trip is an entry in Samuel Curwen's journal on Oct. 11, 1775: "Governor Hutchinson came in his coach with Mr. Copley from Mr. Brom- field's, and took Mr. Pickman and myself to his house, where we dined in company with Mr. Bliss, Mr. W. N. Boylston, Mrs. Copley, and the family" (Ward, *Curwen*, p. 39); "Letters of E. Hutchinson

On his return Copley joined in the round of dinners, teas, and general social interchanges. However, unlike many of his loyalist friends, Copley was not a political refugee waiting until the fires of rebellion were put out before returning to the colonies to resume business as usual. It was art, not politics, that had brought him to Europe, and art was his primary concern. From the beginning he had to turn away from the loyalists, who had ample leisure, to attack the large problem of carving out a career for himself in the London art world.

His first task was to secure a home for his family that would afford him a commodious and well-lighted studio, and a fashionable address suited to the wealthy patrons he hoped to attract. He found what he was looking for in a house at 12 Leicester Square. The Copley family moved there early in 1776. With them went Richard Clarke, Susanna's father, who was to spend the final twenty years of his life in his daughter's household.[2] Twelve Leicester Square, the home of the Copley family for their first seven and a half years in London, could not have been more auspiciously located. Fig. 343 shows the square as it appeared in 1753, and architecturally it was not much altered by the time the Copleys moved in. The first house on the right, with the artist's bust visible above the doorway, was the home of the painter William Hogarth. When the Copleys arrived it was occupied by Hogarth's widow, Jane. Twelve Leicester Square can be seen two doors above Hogarth's house, with four windows on the upper floor and an asymmetrical placement of the door and three windows on the ground floor.

A generation earlier, Leicester Square, or Leicester Fields, had been London's art center, the residence of Hogarth and Sir James Thornhill. Now it was the home of Sir Joshua Reynolds, president of the Royal Academy, the acknowledged leader of the new generation of artists. Reynolds lived across the square from Copley. Next door to him lived the auctioneer James Christie. Athenian Stuart, the engravers David Loggan and Edward Fisher, the architect John Gwynn, and the medalist and antiquarian James Tassie also lived on Leicester Square.[3]

The house at 12 Leicester Square, now destroyed, achieved fame not as the residence of Copley, but (renumbered 28 Leicester Square) as the residence and museum

to His Wife, 1774–1777," British Museum, Egerton Ms. 2668, fol. 81, June 29, 1775, and fol. 83, July 6, 1775; "Diary of Elisha Hutchinson," fol. 24, June 28, 1775; "Diary of Gov. Thomas Hutchinson, 1774–1780," *ibid.*, Egerton Ms. 2662, fol. 219, [June] 28, [1775]; Codman, *Mrs. Amory*, p. 5.

[2] Since Richard Clarke had been a prosperous New England merchant, and since Copley on his return from Italy was relatively poor, it seems possible that Clarke rendered sufficient financial assistance to enable the Copleys to move into their fine new home. This supposition is supported by the fact that when Clarke died in 1795 his will released Copley from a not inconsiderable debt. Principal

Probate Office, Somerset House, foll. 372–73.

[3] Among the lesser known artists in this area were G. K. Ralph, James Nixon, and R. Livesay, all of whom exhibited at the Royal Academy in 1780. On the far or north side of the square to the left of the equestrian statue and set back from the street was Leicester House, the most elegant building on the square. This was the home of Sir Ashton Lever and his museum. To the left of it was Savile House, the home of Sir George Sackville. During the Gordon Riots of 1780, from the windows of their home the Copleys watched the mobs sacking Savile House. E. Beresford Chancellor, *The History of the Squares of London* (London, 1907), pp. 151–63.

of Dr. John Hunter, who took possession in the summer of 1783 and greatly enlarged the property to accommodate his museum. A ground plan of Hunter's house suggests what the building may have been like when the Copleys lived in it. A long passage divided the house, with the hall and the main staircase on the right as one entered, and the parlor and the backstairs on the left. Two rooms shaped to conform to the bow of the rear of the house served John Hunter as a study and an afternoon bedroom. The backyard was also divided in half, one half being a gravel yard and one half a sky-lighted picture gallery. If this gallery stood in Copley's day, it possibly served him as a painting room; otherwise he probably used one or both of the rear rooms.[4]

Once settled in his new quarters, Copley set about establishing his reputation as a portrait painter. Almost immediately he had to decide on which artistic organization to join. While still in the colonies he had been elected to the Society of Artists, on the basis of his portrait of *Henry Pelham (Boy with a Squirrel)*. The general quarterly meeting of the Society of Artists, held on December 5, 1775, resolved, "that Mr. [John] Greenwood do wait on Mr. Copley — requesting the continuance of his attachment to this Society." It was obvious to Copley, however, that his future lay with the newer and more important organization, the Royal Academy, headed by Reynolds and sponsored by George III. With Royal Academy exhibitions held in the spring each year, Copley immediately entered a picture for 1776. Recorded in the catalogue only as "a conversation," this was probably the *Izard* double portrait. Since Copley had still been at work on this picture when the Izards left Rome for England, he took it to England himself and had it on hand at the time of this exhibition. The painting seems not to have made any particular impression on the London critics, but Copley's bid to affiliate himself with the Royal Academy was successful. On November 4, he and William Parry, his friend from Parma, were elected associates out of a field of twenty-three candidates.[5]

While Copley worked to establish himself professionally in London, he by no means turned his back on his loyalist acquaintances. Entries in various diaries and letters reveal the extent to which the Copley's participated in the vigorous social life of the New England loyalists in London.[6] In February 1776, when a group of New Englanders in London met for dinner at the Adelphi in the Strand and founded the

[4] "Hunter Album," Royal College of Surgeons, pp. 38–39, 163, including on p. 39: William Clift, "Ground Plan of 28 Leicester Square as it appeared in 1792, drawn in 1832."

[5] Greenwood, p. 64; "Minute Books, Council," Royal Academy [hereafter RA], I, Nov. 11, 1776.

[6] The Hutchinson Papers in the British Museum (many of which have been published) and the published journals of Samuel Curwen, Edward Oxnard, Samuel Quincy, and Mrs. John Amory are rich sources of such information. The Copleys enjoyed an especially warm friendship with the Hutchinsons. Elisha Hutchinson tells in his diary of going to Buckingham House with the Copleys and two of their children and spending two hours going through the rooms to look at pictures (fol. 42b). In another entry he relates going with the Copleys, Mrs. Hutchinson, and Mrs. Galloway across the square to Reynolds' studio (fol. 6ob). The Copleys dined with the Auchmutys in Haymarket (fol. 33b). When they dined at Judge Sewall's, accompanied by Richard Clarke and Henry Pelham, they took part in a discussion of the possibilities of a French war ("Edward Oxnard's Journal," *New England Historical and Genealogical Register*, XXVI [1872], 259).

New England Club with the avowed purpose of meeting for dinner once a week, Copley was present. However, as the club became more and more a political center, and as Copley became increasingly caught up in his own career, his affiliation tapered off. Before too long the club was jokingly called "The Brompton Road Tory Club," and Copley took no part in it at all.[7] Copley never considered himself a Tory and never filed any claims for support or reimbursement from the British government. He preferred to remain apolitical, maintaining at all times that he had left Boston for professional reasons alone. After he learned that his Boston property was unharmed, and that the occupying British would care for it and pay rent, there was no financial reason for him to proclaim himself a loyalist. It was much better to try to retain the ownership of his property in Boston through political neutrality.

When American loyalists arrived in England, they were generally in a high state of excitement. They rejoiced over their deliverance from the rebellion and their safe arrival "home," but they were deeply concerned about those left behind and the fate of their property. At first there was a great deal of cohesiveness among the loyalists in London as they exchanged information and opinions. This was reinforced by the fact that the Americans were decidedly provincial in speech and manner, a social fact of life that set them apart in sophisticated London society.[8] After the first stage of excited arrival, many of the loyalists found themselves with nothing to do but wait for the force of British arms to restore order in the colonies. So they took advantage of the leisure afforded them to travel about England and enjoy some sightseeing. Yet, as the revolution continued, many of the loyalists began to feel a financial pinch and became increasingly dependent on an annual subsidy from the British government. Discovering that their return to America was much further off than they had anticipated, in disillusionment they left London and gravitated to those provincial cities that resembled their colonial homes — places like Exeter, Bristol, and Birmingham — to set about the task of rebuilding their careers.

Copley was also a provincial, but he had a deep-rooted drive toward success in his field. His attention was not focused on the course of the rebellion, but was directed toward the problem of getting on with his career. With the dispersal of the loyalists, Copley's connections with them decreased, although the presence of Richard Clarke in the household maintained some of the lines of contact. Moreover, there were ties

---

[7] Samuel Curwen records the presence of the following in addition to himself at the first meeting: John Singleton Copley, Richard Clarke, Jonathan Clarke, Joseph Green, Jonathan Bliss, Jonathan Sewall, Joseph Waldo, Samuel Sampson Blowers, Elisha Hutchinson, William Hutchinson, Samuel Sewall, Samuel Quincy, Isaac Smith, Jr., Harrison Gray, David Green, Thomas Flucker, Joseph Taylor, Daniel Silsbee, Thomas Brinley, William Cabot, Nathaniel Coffin, Samuel Porter, Edward Oxnard, Benjamin Pickman, John Amory, Judge Robert Auch-

muty, and Major Urquhart (Ward, *Curwen*, p. 45). The nickname of the club derived from the street where a number of the exiles lived, including Thomas Danforth, Edward Oxnard, and Copley's brother-in-law Jonathan Clarke (*ibid.*, p. 103).

[8] Their form of speech, though less crude than the earthy patois of Somerset or Norfolk, was similar to the country dialects of Bedford, Huntington, or Bucks. Henry C. Van Schaack, *The Life of Peter Van Schaack* (New York, 1842), pp. 162–63.

with families of relatives and close friends, particularly the Hutchinsons, Olivers, and Startins in Birmingham. Copley's provincial background, which he probably revealed by his manner and speech, was something of a liability. He had not come out of the wilderness early enough to be a novelty and a prodigy like West, and thus had to progress largely on the merits of his work. So it was politic that he not orient himself socially toward American expatriates, but instead try to transcend his colonial background.

In 1777 Copley increased the number of pictures that he exhibited at the Royal Academy. In addition to a whole-length portrait and a three-quarter-length portrait of unidentified men, he submitted his *Copley Family* (fig. 344) and *The Nativity* (fig. 347). He had begun the family picture shortly after the move into the new home in Leicester Square, and it is a hymn of contentment on the reunion of the family. The artist calmly regards the viewer from his background niche surrounded by his assets — four lovely children, a beautiful and charming wife, a prosperous and respected father-in-law, and, in his hands, plans or drawings that represent his art, the key to future fame and fortune.

The three older children were born in America and crossed to England on the *Minerva* with Mrs. Copley. Elizabeth Clarke Copley stands in the center between two groups of three figures each. John Singleton Copley, Jr., stands by his seated mother, his left arm bending up around her neck, their eyes almost engaged, in a delightful mother-child relationship. Mary Copley is on the sofa leaning against her mother. On the left Richard Clarke holds an infant on his lap. When Copley began to paint the picture, he intended the child to be the son, Clarke Copley, left behind in America. A loyalist acquaintance, Samuel Curwen, noted in his diary on April 1, 1776, "in passing through Leicester-square, I called in at Mr. Copley's to see Mr. Clarke and the family, who kindly pressed my staying to tea; and in the mean time amused myself by seeing his performances in painting. He was then at work on a family piece containing himself, Mr. Clarke, his wife and four children, of all of whom I observed a very striking likeness." Although the composition included four children, Copley probably knew by then that his infant son had died in Boston on January 19, since Pelham had written him about it on January 27. But having started with four children in his sketch, and knowing that another child was on the way, he presumably let his composition stand. In the final version the baby is certainly Susanna, the first Copley child born in England (October 20, 1776).[9]

In the portrait Copley himself, standing behind his father-in-law in a pose reminiscent of his portrait of *John Amory* (fig. 220), forms the left side of the right-triangle composition. The composition of *The Copley Family* is not only triangular on the surface but is so in depth, with Elizabeth standing in the forefront of a wedge of figures. The setting develops out of the *Izard* double portrait, with the background

[9] Ward, *Curwen*, p. 51; *Copley-Pelham Letters*, pp. 364–65.

screened completely at the right and almost completely by the vase and column on the left, and the landscape distance opening in the center. An oil sketch that studies the three figures on the right (fig. 345) and a complete oil sketch for *The Copley Family* (fig. 346) are spirited and strong, demonstrating for the first time what remains true throughout Copley's English career, that he is at his virtuoso best in his oil sketches. The free handling of the monochrome sketches frequently is unmatched in more rigid and formal final versions.

Unfortunately for Copley, his family picture, although it attracted attention at the academy, did not receive the critical acclaim he had hoped for. The critic of the *Morning Chronicle* on April 26, 1777, had considerable fault to find:

> Mr. Copley, from the size of his family piece, is likely to be as much the subject of observation in the rooms as any artist who has exhibited; as his picture (No. 61) has, in some of its parts, great merit, it is a pity that the whole effect should be destroyed from a want of proper proportion of light and shade. Several of the figures, particularly that of the lady and old gentleman, are well painted. The face of the infant in the lap also has great merit; but the arm round the mother's neck appears to be rather unnaturally turned, and extravagantly long. The figure of the gentleman, leaning behind with some plans in his hand, seems also to be oddly placed, and not properly one of the family. Add to this the settee, the carpet, and the prospect through the window, are all so glaring that the effect of the figures is greatly destroyed, and, after regarding the picture for some time it is difficult for a beholder to guess which object the painter meant to make his main subject. *The portrait of a gentleman*, in the little room fronting the door, is also in part liable to the same objection, the background is not sufficiently kept under.[10]

This was a rather friendly attack in contrast to the lines later penned by Anthony Pasquin about another of the exhibited pictures, *The Nativity* (fig. 347). Pasquin noted that the Infant looks at the Virgin with an "air of despondency, rather than ineffable joy," and remarked that her "white drapery is so inveterately modern, that it furnishes a lively notion of a female haberdasher in the third week of her *accouchement*."[11]

The Nativity is known to us today only through engravings and a few drawings. James Anderdon, who saw the picture at the time of the Lyndhurst sale in 1864, described it as "a sketch." The picture bears some similarity (cows, pointing figure) to Joshua Reynolds' *Nativity* design for the west window, New College Chapel, Oxford. But Copley's picture predates Reynolds' concept by about a year. Reynolds in 1778 spoke of his plan to paint the subject in the manner of Correggio's *Notte*, the famous *Nativity* at Dresden, "making all the light proceed from the Christ." Copley's

[10] The same review may be found in the *London Packet*, April 25–28, 1777. In the case of this review, as with many of the subsequent ones quoted, I first found reference to it in the William T. Whitley Papers, a collection of the cuttings and notes in the British Museum Print Room. But when the citation is to the primary source, the quotation is taken directly from it.

[11] Anthony Pasquin, *Memoirs of the Royal Academicians* (London, 1796), p. 137.

more realistic treatment has the light flooding in from the left and bears only the vaguest resemblance to the Correggio.[12]

There are two drawings for *The Nativity* currently known, both studies for the figure of the Virgin. Fig. 348 is a study of the head and if, as family tradition has it and as seems likely to be true, this is Mrs. Copley, it is one of Copley's few portrait drawings. The entire central composition could, in fact, have a personal basis since Copley's daughter Susanna had been born only a few months earlier. Closely allied to this drawing is a drapery study (fig. 349), executed on sized paper.

There are three oval or circular portraits that also seem to date from this general period. Fig. 350 is a spirited, freely brushed self-portrait, only vaguely related to the artist's likeness in *The Copley Family*. Its restless, almost nervous, vitality contrasts with the bland assurance of the pastel self-portrait the successful young colonial had painted less than ten years earlier (fig. 226). The bone structure of the head is more marked, and one can sense the aptness of Carter's unkind remark about Copley's eyes being "a day's march in his head" when he was fatigued. An oval portrait (fig. 351) has been customarily identified as another self-portrait, but there is no resemblance between this figure and the known likenesses of Copley. However, the strong resemblance between this likeness and the head of Richard Clarke in the family picture suggests that this may be a portrait of one of Clarke's two sons, Jonathan or Isaac Winslow. The third portrait (fig. 352) is of the former colonial governor, Sir Francis Bernard, whom Copley had painted in the colonies in happier days.

In 1777 Copley painted a half-length portrait of young *Squire Hyde of Hyde* (fig. 353). He executed the splendid portraits of an older man, *Robert Hyde, Squire of Hyde* (fig. 354) and *Mrs. Robert Hyde* (fig. 355) in the following year. The portrait of Mrs. Hyde is a restrained and sensitive painting, executed with something of the careful approach of Copley's American manner but with an even higher degree of plastic realization. Its handling and tonality are evidence of the impact of Reynolds' early portrait style on Copley during his first English years. Moreover, the striking portrait of the older Squire Hyde reveals clearly the increased freedom of brushwork and the lightening of the palette achieved without any weakening of coloristic strength in Copley's early English pictures.

In 1778 Copley exhibited three pictures at the Royal Academy: *Sir William Pepperrell and His Family* (fig. 356), a three-quarter-length portrait of a lady (possibly fig. 363), and the picture that brought him his first popular triumph, *Watson and the Shark* (fig. 371).

[12] "James Hughes Anderdon Scrapbooks," RA, XIII, 1808, annotated copy of the catalogue of the Lyndhurst Sale, Christie's, March 5, 1864; Frederick Whiley Hilles, *Letters of Sir Joshua Reynolds* (Cambridge, England, 1929), p. 60. Copley did own a copy of the Correggio *Nativity*, attributed in the Lyndhurst Sale to "Carlo Maratti" (111). One assumes either that Copley acquired the painting after he had painted his *Nativity* or that he ignored it in working out his own composition. This copy of Correggio's *Notte* was among the unsold items remaining in Copley's studio after his death, mentioned in a list Mrs. Copley sent to her daughter, Mrs. Gardiner Greene (Boston Public Library, Ch. F.6.4., received June 23, 1821).

Although the family picture exhibited at the Royal Academy in 1778 was not identified in the catalogue, it was doubtless *The Pepperrell Family*, since the family group exhibited in 1777 was *The Copley Family* and *The Pepperrell Family* bears the date of 1778. Copley and Sir William Pepperrell had not been on good terms in the colonies at the time Copley left for Europe, but they had obviously patched up their differences in London.[13] The production of *The Pepperrell Family* was complicated by the fact that Lady Pepperrell had died in America in 1775. Anna Wells Rutledge has suggested (I believe correctly) that Copley used his own wife as a model in the preliminary drawings for Lady Pepperrell.[14] The crowded and awkward grouping of the earliest sketch (fig. 359), which involves no real likenesses, was rapidly abandoned for a more highly finished sketch (fig. 357), owned by a Copley descendant in England. The background opens up into a landscape. A little blackamoor appears sketched on the far right. Also on the right is one child seated on a table, supported by his sister who plays with him. Another putto-like child stands on the table and reaches up to hold a scarf, held at the other end by Sir William. This figure is not Sir William as he appears in the finished picture, and someone else seems to have posed, just as Sukey Copley may have posed for the late Lady Pepperrell.[15] The eldest girl clasps the figure of Sir William around the waist. The next stage in the compositional development is represented by a drawing owned by another Copley descendant (fig. 358). Here Copley tightens up the composition and returns to the right-triangle arrangement of *The Copley Family*. The blackamoor is omitted, as is any clear landscape indication. The infant now stands on his mother's lap, and the eldest sister moves further into the composition, putting her arm around the infant rather than around her father. Gone too, fortunately, is the scarf. The figure of Sir William here looks at the spectator rather than at his family.

---

[13] *Copley-Pelham Letters*, p. 366. Sir William Pepperrell carried this letter of Jan. 27, 1776, from Pelham, who urged a reconciliation, to Copley.

[14] Anna Wells Rutledge, "American Loyalists — A Drawing for a Noted Copley Group," *Art Quarterly*, XX (Summer 1957), 195–201.

[15] Although this is only conjectural, a likely guess would be that this was Henry Pelham, who had arrived in London in mid-1776 from Halifax and stayed at Leicester Square with the Copleys. In 1777 Pelham exhibited *The Finding of Moses* and several miniatures at the Royal Academy. The following year he exhibited a group of four miniatures, two watercolors and two enamels. He also was one of nineteen candidates for two vacant Royal Academy associateships, but was not elected. William T. Whitley, *Artists and Their Friends in England, 1700–1799* (London, 1928), II, 338.

Pelham had corresponded with relatives in Ireland and England before he left Boston, which Copley did not do, and on his arrival followed up his interest in Ireland. In 1780 or 1781 he married Catherine Butler of Castlecrine, County Clare (Registry of Deeds, Dublin, 338.196.227133, marriage settlement, indented deed, Sept. 12, 1780, reg. March 20, 1781). For the next few years he seems to have centered his artistic activity in Ireland, which included a survey and map of County Clare, an aquatint of Nathaniel Grogan's portrait of the Countess of Desmond, and drawings of Quinn Abbey, Clare Abbey, and Ennis Abbey for Groce's *Antiquities of Ireland* (Walter G. Strickland, *A Dictionary of Irish Artists* [Dublin and London, 1913]). In 1787 Pelham was engaged as agent for the Marquis of Lansdowne's estates in Ireland (Kerry), continuing in this position for eleven years ("Henry Pelham's Agency and Miscellaneous Letters, 1787–1798," Bowood Park, Calne, Wilts). In 1800 he issued a brochure announcing his plan to publish "An History of the Ancient Palatinate of Desmond and the Present County of Kerry" under the auspices of the Dublin Society (brochure with the Pelham Papers at Bowood Park). In 1806 Pelham, who could not swim (Pelham Papers, Pelham to John Cross, March 24, 1792), drowned in the Kenmare River at Bear Island.

Two other extant drawings help to explain Copley's procedure. The study of the central group with the infant in the mother's lap (fig. 360) probably was executed before fig. 358 in order to work out the rather complicated arrangement of the figures and to set down the flow of light from the upper left. A tightly drawn study for the figure of Sir William Pepperrell (fig. 361), with someone else's head lightly sketched in, defines the pose, with the head facing to the right as in the final version. This is primarily a detailed drapery study, with careful attention to the effect of light on the fabric in defining texture. It is a final study and is neatly, almost delicately, squared for transfer. A similar drawing of a man leaning on a balcony (fig. 362) is also primarily a drapery study, with only a faint suggestion of the head sketched in. Like the drapery study for *The Nativity* (fig. 349), it is one of the few Copley drawings on sized paper. In composition it is similar to the portrait of *George Boone Roupell* (fig. 388).

Copley at times indulged himself in the fairly common eighteenth-century artistic practice of "quoting" standard compositional themes in order to give an added dimension to his paintings. In *The Pepperrell Family*, the figures on the left of Sir William, Lady Pepperrell, and the eldest and youngest children comprise a group that is composed like a traditional Holy Family, even to the role of the eldest daughter as a John the Baptist figure. The Holy Family theme also seems to underlie *The Copley Family*. Copley owned an engraving of *The Holy Family* by Boulanger after Annibale Carracci, which has the child somewhat reversed from the Pepperrell format but does have the general idea of one arm around the mother's neck and one arm extended toward the father.[16] In that picture Joseph looks directly out at the viewer, much as Copley himself does in *The Copley Family* and as Sir William does in fig. 358.

Since Lady Pepperrell had died about two years before the picture was painted, Copley was faced with the problem either of projecting her into the present or of trying to subtract two years from the age of each child to recapture the family relationship of an earlier period. If he chose the latter course, which the age of the youngest child suggests, he was for the first time engaging in an attempt to re-create a scene from the recent past, as he was subsequently to do so effectively in his major history paintings. The deceased Lady Pepperrell was Elizabeth, the daughter of Isaac Royall, and had been painted as a child by Copley in a double portrait with her older sister Mary (fig. 83). Copley had painted Isaac Royall in about 1769–70 (fig. 254), and he had begun a companion portrait of Mrs. Royall, left unfinished upon her death in 1770. The unfinished painting was taken to England presumably by Isaac Royall at the time of the loyalist exodus, and Copley completed it there (fig. 364). It is unique in that it combines Copley's English and American styles in one picture, although aesthetically it suffers somewhat from the disparity between these two styles. The face and the forearms were done in America, the rest in England. X rays indicate that a bit of the hair, a cap, some cuffs on the left hand, and a pearl bracelet on the

[16] See appendix, Copley Print Sale (121)

right hand were painted over in the process of completing the picture in England. The English portion of the picture dates stylistically from the early years of Copley's English career, perhaps from 1778 when Isaac Royall and his son-in-law may have commissioned Copley to paint their deceased wives, almost as a ritualistic conclusion to a life in America that was ended. Copley completed *Mrs. Isaac Royall* by copying the clothes and accessories from another portrait he may have just completed, the superb portrait traditionally but not positively identified as *Mrs. Seymour Fort* (fig. 363). The bonnet, the lace around the neck, and most of the dress are borrowed directly. Only the sewing bag is missing. Both the stylistic and the circumstantial evidence point to a date of about 1778 for *Mrs. Fort*, and indeed this picture may well have been the three-quarter portrait of a lady that Copley exhibited at the Royal Academy in that year.

Neither the large *Pepperrell Family* nor the three-quarter-length portrait aroused much critical response when exhibited at the Royal Academy in 1778. A critic writing in the *Morning Post* on April 25, 1778, discussing the opening on the previous day, dismissed Copley's *Pepperrell Family* as "a mere daubing," and observed of his three-quarter-length portrait of a lady that it "deserves neither praise nor censure." But Copley's third exhibition piece, *Watson and the Shark* (fig. 371), caused a minor sensation. The *Morning Post* account stated that this painting "may fairly be estimated among the first performances of this exhibition. The softness of the colouring, the animation which is displayed in the countenances of the sailors, the efforts of the drowning boy, and the frightened appearance of the man assaulting the shark, constitute altogether a degree of excellance that reflect the highest honour on the composer." [17]

[17] The reviewer in the *Morning Chronicle* on the same day discussed *Watson and the Shark* right after his lead comments on Reynolds and Gainsborough. He found *Watson* to be "One of the most striking pictures in the Great Room." He praised the expressions on the various faces, noting that the face of the Negro "is a fine index of concern and horror." But he did comment critically that the shark did not look like a shark or anything else and was not vicious, that his tail did not lash the sea into foam, and that the boat did not tilt even though almost all of the figures were on one side. The critic in *St. James's Chronicle* of April 25–28, 1778, dedicated almost his entire first article on the exhibition to a favorable review of *Watson and the Shark* and disagreed with the *Morning Chronicle* by pointing out that the "Black and two rowers lean back to keep the 'gunnel' up." He praised the expression, the color, and the "correct and firm" drawing. "We heartily congratulate our Countrymen," he wrote, "on a Genius, who bids fair to rival the Great Masters of the Ancient Italian Schools." The *General Advertiser* review of April 28, 1778, was also very favorable, noting that the picture "deserves particularly to be praised." The criticism of details was again factually based — the Negro would act instead of just looking horrified, he would hold the rope in such a way that he could use it, and the wind that blows the hair of the harpooner should also have an effect on the sails in the background and on the sea. The favorable review in the *General Advertiser* evoked a letter to the editor from "A Young Painter," which stated that *Watson* had received the most severe verbal criticism of any picture in the exhibition. The correspondent reported having heard one man hold forth on this subject for half an hour: "The men, he said, were not rowing the right way to approach the body; that the sailors were imperfect, in having their fingers *open* to make a grasp, and the old man in holding by a shirt that hung loose; that the boy was too large, being equal to the boatmen; that he was drawn as if dead, though *they* had lately examined him before their house [that is, they had seen Brook Watson] &c. &c. &c. An objection was started by another gentleman, that the

Although Copley had concentrated on portraiture during his first few years in London in order to support his family, he certainly had not put aside his higher aspirations. His opportunity to depart from portraiture came through a commission from Brook Watson [18] to paint and record that horrible scene from Watson's youth when in 1749, at the age of fourteen, he had been attacked by a vicious shark while swimming in Havana Harbor. The shark's first strike stripped all the flesh below the calf from the victim's leg; the second attack snapped off his foot at the ankle. Then the shark flashed toward the boy for a third assault, but this time was driven off by rescuers. Copley's subject was the climactic moment of the final attack. *Watson and the Shark* may be counted as Copley's first English history painting, although it is atypical thematically of the genre since the subject is one of bizarre novelty rather than historical importance. It is also quite different from Copley's own subsequent history paintings, although it is a significant prelude.

The path Copley hoped to follow as a history painter had been blazed by Benjamin West, whose youthful imagination had been fired in colonial America, like Copley's, with dreams of gaining fame and glory as a painter of historical subjects. West had already made his dreams a reality, since in 1772 he was named history painter to the king. West had a substantial head start on Copley, having left the American colonies for an extended period of study in Italy in 1760, fourteen years before Copley was able to get there. While in Italy, West made copies after the work of the old masters, did study drawings of antique sculpture, and was struck with classical fever to a much greater degree than Copley later was. Copley's case, if we can read the symptoms in the *Izard* double portrait and in his letters home, was rather mild, but West was in Italy at a particularly exciting moment in the eighteenth-century rediscovery of classical antiquity. The eighteenth century was a period of intellectual ferment, and there was increasing concern with questions of human dignity and individual freedom, with the possibilities for man through the exercise of his rational powers to construct a better society for himself. To many, the classical age seemed to represent a prototype of the longed-for ideal society. In a less jaded day, before the corrupting rule of later princes of state and church, the Greeks and Romans had developed standards of law, government, morality, and virtue that could stand as models to the eighteenth century. As a result there was, particularly in the second half of the century, an eager turn to the past that was no dry revival of dusty classical relics, but a vital quest for man's social and political salvation. This was not idle theorizing: before the century was out, two

---

boat had two men leaning over the side, without keeling half a streak. This is true." "Cuttings from English Newspapers on Matters of Artistic Interest, 1686–1835," Victoria and Albert Museum, London, I, 160, May 1778.

[18] Brook Watson (1735–1807) was a prominent London merchant who had earlier spent years as a commissary officer with the British army in North America. Ultimately he rose to become lord mayor of London for one difficult year, 1796. The family tradition that Copley sailed from Boston to London in 1774 with Watson on one of his ships seems incorrect. But Copley's brother-in-law Jonathan Clarke did sail from England for Canada in the spring of 1776 with Watson on his ship, the *Canadian*. Boston Public Library, Ch. J.5.60, Richard Clarke, London, to [Isaac Winslow], Boston, May 4, 1776.

successful revolutions, in America and France, had toppled monarchic rule and established republics that both cloaked themselves in the garb and motifs of classical antiquity.

The first flush of excitement over the rediscovery of the classical heritage was in the air when West was in Italy in the early 1760's. There had been interest in classical antiquity long before, of course, but now there was new intensity, with philosophical and political overtones, as the eighteenth century quite literally attempted to reach back across the span of centuries to touch hands with Greece and Rome. At Herculaneum and Pompeii the earth was scraped away to uncover the buried buildings and objects; at Spalato Robert Adam made careful measured drawings of the palace of the Roman Emperor Diocletian, and Stuart and Revett did the same thing for the antiquities of Athens. In Rome the influential theoretician of the arts of classical antiquity was the German, Johann Joachim Wincklemann, and the prime interpreter of the new classicism into a contemporary artistic idiom was Anton Raphael Mengs. West experienced and absorbed all of this and was particularly affected by Wincklemann and Mengs. The result can be seen in a painting produced after he had begun to hit his stride as a painter of historical subjects, *Agrippina Landing at Brundisium with the Ashes of Germanicus* (fig. 365). The painting takes its subject from Tacitus. The popular Roman hero Germanicus had been assassinated by a political rival in a foreign land. His wife returns with her young family and entourage, bearing the ashes of her husband in a cinerary urn. West's painting is didactic, and its message is that it is sweet and proper to die for one's country and that it is also possible for human beings in the face of great personal loss to carry themselves with stoic calm and dignity. The painting fulfills West's own concept that "the art of painting has powers to dignify man, by transmitting to posterity his noble actions, and his mental powers, to be viewed in those invaluable lessons of religion, love of country, and morality." [19]

The way in which West delivers his message is equally important. History painting up to this time involved the exercise of artistic imagination to reconstruct a scene from the past. But West tries to depict this Roman event in accurate Roman terms. Roman clothing and objects are reproduced on the basis of surviving relief sculpture. The central group, monochromatic and restricted in plane like a relief, is based directly on a section of the frieze of Roman senators and their wives from the *Ara Pacis*. [20] The arcaded facade forming the front plane of the architectural backdrop is taken from one of the plates of Robert Adam, *Palace of Diocletian*. [21] Other figures seem to be taken from classical sculptural prototypes, and the triangular group on the left, one of the two supporting groups that focus attention on the dramatically illuminated processional group in the center of the stage in this theatrical composition, seems based on Greek

[19] William Dunlap, *A History of the Rise and Progress of the Arts of Design in the United States* (New York, 1834), I, 93.

[20] Grose Evans, *Benjamin West and the Taste of His Times* (Carbondale, 1959), p. 5 and plates 1, 2.

[21] My attention was first called to this source by Peter Bohan. The full title of Adam's book is *Ruins of the Palace of the Emperor Diocletian at Spalatro [sic] in Dalmatia* (London, 1764).

pedimental sculpture. West has told an ancient story that had didactic significance for the eighteenth century, and to increase the actuality of the past, to make it more real for an eighteenth-century audience, he used real classical sources for his details. His approach to classical antiquity, then, was not solely imaginative, but realistic as well.

Three years later, in 1771, West painted a much more startling and novel history painting, *The Death of General Wolfe* (fig. 366). In depicting the heroic death of Wolfe on Quebec's Plains of Abraham, West chose as his subject not an event from the classical past, but one that had occurred in modern times, in fact only twelve years earlier. Still, distance in time had been replaced by distance of place. The radical departure in this painting is again in method. This was not the first time that recent history had been depicted, but it was customary in treating a modern subject to put the action in a classical setting and the figures in classical dress. This was a way of saying that this event was worthy of the ancients. West wanted to shift the emphasis by asserting that not only are courage, dignity, and a willingness to die for one's country desirable virtues of the past, but that in fact such virtues were real possibilities in the present. Therefore, against the advice of Joshua Reynolds, George III, and others, West put the figures in modern dress. In his next major history painting he followed the same line of attack. *Penn's Treaty with the Indians* (fig. 367) of 1772 celebrates an event that seemed to the Quaker West to offer strong support for the arguments concerning the innate goodness of man and the possibility of peaceful coexistence among all men. The scene is the signing of the treaty between Penn and the Lenni Lenape chiefs, which provided the basis for Penn's Holy Experiment in Pennsylvania. West in this instance was presenting an earlier scene, the event having taken place in 1682. In an attempt to be realistic, he apparently reached back in his own memory to the Pennsylvania he knew as a boy. The buildings with their pent roofs are of an early Pennsylvania type. The clothes are not of 1680 vintage, but what West would remember as Quaker dress in Pennsylvania. Even the faces, though not those of participants in the events, have some Pennsylvania and Quaker associations as West introduced portraits of his father and brother.

Thus before Copley arrived in London, but while he was corresponding with West from Boston, West had created an important sequence of history paintings that had advanced this branch of art into new ground: not only had he painted modern subjects in modern dress, but he had tried to achieve the proper depiction of the subject matter in realistic terms. Copley had come out of a background remarkably similar to West's, and his aspirations were almost identical. The question was whether Copley would seek to follow in West's footsteps by continuing the development of an increasingly realistic mode of history painting, or whether he would create his own innovations. The test of his realism, in the case of *Watson and the Shark*, would be whether he created an entirely imaginary scene, perhaps treating the subject allegorically, or whether he would attempt the factual re-creation of an event that had taken place almost thirty years earlier.

270

The scene of the action was Havana Harbor, Cuba. A 1785 plan of the city and port of Havana (fig. 368) presents the general layout of the harbor. Morro Castle and Point Castle guard the entrance to the channel leading into the harbor. The city, surrounded by a wall and protected by gun placements, is on a blunt peninsula across from Morro Castle. The Bishop view (fig. 369) looks across the mouth of the channel at the city. Very prominent on the skyline are two towers of the convent and the tower and dome of the cathedral further to the left. The Canot engraving (fig. 370) presents a view from within the neck of the channel, fairly near the Morro Castle shore, looking out to sea. Morro Castle is on the right, Point Castle on the left. Certainly the setting of *Watson and the Shark* is Havana Harbor, with the viewer taken much further into the harbor than in the case of the Canot engraving. The cathedral dome and tower and the two convent towers are quite readily visible on the left, and the tower and fortifications of Morro Castle can be seen in the distance beyond the man with the harpoon (actually a boat hook). The salient features in the background of Copley's picture are not woven out of whole cloth but do have a factual basis. Still Copley has taken liberties. The towers are given rounded cupolas. The low line of Morro Castle is raised somewhat and given a sharp slope to the water, which is compositionally reinforced by flags flying from boats nearby to play against the thrusting diagonal of the harpoon. The high fortification wall so prominent in the Bishop view is presented simply as a lower sea-wall. If this were not done, the low viewpoint of the action would cause the left background to consist largely of wall, and to be correspondingly dull. By setting the action further into the harbor, Copley can introduce the interesting cityscape on the left. Moreover, the standing figures of the Negro and the harpoonist fit into the gap of the harbor mouth and the flats on which Point Castle sits so prosaically in the Canot view.

Since Copley did not travel to Havana, he must have utilized available visual sources for the background of his painting. The Canot engraving had been published. The Bishop view was first drawn in 1762, and although the particular print reproduced here was published after *Watson and the Shark* was painted, it was available earlier. So were plans of the city as well as a whole series of views by Jefferys which, though not of direct relevance to *Watson and the Shark*, could have helped Copley to get a general impression of the topography.

As for the accuracy of other elements in the picture, we can only speculate. Copley had ready access to boats, so visual sources for these posed no problem. The shark, as one critic noted, hardly seems real. It is much too elongated and is not physically accurate, but it fully serves its pictorial purpose as the source of danger. Nor is there any documentation on the individuals portrayed in the boat. The event had taken place almost thirty years before the painting was produced, and it is unlikely that Brook Watson, now a prosperous merchant, had kept track of his early shipmates. Possibly the face of Watson himself may have been a general source for his earlier likeness.

Watson and the Shark greatly extended Copley's reputation. This was a striking and remarkable picture, well calculated to catch the public fancy. Copley apparently painted two initial versions of the picture. Fig. 371, presumably commissioned by Brook Watson himself, was left by Watson on his death to Christ's Hospital. A second version (fig. 372) Copley kept, and it remained unsold in his studio at the time of his death. A small vertical version was painted in 1782 (fig. 373). An engraving of the picture by Valentine Green was published in 1779, seemingly with very good success.

There are five early detail drawings for *Watson and the Shark*. A problematical one is a sketch on the verso of another drawing that appears to be a notation for the head of Watson (fig. 374). The earliest of the drawings for the rescue group (fig. 375) consists of preliminary studies of the harpoonist and the principal oarsman. They are reversed in the final arrangement. The poses are rather static, and Copley soon abandoned this compositional tack. The two drawings relating to the left-hand group in the picture suggest that Copley experimented with having the figure in the stern seated, since in one study (fig. 376) his face is at the same height as the oar. In the other drawing (fig. 377) the stern figure is higher, but not nearly as upright as in the final version. Moreover, Copley was still experimenting with a figure to the right, seemingly the figure that evolved into the man in the center holding his comrade by the shirttail. A more finished drawing (fig. 378) shows the figures in their approximate final relationship to each other. The harpoonist has his general pose, but the dynamic, thrusting position that so energizes the final composition has not yet been achieved. This is brought about by placing the figure lower in the boat so that he steps higher and bends further forward in order to get into position. This gives a more vertical line to the harpoon, and when the hair, like the coat, is blown backward by the wind, the sense of motion is quickened. The grouping on the left has been developed, but the oarsman now is almost in profile and in the finished version looks over his shoulder at the floundering Watson. The group on the near side of the boat is decided upon. No earlier drawings for these figures have yet come to light. A standing figure in the center, not here identified as a Negro, is literally a central figure, competing in scale with the harpoonist. In the end he moves backward in the boat, and his head is lowered to become the central point from which all action radiates. Finally a figure is introduced, as yet undefined, beyond the harpoonist. One presumes that Copley found this to be a late compositional necessity to fill the gap caused by the harpoonist's stride. This connects the harpoonist solidly with the bulk of the rest of the figures so that his thrust carries, in a figurative sense, the weight of the entire group as well as a certain amount of inertia from the forward movement of the boat.

The composition is built on the strong horizontals of the boy and the shark, the boat, the cityscape, and Morro Castle in the background. These horizontals are not exactly parallel on the surface and form a zigzag recession in space. This gentle movement serves as a foil to the violent, vertical accent of the harpoon thrust. The movement of the shark toward the boy, the progress of the boat toward the shark, and the strength of the compositional line of the harpoon invoke a powerful sense of impending impact. The question is whether the impact will be between the shark and the boy or the harpoon and the shark. The effect is amplified by the theatrical light that flows in from the left: it highlights the boy, the shark, and the reaching men; casts the bow and stern into contrasting shadow areas; and then picks up the stem with a triangle of light that accentuates the tip of the harpoon. Yet one does not have an impression of a fugitive scene frozen only for an instant. The solid pyramid of the composition and the inevitability of the poses give a monumentality to the presentation.

Copley's composition for *Watson and the Shark* seems strikingly original, but it is not without its sources. The figure of Watson is a mirror image of *The Gladiator* in the Villa Borghese, placed on its side (fig. 379),[22] an unusual adaptation of classical sculpture that nonetheless does work and subtly carries the overtones of gladiatorial combat between man and beast into *Watson and the Shark*. A general influence may well have been Rubens' *Lion Hunt* (fig. 380), in which a lion receives the thrust of lances while attacking a central figure who is turned almost upside down, his head back, one leg bent and the other out of view. Rubens' composition also contains one Negro figure. Copley did own the Schelte à Bolswert engraving of Rubens' *Lion Hunt*, though not necessarily at this early date.[23]

Although the debt of *Watson and the Shark* to Rubens is quite general, it is significant. Copley's first history picture, which does carry West's realistic approach to history painting a step further by the careful authenticity of the setting, is nonetheless very different from *Agrippina* or *Penn's Treaty*. Copley was not representing a significant or heroic event, but merely the unusual maiming of a quite ordinary individual. Such subjects were customarily the province of cheap, sensational pictorial journalism rather than of history painting.[24] Moreover, *Watson and the Shark* is different from West's production compositionally as well as thematically. West's classical phase, which followed his Italian trip and lasted into the 1770's, was strongly influenced by the work of the seventeenth-century classicist, Nicholas Poussin. *Agrippina* is particularly like Poussin, but all of these early West history pictures have a Poussinesque emphasis on drawing, on planarity, and on a rational, ordered, and carefully measured disposition of pictorial elements. Copley chose the opposite course. When he had arrived in London in December 1775 after his Italian tour, he was keenly aware of West's accomplishments as a history painter. However, unlike most young American artists coming to London,

[22] This source was indicated to me by Professor Benjamin Rowland.

[23] See appendix, Copley Print Sale (189).

[24] This was novel, and it has occasionally caused art historians to point to *Watson and the Shark* as a forerunner of such romantic masterpieces as Gericault's *Raft of the Medusa*. In fact, however, fascination with the distant, the exotic, and the horrible was an integral part of eighteenth-century classicism, and Copley's depiction of these reflects a normal eighteenth-century interest in such matters. It was unusual only in that it was here accorded full history-painting honors. Copley does not seem to have provided new insights into the struggle between man and nature, although the more romantic-minded critics of his day complimented him on his clever stroke in leaving the shark unfinished and increasing the sense of danger and horror through its very indefiniteness (*General Advertiser*, April 28, 1778).

he had no intention of becoming a disciple at the feet of West. He was a mature artist who had experienced considerable success, and he was eager to compete for public favor. His innermost ambition, nurtured since his earliest days as an artist, was to become the leading history painter of the day, the equal of the old masters, and clearly this meant direct competition with West, who was already established as the leading history painter in England. Thus overlapping professional aspirations meant that a clash between Copley and West was inevitable. Still, for the first few years after Copley's arrival in England — perhaps because Copley had the good sense not to talk too much about his hopes, and perhaps because Copley did not pose any immediate threat to the well-entrenched West — a warm professional and personal friendship existed between the two. For the moment West indulged himself in the kind of paternalistic guidance and support that was natural for him, and Copley's ambition and flinty competitiveness were undoubtedly muted by his admiration for West, his gratitude for his help and advice, his awareness of his own position as a tyro in the London art world, and by the warm glow of optimism that accompanies a new start in a new place. It was probably during this period that Copley painted his portrait of *Benjamin West* (fig. 382). Indeed at this moment, especially 1776–77, there was a remarkable but temporary similarity in the portrait styles of the two men.[25]

The honeymoon was to be short-lived, however, and the Rubenesque quality of *Watson and the Shark* is a symptom of what was to come. Aware of West's achievements and of West's classical affinity for Poussin, Copley, with his own great gifts as a colorist, drew upon himself the mantle of Rubens, the traditional antithesis of Poussin. Echoing the seventeenth-century battle of the Poussinistes and the Rubénistes, Copley set out to play the part of Rubens in counterpoint to West's Poussin. Copley's penchant for Rubens is clearly evident in the superb *Head of a Negro* (fig. 381), which for over a century has been known as a sketch for *Watson and the Shark*. Indeed it may have been intended as a sketch for that painting, but the head does not bear any resemblance to the more sober, much less animated face of the Negro in the final picture. This head would have stolen the scene from the harpoonist, and possibly it was not used in the painting so that the harpoonist could clearly epitomize the rescue operation as he prepares to thrust his harpoon into the shark.

[25] For example, West's portraits of *George Drummond with Peter Auriol Drummond and His Wife* (1776, Minneapolis Institute of Arts) and *Sir Thomas Beauchamp-Proctor* (1777, Tate Gallery) are exceedingly close in their handling, especially in the brushwork, to Copley's earliest English portraits. Although Copley may have been influenced by West, which would be natural, zestful brushwork was actually a more deeply entrenched Copley characteristic. This raises the question of whether Copley may not have had some impact upon West, or if the influence was not at least mutual.

XII

The Death of Chatham

1779-1781 Following the successful exhibition of *Watson and the Shark*, Copley was elected to full membership in the Royal Academy in February 1779,[1] although his delay in presenting a diploma picture to the academy deferred his formal elevation to academician for more than four years. In 1779 and 1780 Copley was largely occupied with a much more ambitious history picture, *The Death of the Earl of Chatham*. But he did manage to produce a few other important paintings. The lucid and effective portrait of *Gilbert DeBlois* (fig. 383) dates from this general period. In 1779 he painted the seated portrait of *Mrs. Clark Gayton* (fig. 384) and the strong, three-quarter-length standing portrait of *Admiral Clark Gayton* (fig. 385). Copley painted Gayton in flag officer's full-dress uniform, in a dramatic standing pose with his hand on a scroll of paper inscribed "Vice-Admiral Gayton." In the left distance can be seen the *Antelope*, flying Gayton's flag as Vice-Admiral of the White at Jamaica.

It also may be possible that *Venus and Cupid* (fig. 386) was painted in this year. It is a sketchy picture and may have been intended as a study for something else. If, as has been stated, the young Cupid is a portrait of Copley's son John as a boy, an approximate estimate of his age as six or seven would indicate a date of 1778 or 1779 for the picture. It has also been said that Venus is Mrs. Copley, but a comparison of this head with other portraits of her (*Copley Family, Nativity, Death of Peirson*) fails to reveal any clear likeness.[2] Stylistically the picture could be much later in date.

Copley probably painted the portrait of *Mrs. John Hay* (fig. 387) in 1780, since Samuel Curwen saw it in his studio in December of that year. Although he had exhibited nothing at the Royal Academy the year before, Copley submitted four portraits in 1780. One was a full-length of *George Boone Roupell* (fig. 388) of Charleston, South Carolina. Another, listed only as a *Portrait of an Highland Officer*, has been identified as *Major Hugh Montgomerie*, later Twelfth Earl of Eglinton. There are preliminary drawings by Copley for such a picture (figs. 390 and 390a), but the painting itself remains unlocated. A full-length portrait of Montgomerie in the Scottish National Por-

[1] "General Assembly Minute Books," RA, I, 132, Feb. 9, 1779. There were seventeen candidates. In the final ballot Copley defeated William Pars by two votes. Pars had been an associate academician since 1770 and had previously been defeated in an attempt for full status by James Barry in 1773. Whitley, *Artists in England, 1700–1799*, II, 344.

[2] Frank W. Bayley, *The Life and Works of John Singleton Copley* (Boston, 1915), pp. 10, 88; Amory, p. 23.

trait Gallery (fig. 389), which follows the composition of the drawing, has been considered Copley's portrait. Stylistic examination indicates that it is an imposing, impressive, and early copy. (An 1821 copy by Henry Raeburn hangs in the county buildings, Ayr, Scotland.) These paintings depict the Twelfth Earl of Eglinton in full highland uniform — feathered bonnet, red jacket faced with green and laced with silver, belted plaid or "big kilt" of government or Black Watch tartan, and red and white hose. Although the original picture was painted in 1780 when Montgomerie was in his forties, his uniform has the facings of his American war service of the early 1760's. The pose, as in innumerable eighteenth-century full-length portraits, is an adaptation of the Apollo Belvedere.[3]

In 1780 Copley also painted *Samuel Relating to Eli the Judgements of God upon Eli's House* (fig. 391). His son appears as Samuel, and a maimed beggar who had lost both legs in battle is said to have been the model for Eli. The painting is coloristically pleasant, with rather heavy Rembrandtesque impasto, especially in the gold of the breastplate and the vessels on the table, in the sashes and on the footstool. There is a considerable amount of life and interest in these painterly passages, but much of the picture surface is flat. Surprisingly enough, the heads themselves, particularly the boy's, lack vitality. One wonders why Copley bothered with this particular picture at a time when he must have been deeply involved with the much more important *Death of Chatham*. It is possible that he intended it as his diploma piece for the Academy but, finding a purchaser, decided to sell it instead.[4]

Copley's large history painting *The Death of the Earl of Chatham* (fig. 392), which claimed most of his attention during 1779–80, commemorated an event that had occurred in the House of Lords on April 7, 1778. The House was then meeting in a Committee on the State of the Nation, and the Duke of Richmond had offered for consideration an address to the king which urged the withdrawal of British armed forces from the American colonies. Richmond argued that the attempt to enslave the American colonies was immoral and that American resistance to the repressive measures was justified. He further argued that Britain's attempt to equip an adequate army on the other side of the Atlantic was a folly, and that British losses and the unimpressively

[3] Ward, *Curwen*, p. 296; Whitley, *Artists in England, 1700–1799*, II, 376; Algernon Graves, *The Royal Academy of Arts* (London, 1905–6), II, 159; Scottish National Portrait Gallery Records. Copley's portrait was owned by the Eglinton family. After Raeburn copied it, he returned both the original and the copy to Coilsfield, Ayrshire, the family home (Henry Raeburn to Hamilton Douglas-Boswell, Dec. 6, 1821, Scottish National Portrait Gallery, photostat of original in Scottish Record Office). A version of the picture said to be signed and dated by Copley has recently been located in a private collection in Scotland. My attempts to communicate with the owner and to secure a photograph have been unsuccessful.

[4] Further evidence of this is found in a 1780 letter to the editor of the *Morning Post* from "No Conjuror," which discusses the new building of the Royal Academy. The letter prudishly complains that females visiting the academy must pass by naked Greek statues in order to arrive at the room containing Reynolds' portraits of the king and queen, the ceiling painted by West and Angelica Kauffmann, and that "masterly picture of Eli and Samuel by Copley." "Cuttings on Art," Victoria and Albert Museum, I, 191, 1780.

small amount of territory now under British control was ample proof of the inadequacy of the British forces and the magnitude of the undertaking. The alliance of the colonies with France had not only made the situation more impossible, but it meant that the continuation of armed conflict would only serve to drive the Americans into a tighter liaison with France. Moreover, the further diversion of British troops from elsewhere in the empire to America would seriously debilitate defenses closer to home. Viscount Weymouth, who does not appear in Copley's picture, spoke at length in opposition to Richmond. When he had finished, the infirm William Pitt, Earl of Chatham, rose. He had entered the House earlier on crutches and had been assisted to his seat. Chatham's political philosophy, for which he had long fought, was based on a belief that England should pursue an adventurous policy abroad, relying on naval supremacy to control the seas in the race for trade and wealth. He believed that England's power should be founded on prosperity, not on vast land holdings. Rather than a land empire, Chatham advocated securing "strategic focal points of trade." During his first ministry, beginning in 1757, British arms had won an impressive series of victories over the French, which assured English commercial primacy in North America. In 1762 Chatham violently opposed the Treaty of Paris, which once more gave France a maritime foothold in America, in the West Indies and the Newfoundland fisheries. He was certain that this would enable France again to become a naval threat in the New World. As leader of the opposition during the succeeding years, and during a second brief ministry in 1766, Chatham made America his great cause. He saw the issues as commercial, not constitutional. America was a source of wealth, naval strength, material, and manpower, as well as an important market for English goods. So he favored every compromise short of granting independence to hold America in the empire. Because Chatham favored an adventurous policy, he had the support of the military; because he was primarily concerned with commercial expansion and prosperity, he had the support of the City; because he favored a liberal policy toward America that would prevent rebellion, he had the support of moderate Whigs and Tories alike; and because he espoused the cause of freedom from excessive governmental control in the pursuit of private interests, Pitt as the "Great Commoner" had the support of the people. During the 1760's Pitt became increasingly ill in body and mind. His infirmity and his madness combined with an innate theatricality to give his orations particular force and an aura of prophecy.

When Chatham rose to rebut the Duke of Richmond and to urge the extension of the war effort in America, it was not because his sympathy for America had lessened but because to him the greatest tragedy for England would be the severance of all ties with the colonies. He felt that the independence of America must ultimately lead to the decline of England as a world power. In an effective speech he recalled the previous adventurousness of English foreign policy and deplored the defeatism implicit in Richmond's argument. Richmond in his reply paid effusive tribute to Chatham, noting that his name "will ever be dear to Englishmen." But he averred that times had changed and that the realities of the present situation clearly indicated that England could not win the American war. It was prudent to end the action and treat for peace in order to cut losses, to salvage the good will of the Americans, and to strengthen the nation's defenses against possible continental aggression.

Chatham, wishing to speak further, tried to reach his feet but fell backward in a faint. He was immediately assisted by the Duke of Cumberland, lords Temple and Stamford, and others who were nearby, including his son James Pitt. He was removed to the prince's chamber where he was attended by the royal physician, Richard Brocklesby. In the House, after the confusion had subsided, Richmond rose once more, again gave "warm testimonial to the great political abilities and integrity of the noble earl," said that Chatham's indisposition was believed to be temporary, and moved the adjournment of the debate until the following day.[5]

Although Chatham clung to life for another month, he had in fact been struck down in the House in the fight that had long engaged him and that had won him ardent support as well as bitter opposition. Like most Americans, Copley greatly admired Chatham.[6] As an aspiring history painter, he saw in Chatham's dramatic stroke an opportunity to follow up the successful *Watson and the Shark* with a painting that would deal with an event of real historic importance. By the time of the Royal Academy exhibition in the spring of 1779, Copley was at work on his large picture. When the London Court of Common Council met in December of that year "to consider what Mark of Respect is most fit to perpetuate the Memory of the late Earl of Chatham,"[7] Copley, with the subject already in hand, was able to submit a design for consideration. The other competing artists were the sculptors John Bacon and Nicholas Read. A contemporary account noted that "Mr. Copley's is a Sketch in Colours, representing Lord C in the unfortunate moment when he was apprised of his Dissolution in the House of Lords, attended by his Sons and the Minority Lords. The Duke of Richmond is a principal Figure in the Groupe, which comprises fifty-six different Figures, all executed in a masterly manner."[8]

After much debate the commission was given not to Copley for a history painting, but to Bacon for a memorial statue. According to the stated purpose of the Court of Common Council, suitability or appropriateness was a prime factor in the choice. Copley's proposal for a realistic painting containing the portraits of fifty-six noblemen was a much less traditional memorial; indeed it was quite radical. The projected picture was not to be a group portrait, like Frans Hals's *Syndics*, Rembrandt's *Nightwatch*, or,

[5] J. H. Plumb, "The Earl of Chatham," in *Men and Places* (London, 1963) pp. 107–114; *The Parliamentary History of England*, XIX (London, 1814), 1012–31.

[6] When Charles Willson Peale had sent Copley a copy of his mezzotint of Pitt in 1770, Copley first of all liked the print "because it is the portrait of that great Man, in the most exalted carractor human [sic] can be dignified with, that of a true Patriot vindicateing the rights of Mankind." *Proceedings of the Massachusetts Historical Society*, XLVIII (Feb. 1915), 292, John Singleton Copley, Boston, to Charles Willson Peale, Annapolis, Dec. 17, 1770. A draft of the letter is printed in *Copley-Pelham Letters*, pp. 100–01.

[7] *St. James's Chronicle*, Dec. 16–18, 1779.

[8] *Ibid.*

more contemporaneously, James Barry's 1778 project to paint forty or fifty members of the Society of Arts taking part in a prize distribution of paintings; in these the making of specific portraits was the avowed purpose of the paintings.[9] *The Death of Chatham* was to be a group portrait after the fact, created not for the sake of the portraits but to commemorate the event. This stress on the significance of the event provided the basis of Copley's novel position in going before the City Council: he intended to carry the revolution in history painting one more step in the direction of increased realism. Fortunately, although the proposal was too radical for the council and he did not gain the commission, Copley continued with the picture.

The depiction of current events was in itself no novelty. Dutch masters of the seventeenth century had reveled in scenes of everyday life; and in England in the eighteenth century Hogarth had continued the tradition, giving the genre scenes a moralizing twist. Crude reportorial engravings of current events were common throughout the eighteenth century. West's radical innovation in *The Death of Wolfe* lay in elevating the realistic treatment of a current event from painted genre scenes or six-penny engravings into a carefully composed, expertly executed, large-scale history painting. Although West presented a contemporary hero in modern dress, he cushioned the shock of immediacy by representing a scene that was at least far removed geographically. Copley now proposed to strip away even that distance between viewer and object. The death scene he proposed was recent in time and local in place, and the realism of the presentation, which included actual portraits of people who were there, would have all the shock of a photograph on a pre-camera audience.

Copley in *The Death of Chatham* consciously combined two distinct branches of painting — history painting and portraiture. Other artists, notably Joshua Reynolds, had emphasized portraiture, sometimes simply by stressing classical accessories and putting the figures in a classical pose, but sometimes by presenting the subject in a specific classical role.[10] Copley, however, was not painting historically flavored portraits, but portrait-laden history pictures. In theory this should have lowered the status of his history paintings since, according to accepted standards, portraiture marked a lesser level of artistic achievement. Copley tilted his lance at this particular doctrine, and set out to prove that a factually accurate history painting was more meritorious than a work based on imagination alone. With *The Death of Chatham* Copley broke new ground in the development of history painting in the eighteenth century, and he won a place alongside Benjamin West as one of the two leading English history painters of the day.

It is significant that both of the leading English history painters of the last quarter of the eighteenth century, practitioners of the noblest form of painting, were born and achieved their artistic maturity in the American colonies, where their imaginations had

[9] Robert R. Wark, "James Barry" (unpublished dissertation, Harvard University, 1952), pp. 150–52.
[10] Copley did paint at least one portrait in which the sitter was assigned a role, *Mrs. Derby as St. Cecilia*, 1806, which was based directly on Reynolds' portrait of *Mrs. Sheridan as St. Cecilia*, 1775.

been kindled by books — descriptions of art and artists and the special glories reserved for the painters of historical subjects — rather than by art itself. It is if anything more significant that West from Quaker Philadelphia and Copley from Puritan Boston emerged from provincial societies that were singularly materialistic and pragmatic, concerned more with the tangibles of this world than with the possibilities of the next. As history painters West and Copley were innovators, and their work moved steadily in the direction of realism. Certainly it seems possible that the impulse toward realism manifested in their most creative artistic statements reflects values and outlooks traceable to their common provincial origin. In fact, the realism introduced into history painting by West and Copley can be placed among the first direct American contributions to Western art. West's influence has long been recognized as seminal in the development of French neoclassicism; and Copley's influence on later neoclassicism, particularly such portrait-filled recordings of contemporary history as Jacques Louis David's *Tennis Court Oath*, is equally significant.

Copley's materialistic background conditioned not only the nature of his paintings but also the very circumstances that led him to choose to paint such pictures in the first place. Copley did not have a commission to paint *The Death of Chatham*, but undertook the picture as an entrepreneurial effort. In addition to his wish to pay tribute to Chatham, Copley saw a practical opportunity that induced him to abandon his earlier resolve not to paint history pictures except on commission. The project involved painting portraits of over fifty of the most prominent and influential noblemen in England; out of respect for Lord Chatham, it would have been difficult for any of them to refuse to sit for this work. Therefore Copley, a relative newcomer to the English artistic scene, would have a chance to meet and paint a large group of important people, making contacts that might lead to further commissions. Moreover, after the picture was painted there would be a natural market for the sale of engravings of the picture, beginning with the friends, relatives, and admirers of the figures included. Additional income from exhibiting the picture to a general public curious about the tragic event was another potential source of income.

The compositional beginnings of *The Death of Chatham* are obscured by the fact that the subject obviously had a similar appeal for Benjamin West, whose American background probably made him equally sympathetic to Chatham; his position as history painter to the king prompted caution, however. West apparently began a depiction of the same subject with the king's approval, but he abandoned the project. Several years later Horace Walpole recalled: "Mr. West made a small Sketch of the death of Lord Chatham, much better expressed & disposed than Copley's. It has none but the principal person's present; Copley's almost the whole peerage, of whom seldom so many are there at once, & in Copleys most are meer [*sic*] spectators. but the great merit of West is the principal Figure which has his crutch & gouty stockings, which express his feebleness & account for his death. West wd not finish it not to interfere with his friend

280

Copley."[11] A drawing for *The Death of Chatham* in the collection of John Davis Hatch (fig. 399) has on occasion been attributed to West. A similar drawing ascribed to Copley in the British Museum (fig. 400) is very closely related compositionally, but the viewpoint is further to the left, more as in Copley's final painting. Both drawings are undoubtedly by the same hand. They may tentatively be accepted as by Copley, although they are a trifle mannered and do seem to have some relationship to West's initial project as described by Walpole.[12]

A study for the central group at the British Museum (fig. 401) represents a marked alteration from the arrangement set forth in the two earlier drawings. Chatham is no longer supported in a seated position, but collapses to the right into a group of men, some of whom grasp him under the arms and about the legs. An oil sketch in the Tate Gallery (fig. 402) is evidently the next step in the compositional development. There are about thirty figures now included, and some of the heads — notably the Duke of Richmond (51 in the key, fig. 393) on the right, Earl Bathurst (22) on the left, Lord Camden (32) in the center mid-distance, and possibly the Duke of Portland (44) behind Chatham — suggest that portrait sittings had begun. These figures, with the exception of Bathurst, are in much the same general position that they occupy in the final version, although the specific poses will be altered. The figures of the Duke of Cumberland (45), the Earl of Shelbourne (47), and Earl Temple (48) are in their final grouping, although the pose of Shelbourne is transferred to Lord Ferrers (50) in the subsequent versions. The individual groups are self-contained in comparison to the final version, in which the groups are better integrated with the death scene.

The next oil sketch (fig. 403), also in the Tate Gallery, has about five more figures in it and repeats some of the elements found in the early drawings. The throne with its scalloped canopy is reintroduced on the left, but only as a simple affair. In the earliest two drawings a group of two figures, one of whom leans against the wall, had appeared in the upper right. These figures were placed behind the recumbent Chatham in the small British Museum study of the central group (fig. 401). They were moved still farther to the left in the first oil sketch, and a figure to the right of Chatham leaned against the wall. Here in the second oil sketch a group is introduced above and behind that figure, approximately in the same location as the group in the earliest drawings, and it assumes the important compositional role the first group had played, bringing the wheel full circle. There are no new portraits, which leads us to believe that Copley was now concentrating on the composition, intending to perfect it before finishing the heads. A few more figures have been added behind the Duke of Richmond (51) on the right to form a balancing group to the figures on the left, who have become peers. The group moves closer to the center of the picture and opens up a bit to let the space circulate more freely as an ambient in which the figures exist. Yet the clear contrast

[11] "Walpole's Book of Materials, 1771," p. 113 (1785), Lewis-Walpole Library, Farmington, Conn.; Whitley, *Artists in England, 1700–1799*, pp. 355–56.

[12] Professor Helmut von Erffa, who is writing a study of West, does not believe the two drawings to be by West (letter to the author, July 26, 1960).

between foreground and background deteriorates. From the first drawings through the two oil sketches, there has been a continual retreat of the action from the viewer. The oil sketch in the National Gallery of Art, Washington (fig. 404), carries this further. In a theatrical setting marked by a drawn curtain on the right, a flood of light pours in through an opening in the end wall above the throne to function almost as a spotlight. Much of the coffered, barrel-vaulted ceiling can be seen. The general disposition of the figures is very close to the final arrangement, although there will still be changes, as in Richmond's (51) left hand and Cumberland's (45) knees. Only the Duke of Devonshire (43), Lord Westcote (15), and the Earl of Eglinton (16) are clearly missing, but there are a few additional heads in the sketchy group beneath the canopy. The handling suggests that life portraits of perhaps half of the figures had been taken and introduced. The number of figures appearing in this sketch for the first time approximates the number in the sketch shown in December 1779 to the Court of Common Council, and this may have been the actual sketch Copley submitted. One of the portraits introduced here is that of Lord Temple (48). On May 27, 1779, the late Lord Chatham's daughter, Lady Harriot Eliot, noted in her diary, "We dined with Ld Temple yesterday . . . he has been sitting to the man who has been painting the great and melancholy scene at the House of Lds and I am told that his likeness is most striking." [13] The likeness, indeed striking, is one of the best heads in the picture. Copley's cool and fluid style was well suited to representing the hoary mantle of age that Lord Temple seems to have worn so handsomely.

This sketch also includes a different treatment of the canopy, which relates to a drawing at Utica (fig. 417). These drawings of the throne suggest the error in Oskar Hagen's unlikely observation, based on a critical review of the final painting, that Copley never set foot in the House of Lords.[14]

Copley presented on March 29, 1780, a proposal for publishing an engraving of *Chatham* by John Keyse Sherwin on a subscription basis. The announcement described the painting, on which the artist was then engaged, as depicting the moment when Chatham received his fatal stroke in the House of Lords. The fallen Chatham is surrounded by his three sons and his son-in-law (Lord Viscount Mahon) and supported by the Dukes of Cumberland and Portland. The Duke of Richmond, who has just finished speaking, stands nearby. The composition is divided into three groups of figures. More than half of the picture, the right side, contains one group — the figures around Richmond and Chatham. The great officers of state form a second group in the left rear. The bishops and other peers in the foreground on the left side of the picture form the

[13] Cuthbert Headlam, ed., *Letters of Lady Harriot Eliot, 1766–1786* (Edinburgh, 1914), p. 32. The day and month are noted in the diary; the year is uncertain. But the head of Lord Temple must have been painted before the oil sketch in Washington (fig. 404) was made, since it is included there. Because that sketch was apparently the one shown to the Court of Common Council before December 1779, it seems safe to date this letter 1779.

[14] Oskar Hagen, *The Birth of the American Tradition in Art* (New York, 1940), p. 137. For the review in question, see text below.

third group. The Lord Chancellor and judges are seated on the wool pack, and the sons of peers appear on the steps of the throne. There are, according to the brochure, sixty figures in the picture.

In soliciting subscriptions for the engraving Copley noted, "This is the most arduous work of the kind hitherto undertaken in any Capital country," adding that "The uniting the value of living characters to the dignity of an Historical Fact [gives the picture] an advantage that will be rising in estimation in every succeeding age and which no other picture extant has to boast of in any degree equal to this." This is the core of Copley's argument that, although portraiture is a lesser art than history painting, the union of the two produces a new type of history painting, which should be considered the most elevated of all. Copley rested his solicitation for subscriptions on three factors — the character of Chatham; the singularity of incident, time, and place; and the representations. He listed the people who would be included, omitting only ten who appear in the final version.

After he had almost all of the figures finished, Copley wrote to the Duke of Rutland requesting an appointment to take his portrait. "Mr. Copley has reserved two figures that the Duke may have that which he prefers, and he wishes to know which that will be, that he may make use of the other before the pears [sic] leave town." [15] However, Rutland apparently did not oblige Copley since he does not appear in the final picture. Copley must have been faced with the necessity of locating a few last-minute sitters in order to put likenesses on all of his figures. Samuel Curwen, the loyalist, may have come upon one of these final sitters when he arrived at Leicester Square to visit Richard Clarke on April 2, 1781: "Seeing a nobleman's carriage at the door, presumed he was sitting to Mr. Copley, and that therefore my company may be inconvenient." [16]

Since persuading fifty-five noblemen to sit for their portraits was something of a *tour de force*, one wonders whether or not Copley cut corners by using contemporary prints as source material. But a survey of contemporary engraved portraits of the figures in the picture suggests an almost complete independence of them. Occasionally there is a similarity between a head in a print and in the painting, but this seems to result from random similarities in expression and pose, and there is no evidence of Copley's reliance upon prints here. Further, the descriptive brochure of the picture that was distributed to those who came to the exhibition states that the fifty-five portraits in the picture were "taken from life." [17] A necessary exception would be the portrait of the dead Earl of Chatham: it may have been taken from a secondary source such as the portrait by Brompton, engraved by Bocquet, in which there is not only a general similarity of likeness but also a related pose of hand on breast.

Copley's *Death of Chatham* was completed by the spring of 1781. It had occupied

[15] Royal Commission on Historical Manuscripts, *Fourteenth Report*, "The Mss. of the Duke of Rutland, K.G.," III (London, 1894), 70.

[16] Ward, *Curwen*, p. 311.

[17] This brochure includes the same description of the painting that had been set forth in the engraving proposal of the previous year.

much of his time and effort for two years. Now the moment was at hand for him to reap his rewards in fame and money. Since the painting had not been executed on a commission basis and the Corporation of London had not elected to acquire it as a memorial, the picture was a pure financial speculation for Copley. Since income from exhibition promised to be a major source of revenue, Copley decided not to exhibit the picture at the Royal Academy. Instead, several days after the 1781 academy exhibition opened, Copley presented a competing exhibition of *The Death of Chatham* at Spring Garden. The printed brochure that was given to visitors at the exhibition also served as a press release for the newspapers, many of which printed large sections of it as a ready-made article on the opening.[18] This afforded the exhibition much good publicity that, coupled with favorable or provocative reviews, contributed toward the success of Copley's independent effort. On some days over eight hundred people came to see the picture, and by the end of the first six weeks of the exhibition, almost twenty thousand people had seen it. In the face of such competition, the Royal Academy did not do well, and income from its 1781 exhibition declined almost one thousand pounds from the previous years.[19]

Copley's rival show was not kindly entertained by some members of the Royal Academy. It had been Copley's initial plan to exhibit the picture in Pall Mall in the exhibition gallery formerly used by the Royal Academy. This gallery was currently used as an auction room by Copley's neighbor, James Christie. The architect, Sir William Chambers, led Royal Academy opposition to Copley's plan, and he exerted sufficient pressure on Christie to cause him to refuse the gallery for what Chambers called a "raree-show." Copley angrily published a statement describing the way in which Chambers' interference had caused him to alter his plans. He twitted Chambers on his fear that one picture would hurt the Royal Academy exhibition, noting that he himself never could be presumptuous enough to make such a claim for his picture.[20]

Reactions to *The Death of Chatham*, favorable and unfavorable, were uniformly based on two factors: the verisimilitude of the likenesses and the political implications of the expressions and reactions of the various lords depicted. Dr. James Beattie and his son, James Hay Beattie, two early visitors to the picture, noted the acceptability of the likenesses, but objected to the absence of expression that seemed to reflect a lack of concern on the part of some individuals.[21] The *St. James's Chronicle*, June 9–12, 1781, was concerned with the political grouping. Noting that visitors to the exhibition were affected by the scene "as at the Bed of a sick Person," the reviewer's opinion was that the group around the stricken Chatham and the surrounding leaders of the minority

---

[18] For example, the description and list of portraits was printed intact in *London Courant*, May 2, 1781; *Morning Chronicle*, May 4, 1781; *Morning Herald*, June 8, 1781; and *London Chronicle*, May 3–5, 1781.

[19] *Public Advertiser*, May 29, 1781; *Morning Herald*, June 8, 1781; Whitley, *Artists in England,*

1700–1799, I, 357.

[20] Whitley, *Artists in England, 1700–1799*, I, 357.

[21] Sir William Forbes, *An Account of the Life and Writings of James Beattie* (New York and Boston, 1807), p. 338; "Journal of James Hay Beattie," University of Aberdeen, entry for Thursday, May 3, [1781].

had been painted "to the utmost Advantage," while the group around Lord Mansfield had been given, either by nature or the artist, the appearance of "sharpers." It was also noted, though probably inaccurately, that Lord Mansfield was the only man included who would not sit to Copley, and that Copley therefore felt that Mansfield was unconcerned about the death of Chatham and painted him seated to express this lack of concern.

In painting *The Death of Chatham* Copley was in political waters a little out of his depth. He apparently failed to realize that by honoring Chatham he could hardly help giving offense to those who opposed Chatham, a powerful group that included the ministry in power and other influential figures at Court and in Parliament. Perhaps this explains why the politically acute West was so agreeable to abandoning his project for the picture, leaving the field to Copley. The task of painting *The Death of Chatham* was surrounded by political booby traps, and in the case of the representation of the Earl of Mansfield Copley may have tripped one. Mansfield had been a bitter lifelong opponent of Chatham, and "on the occasion of Lord Chatham's final scene in the House of Lords, on 7 April 1778, Mansfield disgraced himself by exhibiting an ostentatious indifference." [22] By painting Mansfield seated, Copley called attention to this calloused attitude, whether he intended to or not. That Mansfield probably did pose for his likeness is suggested by a scaled drawing of his head in the Boston Athenaeum (fig. 406). But he may have regretted it when he saw the completed picture. What is puzzling is that less than two years later Copley painted a full-length seated portrait of Lord Mansfield, in which the expression and the head position are substantially different from the figure in the history picture. Mansfield could hardly have been pleased by Copley's dramatization of his indifference, and it is almost inconceivable that he would subsequently commission a portrait by Copley. Perhaps Copley, realizing the extent of his tactlessness and the professional danger of offending great and powerful lords, painted the portrait gratis as an act of contrition.

The most vigorous critical response to the picture occurred as a letter to *The Gazetteer* dated May 5, 1781, from "A By-Stander." The writer was an eyewitness to the event, and the tone of the letter suggests that he was a peer or some official of the House of Lords. His first objection was that the interior of the chamber was inaccurately drawn. Allowing no quarter for artistic license, he attacked on the ground that at no point in the room is it possible to see all of the elements that are included in the painting. He suggested that Copley had never been inside the House of Lords, which seems unjustified (see fig. 417). He noted that, if the painting were worth the estimated eight to twenty thousand pounds, it would have been worth more if it had been accurate. Copley, the correspondent suggested, could have used a view of the interior that had been published in a cheap periodical a few years before. The only realistic elements he found in the picture were the faces themselves, and he had some severe reservations

---

[22] *Dictionary of National Biography*, XIII, 1310.

about these. Strangely enough, he felt that the best portrait likeness was that of Lord Mansfield.[23] Lord North, the critic noted, is considered to have been "ill-treated," and Lord George Germain "made to look like a buffoon," while Lord Coventry, an athletic man of between fifty and sixty, is turned into a slender young man with a vacuous expression. The figure of the Duke of Richmond came in for a particularly vigorous onslaught.

> The Duke of Richmond, one of the *principal* figures in the piece, preserves a likeness, but *such* a likeness as I never desire to see again on canvas; such a likeness in my opinion, as I have seen more than once drawn with a piece of *charcoal* by the *aid* of a *candle*. It is indeed a profile, but a profile of the *first* impression. The position of his body is as *unnatural* as his *place* is *fictitious*. He is made to stand on canvas, as I will venture to say, he never stood on *his own* legs.

It is obvious that Copley did have difficulty with the figure of the Duke of Richmond. It was one of the first to be placed in the composition, but it was altered many times. There are numerous extant drawings for the figure (figs. 407–411), all relating to a changing pose between the fully developed last oil sketch and the final format. Copley was concerned not only because the Duke of Richmond had figured prominently in the scene, having just finished the speech to which Chatham was rising to reply when he was stricken, but also because he was a prominent and powerful patron of the arts. Copley would have liked to make a favorable impression upon him; unfortunately the final result was rather stilted.

As for others of the portraits, Mr. B. Leacroft wrote to a friend that he was "quite affronted at the painter for placing Lord Scarsdale just as if he were playing at hide and seek whilst Lord Chatham was expiring." He added, however, that some of the portraits were very good and noted that Lord Ferrers, who "was once so genteel and thin a gentleman," here "looks like a fat Dutch mastif."[24] One of the earliest drawings

[23] After Lord Mansfield, the "By-Stander" liked the portraits of Lord Camden and Lord Amherst (which are indeed splendid), followed by such "capital" portraits as those of the Bishops of St. Asaph and Peterborough; Lords Gower, Dudley, Loughborough, Thurlow; Earl Ferrers; and Mr. Shirley. Classified as "good" are the portraits of Lords Bathurst, Edgecumbe, Mahon, Temple, Fitzwilliam, and Bessborough, Mr. W. Pitt, Dr. Brocklesby, the Duke of Grafton, the Archbishop of York, Chief Baron Skinner, and the Duke of Cumberland. "Tolerable" are the heads of the Marquis of Rockingham, Lords Shelburne, Radnor, Effingham, Cholmondeley, the present Lord Chatham, Scarsdale, Sandwich, Harcourt, Westcote, and Robert Bertie, and the Dukes of Portland and Devonshire. The final category, "execrable," included Lords North, Germain, Fauconberg, Westmorland, Dartmouth, Coventry, Courtenay, and Spencer, the Dukes of Montague and Manchester, "and all the others." The "By-Stander" also felt that Copley had committed a gross inaccuracy in painting the peers in robes, since they were not wearing them at the time. But he conceded that the painting of the drapery was very good and may have been why the robes were incorporated. He repeated the observation made by the Beatties that the figures are deficient in "expression." The critic in the *Public Advertiser*, May 19, 1781, agreed with the "By-Stander" on the merits of Lords Thurlow, Loughborough, Hinchcliffe (Peterborough), and Amherst, and also listed the Archbishop of York and Lord Bathurst who were considered merely "good" by "By-Stander," the Duke of Portland who was "tolerable," and Lord North who was "execrable." The *Public Advertiser* critic also liked the portrait of Richard Brocklesby, but asked, "Where are Lord Clarendon and Lord Godolphin? They should have been pictured in the Situation they really were, supporting the drooping Body of Lord Chatham." He also noted that Copley took careful pains to "give a very intelligible Idea of the *particular Furniture* of the House of Lords, and the *Shipping* in the *Hangings*."

[24] Royal Commission on Historical Manuscripts,

for the picture, early because the representation of the figure appears in its final form in the first oil sketches, is the head of Earl of Bathurst (fig. 413). Later portrait drawings exist of Richard Brocklesby (fig. 405), the Bishop of Peterborough (fig. 412), and the Earl of Stanhope (fig. 414).

The Death of Chatham is an impressive painting. It is well composed and facile in execution. Strong value contrasts flicker over the surface, enlivening and illuminating the action. Coloristically there is a bold red-white contrast, just as in the subsequent *Death of Major Peirson,* and a good part of the forcefulness of the painting resides in the strength of this color combination and in Copley's skill in placing the scarlet robes and ermine capes throughout the pictorial space in such a way that they are controlled and enhanced by a restrained array of blues, greens, and browns in the uniforms and suits, and by the gray-black-white tonalities in the bishops' robes. Just as Copley manages to use a great deal of red in the draperies without painting a red picture, so too he uses quite a bit of red in the faces without getting red faces, allowing old Lord Temple's frosty white hair and the stricken Chatham's yellow pallor to stand out with particular strength.

The successful portraiture in the painting is its most important asset. Copley intentionally kept careful rein on the gamut of expression, risking the criticism that followed, because too much emotion would have ruined the likenesses. Real concern is shown only by the relatives who are close to the stricken Chatham. The other portraits show the individuals at their best, controlled and yet deeply involved in an affair of great moment. Despite some amount of idealizing, the faces reveal character, strength, and individuality. The background treatment is kept broad and restrained in order not to compete with the main areas of the picture. Brushwork in the foreground is tight and crisp, although freely applied. Political considerations aside, the composition is very much enhanced by the seated figure of Lord Mansfield in a niche on the left, serving as a minor echo of the Chatham group in the larger niche of figures on the right. This heightens the effectiveness of the broad sweeping movement to the right that carries to the reclining, spotlighted figure of Chatham, before its energy pours off through the up-raised hand of Lord Ferrers (50) and the group of figures behind the Duke of Richmond (51).

The exhibition of *The Death of Chatham* was an unqualified success, both financially and in terms of the publicity it brought Copley.[25] When the exhibition at Spring

---

Ninth Report, appendix 2 (London, 1884), p. 402, B. Leacroft, Little Wild Street, Lincoln's Inn Fields, to Philip Gell, Esq., Hopton, July 16, 1781.
[25] Allan Cunningham said that the picture strongly affected the public, some seeing in the death of Chatham an omen of bad days ahead and reading Chatham's final speech as "a prophetic admonition to Britain" (*The Cabinet Gallery of Pictures by the First Masters* [London, 1834], I, 50). Various other reactions to the picture indicate the range of its reception. Thomas Dibdin called it a "highly

wrought and thoroughly rational picture," with "harmonious light and shade," and noted that the "resemblances are considered perfect" (*Reminiscences of a Literary Life* [London, 1836], I, 151n). Mrs. Philip Powys thought that it would be a shame if Chatham's family did not buy this "charming picture" (Emily J. Climenson, *Passages from the Diaries of Mrs. Philip Lybbe Powys, 1756–1808* [London, 1899], pp. 233–34). From Romney's supreme admirer, William Hayley, Copley's performance elicited the following poetic encomium

Garden closed after two and a half months, the picture was placed in the Gresham lecture room over the Royal Exchange for the convenience of viewers in the City, where Chatham had many admirers.[26] Now Copley looked forward to even more income from the sale of the picture and the publication of the engraving. Yet in both regards he was to experience considerable difficulty before capitalizing on his work.

While Copley was painting *The Death of Chatham*, the Marquis of Buckingham expressed his desire "to have the refusal of it and caused him to introduce several figures of particular persons." When the picture was done, Copley offered it to him for two thousand guineas. The Marquis asked twenty-four hours to consider the matter and then delayed, always being "engaged" when Copley called. Copley later heard that the Marquis simply felt that two thousand guineas was too much to give for any picture.[27]

Another false alarm, this time a public one, occurred on June 20–21, 1781, when the *Morning Chronicle* and the *Public Advertiser* reported the sale of *The Death of Chatham* to Lord Temple for a thousand guineas. The *Advertiser* speculated that with another thousand for the exhibition, plus whatever might come from the sale of the engraving, Copley would net over three thousand guineas for the picture, "a very handsome Reward for his Labour." But the report of this sale was incorrect, and the story was retracted immediately. In 1788 Copley put the picture up for sale but with no results. The *World* observed that the painting, valued at twenty-five hundred guineas, never had been shown to greater advantage and expressed surprise that the picture was not yet sold.[28]

Ultimately Copley disposed of the picture by raffle. In 1806 he induced twenty subscribers to put up one hundred guineas apiece in advance. He wanted to get twenty-five subscribers, but decided not to delay and run the risk of losing those already signed up. The drawing was held on June 27, 1806, and the winner was Alexander Davison, who immediately declared that he would not take less than five thousand pounds for the picture.[29]

("An Essay on Painting," *Poems and Plays* [London, 1788], vol. I, epistle 2, pp. 35–36):

"With kindred power a rival hand succeeds,
For whose just fame expiring Chatham pleads,
Like Chatham's Language luminous and bold,
Thy colours, COPLEY, the dread scenes unfold,
Where that prime spirit, by whose guidance hurl'd,
Britain's avenging thunder aw'd the world,
In patriot cares employ'd his parting breath,
Struck in his field of civick fame by death:
And freedom, happy in the tribute paid,
By art and genius to so dear a shade,
Shall own, the measure of thy praise to fill,
The awful subject equal'd by thy skill."

This stanza and the preceding one devoted to Benjamin West (which explains "a rival hand" in the first line) were published by the *Massachusetts Centinel*, May 28, 1788, with the following commentary, "We are ever happy when it is in our power to give circulation to the just tributes of applause paid to genius — on the present occasion our happiness is increased, in the reflection that the artists here panegyrized are our countrymen, and that their panegyrist is Mr. Hayley."

[26] *Morning Post*, July 10, 1781. The exhibition in London closed on Sept. 1, 1781. Frederick W. Hilles and Philip D. Daghlian, eds., *Anecdotes of Painting in England* [1760–1795] . . . *collected by Horace Walpole*, V (New Haven, 1937), 26–27.

[27] Joseph Farington, "Diary," typescript copy in the British Museum, Department of Prints and Drawings, of the manuscript original at the Royal Library, Windsor Castle, p. 2172, Jan. 30, 1803.

[28] March 24, 1788; April 10, 1788.

[29] "Farington Diary," pp. 3219 (April 16, 1806), 3324 (June 18, 1806), and 3341 (June 28, 1806); *Times* (London), June 30, 1806.

As difficult as it was to sell the painting, the process of getting it engraved caused even more complications. Although the engraver in the 1780 brochure had been announced as John Keyse Sherwin, Copley on August 21, 1781, advised the subscribers that the task was turned over to the more renowned Francesco Bartolozzi, who undertook to produce the engraving in four years. The print seems to have been eagerly awaited, and there was a brisk black market in subscriptions for proofs.[30]

In 1788 a report came out that the long-awaited engraving was far enough along to tell that it would be the "first plate in point of merit in the universe." Then word came that Bartolozzi was engaged in executing the last touches. Still, by the end of the year, the plate was having extensive alterations and would take Bartolozzi at least another year. The delay in this engraving, which in the first proposal had been promised in two and a half years, hurt Copley when he sought subscribers for engravings of subsequent pictures. Thus when he solicited subscribers for an engraving of *The Siege of Gibraltar* in 1789, it was pointed out publicly that he had received subscriptions for *The Death of Chatham* eight years before and for *The Death of Peirson* two years later; since neither plate had been delivered, the conclusion was that almost anyone else could ask for subscriptions with better grace than Copley could.[31]

In September 1790 an "unforeseen or unexpected accident" put off completion of the plate for another six months. It was finally published in 1791. The quality of the engraving was up to expectation, but Copley was disenchanted with Bartolozzi. In one day, eighteen months of work had been beaten out, and as a result of "its having been so often beat up" the plate yielded only twenty-five hundred impressions and could not be retouched. According to Josiah Boydell, it should have stood two or three retouchings.[32] Even though the engraving was completed, Copley's troubles with it did not cease. Unsigned reports came out in the newspapers and private rumors circulated to the effect that too many proofs had been pulled from the plate and that the plates were not being given to subscribers in the order of subscription. Copley advised in the *Morning Herald* on May 1, 1792, that in view of these charges he had asked three "respectable gentlemen" and "an eminent engraver" to investigate. Their signed state-

[30] Hilles and Daghlian, *Walpole*, 25–26. Some receipts that had cost three guineas brought twenty-five guineas in 1785 (*Public Advertiser*, June 7, 1785). A visitor in London, who thought West had painted *The Death of Chatham*, went to see Bartolozzi's studio in Fulham and reported, "an Italian already shows a masterly hand on the completion of Lord Chatham's portrait after West, at the moment when the count, speaking emphatically for the common good, swooned away" (Clare Williams, trans., *Sophie in London, 1786, being the Diary of Sophie v. la Roche* [London, 1933], p. 232). The Italian at work on the plate may have been Testolini, who Bartolozzi sent for in Italy to assist him and who proved "unequal to the task" (Pasquin, *Memoirs*, p. 106). Although the job was taken away

from Sherwin, he nonetheless continued a similar project on his own. On June 4, 1794, Robert Wilkinson published "The House of Peers on the 7th April 1778 when the Earl of Chatham was taken Ill," which had been "Painted by the late J. K. Sherwin, historical engraver to the King and the Prince of Wales, and partly engraved by him, finished by others on his decease." This composition was based heavily upon Copley's.

[31] "Cuttings on Art," II, 415 (Jan. 4 [?], 1788), 422 (May 28, 1788), 387 (Nov. 27, 1788), 512 (April 13, 178[9?]), and 611 [incorrectly dated 1792].

[32] *Ibid.*, II, 575; "Farington Diary," p. 244, Nov. 21, 1794, and p. 347, May 29, 1795.

ment that fewer proofs than usual were drawn and that the subscription order was being followed as closely as possible could be seen at his house.[33]

Copley had even further engraving problems. The Bartolozzi plate had taken a long time; it had yielded only a limited number of impressions; it had been costly to produce and the print was expensive to buy. So Copley commissioned one of Bartolozzi's assistants, Jean Mari Delattre, to make a smaller, less expensive print. The terms were one hundred and twenty pounds in advance and six hundred and eighty pounds on completion of the plate — a total of eight hundred pounds as against the two thousand pounds that Bartolozzi had received. However, when the plate was finished Copley considered it so bad that it could not be published without severe damage to his reputation. He refused to pay Delattre the remaining six hundred and eighty pounds. The result was a lawsuit in 1801, with Delattre as plaintiff. There was a major professional point at issue — should the engraver or the painter judge an engraving? Accordingly the engravers rallied behind Delattre, and the painters, despite the fact that some of them disagreed with Copley over other matters, closed ranks behind the artist.[34]

The defense argument was that the engraver had failed entirely to reproduce correct likenesses following Bartolozzi's plate, and to publish these impossible likenesses would harm Copley's reputation. The plaintiff charged that the plate was acceptable and that he should be paid for work accomplished. Bartolozzi testified that, although the plate was not excellent, it was acceptable. It had been based on his engraving, which in turn had been based on a drawing by Cipriani after Copley's original. The engravers, among other things, objected to being dismissed as mechanics and this may have helped them with the jury, chosen as it was from haberdashers, cheesemongers, saddlers, and so on. Lord Kenyon, the presiding judge, in summation noted that it was odd that Copley had not said anything while the engraving was being executed. He professed no competence whatsoever in artistic matters, however, and said he would tend to rely on the word of West, who had supported the artist. Nonetheless, to everyone's surprise, the jury returned in ten minutes with a verdict for Delattre. The engravers in jubilation retired to the Spring Garden Coffee House for dinner, while the painters retired to their second guesses. Farington's opinion was that West, Cosway, and Beechey had hurt Copley by going too far in their statements. So ended, to Copley's distress, the Delattre affair.[35]

[33] According to C. Reginald Grundy, "British Military and Naval Prints," *The Connoisseur*, XL (Oct. 1914), pp. 70, 72–73, some 320 proofs and 2,118 prints were pulled. After the print was ready, Copley sent two copies to Vice President John Adams, the second one being for President George Washington. Adams sent his thanks to Copley on Nov. 16, 1792, and promised to give the other copy to the president, who was away at Mount Vernon (Boston Public Library, Ch. F.6.3a). Washington sent his thanks to Copley on Dec. 12, 1792, observing, "The work, highly valuable in itself, is rendered more estimable in my eye when I remember that America gave birth to the celebrated artist who produced it" (Amory, p. 86).

[34] The Delattre engraving was eventually published in London, March 1, 1820, by William Johnstone White. It is as bad as Copley claimed. Bartolozzi, Byrne, Landseer, Neagle, Smith, Tomkins, and Bromley testified for Delattre. West, Beechey, Hoppner, Opie, and Cosway testified for Copley, as did the engravers Fittler, Dunkarton, Boydell, and Holloway (*Morning Herald*, July 3, 1801).

[35] *Ibid.*; *Morning Chronicle*, July 3, 1801; *Morn-*

The Death of Chatham, despite the extended difficulties Copley encountered in getting it engraved and in finding a purchaser, won for the artist at the time of its triumphant first appearance wide recognition as a leading history painter. For the next few years Copley rode the crest of his career.

ing Post, July 3, 1801; "Farington Diary," pp. 1982 (July 1, 1801) and 1986–87 (July 5, 1801); Amory, p. 222, Susanna Copley, London, to Mrs. Gardiner Greene, Boston, Jan. 8, 1802; Court Records, Middlesex County Council Record Office, D.D.X. 7/17–7/20, which include the certified copy of enrollment on the King's Bench Roll of the case between Copley and Delattre, the jury list, and the directions to the sheriff to assemble the jury.

XIII   The Laurels of Success

1781-1783 COPLEY'S SUCCESSFUL EXHIBITION OF *The Death of Chatham* IN
1781 served to cement his ties with England. His dream of
winning fame as a history painter had come true. Reputation and fortune could be
attained in London, and there was little temptation to return to the relatively barren
artistic climate he had left behind in Boston. Of course, many of the American loyalists
in London went to see Copley's exhibition.[1] Of these, perhaps the one most interested
in Copley as an artist was Peter Oliver, Jr., who, noting in a letter of May 22, 1781, to
Elisha Hutchinson that he had faithfully carried out Mrs. Copley's request to "puff
about Lord Chatham's Picture," gave the following advice:

> I rejoice with Mr. Copley on his Success; tell him not to be exalted above measure, lest he
> should receive a Thorn in the Flesh to buffet him, & as he hath begun historical Painting, I
> urge him to draw Aeneas's Shield as described in Pitts Virgio: if he executes it well, he
> will then add Immortality to his present Fame, & some Noblemen of Classic Taste will
> purchase it to add to his own Fame — it is a pleasing & grand Subject.[2]

If Copley was at all tempted by this suggestion, he managed to resist successfully.

As he prospered in England, Copley's ties with former loyalist friends slackened.
Some had died, some had scattered, and a few friendships formed during the flush
of the loyalist influx had faded with time. The Copley's closest loyalist friends were
the Hutchinsons. The governor had died in 1780, but his son Elisha lived in London
with his family, and the families of Thomas Hutchinson, Jr., and of Peter Oliver were
in Birmingham. The Copleys on occasion exchanged visits with them, especially during
the time Mrs. Copley's sister, Sarah Startin (fig. 476), was in Birmingham; Sarah
followed her husband back to New York in October 1783.[3]

---

[1] Ward, *Curwen*, p. 323; "Diary of Elisha Hutchinson," fol. 97b, [May] 3, [1781]. Some of Copley's friends in America wrote to him after the success of *The Death of Chatham*. Mather Byles affirmed, "I delight in the fame you have acquired, and in being ranked among your earliest friends" (Amory, p. 85). John Scollay more soberly wrote, "I trust amid this blaze of prosperity you do not forget your dear native country, and the cause it is engaged in, which, I know, lay once very near your heart, and I hope does still" (*ibid.*).

[2] British Museum, Egerton Ms. 2659, foll. 330–31.

[3] British Museum, Egerton Ms. 2660, fol. 7; see also n. 14 below. In various diaries and letters of the period, there are many verbal snapshots of the family — Richard Clarke riding in Hyde Park or leaving for a stay at Tunbridge Wells; Henry Pelham stopping by Birmingham en route to Ireland, having left Mrs. Pelham in London at the Copleys'; Copley taking a letter from Elisha Hutchinson in London to Thomas Hutchinson in Birmingham while

In 1782 Copley painted two portraits of Americans in London. One was a portrait of *Elkanah Watson* (fig. 419). Watson recorded in his diary that, while Copley was at work on this portrait, the two of them went to hear George III make the announcement of American independence. Afterwards, according to Watson, Copley rushed back to his studio and painted an American flag on the ship in the left distance of the picture, thus raising the first American flag in England after the colonies had won the war.[4] The other picture of an American was a full-length portrait of *Henry Laurens* (fig. 416), which was engraved by Valentine Green, the engraver of *Watson and the Shark*.[5]

Green also engraved another picture for Copley that year, *The Tribute Money* (fig. 420), which was Copley's "tribute" to the Royal Academy. Although Copley had been elected to academy membership in February 1779, he failed to submit his diploma picture promptly. As he became increasingly involved with *The Death of Chatham*, it apparently became more difficult to find time to paint anything for the academy. At a meeting of the general assembly of the Royal Academy held on December 10, 1781, it was enacted that if an academician did not take up his diploma within a year it would be considered to have been declined. Although Copley in 1781 had exhibited *The Death of Chatham* in competition with the annual academy exhibition, he had no desire to remain outside this important organization. So in 1782, though once more he did not participate in the annual exhibition, he did paint his diploma picture. The minutes of the governing council of the academy for December 31, 1782, note that Copley had submitted a "Specimen of his Abilities" and that the council recommended to the king that he be granted his diploma. On February 11, 1783, four years after his election, Copley was approved as an academician and attended his first meeting. In December of that year, as was the custom with new members, he was elected to the governing council of the academy and was also elected a visitor.[6]

---

on a trip; etc. Ward, *Curwen*, pp. 286, 293; "Hutchinson Diary," foll. 115b, 114, 147b; British Museum, Egerton Ms. 2659, foll. 328, 340; *ibid.*, Egerton Ms. 2660, fol. 7.

[4] Winslow C. Watson, ed., *Men and Times of the Revolution, or Memoirs of Elkanah Watson, 1777–1842* (New York 1856), p. 177.

[5] "Anderdon Scrapbooks," RA, V, 1783. An unidentified newspaper cutting of Nov. 12, 1782, announces the publication that day of a full-length engraving of Henry Laurens, president of the American Congress, 1778, painted by Copley, engraved by Valentine Green, published and sold by I. Stockdale, Bookseller, no. 181, opposite Burlington House, Piccadilly. This representation of Laurens was intended as a companion to a portrait of Washington, also engraved by Green. Purchasers of either print could see the Copley painting of *Laurens* at Stockdale's.

[6] "Assembly Minutes," RA, I, 155, 165, 174; "Council Minutes," RA, I, 334, 352. As Whitley (*Artists in England, 1700–1799*, II, 339) points out, the new diploma regulations were enforced. George Stubbs was elected to the academy in 1781 and was voted out on Feb. 11, 1783, because of failure to submit his diploma picture. Copley attended his first council meeting on Jan. 7, 1784. The council was soon afterward involved in a dispute with Gainsborough, who sent in his pictures late for the annual exhibition and claimed the right of dictating the hanging height. The *Morning Post* observed that, if Gainsborough could stretch the rules, the members of the council, "gentlemen of the most distinguished abilities — Sir Joshua Reynolds, West, Copley, Loutherbourg, &c." might claim the same privilege. William T. Whitley, *Thomas Gainsborough* (London, 1915), pp. 213–15.

The picture that Copley submitted to the academy as his diploma piece, *The Tribute Money*, was one of his infrequent religious pictures.[7] The composition and the chiaroscuro recall seventeenth-century prototypes, such as Guercino's *The Betrayal* (Fitzwilliam Museum, Cambridge) or Rubens' *Christ Giving the Keys to St. Peter*, engraved by Pieter de Jode (fig. 421), in which the figures are similarly disposed with Christ on the right raising one hand, a slightly stooped and elderly St. Peter on the left receiving the keys in his hand, and four figures behind him looking on. Copley's handling is pure eighteenth century, however, and in fact pure Copley. The colors are strong, especially on the right where the figure of Christ with arm raised, garbed in brilliant red and blue and flooded by the light from the left, balances the entire group of five figures on the left. The cool coloration, the clarity of outline, the strong chiaroscuro, and the somewhat unfortunate fixed expressions are familiar Copley trademarks. The picture, broadly brushed, is more effective from a moderate distance than at close range, where a certain rough, slap-dash quality mars the effect. A drawing of the two main characters (fig. 422) — the verso of which (fig. 418) is a study for *Elkanah Watson* of the same year — shows that considerable evolution took place in the composition of the picture. The drawing places greater emphasis on the single figure receiving the money and less on the figure of Christ. In the development of the composition, the receiving figure is turned into the space slightly and his role is reduced by the addition of other figures. The figure of Christ is turned out toward the viewer slightly with the position of the arms reversed, and is made to dominate the composition by being moved closer to the picture surface so that the single figure balances the other five.

During the same period Copley also painted two superlative portraits of young boys. The better known of these is *Midshipman Augustus Brine* (fig. 423). The strong light and dark contrasts, the brilliance of the colors, and the bravura of the brushwork all contribute to its success. Another portrait of the same vintage is the excellent 1782 portrait of *Richard Heber* as a young boy leaning on a cricket bat (fig. 424). After he had completed the portrait, Copley wrote twice to Richard Heber's father, Reverend Reginald Heber, as follows:

> London
> Aug 9th. 1782
>
> Sir,
>
> I had the honor of your favor dated 5th instant, containing a Draught for forty two pounds. The Picture is intirely finished and framed, and I will send to the frame maker and as soon as he can make the case, and pack up the Picture, it

---

[7] There is no evidence about why Copley chose this particular subject. Perhaps the idea was formed when he learned that the Royal Society of Arts contemplated the awarding of a premium for a religious painting based on the Scriptures, "Suitable for Altarpiece in Protestant Church." The picture was to contain no less than five figures, with the main one at least six feet high; the canvas had to be at least ten feet high and seven feet wide; and the picture was to be due in April 1782. But no competition was ever opened, and the size and proportions do not seem to accord. Royal Society of Arts, "Minutes of Committees, 1780–1781," Committee on Polite Arts, Jan. 18, 1781, p. 96ff.

shall be sent as you direct; I think you may expect it some time in the next weeks, but of this I will write you when it is ready; My best respects attend your self and Family.

I am, Sir, your most Obt.

Humble Ser^t

J. S. Copley

- - - - -

London

Sir,

Sept 7th 1782

I have the pleasure to inform you that your son's portrait goes off tomorrow morning in the Waggon for Whitchurch, where I hope it will arrive safe, every precaution has been taken to secure it from Accidents, I am sorry it has been detained so long. I am afraid you have been expecting it some time past, but assure you it has not be owing to neglect but Accidents. I enclose the frame-maker's bill as you desired. I request you [will] inform me of the arrival of the picture at Malpas, and weither it gets there safe and Meets your approbation. My best respects attend your two sisters and the young gentleman. I am, Sir, Your Obe^t

Hum^{ble} Ser^t

J. S. Copley [8]

The portraits of *Augustus Brine* and *Richard Heber* make it clear that Copley had achieved a vigorous, highly successful portrait style which, in the freedom and dash of the brushwork and the ebullience of a lightened palette, rivals the more sober triumphs of his American style. If further proof is needed, there are several superb female portraits of the same general period, which with apparent feminine perversity resist precise dating and keep their ages secret. The earliest of these, perhaps dating from 1778, is the vibrant portrait of *Mrs. John Montresor* (fig. 426), whose husband Copley had painted in America several years earlier. Her red jacket, black lapels, and gold epaulets echo the colors of her husband's portrait, but the results of the bold, cool color scheme are much more dramatic and successful in this exciting portrait.

The portrait of *Mrs. Thomas Hooper* (fig. 427) is given particular interest by the high placement of the sitter, which yields an unusual angle of view. As in only a few of the American portraits, and even fewer of the English, there is less emphasis on

[8] Both letters are in the possession of Charles C. Cholmondeley, Yeovil, Somerset (typescript courtesy of the late Richard H. Cholmondeley). The composition involving a cricket bat was not unusual in the eighteenth century. For example, Francis Cotes had used these elements to create a much different kind of informal portrait of *The Young Cricketer* in 1768 (*British Painting in the Eighteenth Century* [British Council, 1957–58], p. 28, no. 5, illus. p. 112), while Joseph Wright of Derby's group portrait of *The Children of Hugh and Sarah Wood* in the Derby Museum is in part fairly close in style and composition to the portrait of *Richard Heber*.

That *Richard Heber* possesses Copley's most salient characteristics is indicated also by the observations of a skilled nineteenth-century observer, Sir George Scharf, who saw the picture on exhibition at the British Institution in 1865 and noted its "rich dark strong colours, deep shadows, sharp lights" (National Portrait Gallery, London, "Scharf Sketch Books," vol. 72, p. 31). Dibdin in his *Reminiscences* spoke of his liking for this picture and also noted the "play of light and shadow" (I, 152n). Copley's use of strong contrast has always been one of the stylistic traits frequently remarked by subsequent observers.

externals and more on the character of the individual portrayed. Finery is conspicuously absent, and our attention is irresistibly drawn to the slightly pinched and pensive face of the woman. The portrait of *Mrs. Daniel Denison Rogers* (fig. 428) is in Copley's more familiar idiom, concerned not only with the individual as individual, but the individual as a social entity. Here Copley's style can best be described as exuberant. The flying brush traces ridges of impasto along its path, and the color and texture of pure pigment carries much of the visual appeal. A lovely woman, Copley's stepniece, is memorialized not in terms of her actual physical being and accessories, as would have been the case back in Boston, but in terms of abstract qualities — youth, beauty, quick vivacity — that are conveyed by their pictorial equivalents in color, texture, light, and composition.[9]

In 1782 Copley was probably already doing preliminary work for his great history painting, *The Death of Peirson*, although it was not completed until 1784. One of his early projects for 1783 never came to fruition. This was to be a depiction of "The Installation of the Order of St. Patrick." Many Irish lords had been active in attempts to secure greater freedom for Ireland in 1781–82. In an attempt to smooth the troubled waters, George III early in 1783 offered to establish the Order of St. Patrick and to create Irish knights. The installation took place on St. Patrick's Day, 1783. One of the Irish leaders was Lord Charlemont, and Copley wrote him on March 22, 1783:

> The subject that now presents itself for the exercize of the pencil, and is one of the finest that modern times has given birth to, is the institution of the new order of St. Patrick, a subject replete with every picturesque beauty, and invaluable from the portraits it will contain. I should feel much regret should I meet with any impediments that should deprive me of the honor of making it one of the monuments I am ambitious to leave behind me.

Copley added that Henry Pelham would be in Ireland shortly and "is well qualified to transmit to me sketches of the buildings where the scene lay, of the dresses, etc."[10]

Copley chose to write Charlemont not only because this nobleman had been instrumental in the affair politically, but also because he was interested in the fine arts. Since Copley boasted an Irish background and still had relatives in Ireland, there were extra-artistic factors in his favor. The reason why Copley did not paint the projected picture is suggested in a letter to one of the Irish noblemen concerned (not identified), a letter that constitutes a unique statement of Copley's attitude toward the history paintings he was now creating:

[9] It is quite possible that Copley painted this portrait in the autumn of 1784 when he was at work on *The Daughters of George III*. At that time Mrs. Rogers was staying with the Copleys at Windsor while recuperating from an illness. Clarke-Bromfield Papers, Historical Manuscripts and University Archives Collection, Yale University Library, Mrs. Copley, Windsor, to Daniel Denison Rogers, London, Oct. 13, 1784.

[10] Royal Commission on Historical Manuscripts, *Twelfth Report*, "The Mss. and Correspondence of James, First Earl of Charlemont," I (London, 1891), 425. This source misprints Pelham as "Letham."

My Lord

Being fully persuaded that modern subjects are the properest for the exercize of the pencil and far more Interesting to the present Age than those taken from Ancient History I have as much as possible employed myself in Events that have happened in my own time and intend pursuing the same Idea and I shall think myself happy in adding to those I have already done, a Picture of the Installation of the Illustrious Order of St. Patrick. I think it a most magnificent subject for painting; and my desire is to treat it in an Historical Stile and make it a companion to the picture of Lord Chatham, and the English House of Peers, filling the Group with the portraits of the Illustrious Knights and other great Charactors; the Idea originated with myself, and I mean to paint it on my own Account, and to publish a print from it of the same size with that now Engraving for for me by Bartolozzi of Lord Chatham. From this sketch of my Plan your Lordship will set [sic] the magnitude of the undertaking, and I cannot doubt the Noble Knights of the Illustrious Order will so far countenance a work which will afford so much satisfaction to posterity as to honor me by sitting for there portraits, and as the original portraits will give a stamp of peculiar value to the picture and prints, the prospect I look forward to, as the source from whence I may hope to draw a Recompence Adequate to so great a work, and as your Lordship must be sensible that such a work must be attended with great Labour and Expense, if therefore any other Artist should be permitted to take the portraits with a view to Anticipate the Subject, it will defeat my purpose, but if I can be assured that no such permission will be allowed by the Illustrious Knights I shall enter on the work with ardour, and shall hope that the perform-ance will prove no discredit to myself or the Noble Personages whose portraits will appear in it, — I am happy to inform your Lordship that I have waited on the King and laid before him my intended plan, which his Majesty was Pleased to honor with his Royal Approbation and Most graciously said, whenever you are ready Prince Edward you may be assured shall sit for his.[11]

Copley stressed the fact in this letter that his purpose would be compromised if "any other Artist should be permitted to take the portraits with a view to Anticipate the Subject." But the scene was painted in 1783 by John Keyse Sherwin, the jilted engraver of *The Death of Chatham,* and this may explain Copley's abandonment of the idea. If Sherwin had painted the portrait heads first, the commercial edge would have been taken off of Copley's undertaking and he would have scuttled the project.

In 1783 Copley resumed exhibiting at the Royal Academy, submitting a portrait of *William Murray, Earl of Mansfield* (fig. 429) and a double portrait of *The Western Brothers* (fig. 436). *Mansfield* is the first of a few portraits related to the likenesses

---

[11] I am indebted to Dennis Farr for showing me a copy of this letter made from the original manu-script, owned in 1955 by the London firm of Chas. Higham & Son, Ltd. The letter was published in part in Cunningham, *Eminent Painters,* IV, 151.

in *The Death of Chatham*, others being representations of *John, Second Viscount Dudley and Ward* (fig. 630), *William Ponsonby, Second Earl of Bessborough* (fig. 590), and, to a slight degree, *Richard Brocklesby* (fig. 618). In this case the *Chatham* representation served only as a point of departure. All of the extant drawings of Lord Mansfield, except the head in the Boston Athenaeum (fig. 406), seem to be studies for the portrait rather than for *Chatham*. These drawings (figs. 430–435) reflect a considerable amount of indecision on Copley's part as to the best pose. He seems to have been constant in his desire to have the face to the right but less in profile than in *Chatham*. The body in the sketches is pivoted in a great number of positions. The drawings reflect indecisiveness rather than progress toward a compositional solution.

Copley may have painted this portrait of Mansfield on his own initiative to propitiate a powerful nobleman who possibly was angered by his treatment in *The Death of Chatham*, or he may have simply received a regular commission for it — but in either case it ranks as one of Copley's best portraits. It combines grandeur of scale, boldness of light and dark contrasts, luminosity of background space, strength of character in the likeness, and a vibrant use of color. The scarlet robe and white ermine make a vital contrast (as in *Chatham* and in the later *Death of Peirson*) that Copley moderates and subdues through the chiaroscuro. Although there is a much more convincing spatial ambient in this picture than in most Copley portraits, the figure itself remains, except for the out-thrust scroll, largely biplanar — with major accents on the ascending ladder effect of the ermine facing and on the forcefully painted gray hair, which forms a nimbus around the face that Edward Oxnard described as having "something stern in [the] countenance, that strikes one with awe." [12]

Critics of this painting found the likeness very good, but objected to the high color, particularly in the face. The reviewer in the *Public Advertiser* of May 1, 1783, observed that Mansfield had been moving up in his choice of portrait painters. He pronounced Copley a definite improvement on Martin and Ramsay, and expressed the hope that Mansfield would continue to better his taste by ultimately sitting for such really good artists as Romney, Gainsborough, and Reynolds. Any comparison of artists like these or Angelica Kauffmann with Copley:

> shews not only comparative inferiority, but positive Deficience in some of the greatest Requisites of the Art — and, it is also visible, that the late accidental Vogue of Copley has arisen much more from a lucky Selection of Subject, than from any ascendant Skill in the Manner of treating it. — The instances are, the Death of Chatham, the Shark, &c.&c.[13]

[12] "Oxnard's Journal," p. 116.
[13] "Guido," who reviewed the Royal Academy exhibition in the *Morning Herald*, May 5, 1783, thought the Mansfield portrait "an admirable performance," noting that the "likeness is very strong, but there is rather too much *vigour* in the complexion for his Lordship." The *London Courant* of May 2, 1783, said that with this picture Copley "has not added to his reputation." It noted that the portrait "certainly is a strong likeness, but has neither truth of colouring, nor dignity of character; the drapery is, moreover, ill disposed, and the figure ill proportioned."

The pleasing double portrait of *The Western Brothers* (fig. 436) did not draw much critical attention at the academy, although one reviewer said it "is a better picture than most of [Copley's] private portraits generally are." [14]

In 1783 the Copleys moved from their first London home at 12 Leicester Square to the George Street home that was to be the scene of their family life not only for the rest of Copley's days, but throughout the long and distinguished career of his son. The new house was not particularly large, but it was "elegant & well-furnished," and suitable for Copley's business needs. In the center of the house was a large high room with skylights, which was used for the display of paintings. Copley's painting room was connected to the rear of this larger room. [15]

The house, 24 George Street at the time of purchase but later renumbered 25, was about five doors up from St. George's, Hanover Square, in the direction of the square. It was an attractive and desirable location, as may be seen in the 1787 Dayes view (fig. 437), which looks southward across the square toward the church. [16] There were some splendid houses around the square and on George Street, but actually only four or five of the houses had a higher tax rate than Copley's. [17] At the time of the move, the family consisted of Copley, who was forty-five, his wife Sukey, thirteen-year-old Elizabeth, eleven-year-old John, Jr., eight-or-nine-year-old Mary, seven-year-old Susanna, and Jonathan, who had been born in February. Mrs. Copley's father, Richard Clarke, also came with the family to George Street. [18]

[14] *Morning Chronicle*, May 30, 1783. This review, signed by NOSAM (presumably an anagram for Mason), identifies the sitters as the sons of Mrs. Weston of Essex, the elder of whom attended "Newcomb's school."

[15] "Diary of Elisha Hutchinson," foll. 102, 105b (Aug. 27, [1783] — an incorrect date of 1781 was added to the manuscript in the nineteenth century); British Museum, Egerton Ms. 2660, fol. 7, Peter Oliver to Elisha Hutchinson, March 5, 1784; Amory, p. 99.

[16] "I must own that the view down George Street, from the upper sides of the square, is one of the most entertaining in the whole city: the sides of the Square, the area in the middle, the breaks of building that form the entrance of the vista, the vista itself, but above all the beautiful projection of the portico of St. George's Church, are all circumstances that unite its beauty and make the scene perfect." Ralph, *Critical Observations on the Buildings in London*, as quoted in Chancellor, *Squares of London*, p. 61.

[17] Westminster Public Library, Tax Rate Books, St. George's, Hanover Square. A householder list of about 1790 for St. George's, Hanover Square (Middlesex County Record Office), gives an idea of Copley's neighborhood. On George Street lived a tavernkeeper, a baker, a French hairdresser, an apothecary, a surgeon, an upholsterer, a physician,

a milliner, the Earl of Salisbury's steward, Earl Fauconberg, and the Lord Bishop of Peterborough. The site of Copley's house, now occupied by the Caxton Publishing Company, was directly across the street from the still-standing residence of Earl Fauconberg, whose portrait Copley painted. A nearby house at 8 George Street frequently had artistic associations. It was occupied about the time that the Copleys arrived by Mrs. Hadfield, the mother of Maria Cosway. In the 1790's William Beechey lived there and during that period was Copley's ally at the Royal Academy. The tenant in the same house in about 1805–1845 was Thomas Philips, R.A. Other interesting neighbors were Richard Brinsley Sheridan and his son Thomas, who in 1803 were at 9 George Street, and Madame de Staël, who was at no. 3 in 1813. Henry B. Wheatley, *London Past and Present* (London, 1871), p. 93.

[18] Elisha Hutchinson ("Diary," fol. 105b, Aug. 27, 1783) records of a visit to the Copleys at George Street that "Mr. Clarke is rather sick & complaining — the Death of his Son Jonathan of a Disorder in his Liver in Feby last of which he has but lately heard seems to lay very heavy upon him." Clarke's son died in the month that also saw the birth of his short-lived grandson with the same first name.

One of the first pictures painted by Copley at George Street was the full-length portrait of *John Adams* (fig. 438). Adams was in London only during October and December of 1783, and he paid Copley one hundred guineas on December 10 as payment in full for his portrait. In June of the following year, the picture still not sent off, John Adams wrote to his son, John Quincy, "Desire Mr. Copley to get a Frame made for my Picture and do you give him the Money. He will tell you how much and give you a Receipt. The Frame should be made, to take to Pieces, so that it may be removed to the Hague or to Boston, in time. Thus this Piece of Vanity will be finished. May it be the last." In July Mrs. John Adams went to see the painting at Copley's house and concluded that it was "a very good likeness" and "a most beautiful picture." She noted that it "was taken at the request of Mr. Copeley." [19]

A drawing for the *John Adams* portrait (fig. 439) is close to the final composition except for the position of the left hand. The statue in the upper left corner of the painting evokes memories of *Mr. and Mrs. Ralph Izard* (fig. 342) with its sculpture group centrally located, but in a similar scale to the figures, and with a vase in a position similar to the statue here. In 1782–83 Copley turned out a spate of similarly composed pictures. The portrait of *Henry Laurens* of 1782 (fig. 416) has scrolls and papers on a carpeted table to the left, an opening in the upper left, and drapery in the upper right; *Elkanah Watson* (fig. 419) of the same year is similar, but without the scrolls; *Earl of Mansfield* (fig. 429) of 1783, the same year as *John Adams*, has scrolls and papers on a carpeted table, the figure also holds a scroll, though in the other hand, and the right hand is extended to the table; and a recently located unidentified portrait of *A Cleric* [?] (fig. 441) is closely related compositionally to *Mansfield* and probably dates from this same general period.

[19] Amory, p. 87; Adams Papers, Massachusetts Historical Society, has the receipt for this painting; *ibid.*, John Adams to John Quincy Adams, June 7, 1784; Abigail Adams to Mary Smith Cranch, July 25, 1784, American Antiquarian Society, Worcester, Mass. Copley had the large Adams portrait on his hands for many years, even though it had been bought and paid for. On March 28, 1788, the *World* commented on the picture in Copley's studio as "a whole length of *Adams* the late Embassador from America — Having lost this situation, a Terrestrial Globe is painted under his eye, signifying the World is before him — And as he stands, he is on the *right* side of the Atlantic!" Copley subsequently planned to have the painting engraved by James Heath. He wrote to Adams in America in March 1800, asking him to sit for Gilbert Stuart so that a sketch without a wig could be made for use in the engraving. Also the aid of Copley's son-in-law in Boston, Gardiner Greene, was enlisted to get a print after Stuart's *Adams* or some other likeness. The efforts were not immediately fruitful, and in July 1801 Mrs. Copley wrote to her daughter: "Mr. Heath is going on with the engraving of Mr. Adams's portrait, but he is much in want of some painting or sketch that will give some idea of his present character; we understand that he is much altered from the likeness your father took of him. He hears that there are several pictures of him in Boston, and will be obliged if Mr. Greene will get some person to make a copy of one of them, and, if it could be obtained, a sketch from Mr. Adams's head; in short, anything that would give an idea of his present character, hair, etc. He thinks an inferior artist can do either, and the sooner they can be procured the more will be the advantage derived in the finishing the print" (Amory, pp. 210–11). By 1811 Adams still had not taken possession of the picture, although John Quincy Adams was very much interested in it as a unique, full-sized representation of his father. He told Copley that it should be turned over to Ward Nicholas Boylston (Amory, pp. 89–90). However, in 1815, the year of Copley's death, the picture was in the hands of the engraver Heath (Adams Papers, D/JQA/29.1372). John Quincy Adams finally took the picture, along with the portrait of his sister, *Abigail Adams* (fig. 440), to the United States in 1817 (Amory, p. 328).

Copley presumably painted his portrait of John Adams' daughter Abigail (engraving, fig. 440), subsequently destroyed by fire, at this time as well. It is known to have been painted prior to her marriage on June 11, 1786 — Copley was one of the witnesses — to William Stephens Smith.[20]

[20] Adams Papers, M/TBA/2, T. B. Adams, Journal, Oct. 24, 1794; John H. Chapman, ed., *The Register Book of Marriages Belonging to the Parish of St. George, Hanover Square, in the County of Middlesex* (London, 1886), I, 389; Bayley, p. 230.

XIV *The Death of Major Peirson*

1783-1784   ON THE NIGHT OF JANUARY 5, 1781, A FRENCH FORCE OF SOME nine hundred troops landed on the English island of Jersey. The invaders quickly seized control of the capital, St. Helier, and imprisoned the commandant of the British forces. The ranking officer of the uncapitulated British troops on the island, twenty-four-year-old Major Francis Peirson, took command and marched on St. Helier. After a brisk pitched battle, Peirson's men recaptured the town and crushed the invasion. At the point of his triumph, Peirson was mortally wounded by enemy fire.[1] This moment of Peirson's death, and the exacting of revenge by his black servant on the Frenchman who had fired the fatal shot, was the theme of Copley's next history painting, *The Death of Major Peirson* (fig. 442).

The Death of Peirson is certainly Copley's boldest and most successful history picture. The brilliance of the color, the strong light and dark contrasts, and the vigor of the composition all enhance the total effect. The central group echoes *The Death of Chatham*, but the total scene is enlarged with peripheral figures and activity. At the left, a detachment of troops moves on to the scene, while at the right two women, a child, and an infant flee from it. Between each of the outside groups and the central group lies a dead or dying figure, above whom a gap into the middle distance reveals English troops pouring fire into the hapless French. The action is defined carefully by buildings to the left and right and at the rear of the square. In the upper left a detachment of Highlanders is seen on Town Hill.

In the picture Copley emphasizes the confusion of battle, with all its color, smell, and stir. In later years the Duke of Wellington told Lord Lyndhurst, Copley's son, "It was the only picture of a battle that ever satisfied him or displayed the reality of the scene, inasmuch as the artist had only attempted to represent *one* incident and but a small portion of the field, — the rest being necessarily concealed by smoke and dust." [2] Copley added the spice of realism through an accurate portrayal of the locale and the participants, and the representation is further flavored by the emotional overtones of a subject which records the triumph of British arms rebounding from

[1] E. Durell (P. J. Ouless illus. and pub.), *The Death of Major Frs. Peirson* (Jersey, 1881); *The Annual Register, or A View of the History, Politics and Literature for the Year 1782* (London, 1783), p. 99; M. C. Green, "The Invasion at La Rocque, 1781," *Bulletin of the Société Jersiaise*, XVII (1957), 66–69.
[2] Amory, p. 92.

the brink of defeat, the poignancy of the death of a young hero cut down at the hour of his glory, and the just vengeance exacted by the Negro servant. Brilliant scarlet uniforms, stirring ensigns flying amidst the smoke of battle, fearful women and children fleeing the scene of turmoil and death, a royal statue (George II), the self-less devotion of an expiring British drummer who ignores his own wound to lament his lost leader — how could any red-blooded eighteenth-century Englishman fail to be stirred by this painting? To gauge the impact of the picture on viewers in 1784, we would have to visualize a battle scene closer to our own time, a twentieth-century attack with soldiers bleeding and dying, and women and children fleeing in horror. Even then it is difficult to imagine the effectiveness of this violent, realistic, contemporary scene in a pre-photographic age, when pictures were not commonplace and the audience was not flooded with an endless parade of visual images.

It is not known whether Copley visited St. Helier to make sketches, whether he sent an emissary such as Henry Pelham to take sketches as had been intended for the projected *Installation of the Order of St. Patrick,* or whether he relied on prints for topographical data as in the case of *Watson and the Shark.* In all probability he or an emissary did make the trip. The houses on the right and left, the statue, the Royal Arms over a door, the Town Hill in the background, and the Royal Courthouse are all accurately delineated.[3] When the picture was exhibited in May 1784, it was accompanied by a brochure that was both a description of the picture and a proposal for an engraving to be executed by James Heath. Here Copley claimed topographical accuracy: "The back-ground is an exact view of that part of the town of St. Heiller's [*sic*] where the battle was fought."

In the same brochure Copley told of similar adherence to fact in the likenesses. He pointed out that the central group "consists entirely of the portraits of Officers of the 95th Regiment, and Officers of the Jersey Militia, and of the said black servant" (fig. 443 is a key to the portraits in the painting). A drawing for the picture's central group (fig. 447) in the Tate Gallery gives an interesting insight into Copley's procedure in taking portraits and in developing the composition. Although the scheme is fairly well developed, only three of the identified figures are in the position they occupy in the finished picture. Two of these figures, Captain Macneil (2) with the sword in his right hand and Lieutenant Drysdale (5) who supports the lifeless body of Major Peirson, apparently had already sat for Copley and had their likenesses painted into the canvas. The pattern of light and shade on their faces as it appears in the finished painting is already established in the drawing. The third figure in a final position is Peirson's Negro servant. In the drawing this figure is identified not as Peirson's servant, but as "Captn Christies Black Servt," suggesting that when painting the figure Copley did not actually locate Major Peirson's servant, but simply reached no further than the other side of Leicester Square for the servant of James Christie,

---

[3] Letter to the author from Ralph Mollet, Secretary, Société Jersiaise, Isle of Jersey, June 13, 1959.

the auctioneer. The remaining figures in the drawing are still tentative in identification, and several more are added in the final version.

This central group, if we include Major Peirson, consists of eleven characters. A contemporary review of the painting states that eleven of the fifteen major figures are real portraits, but this is probably derived from the list of eleven names in Copley's brochure. The group on the right is also said to consist of portraits: the figure on the far right with upright arms is Mrs. Copley, the other woman is a family nurse, the child is John Singleton, Jr. (born May 1772), and the babe in arms could be the infant Jonathan (born February 1782).[4] With the addition of these four figures, Copley departs from fidelity to the facts of the event in order to get closer to its spirit. As a history painter, not as a reporter, Copley wanted to arouse in the viewer a sense of the terror inspired by the battle, thus adding to the general realism of the effect. By including real women and children in contemporary dress, he was able to convey the feeling that these might be people the viewer knew, even his own family.

The drawings extant for this picture do not reveal much concerning the genesis of the composition. In the two earliest known drawings (figs. 448 and 449), the general idea of the central death group has already been determined — a crouching figure at the head facing forward, a standing figure at the feet facing rearward, and a central figure supporting the torso. The composition also includes in this early stage a figure with sword upraised leading a detachment of troops on the left, a figure firing his musket at the French officer, a preliminary notation for the French officer group, and the fleeing group on the right. These early drawings suggest the corner of a building projecting a considerable distance into the space on the left as well as on the right — framing the action more tightly and giving a realistic tunnel-like effect as the viewer looks down an alley to the square. In the final version this building on the left is only slightly visible, thus bringing the viewer into much closer contact with the action.

An oil sketch (fig. 450) marks a development in the composition beyond the two early drawings. The building on the left no longer obtrudes on the scene. The avenger with the musket has been incorporated into the central group, as has the large banner. The figure furthest to the right in the fleeing group appears to be a man, and one wonders whether Copley's early idea was to include his own portrait as well as his wife's. An exceptionally interesting drawing (fig. 455) depicts the figure with sword over his head, Captain Clephane, striding over slain figures and also contains a rough approximation of the French group, squared for transfer, as it appears in the finished painting. There is a scale in feet in the lower right. Over the drawing are jotted notations on the color and style of the uniforms of the British, the French, and the Jersey militia — the lapels, the cuffs, the facings, the cockades, the coats and linings, the hats; and in the case of the dying French officer group, a color code is given on the

---

[4] "Cuttings on Art," Victoria and Albert Museum, I, 238, May 25, 1784, reprinted in *Massachusetts Centinel*, Sept. 8, 1784; Amory, p. 23; Bayley, pp. 82–83.

left to accord with marks placed on the uniforms. This methodical procedure in an effort to be as factually accurate as possible is typical of Copley's approach to history painting, as it was of his approach to portraiture in colonial Boston.

In gathering data, Copley certainly had recourse to verbal accounts of the circumstances. There were also reportorial visual sources, on-the-spot renderings or cheap imaginings, poorly but rapidly done, and set before the public while the story was still news. Thus the aquatint reproduced here (fig. 464), although lacking virtually all of the qualities of Copley's picture, includes such elements as the projecting building on the left found in Copley's early plan, the receding movement of action diagonally from left to right, the prostrate figures and drum in the foreground, the figure with the sword over his head, and the flags. Visual material such as this could well have supplied subconscious ideas and motifs that reappeared in a much more sophisticated fashion in Copley's final work.

Even though *The Death of Peirson* represents an event depicted with a high degree of realism in the setting, the uniforms, and the likenesses of participants, Copley was nevertheless very much concerned that this picture be more than a mere reportorial image. He was trying to create a new type of history painting that would still have all the virtues of the great history pictures of the past. Far from isolating his new efforts from traditional history paintings, Copley went to great lengths to associate his pictures with them. Like West in his *Death of Wolfe*, with its compositional evocation of countless crucifixion, deposition, and lamentation scenes, Copley cast the analogue of a Christian martyrdom over Peirson. Here a close source typologically for the central group would be something like the Pieter Soutman engraving of a drawing by Copley's favorite, Rubens, after Caravaggio of *The Entombment of Christ* (fig. 465). Although the composition is reversed, many elements overlap. One figure wraps his arms around the legs of the dead body; another figure supports the head and shoulders with one hand showing beneath the shoulder and upper arm; the moribund figure has his head back, his hair flowing down, and a free arm dangling; and in the background mourners peer over the shoulders of the figures supporting the body. The closest specific source for the whole picture seems to be the Paulus Pontius 1643 engraving, again after Rubens, of *The Massacre of the Innocents* (fig. 466). There is a similar three-part composition, with a gap into the distance between each group and fallen figures in the left and right foreground. In the upper center the soldier's lances descend from vertical to horizontal as they move from left to right into the action, like the bayonets of the advancing British troops in *The Death of Peirson*. In the lower left a Negro woman is bent to the right into the action as she pulls the hair of a soldier attacking her mistress and her mistress' child, manifesting the same fierce loyalty as Peirson's Negro servant. In the lower right a figure holds a sword above his head, as Captain Clephane does. The adjacent male figure strides over fallen figures, as the boy appears to do in *Peirson* and as occurs in one of the drawings (fig. 455). In the center a woman raises both arms in anguish, like the fleeing woman on the far right in *Peirson*. A female figure to the left of this one in each picture wraps both arms protectively about an infant. In the lower left the hair of the woman warding off an attacker falls like Peirson's. In the center right distance there is a dome placed like the belfry in Copley's picture.

Another similar *Massacre of the Innocents* is the fifth plate in "St. Matthew" in Antonio Tempesta's *The Four Evangelists*, which also has a fleeing figure with a babe in arms at the right, a figure with a sword held horizontally above his head, and so forth. Still another *Massacre of the Innocents*, by Alessandro Turchi at Corsham Court, also has two fleeing women. Obviously the "Massacre of the Innocents" is the principal thematic source for Copley's entire picture.

In relation to Copley's own works, *The Death of Peirson* combines the best qualities of *Watson and the Shark* and *The Death of Chatham*, its two predecessors. With *Watson* it shares a concern for fidelity to the actual physical background, a Negro as a romantic central figure, a primary focus on exciting action, and some degree of spectator involvement. With *Chatham* it shares some of these elements, but above all the theme of a stricken and dying central figure supported by a group of other figures present at the event, whose life portraits are incorporated into the composition.

Unlike *The Death of Chatham* this picture was not painted on speculation. Copley had obtained a commission to paint *Peirson* for £800 from John Boydell,[5] who subsequently published the engraving by James Heath. This engraving did not appear until 1796, twelve years after the subscriptions were first taken.

Copley did not enter anything for exhibition at the Royal Academy in 1784, and on May 22 *The Death of Peirson*, went on exhibition at the great room in number 28, Haymarket. With it was *The Death of Chatham*, being shown to the public still

[5] A signed receipt dated May 15, 1783, for part payment of £200 is in the Karolik Collection, Boston Museum of Fine Arts (Edwin J. Hipkiss, *Eighteenth Century American Arts: The M. and M. Karolik Collection* [Boston, 1941], p. 318). Boydell's final payment to Copley after the exhibition of the painting was £164 5s made on August 17, 1784 (Microfilm, Archives of American Art, Detroit, ALSO / D8 / 487–8 / Feinberg). Copley's original commission from Boydell was to paint *Charles I Demanding the Five Impeached Members* (fig. 599), but this subject was set aside in favor of *The Death of Peirson*. It is not clear whether Copley or Boydell chose the subject, although the choice was probably Copley's and Boydell approved it. Copley's original idea to paint the subject may have been rooted in the decision of the States of the Isle of Jersey on April 21, 1781, to commission a memorial to Peirson. This commission was awarded on August 20, 1781, to the sculptor John Bacon (Durell, pp. 26–27) who, it will be recalled, also won the commission over Copley in 1779 from the London Court of Common Council for a memorial to Lord Chatham.

Although Copley chose the central square of St. Helier as his *mise en scène*, this may not have been the actual location of Peirson's death. When Henry Angelo visited Jersey in 1825 and stayed in a room overlooking the square of St. Helier, he gazed out musingly on the scene that was familiar to him from Copley's painting and the engraving of it by his friend James Heath. He noted that he had been told that Peirson actually was not killed in the square, but on the corner of the nearby street. Henry Angelo, *The Reminiscences of Henry Angelo*, introduction by Lord Howard de Walden, notes and memoirs by H. Lavers Smith (London, 1904), II, 343.

At one point Boydell also apparently considered commissioning work from Copley for his Shakespeare Gallery publications. The earliest prospectus announced that "The first number will contain Macbeth, and As you like It; the four designs of this number by Sir Joshua Reynolds, Mr. Romney, Mr. West and Mr. Copley." William Hayley, *Life of Romney* (London, 1809), p. 110.

another time. The exhibition was open each day from 8 A.M. to midnight, and admission cost one shilling. An explanation and key to the picture was attached to the proposal for the engraving given to each visitor.[6]

The day before the exhibition opened, the picture was sent to Buckingham Palace for the king's perusal. He returned earlier than usual from his morning ride in his eagerness to see it. The *Morning Herald* reported on the following day that "His Majesty continued examining it with the minutest attention for near three hours, and in commenting on its various excellencies, in point of *design, character, composition,* and *colouring,* expressed himself in the highest terms of approbation." The report added that the queen and the young princes and princesses were also pleased with the picture, and that the picture was said to be an honor to the gallant officer who had died and to the artist who had created it. The king also praised Boydell for his public spirit and his encouragement of the arts by this commission.

A laudatory review appeared on May 25, noting that "Mr. Copley has grouped the *figures* with spirit, and in the whole *composition* has discovered great science." The reviewer noted that the "fierceness" of the scarlet uniforms had been softened effectively by the light colored facings and linings, the blue drapery of the Negro and the French officer, and the highly finished arms and accoutrements. Note was also taken of the strong chiaroscuro: "the lights and shades throughout the picture is in fine keeping." [7] The *St. James's Chronicle* of April 24–27, 1784, cited Sir William Chambers and the "illiberality" of the council of the Royal Academy as the cause of not having Copley's "wonderful" *Death of Chatham* and "yet more wonderful" *Death of Peirson* exhibited at the academy, recalling the open dispute between Chambers and Copley that had occurred at the time of the *Chatham* exhibition and suggesting that Copley would have exhibited his large picture at the academy if he could have charged a private admission fee.

After the exhibition closed, the picture went to Boydell's house in Cheapside, where it hung in a sky-lighted second-floor gallery. On August 6, 1784, the *Morning Herald* noted:

> The celebrated picture of the death of Major Pierson is fixed up in Mr. Boydell's gallery. The frame in which it is placed is a beautiful piece of carved work. Three ovals are placed on the top of the frame, in the centre of which is Mr. Copley's portrait, painted by that able artist, Mr. Stuart [fig. 467]. The portrait of Mr. Heath, who is to engrave the subject, is on one side of the frame, and that of Mr. Josiah Boydell, who is to make the drawing, on the other.[8]

[6] *Morning Herald,* May 21 and 22, 1784; *Morning Chronicle,* May 21, 1784; British Museum, Egerton Ms. 2660, fol. 14, Peter Oliver [Jr.], Birmingham, to Elisha Hutchinson, France, May 17, 1784.

[7] "Cuttings on Art," I, 238, May 25, 1784, reprinted in *Massachusetts Centinel,* Sept. 8, 1784.

[8] Quoted in Whitley, *Gilbert Stuart,* p. 48. When Sophie Viscountess la Roche visited Boydell's gallery, she compounded her former slight of Copley in attributing *The Death of Chatham* to West (Chapter XII, n. 30, above) by reporting that she saw "the large canvas by Mr. Cosway, of General Piereson's death in Guernsey" (Williams, *Sophie,* p. 239, Sept. 28, 1786). Dibdin in his *Reminiscences*

A month after the highly successful exhibition of *The Death of Peirson* had opened, the young American artist, John Trumbull, came to England to advance his studies. As a young Harvard student with artistic ambitions, Trumbull had known Copley in Boston. Several years later, after Copley had gone to England, Trumbull began his own artistic career. After resigning from the Continental Army in 1777, he moved into Smibert's old studio and began to paint actively. Although Copley had gone, his paintings remained behind and Trumbull was profoundly influenced by them. His portrait of his brother *Jonathan Trumbull and His Family*, 1777 (Yale University Art Gallery) closely followed the composition of Copley's *Mr. and Mrs. Isaac Winslow* of three years earlier. His double portrait of his parents *Mr. and Mrs. Jonathan Trumbull Sr.* (Connecticut Historical Society) reverses the image of the *Winslow* double portrait and also clearly reflects the direct influence of Copley's *Mr. and Mrs. Thomas Mifflin* of 1773 and the full-length portrait of *Nicholas Boylston*, painted by Copley for Harvard while Trumbull was a student there. Even Trumbull's 1777 *Self-Portrait* (Boston Museum of Fine Arts) reflects Copley's portraits of *Nathaniel Hurd* and *Paul Revere*, all being portraits of artists with relevant objects placed on the table before the similarly posed sitters.

Trumbull wanted to study with West, and in May 1780, despite his prior service in the Continental Army, the English permitted him to come to London with the proviso that he keep clear of politics. Trumbull immediately began to study in West's studio, joining Gilbert Stuart who had been West's chief pupil for several years. He also saw Copley, currently at work on his *Death of Chatham*. In November 1780, Trumbull was suddenly imprisoned as an act of reprisal for the arrest of Major André in the colonies. Trumbull was in no great danger, having some powerful friends, including West, history painter to George III, and he could continue to copy some of West's pictures while in jail. He was finally released in June 1781, with West and Copley each posting one half of the required £200 release bond. Trumbull was immediately deported, but in June 1784, the war over, he returned to London to resume his studies.

Trumbull was undoubtedly aware of the achievements of his fellow Americans in history painting. He knew West's pictures intimately from his earlier apprenticeship, and he certainly saw *The Death of Chatham* while Copley was at work on it. The picture was enjoying its successful exhibition in the summer of 1781 when Trumbull was released from prison and deported. Now, on his second arrival in London, Trumbull found Copley in the midst of still another great success with an even finer painting,

---

recounted his stealing off to Boydell's back room to contemplate the picture. "From latest boyhood I loved this picture — as the most perfect, on the score of picturesque treatment, of all its author's productions" (I, 151n). The nineteenth-century historian of English art, Allan Cunningham, said that an engraving of the picture was the first print he ever saw, at the age of ten years. He liked it then and still liked it when he wrote, "It is stamped with true life and heroism: there is nothing mean, nothing little" (*Eminent Painters*, IV, 149–50).

The Death of Peirson. Trumbull clearly perceived that West and Copley had created a new type of history painting that included realism of setting and actual portraits of participants while celebrating important contemporary events; moreover it had elicited broad popular acclaim and could be highly profitable. Trumbull also realized that there was a large area of colorful current history that West and Copley could not touch: the American revolution. It would have been neither tactful nor wise of Copley, West, or anyone else to exhibit battle scenes from the American revolution in England. The war was unpopular, with strong support for both sides, and there was of course little public appeal in scenes of Englishmen killing Englishmen. This was the basic reason for Copley's choice of a subject like *The Death of Peirson* and for the picture's considerable success. Here was a glorious scene that depicted courageous English soldiers achieving a notable victory, a victory involving not the slaughter of English colonials but of Frenchmen, always a popular subject in London. But Trumbull did not labor under such restrictions, and he was not wedded to a career in London. Also he had actually served in the revolutionary army as an officer and knew a large number of the participants. Certainly there would be a ready market for the exhibition of paintings and the sale of engravings in America and France. The path was clear, and both West and Copley encouraged Trumbull to pursue it.

The first picture that Trumbull produced in his series of scenes from the American revolution was the *Death of General Warren at the Battle of Bunker's Hill, June 17, 1775* (Yale University Art Gallery). The picture was completed in March 1786. There is little question that Copley's *Death of Peirson* had been much on Trumbull's mind, for his picture repeats a number of elements found in Copley's work — the death of a hero, a figure with a sword above his head held parallel to the ground, a fleeing group on the right, a Negro servant in a prominent pictorial role, a dead figure in the lower left, ensigns overhead, baroque diagonals and alternating bands of light and shadow, and a general sense of confusion pervaded by the smoke of battle. The soldier seizing the British bayonet to protect the moribund Warren repeats the motif in the lower left of the Rubens *Massacre of the Innocents* (fig. 466) of the mother grasping the soldier's dagger to protect her child, suggesting that Copley may even have indicated his own source to Trumbull. For the second picture in Trumbull's series, *The Death of General Montgomery in the Attack on Quebec, Dec. 31, 1775* (Yale University Art Gallery), completed in June 1786, the obvious prototype was West's *Death of Wolfe* and Trumbull availed himself of it.

Although Trumbull never studied with Copley formally, he more than any other painter was influenced by Copley, in both America and England. Trumbull was like Copley in many ways: both were rather stiff, formal, cool, devoted to their own interests, rarely warm or generous outside their family circles, and in later life frequently in bitter conflict with other artists. Artistically, in addition to an interest in history, both were strong colorists and saw themselves as operating in the tradition of Rubens, although this too may have been another of Copley's effects on Trumbull. Up to the mid-1780's the relationship between the two consisted of admiration and emulation on the part of Trumbull, and encouragement and occasional assistance from Copley. But their friendship had deteriorated by 1787 when Trumbull, in order to work on a subject that would have some appeal in England and bring in some income to tide him over until his American scenes were completed, followed West's advice and chose a scene from the action at Gibraltar; this threw him into competition with Copley who was working on the same general theme.[9]

Copley had virtually no other pupils. Unlike West and Reynolds, who ran ateliers and were surrounded by young pupils and apprentices, Copley was a lone wolf. In this regard he was quite different from his hero Rubens. The only artist who worked intimately with Copley seems to have been his half brother, Henry Pelham, who did on occasion assist Copley toward the very end of his American years and who, after his arrival in London in 1776, lived with the Copleys in Leicester Square and submitted a few items for Royal Academy exhibitions. This artistic relationship ended when Pelham married and moved to Ireland.[10]

Another young American painter who worked a little with Copley was the rather eccentric Mather Brown, who came to London early in the 1780's. Copley had painted his mother in oil and pastel about twenty years earlier (figs. 110 and 111). Brown carried letters of introduction to Copley, including one from his grandfather, Mather Byles, who was also painted years earlier by Copley (figs. 199 and 200). After his arrival in London, Brown reported to his grandfather that "Mr. Copley, who is particularly kind to me, welcomed me to his house and lent me his pictures, etc."[11] But Brown studied more extensively with Benjamin West. Copley, ambitious and hardworking, preferred to keep to his own devices.

[9] Years later, when Trumbull was in England on diplomatic rather than artistic business, Copley borrowed almost £50 from him to reimburse Richard Codman for paper purchased in Hamburg. Although Copley agreed to repay the debt in several months, it was still outstanding after two and a half years, and Trumbull requested his money. Copley replied rather testily that he could not pay the debt and would already have paid it if he could. Trumbull answered that he had only advanced the money as a favor, that if necessary Copley could sell the paper which had gone up in value, and deftly concluded that Copley seemed to think it more just for Trumbull to borrow money to lend him than to borrow money himself to repay Trumbull: "Whether this is strictly consistent with the great Principle of Christianity, which commands us to do to others, as we would that they should do

unto us: — I leave to be decided by you who are an older, and ought therefore to be a better Christian than/Your very obedient Servant/Jnº Trumbull." Trumbull-Copley Account and Letters, July 16, 1797–July 18, 1799, Historical Manuscripts and University Archives Collection, Yale University Library.

[10] See Chapter XI, n. 15, above.

[11] Ward, *Curwen*, pp. 495–96. Massachusetts Historical Society, photostat, Mather Brown to his Aunt [Miss Byles], June 19, 1780, "I . . . have one particular Favour to beg of you which is to write me a letter of recommendation to Mr. Copley; as I am determined to go to London." *Ibid.*, photostat, Mather Brown to his Aunts, July 28, 1784, "Your last Favour by Callahan I thank you for, nothing could oblige me more than that to Mr. Copley who received it in the most affectionate manner."

A Time of Trial

1784-1789 IN 1783, THE YEAR HE MOVED TO GEORGE STREET, COPLEY WON A commission from the Corporation of the City of London to paint a large history picture commemorating the victory of the British over the Spanish and French at Gibraltar in the autumn of 1782. The Court of Common Council of London, meeting on February 6, 1783, had formed a committee of eight aldermen and sixteen commoners to consider "the most suitable mode" to honor Sir George Augustus Eliott, the commander of the defending forces at Gibraltar; Admiral Howe, who commanded the relief fleet; and other participants. The committee met later that month and recommended giving the keys of the city to Eliott and Howe in gold boxes worth one hundred guineas. It also resolved that "an Historical Painting will be the most suitable mode for the Court of Common Council to express its respect to the Gallant Conduct of General Elliot, Governor of Gibraltar, Lord Viscount Howe, Commander of the Fleet, and the rest of his Majesty's Officers, Solders and Sailors employed in its [Gibraltar's] defence and relief"; West and Copley were to be called in "to consult them for a design for the above purpose."

The artists appeared before the committee on the last day of February 1783. West's opinion was that it would be better to treat the defense and the relief of Gibraltar as two subjects in separate paintings. Copley took the position that a picture large enough to fill one of the side windows of the Common Council Room with figures of half life size could successfully combine the events. Copley's opinion was probably more agreeable to the committee than West's, since it involved only one picture. Moreover, Copley had an inestimable advantage because, as he told the committee, he had already decided to execute such a picture before having learned that the city planned a commemorative work. Copley also told the committee that the picture could be done for £1500, or even for £1000 on a smaller and less magnificent scale. In either event he promised to paint it to the best of his ability, for "he would not find his Interest promoted by a Picture that was deficient."

On March 6, 1783, the members of the committee visited Copley's Leicester Square studio and saw *The Death of Chatham* and *The Death of Peirson*, the artist being engaged on the latter picture. The committee met on the following day but did not reach a decision because West had called on one of the aldermen and left word that no decision should be reached until he had been seen. West was fighting a losing battle, however, and on March 18, 1783, Copley signed an agreement that "Mr. Copley, desirous of receiving so honourable a commission from the City of London as the one proposed, and willing to meet the wishes of the committee, will undertake the work for one thousand guineas, hoping the advantages of an Exhibition of the Picture and the publication of a Print from it will compensate him for the time and study requisite for completing so large a work." Satisfied with the adequacy of this tribute to Eliott and Howe, the committee also rescinded the vote to give them the gold boxes. The Court of Common Council approved the decision of the committee which, in recommending the acceptance of Copley's proposal, noted that the opinion "of two of the first artists in this Kingdom had been sought." Thus Copley won the largest commission of his career: it took him almost eight years to discharge it, although he had given the committee an estimate of only two years for the task.[1]

When Copley returned to his easel after the successful exhibition of *The Death of Peirson*, he was at the zenith of his career. He had achieved the dream of his youth to become a renowned painter of historical subjects, and he had achieved some measure of financial success. The popularity of the exhibitions of *Chatham* and *Peirson*, and the flood of subscriptions for the projected engravings, had already netted him a sizable income, and he would receive the remaining subscription income when the engravings were published. His success had enabled him to move his family into the fine new house on George Street. With the Gibraltar commission in his pocket, the future indeed looked bright for Copley. And now a new opportunity arose, which tempted him to put off the Gibraltar project. Royal approbation of *The Death of Peirson* apparently resulted in a grant of permission to paint a conversation piece incorporating portraits of the English princesses. Although this does not seem to have been a commission, it gave the artist a splendid chance to extend his reputation: such a painting would lead to commissions from others wishing to sit for the painter of successful royal portraits.[2]

[1] James L. Howgego, "Copley and the Corporation of London," *The Guildhall Miscellany*, IX (July 1958), 35, 38; "Committee Minutes," first draft, Corporation of London Record Office, Guildhall, Mss. 195.5, [Feb. 28], March 8, April 1, 1783. West was not the only disappointed contender for this commission. On the day after Copley signed his agreement with the committee, his erstwhile incompatible traveling companion, George Carter, wrote to the Corporation to apply. He noted that he had been working on such a picture since the event, had finished it a month before, and had engaged to have it engraved. He further claimed that in order to achieve accuracy in his presentation he had gathered information from state papers and from Sir Roger Curtis, whose portrait was included and who superintended the composition (*ibid.*, March 19, 1783). Carter's petition was set aside. It seems likely that his painting was not as far advanced as he claimed, since in the following year he visited Gibraltar and took life portraits of the Hanoverian officers there (Heathfield Papers, National Maritime Museum, I, 28, 30). Carter's sketch for "The Siege of Gibraltar" (fig. 491) also dates from 1784.

[2] Payments for royal portraits ordinarily appear in the "Warrant Books, Declared Accounts," Records of the Lord Chamberlain's Department, Public Record Office, London. These Warrant Books record payments to Ramsay and Reynolds, the official court painters, but no payments for 1785 are listed to Copley. Further evidence that this was not executed on commission is found in "Farington Diary," p. 1198, Jan. 13, 1798. At this time, when Copley

The surviving drawings for *The Three Youngest Daughters of King George III* (fig. 468) reveal an almost frantic compositional search. There seems to be no consistent development, but instead gigantic leaps from one scheme to another. One early drawing (fig. 469) contains six figures and suggests that the initial plan was to include Queen Charlotte, three princes, and the two older princesses. A drawing at Worcester (fig. 470), presumably of Queen Charlotte and Princess Amelia (the middle princess in the painting), explores further the right-hand portion of this initial composition, reminiscent of the arrangement in *The Tribute Money*. Fortunately this static format was abandoned. A sheet of studies of Princess Mary (fig. 471), the eldest daughter, shows Copley groping toward another compositional solution. A drawing in the Victoria and Albert Museum (fig. 472), executed after the design had been formulated, is a calculation sheet; the figures, only cursorily sketched, are liberally peppered with measurements. Both the broad range of compositional shifts and the careful measuring of the last drawing indicate the importance Copley attached to this picture, and the pains he took to make it as good as possible. Small wonder that the princesses grew exasperated with this painter who demanded so much of their time.[3]

The end product justifies Copley's efforts. Despite the changes of pose and the careful measurements, the final result is fresh and spontaneous. One of the most exuberant of all Copley paintings, it is one of the few instances in which Copley's finished painting is just as engaging as his oil sketches. The colors, predominantly light in value, float on the surface, in evidence of the freedom and dash with which the pigment was applied. Princess Mary's face is largely cast into shadow, but loses none of its clarity or force. This is one of Copley's favorite devices, to paint the face in shadow but to infuse it with an inner glow so that it still dominates its area. In *The Death of Peirson,* he did this with the faces of Captain Macneil, Lieutenant Drysdale, Ensign Smith, and the soldier leading the group on the left, and in *The Death of Chatham* with Lord Dudley and Ward and Richard Brocklesby. The hat of the baby Sophia is an effusion of white froth. Amelia, behind her, wears a dress of delicate pink with a white border and cuffs under a fine white netting. Mary, in white and yellow with a lavender sash, rests one hand on the handle of the red and gilt go-cart bearing the younger princesses and, with the other hand, holds aloft her red, white, and blue tambourine. The faces — Mary's in shadow, Amelia's in full light, Sophia's half in light and half in shadow — are all suffused with the same warm pinkish tones that rise to a charming flush in the cheeks. Surrounding the figures is a lush aureole of flowers and vines, enlivened by parrots above and bouncing dogs below. The well-

---

was in financial straits, Joseph Farington received a visit from Sir William Beechey, portrait painter to the queen: "He spoke of Copleys picture of Princesses favorably — Copley heard of it — asked if possible to get money — Beechy bid him deliver in acct. & wd. be paid, Copley did so abt 3 months ago & rec⁴ draft on Coutts. made acknowledgement to Beechy." A record of this draft on the royal account at Coutts Bank has not been located. The fact that Copley tried to secure payment during hard times in 1798 suggests that he had not received payment in 1785.

[3] Amory, p. 13.

painted still life in the lower right is unusual in Copley's work. In the distance a blue sky above Windsor Castle is touched with light reds, yellows, and pinks of the sunset. The V-shaped composition provides equilibrium and yet implies the potentiality of movement.

One of the surprising elements in Copley's style at this point is that, despite his remarkable agility with the brush, he was still laying out his pictures area by area, as in his colonial works. The color areas remain distinct, creating a pattern of their own on the surface, and do not fuse into one another to create a unified, homogeneous picture. It is this trait that enables Copley to achieve the brilliance of color and strong contrasts of light and shadow that mark his style. The important difference in the products of Copley's American and British periods is not one of technique but of concept, although there is of course some technical development. Throughout Copley's work, the nature of his artistic means is consistent. Free brushwork, bold color harmonies, strong value contrasts, and the use of discrete color areas can all be traced from the earliest paintings to the late productions of his English years. The changes over time take place more in terms of pictorial ends than in pictorial means. And in both America and England these ends were determined not by Copley alone, but by the artist in response to the requirements of his patrons.

In colonial America the demand from a limited patronage was for the realistic delineation of the individuals portrayed. The emphasis was on the likeness of the sitter, not necessarily on the convincing presentation of a human form in space.

In England Copley encountered or solicited several different kinds of patrons. The audience for history paintings was the public that came to see his exhibitions and subscribed to the engravings. These pictures had to be sources of pure visual pleasure as well as meaningful representations of particular themes. For this, Copley's major talent as a colorist, his sensitivity to the decorative possibilities inherent in the arrangement of colors and designs on the picture surface, and his sensual delight in pigment were well suited. His clientele for portraits in England was largely drawn from the lower nobility, the landed gentry, and the military; only rarely did he paint royalty or the higher nobility. Whereas his Boston patrons might be equated with their counterparts in Britain's provincial centers — Bristol or Birmingham, Edinburgh or Dublin — his English sitters who lived in London, or came there to be painted, represented a somewhat higher social echelon. His portrait style in England, reflecting the popular manner shared by the leading portrait painters of the day — Reynolds, Romney, and Gainsborough — became more idealized and more imaginative than it had been in Boston, and more concerned with a convincing realization of the three-dimensional human figure in space than with realism of specific details. If Copley had chosen to live outside of London, his portrait style might have been more closely allied with that of painters like Tilly Kettle or Joseph Wright of Derby (in his early years). Significantly, it is only his American paintings that resemble the work of these provincial artists. Yet his English portraits remain essentially simple, less elaborate and less flamboyant than the productions of Reynolds and Gainsborough. His English portrait style finds its closest affinity with the art of George Romney. Like Romney, Copley grew out of his provincial background without ever completely losing a deep-rooted sense of realism. Unlike Gainsborough and Reynolds, who did paint sitters of the highest social levels, Copley did not indulge in creative elaborations of dress, setting, pose, or iconography, which would have been less pleasing to his clients. When he did receive an opportunity to paint for an elite audience, as in the case of *The Daughters of George III*, he lost a good deal of his restraint (but not all) and, after much casting about for a compositional solution, created a beautiful object that suggests the heights he might have achieved in this direction — a direction for which his decorative skills were eminently appropriate. Even though his serious turn of mind was an ever-present force that kept him headed toward history painting, it seems to have been strictly external factors that turned him away from social portraiture.

The Daughters of George III was a crucial test for Copley. A complete success with this informal conversation piece, a type of painting quite different from the formal *Izard*, *Pepperrell*, or *Copley* family groups, could vault him into the ranks of fashionable portraitists. The picture was Copley's only offering to the Royal Academy exhibition in the spring of 1785, although he had at one time considered submitting the portrait of *Winslow Warren, Jr.* (fig. 473).[4] The art critic of the *Morning Post* in 1785 was the artist John Hoppner, which was unfortunate for the harmony of the London art world, and particularly unfortunate for Copley. Hoppner, who on May 5 reviewed the Royal Academy exhibition in which Copley presented *The Daughters of George III*, had painted for the same exhibition individual portraits of the princesses Sophia, Mary, and Amelia, and he was hardly unbiased:

[4] Copley probably painted this portrait late in 1784. Warren wrote to his mother in Boston on March 7, 1785, "Mr. Copley in London treated me with the greatest attention and politeness and after we had taken my picture told me of his own accord that London was a place that took away money very fast and that if I found it inconvenient to pay him then I might make it convenient to myself and give him a draft upon Prentiss payable in 4 months which I am fearful is not paid. I will not write to London just now because of the uncertainty and my inability to remit 25 guineas — but it shall be sent to Boston this Spring. If it remains in London until April it will be at the exhibition at Somerset House with the rest of his works" (Boston Museum of Fine Arts, extract of letter from Winslow Warren to his mother, Mercy Otis Warren, March 7, 1785). Either Warren found the twenty-five guineas or Copley decided not to detract from the effect of *The Daughters of George III* by exhibiting anything else at the same time. Another American in London, the budding architect Charles Bulfinch, found Copley too expensive and chose to have his portrait painted by Mather Brown. He wrote to his mother on Sept. 17, 1786, in regard to the portrait, "you will find it very rough, but that is the modish style of painting, introduced by Sir Joshua Reynolds. Mr. Copeley indeed paints in another manner, his pictures are finished to the utmost nicety, but then — they are *very dear*" (Ellen Susan Bulfinch, ed., *The Life and Letters of Charles Bulfinch, Architect* [Boston and New York, 1896], p. 57). Copley's price scale in the mid-1780's seems to have been the same as that of George Romney — twenty-five guineas for a 30" x 25," fifty guineas for a 50" x 40," and one hundred guineas for a full-length — and considerably below Reynolds' scale (Maxwell, *Romney*, p. 70). Copley received one hundred guineas for the portrait of *John Adams* and the same amount for the conversation piece of *The Sitwell Family*. Presumably his price scale was lower when he first arrived in England; subsequently, at the time of the Knatchbull dispute in 1803–1804, he was getting one hundred and twenty guineas for a full-length portrait.

So, Mr. Copley, is this the fruit of your long studies and labours? Is it for this you have contemplated the Iris and the Prism? Is it because you have heard *fine feathers* make fine birds, that you have concluded *fine cloaths* will make *Princesses*? What delightful disorder! Why, you have plucked up harmony by the roots, and planted confusion in its stead! Princesses, parrots, dogs, grapes, flowers, leaves, are each striving for pre-eminence, and opposing, with hostile force, all attempts of our wearied eyes to find to repose.

The review was patently unfair, but its opinions were contagious. Two weeks later the normally friendly *Morning Chronicle* stated: "*Copley* has nothing to do, but to obliterate all the profuse decoration about the portrait of the princ's [*sic*], to make it a very picture — when unadorned, adorned the most. This is precisely the case, with such beautiful objects, as the figures are, and of such ugly objects, as are the ducks, the dogs, the red flowers, and the green leaves, &c. &c. &c." [5]

Hoppner's portraits did not receive favorable reviews either, but this was small comfort to Copley or to West and the Cosways, whose pictures were also attacked. Hostility at court from the royal painters — West, Ramsay, Reynolds — could also have been a factor working against a favorable response for Copley's picture. Ramsay, a staunch colonialist, may have felt good reason to oppose Copley on political grounds alone. Copley had alienated some of the academicians, presumably including Reynolds, the president of the academy, by his successful private exhibitions of *The Death of Chatham* in 1781 and *The Death of Peirson* in 1784. And Copley's relations with West, though not yet at the point of enmity, were already strained. One reason for this was that, whenever West would give an opinion at a meeting of the Royal Academy, Copley would invariably speak in opposition. This was perhaps a psychological necessity for Copley, who was seeking to achieve at least a parity of prestige with West, but such actions were not calculated to create good feelings on the part of the academicians who had to sit through these proceedings.[6] Dissatisfaction with the rococo flamboyance and opulence of *The Daughters of George III* in a period of classical restraint and simplicity may also have contributed to its lack of popular favor.

Still, whatever the reasons for the failure of the picture, it unleashed no flood of commissions from the royal family or the upper nobility. The world of fashion remained the preserve of Reynolds, Gainsborough, and, for all his stylistic similarity to Copley,

[5] May 18, 1785. The tenor of other criticism was the same, following Hoppner's lead. One reviewer felt that Copley's atypical coloring of the children was very successful, but that all the highly finished birds and plants resulted in a heavy effect ("Cuttings on Art," Victoria and Albert Museum, I, 255, "RA 1785," no. II, 80). Another suggested that Copley should use the exotic flowers in a May garland, put the vines on the poop of the Vintner's barge, and send the birds to Brook's Repository in Holborn. This same reviewer praised the head of Princess Mary, but felt that the other two figures were submerged in the surrounding stuffs and made the strange observation that, although the dogs were well painted, they were seen from unpleasing angles (*ibid.*, I, 260). Pasquin in his *Memoirs* fired a fusillade of unfavorable comment at the picture, whose high color caused one to "wink involuntarily": "All flutter and folly, flowers and ribbands," "more calculated for the meridian of taste at Coventry or Cranbourn-alley than a Royal Palace," "overcharged style of tinting," "levity of pencilling," and "a sedulous attempt to make finery overthrow truth" (p. 137).

[6] Whitley, *Artists in England, 1700–1799*, II, 47.

Romney. During his career in England Copley was to paint few sitters of social eminence. The high-ranking sitters he did paint were usually men who had achieved political, professional, or military prominence. *The Daughters of George III* was Copley's moment of truth with the world of English fashion. The painting was not a success and Copley turned back to familiar ground; the painting of *The Siege of Gibraltar* that had been commissioned two years earlier awaited his attention. His patrons would be the city aldermen who had given the commission, the Londoners who would come to see the picture when it was put on exhibition, and the people who would subscribe to the engravings. Portraits were not to be Copley's artistic way of life in England, but only a source of additional income or prestige between entrepreneurial efforts at history painting. Portraits were money in the bank and would get preference when commissioned, but only a few opportunities followed in wake of *The Daughters of George III*. Copley was no longer a rising young painter: at the age of forty-seven he had painted his royal portrait and failed to kindle the enthusiasm of the elite. So Copley, it seemed, had gone as far as he could in the realm of social portraiture.

The year 1785 held much greater tragedy for Copley than the unenthusiastic reception accorded his *Daughters of George III*. On October 24, four days after her ninth birthday, Susanna Copley died of what Mrs. Benjamin West called a "putrid sore throat." She was buried at the parish church in Croydon on October 30. Ten days later, the youngest member of the family, three-and-a-half-year-old Jonathan, succumbed to the same disease and was also interred at Croydon. The Copleys had lost in one blow the two children born to them in England.[7] A splendid oil sketch of *Susanna Copley* (fig. 475) must have been painted only shortly before her death, if indeed it is not a *memento mori*. Copley occasionally painted relatives when they were about to leave the family circle for one reason or another, such as the portrait of his sister-in-law, *Mrs. Charles Startin* (fig. 476), probably done just before her departure to rejoin her husband

[7] "Mrs. Benjamin West's Account Book," Swarthmore College, Oct. 24, 1785, and Nov. 9, 1785. Susanna Copley was born Oct. 20, 1776, and baptized Nov. 12, 1776. Jonathan Copley was born Feb. 23, 1782, and baptized March 24, 1782 (Register of Baptisms, 1775–1791, St. Martins in the Fields, London). The Croydon parish burial records (contemporaneous copy in the Croydon Public Library) show that both Susanna Copley (Oct. 30, 1785) and Jonathan Copley (Nov. 13, 1785) from London were interred in the Heron Chancel of St. John's church. Copley himself was eventually buried on Sept. 19, 1815, inside the church on the north aisle. The church has since been destroyed and rebuilt, and the interment site has been marked by Copley's descendants. The reason for interment in Croydon rather than through the Copley family's own parish church, St. George's, Hanover Square, probably lies in the fact that members of Thomas Hutchinson's family had been buried there, including the governor himself in 1780, and the Hutchinsons and Copleys were both relatives and friends. The Hutchinsons had probably gone to Croydon to bury their dead because the vicar was the Reverend East Apthorp, who until 1764 had been rector of Christ Church, Cambridge. There is also a possibility that family ties in Croydon may have existed. A large number of Singletons did live in Croydon, though the connection remains unproven.

In *St. James's Chronicle*, Oct. 29–Nov. 1, 1785, there appeared "Lines by a Lady, on a recent Loss in the Family of the celebrated Painter of the Death of Major Peirson," signed by "The Cottage Mouse." The poem consisted of twelve four-line stanzas, beginning: "Ah! what avails the Master's Art,/ Which strews fresh Laurels O'er the Brave;/ Can Genius blunt Affliction's Dart,/ Or snatch one Blossom from the Grave?"

in America in 1783, or the portrait of his daughter Elizabeth, *Mrs. Gardiner Greene* (fig. 634), done just before she married in 1800 and returned to America. The portrait of Susanna might be a particularly poignant memorial, although the freshness and vitality of the sketch make it difficult to associate the portrait with such a somber purpose. It is very broadly painted against a freely stroked light blue background, which is whitened in places for a cloudlike effect. The deep-brimmed hat casts a shadow over Susanna's eyes and the bridge of her nose, very much like the shadow cast by Princess Sophia's hat in *The Daughters of George III*, painted shortly before.

During the next few years, Copley's painting activity was very much limited by his major project, *The Siege of Gibraltar*. But he did have some private commissions. *Jonathan Jackson* (fig. 474) was painted in about 1785, while Jackson was in England, in an oval portrait resembling the slightly larger one of his compatriot *Winslow Warren, Jr.* (fig. 473). At the Royal Academy in 1786, he exhibited another conversation piece, entitled "Portraits of a Young Lady and Her Three Brothers" — the group known more familiarly as *The Sitwell Family* (fig. 477). It reproduces the small-scale figures familiar in paintings by Devis, Stubbs, or Zoffany, but infuses the scene with action. It is more of a snapshot, of a particular moment of play, and has the instantaneous quality of *Chatham, Peirson, Watson*, or, on this particular level, *The Daughters of George III*. It has neither the generalized, unmotivated pose of the standard English conversation piece, nor the formality of his own *Izard, Pepperrell*, or *Copley* family groups. Copley was clearly ill at ease with this genre, however. Although the canvas of *The Sitwell Family* is more than five feet high, the figures fill less than half of it and seem to rattle around like tiny puppets in an oversized dollhouse. Copley, whose attention always centered more on color and pictorial possibilities than on the creation of a three-dimensional visual effect, needed the scale of life, or the approximate scale of life, to maintain the proper illusion. This picture might have been more successful if twice as large, for it is generally true that Copley throughout his career has happier results with canvases that approximate the size of life than with those requiring a reduction in scale. During the latter years of his life, Copley rarely deserted the life scale, creating a series of elephantine pictures that, although depressing in their vastness, are actually much better than they would have been on a smaller scale.

One has the feeling that in *The Sitwell Family* Copley fell prey to the same sort of insecurity that resulted in the 1767 portrait of *Mary Warner* [?] (fig. 164) when, in an attempt to correct the shortcomings of his *Henry Pelham* (fig. 163), he created an infinitely poorer picture by a too literal adoption of the suggestions of his critics. *The Daughters of George III* had been criticized for the profusion of bric-a-brac that surrounded the princesses. In *The Sitwell Family* the figures are at play in a classically austere Adam interior. Two slender vases on the narrow mantel balance one pot of flowers on the left. A lonely pair of tassels dangles above the head of the young lady like the sword of Damocles. It is as if, in one year, Copley had moved from complete rococo

318

exuberance to complete neoclassical restraint. The reviewers tore the picture to shreds. The *Morning Post*, frequently hostile, wrote of it on May 16, 1786:

> It is with reluctance that we criticize with severity; yet, to pass over Pictures of such uncommon demerit, as frequently disgust our eye, and issuing too from the pencil of such that are expected to execute with a degree of excellence to entitle them to the Academic honours, would be doing an injustice to the public, and disgracing the province of criticism. The picture before us is, in every part, such a stranger to the inspiration of genius, that in spite of the meretricious glare which flashes on us, and seems intended for delusion, that did we not know others of the distinguished order of Academicians capable of exhibiting things of *equal* mediocrity, we should pronounce it the performance of a mere Tyro in the art.

A kindlier voice criticized the tameness of the pyramidal composition and the lack of coloristic harmony, concluding that the picture was the "result of labour, not genius" and that, if the catalogue had not stated otherwise, "we should have determined the picture to have been merely an humble imitation of Mr. *Copley's* manner." An unidentified half-length portrait of a lady that Copley also exhibited was criticized by the same reviewer for its hard coloring, the unpleasing drapery, its "sky as cold as marble," and was classified as "a *mechanical* effort, in which neither genius nor fancy have contributed assistance." Another review simply dismissed both pictures as unattractive and unimportant.[8]

After the personal blows and the critical buffets of 1785 and 1786, Copley was probably content to retreat to the sanctuary of a few years' labor on a large historical canvas, *The Siege of Gibraltar*, the type of picture that had brought him so much popular, critical, and financial success. From 1786 on, he was primarily occupied with this task, although he did have a few other projects during this period. In 1786 a commission was given to West to paint a series of scriptural subjects for Greenwich Hospital Chapel. According to newspaper reports, Lord Sandwich had originally selected Copley for the commission, but West was chosen through the intercession of Lord North. Another newspaper attributed the change directly to the intervention of the king.[9] There had been open competition between West and Copley before with *The Death of Chatham*, when West abandoned his scheme to leave the field to Copley, and *The Siege of Gibraltar*, when Copley secured the Corporation's commission over West. Relations between West and Copley had been strained as early as 1785, and this must have added to the tension. However, West and Copley exchanged social calls at least until 1788.[10]

[8] "Cuttings on Art," Victoria and Albert Museum, I, 279, 280 ("Review of the Royal Academy, 1786," no. III, 423), and 285 (unidentified review of May 2, 1786).

[9] Whitley, *Artists in England, 1700–1799*, II, 98. Commenting on this, one pundit could not resist a jibe at West's expense: "Is it decided, that *Copley* is rejected, and *West* the artist fixed on to paint the subjects for Greenwich Chapel? — *Wisdom* of old went to the East, we suppose *Folly* reverses the course!" "Cuttings on Art," I, 298.

[10] "Mrs. Benjamin West's Account Book," March 10, 1786; Aug. 29, 1786; June 14, 1787; June 15, 1787; March 14, 1788; March 20, 1788.

By 1788 Copley was deeply involved with *Gibraltar*, but the *World* noted on March 28 that he was working on several other pictures. One cited was a family portrait of Lord Westcote, his wife, and his daughter. Lord Westcote, who became Baron Lyttelton in 1794, had been created a baron in the Irish peerage in 1766. Previously he had served in 1755–1760 as governor of South Carolina and in 1760–1766 as governor of Jamaica. Copley may have received the commission through American or Irish connections, or perhaps Westcote simply wanted to have a conversation piece of his family done by the painter of *The Daughters of George III* and *The Sitwell Family*.[11] The completed *Lyttelton Family* (fig. 478), representing full-length figures in a landscape, hung at Hadley Hall until it was destroyed by fire in 1925. Several drawings are extant. One (fig. 480) reveals an unusual compositional formation in which the two older figures swing into the picture on the right and the girl and her dog swing out on the left. The two inside figures, mother and daughter, stretch their arms out toward an imaginary central axis, so that the pairs revolve as on a merry-go-round or as if performing some formal dance, each participant gazing intently at his partner. All motion is to the left, and the figures are rather small in relation to the total area. A single study of the figure of the daughter (fig. 479) is certainly one of Copley's better drawings. For Copley a drawing was a working tool, only a means to an end. He used drawings to work out compositional ideas, to plan the flow of light on the forms, and to set a scale of measures for the final picture. Distortions are frequent in Copley's drawings, even in his oil sketches, but usually all is smoothed out in the finished paintings. Inevitably the final artistic thinking was done in paint, and the drawings are only occasionally effective as independent art objects. This drawing is one such instance, though even here there is a lack of plastic realization in the body and a disassociation of the various pictorial elements so that, for example, the head is simply set sideways on the shoulders and the articulation is physiologically unconvincing.

Figs. 481 and 482 may be early studies for *The Lyttelton Family* (the dog in the lower right of fig. 481 is a mirror image of the dog in the lower left of the *Lyttelton* drawings) or for *The Daughters of George III*; or they may be related to fig. 483, which contains a similar girl and dog. That drawing, in turn, is freely related to the somewhat slap-dash *Thomas Lane and His Sister Harriot* (fig. 484), although the sitters in the drawing appear to be considerably younger.

Henry White (fig. 485) and *John Burgwyn* (fig. 486) were among the substantial number of Americans who had their portraits painted by Copley in the 1780's, and he also painted *John Penn* (fig. 487) in London. It is uncertain whether Copley ever

---

[11] Copley had included Lord Westcote's portrait in *The Death of Chatham*. Contact between artist and patron may have been renewed when Copley began to track down seventeenth-century portraits for his projected *Charles I Demanding the Five Impeached Members*. In a letter of Jan. 4, 1782, Edmund Malone advised Copley that for a portrait of Sir Edward Littleton, one of the king's men, Copley should "Enquire of Lord Westcote" (Boston Public Library, Ch. I.3.11). A partial or final payment of £35–15–0 for *The Lyttelton Family* was made by Westcote to Copley on April 11, 1791 (letter to the author from Reginald Winder, Curator, C. Hoare & Co., London, August 2, 1960).

painted a separate portrait of young William Pitt based on the likeness in *The Death of Chatham*, but apparently he did make a drawing that served as the basis for an engraving by Bartolozzi published in 1789 (fig. 488).

In 1789 Copley received more bad news, learning of the death of his ailing mother whom he had not seen since he had left Boston fifteen years earlier. Only the year before she had written to him proudly, "Your fame, my dear son, is sounded by all who are lovers of the art you bid fair to excel in." [12] Despite this fame, resting upon earlier triumphs with *Chatham* and *Peirson*, the previous few years for Copley had been marked by professional disappointments. Still he had high hopes of recapturing his past glory with *The Siege of Gibraltar*.

[12] Amory, p. 83, Feb. 6, 1788; Massachusetts Historical Society, Copley to Mercy Scollay, Aug. 28, 1789.

XVI   *The Siege of Gibraltar*

1785-1791   THE SPANISH AND THEIR FRENCH ALLIES BEGAN THE SIEGE OF
Gibraltar in July 1779, bombarding the English-held rock con-
tinually and blockading against the relief ships bearing food and munitions. In 1782 the
Spanish brought into play a fleet of ten specially built floating batteries, sometimes
called battering ships, with which they intended to subdue the garrison. The floating
batteries moved against Gibraltar on the morning of September 13, 1782. Approaching
slowly, they dropped anchor at a range of about 900 to 1200 yards. A heavy artillery
exchange started as the batteries attempted to knock out the British gun emplacements
nestled in the rocks, and the British in reply poured a constant stream of red-hot shot
into the enemy ships. From his command post on King's Bastion, General Eliott
directed the British fire as his men rushed the fiery shot from furnaces to cannon. The
heavy barrage continued back and forth through the morning and the battle appeared
stalemated until smoke, which had begun to appear from the closest Spanish ships,
became steady during the afternoon. At the same time, the return fire from the Spanish
ships slackened and by evening had almost ceased. The British bombardment continued
at a moderate pace. At about 1:00 A.M. the battering ship that had absorbed the largest
amount of incendiary shot burst into flames. An hour later the ship was a torch from
stem to stern, lighting up the harbor and permitting the British gunners to fire with
greater accuracy at their targets. The scene of the harbor and the surrounding land
was, according to an on-the-spot historian, Colonel John Drinkwater, "highly illuminated; forming, with the constant flashes of our cannon, a mingled scene of sublimity
and terror." [1]

At 3:00 A.M., with the sea calm, Sir Roger Curtis set out with his gunboats to capture the launches fleeing from the stricken ships and to take seamen off the ships themselves. Two hours later fire touched the magazine of one of the Spanish ships and it blew
apart. Soon a second ship exploded. These explosions put Curtis' rescue boats in danger,
and one of them went down. The crew was saved, but on Curtis' own boat the coxswain
was killed and the strokesman wounded. Curtis continued to pick up enemy survivors

[1] John Drinkwater, *A History of the Late Siege of Gibraltar* (4th ed., London, 1790 [1st ed. 1785]),
p. 287.

322

and in all brought in "five officers, two priests, and three hundred and thirty-four private soldiers and seamen." [2]

The scene at daybreak following the explosion of the two battering ships was described in the *Annual Register* for 1782: "Numbers of men were seen in the midst of the flames, crying out for pity and help; others floating upon pieces of timber, exposed to an equal, though less dreadful danger, from the opposite element. Even those in the ships where the fire had yet made a less progress, expressed in their looks, gestures, and words, the deepest distress and dispair; and were no less urgent in imploring assistance." [3] This, the climax of the events at Gibraltar, was the scene that Copley painted in his *Siege of Gibraltar* (fig. 489).

With the defeat of the floating batteries, the back of the siege was broken, although it was not actually ended until a large relief fleet under Admiral Howe pierced the blockade in the following month. [4] The gallant and successful defense of the rock, which had culminated in the destruction of the battering ships, had a great impact on the English public. In contrast with the disgrace of British arms in an unpopular struggle against the American colonies, this was a brilliant victory achieved against the massed might of England's traditional enemies, Spain and France. People were eager to know more about what had happened. A backlog of earlier prints and maps of Gibraltar was available, but fresh views and information were wanted. To meet this demand, a steady stream of accounts and prints describing events at Gibraltar was published during the next few years, not only in England but also in Germany, where there was considerable interest since Hanoverian mercenaries had played an important role alongside the British. Copley had ready access to these materials, and, having received his commission to paint the event in March 1783, he undoubtedly made it a point to be familiar with them. [5]

[2] *Ibid.*, p. 289.

[3] *The Annual Register, 1782*, p. 238. This account, although somewhat more dramatic in style, so closely parallels that given in Drinkwater (*History*, p. 289) that it certainly was written by Drinkwater himself or based upon his written report. My general account of the events at Gibraltar is based on Drinkwater, *History*, pp. 279ff.

[4] Admiral Howe sailed "from Spithead, September the 11th, with 34 sail of the line for the relief of Gibraltar. This he affected, October the 11th, in spite of the combined fleet of France and Spain, (46 sail of the line) . . . It was the action Lord Howe always spoke of, to his dying day, as the greatest he had ever performed, and as the only one, of which he claimed the sole merit to himself." *The Annual Register, 1805*, p. 759.

[5] Colonel Drinkwater's *History* provided the most comprehensive contemporary account of the subject. His clear and complete narrative, illustrated by a number of maps and engraved views, gives the reader a comprehensive and exciting description of the events at Gibraltar. Other accounts that Copley may have found useful are S. Ancell, *A Journal of the Blockade and Siege of Gibraltar* (5th ed., Dublin, 1802); anon., *A Description of Gibraltar* (London, 1782); and anon., *An Authentic and Accurate Journal of the Late Siege of Gibraltar* (T. Benchley: London [1785?]).

Early views may have been of particular help to Copley in visualizing the scene he planned to paint. Shortly after reports of the battle reached England, a crude print was published by G. S. Queen on Oct. 26, 1782, to capitalize on the strong interest in the subject. Called "A View of the Rock and Town of Gibraltar," it is a half-humorous, half-factual view from the French and Spanish camp that indicates the general topography of the peninsula and the rock, the location of fortifications, and the placement of the floating batteries, providing a rough but easily absorbed impression of the physical layout at Gibraltar. Dominic Serres painted a view of "The Destruction of the Floating Batteries Before Gibraltar, September 14, 1782," based on

When Copley first conferred with the committee appointed by the Court of Common Council in February 1783, he had informed them that "he had collected Materials from General Elliots aid du Camp Sir Roger Curtis and fixed in his own mind upon the Size of a Picture, representing the Rock in the back Ground, bringing the Floating Batteries & Gun Boats forward & giving a View of the Relief of the Fortress by the Fleet under Lord Visc^t Howe." [6] Clearly Copley intended to concentrate upon the "sublime and terrible" aspects of the scene: the conflagration of the stricken battering ships, the turmoil of writhing figures in the flames and water, and the heroic rescue undertaken by Curtis and his men in the gunboats. The view of the rock, where General Eliott, his officers, and the British emplacements were located, was to be relegated to the background. The matter in which the "relief" was going to be incorporated into the picture was not spelled out, but Copley noted that it would be included. On the basis of this proposal, Copley received the commission.

By 1786 Copley had advanced his *Gibraltar* to the point where he had sketched the design on the gigantic canvas that had been prepared to receive it. A visitor to his studio reported, "The picture was immense; and it was managed by means of a roller, so that any portion of it, at any time, might be easily seen or executed. The artist himself was raised on a platform." A writer in the *Morning Post* on October 2, 1786, described Copley in his studio as "literally laying siege to Gibraltar, as he has models not only of the fortress, but of gun boats, ship-tackle, men, and every instrument of destruction arranged before him in all the stages of his progress." The picture was advancing smoothly. A sketch of the composition had been completed and sent to the king, who had approved of it. When the committee of the Court of Common Council met on January 23, 1787, to see how the picture was progressing and went to George Street to view it, they found it "in a great forwardness." [7]

---

information from "Sir Roger Curtis and other Principal Officers" who had returned from Gibraltar, which was engraved by F. Jukes and published by R. Wilkinson on Feb. 10, 1783. In stiff and restrained fashion it depicts the activities of Curtis' gunboats around the exploding battering ships, with a smoke-shrouded view of the rock on the right. The sea is calm, as reported, and the scene lighted by the burning ships, but little is depicted other than great billows of smoke. A much more dramatic presentation of this scene, complete with fighting figures in the boats and victims falling or fallen into the sea, was engraved and published the following month, March 25, 1783, by Archibald Robertson after a painting by William Hamilton. Still more accurate and exciting was the picture painted, engraved, and published on Sept. 14, 1784, by John Keyse Sherwin, "under the immediate directions of Sir Roger Curtis" and avowedly based on the report of the action by General Eliott of September 15, 1782, which was published in the *Gazette*. There is a much closer view here of Curtis in his gunboat,

with one arm extended, giving directions to his men as they pluck the Spanish seamen from the water. On the left is the burning file of battering ships with the bastion of Gibraltar in the right distance. An undated engraving by John Emes after James Jefferys, published by Emes, Jefferys, and E. Woolett, bears the closest relationship of all these views to Copley's treatment of the battle. As in the left side of Copley's picture, the scene is full of struggling figures sprawled on wreckage and being pulled from the water into the boats, and a confusing array of masts, chains, ropes, harpoons, canvas, flames, and smoke. A large collection of other prints dealing with the siege of Gibraltar may be found in the Department of Prints and Drawings, British Museum, "Naval History Folder, 1782."

[6] "Committee Minutes," first draft, CRO (Corporation of London Record Office, Guildhall), Mss. 195.5 [Feb. 28], 1783.

[7] Dibdin, *Reminiscences*, p. 151; "Cuttings on Art," Victoria and Albert Museum, II, 307, 1786; "Committee Minutes," CRO, Mss. 195.5, Jan. 23,

This "forwardness" was deceptive, since a major hitch in the project had developed. Copley's design at this stage, in accordance with the plan he had described to the committee, placed the spectator in the harbor beyond the scene of carnage and destruction, looking back at it with King's Bastion and the English officers visible on the rock in the distance. Some of the officers who had participated in the event, on seeing what Copley felt to be a finished sketch in 1786, objected that, while this might be a fine and imaginative piece of creative painting, it did not meet the primary object of the commission, which was to honor the garrison that had defeated the attacking force at Gibraltar. Undoubtedly the thinking of the officers was strongly influenced by George Carter's *Siege of Gibraltar* (fig. 491; a sketch), which had been exhibited in London in 1785.[8] Copley, of course, defended the composition on which he had already spent so much time and effort. However, according to Drinkwater, who was one of the officers involved, even some of the artist's own friends agreed with the objections set forth. Copley was persuaded to confer with General William Picton and other ranking officers, who also had disapproved of his first design, in order to make the picture more accurate and to include a more advantageous portrait group of the officers. One of Copley's strongest arguments for retaining the original design was the difficulty in selecting a topographical vantage point at Gibraltar that would allow him to present a factual view while also permitting the combination of good composition and dramatic effect necessary for a successful history picture. With the officers Copley considered a variety of vantage points, hoping to retain as much of his first composition as possible. Finally they agreed on South Bastion as the best setting from which to view the action and in which to place the officer group, even though Eliott had actually been on King's Bastion. Colonel Drinkwater had made a sketch of the harbor and the burning ships from South Bastion on the morning after the battle (fig. 493), and he made this available to Copley.[9]

1787. Copley may also have made use of the model of Gibraltar which was one of a number of models of English ports in the queen's palace. It showed "Gibraltar's rocky fastness, the Spanish encampment, all on a table ten feet long — and next to it the royal entrenchment with the bomb-proof casemate, all worked in natural Gibraltar rock" (Williams, *Sophie*, p. 146). Copley was undoubtedly somewhat influenced in the early stages of composing his picture by West's large *Battle of La Hogue* (National Gallery of Art, Washington, D.C.), exhibited at the Royal Academy in 1780; — an engraving of it by William Woolett had been published on Oct. 18, 1781. Copley's project quickly transcended West's peculiarly wooden prototype, although some specific pictorial ideas were retained and elaborated.

[8] "Cuttings on Art," I, 251, 1785. Carter's *Siege of Gibraltar* was exhibited at the old Royal Academy along with the life portraits he had made for it. In the same year, 1785, Joseph Wright of Derby also

exhibited publicly in London his *Destruction of the Spanish Floating Batteries Off Gibraltar*, now unlocated, along with his other pictures.

[9] Although Copley was not an original subscriber to Colonel Drinkwater's book, he certainly was familiar with it. Copley's subsequent personal relationship with Drinkwater undoubtedly gave him access to the author's unpublished Gibraltar material, pictorial and written, much of which is interleaved in Drinkwater's personal copy of the *History*, now in the library of the National Maritime Museum, 32MS9777. This drawing from South Bastion is in this volume, opp. p. 288. Much of the information given above on Copley's dispute with the officers is derived from Drinkwater's manuscript account in the grangerized volume at the National Maritime Museum and in another Drinkwater autograph manuscript, "Recollections, Book I, Gibraltar, England, Toulon," in the National Library of Scotland, Ms. 1836. These sources also give suggestions of the appearance of Copley's

It would probably be incorrect to assume that Copley was unhappy as a result of his wrangle with the officers, or to conclude that he was reluctant to introduce the portrait group. The incorporation of portraits was precisely what he had chosen to do in his previous major history pieces, and it would ultimately enhance the proceeds from the exhibition of the picture and the sale of the projected engraving. Early in 1787, after the decision to add portraits had been made, Copley appeared before the committee and reported that the picture would be completed in a year. He requested an advance of 500 guineas on account, which was granted, and the committee noted that it did "desire Mr. Copley to wait on the illustrious characters whose portraits he wishes to have to complete the picture and in the name of this Committee to request them to sit for that purpose."

In July 1787 Copley wished the committee to see the proposed changes in the composition, and the members "accordingly proceeded to Mr. Copley's and viewed the addition proposed by him, whereby the General (in the attitude of giving directions, and applauding the succour afforded the vanquished foe, after the destruction of the floating batteries) and a number of the principal officers concerned in the defence of Gibraltar, are brought forward in a group the size of life upon one of the bastions of that fortress." The committee was pleased with the change in plans.[10] The alteration that Copley had made was to compress his earlier design of the events in the harbor into the left half of the picture, and to introduce the officers on the right as if they were gathered on South Bastion overlooking the action in the harbor. This bifurcated composition, obviously based on Carter's picture, was pretty much what the officers had requested.

The combination of the harbor scene and the portrait group forced Copley to scrap whatever thoughts he had originally entertained of including a view of the relief fleet under Admiral Howe. His first plan might have allowed, by artistic license, the introduction of the relief fleet in the background, since this was to be a dramatic, imaginative history piece with emphasis on the carnage in the harbor, and the officers and the rock would have appeared only in the distance. Now the picture was going to be a factual report of a specific moment, complete with portraits of the participants; the presence of the relief fleet would be a glaring anachronism. Still, the original intent of the commission had been to honor Admiral Howe and his fleet, as well as General Eliott and the land forces, and their contribution had to be marked in some way. Copley preferred not to accept the alternative of two separate paintings, since he had initially persuaded the committee, against the contrary advice of Benjamin West, that it would

original composition before his encounter with the officers. Both manuscripts contain an account of Drinkwater's difficulty, almost twenty-five years later, in obtaining the engraving of *Gibraltar* to which he had subscribed. When Drinkwater called for his engraving, Copley, whose embarrassed affairs "were in the hands of Trustees," had received him

warmly. But Drinkwater's name was not listed as a subscriber, and Copley said he could not give him the print. This annoyed Drinkwater, since at the time the painting was done Copley had offered him a free subscription to the engraving while he had insisted on becoming a regular subscriber.

[10] Howgego, p. 40.

not be necessary. So he conceived a compromise solution: *The Relief of Gibraltar* would be painted as a long low scene and introduced as a predella below the large *Siege of Gibraltar*, flanked by medallion portraits of Admiral Howe and his second in command, Admiral Barrington.[11]

After the new composition had been determined, Copley's next task was to take portraits of the officers involved. The vigorous and virile oil sketch of General Eliott (fig. 495), with the bold profile silhouetted against a column of yellow flame in the background, is one of these. Copley faced a particularly thorny problem in obtaining portraits of the Hanoverian officers who had commanded regiments of mercenaries under Eliott and who had returned to Germany. On August 1, 1787, he informed the committee of his desire to secure portraits of Lieutenant General de la Motte, Colonel Dachenhausen, Colonel Hugo, and Colonel Schleppegrell. He felt that they should not be asked to come to England at their own expense to be painted, but pointed out that General Eliott, now Lord Heathfield, did recommend their inclusion. On rather short notice it was decided that Copley should go to Hanover to take the portraits, and Lord Heathfield and Alderman John Boydell contributed toward his expenses. Heathfield also wrote letters for Copley to the officers concerned.[12]

Copley left London toward the end of August for his trip to Hanover. He was accompanied by his wife and his daughter Elizabeth on what was to be a combined "pleasurable and professional excursion." The *World* reported, "Mr. Copley makes the tour of Flanders; and it is presumed, that his view of *Rubens's* great works, may not prove unserviceable in his destruction of the floating batteries before Gibraltar." [13] The stress on Rubens, undoubtedly originating in Copley's own statements about his forthcoming trip, is further proof of Copley's strong and continuing admiration for Rubens. Very little information about the continental trip of 1787 survives, although the splendid oil sketches of the four Hanoverian officers (figs. 496–498), prove that the primary purpose of the journey was carried out. But there is an extant diary fragment covering part of the journey, which gives an added indication of Copley's interest in studying Rubens. The fragment covers the period from September 1, 1787, when the party arrived in Ghent, to September 5, when it arrived at Antwerp, and Copley specifically takes note of six Rubens paintings, four Rubens oil sketches, and two paintings by Van Dyck.[14]

[11] The *World* of March 28, 1788, referred to *The Relief of Gibraltar* as if completed, reporting that it was to go into a small compartment below the large picture and that a portrait of Lord Howe was sketched to accompany it in profile medallion. Omission of any mention of Admiral Barrington suggests that his inclusion was a later idea.

[12] Payments of £105 were made from Lord Heathfield's account at Drummond's Bank (now the Royal Bank of Scotland) to Copley on Aug. 27, 1787, and Aug. 1, 1788 (information courtesy of David Erskine). John Boydell, the engraver, had been appointed to the committee on general purposes of the Court of Common Council in 1784 (Howgego, p. 39). Heathfield's letter of introduction for Copley to General de la Motte, Aug. 24, 1787, written in French, is in the Royal United Services Institute, Mss. vol. 133, and is published in its entirety in *The United Service Magazine*, II (1842), 238–40. I am indebted to David Erskine for calling this letter to my attention.

[13] Aug. 28, 1787. It was also reported that the Copleys would be accompanied by "Mr. Green Jr., of Newman-Street."

[14] In Ghent in the church of St. Bavo, he saw Rubens' "S. Bavo distributing Charity to a group

When Copley traveled to Hanover in the autumn of 1787, he must have had the composition of the officer group virtually complete, since the oil sketches of the Hanoverian officers show that they were painted in predetermined poses. After all of the portraits had been taken, Copley was able to combine the former sea piece with the completed officers in an oil sketch (fig. 499). Support for a date early in 1788 for this sketch is found in a notice which appeared in the *World* on March 28, 1788, stating that Copley was then at work on *Gibraltar* and that "the well-known alacrity of Major Lewis *not waiting for* his boots, is properly remembered on the canvas." The seated figure of Major Lewis in this sketch is missing one boot.

This oil sketch provides the key clue to the appearance of the original picture Copley had planned and begun before his confrontation with the officers. The left side of the sketch gives an indication of the initial design, and permits identification of a large body of drawings that relate to it rather than to the final composition. Most of these drawings probably date from 1785–86, although some could have been made as early as 1783, when Copley told the Court of Common Council that he had already begun work on the subject.

A dominant element in the initial design was to be a sinking Spanish longboat in the foreground, with figures clinging to the mast, to each other, and reaching for help from a nearby English gunboat. In the gunboat some of the English sailors turn their attention to rescue operations, while others encourage or actively assist their comrades in the bow of the floating battery above to pull down the Spanish colors. In the middle distance is another gunboat, beyond which is the giant hulk of a completely shattered battery, swarming with figures in various stages of distress like the damned in a Last Judgment. Sir Roger Curtis, in the Apollo Belvedere pose previously used in the portrait of *Major Montgomerie*, directs operations from his gunboat in the right distance, including the rescue of Spanish sailors from a drifting spar.

By introducing the officer group on the right, Copley repeats the scheme George Carter had utilized in 1785. General Eliott, astride his horse, is raised above the other figures. The pose of Eliott was probably influenced by the general's figure as it appeared in an engraving after an on-the-spot drawing by Lieutenant G. F. Koehler (fig. 494). Colonel Drinkwater, actively advising Copley at this point, owned a copy of the engraving, which he later interleaved near the beginning of his personal copy of his *History*, noting that this picture "gives a totally correct idea of the figure and dress of

---

of poor people" and "Charles V receiving Pope's benediction before setting out on Campaign," and he cited the Van Dyck *Crucifixion* in the church of St. Michael as being in bad condition. He admired Rubens' "St. Roach Stopping the Plague by his prayers to Christ who appears" in the parish church in Alost. In Brussels at the cathedral of St. Gudule, he noted Rubens' "Christ's Charge to Peter" and Van Dyck's portrait of Maria Anna Schotti. He commented on Rubens' use of Raphael's composi-

tion for his "Entombing of Christ" in the church of the Capuchins. He also recorded that Mr. Denoote in Brussels had Rubens oil sketches of the "Rape of the Sabines," "Romans and Sabines preparing for Battle, with wives and children interposing," "Charles V taking Oath to preserve Liberty of City of Antwerp," and "Finding Remus & Romulus." In Maechlin he commented upon the bad condition of Rubens' "Last Supper." The diary fragment is in the Boston Public Library, Ch. I.3.12.

Lord Heathfield."[15] Copley at first planned to encompass in his officer group an active scene of a cannon being readied for discharge, but this was resolved into a calmer composition of a group of officers behind the cannon viewing the action, with a kneeling officer, Major Vallotton, turning to report what he has observed through the telescope that he steadies on the cannon. Copley seems to have taken the idea of placing a colorful Scot in the right foreground directly from Carter's sketch. Also like Carter he portrayed Major Lewis as the only seated figure. But beyond these similarities, and the major common factor of the split composition, the comparison ends. Whereas Carter held to a considerable degree of realism and topographical accuracy, Copley distorted, dramatized, and enlivened his composition. Copley's painting is much more exciting visually than Carter's. His officers are not the restrained, unconcerned puppets of Carter's version, but rather through their poses, gestures, and expression, as well as through the artist's technical mastery of color and patterns of light, are much more vitally involved in the action and with each other. Thirteen of the officers depicted appear in both pictures, and in every case Copley's treatment is considerably better than Carter's. In Carter's group the hatless officers are clearly posed by rank, with the lesser officers in the right background and the major officers nearer the front attended by their aides-de-camp. In Copley's treatment the officers are grouped with greater subtlety, and there is much less difference between good and bad placements.[16]

When Copley combined his original scheme with the new officer group, he found that the first composition for the scene in the harbor was no longer satisfactory. What had been a well-balanced composition in itself would no longer work with the added mass of officers on the right. Moreover, since the emphasis had switched from action to personalities, there was now an opportunity to introduce portraits of Sir Roger Curtis and Captain Bradshaw Smith in their gunboats, which meant bringing these figures forward. It was thus necessary to recompose the action part of the picture, and Copley returned to his labors once more.

In the revised left-hand portion of the final painting, Copley retained some of the main elements of his sea piece — the sinking boat in the foreground, the prow of a battering ship on the left, and the shattered mast covered with figures aloft in the distance. These received different treatment, however, the sinking boat in the foreground in particular being almost completely repopulated with anguished figures. The gunboats

[15] Drinkwater, personal copy of *A History of Gibraltar*, National Maritime Museum.

[16] While Copley was revising his composition, young John Trumbull completed his own picture of an earlier event at Gibraltar, *The Sortie of the British Garrison from Gibraltar*, a daring British sally during the night of Nov. 26, 1781. The painting, clearly indebted to Copley in its general approach and style, was exhibited to the London public in 1789. But it is not related as closely to Copley's *Gibraltar* as to his *Death of Peirson*: the wounded figure reclining like the dead foreground figure in *Peirson*, the figure on the left summoning his men to attack with a gesture of his sword, and the action in the upper left like that on Town Hill at St. Helier. Trumbull's picture includes four figures who also appear in the Gibraltar paintings of Carter and Copley: Eliott, Hugo, Trigge, and Vallotton. He also introduced a Scot to add color to the scene, presenting Capt. Alexander Mackenzie, the same officer painted by Carter. Trumbull, even more slavishly than Copley, relied on the Koehler depiction of General Eliott in King's Bastion (fig. 494).

on the left and in the middle distance were eliminated, as was the pile of figures in the center. Instead the flank of a battering ship was introduced on the left, with two English gunboats below it taking part in the rescue operation.

This new composition brought forth a spate of drawings. Since the swamped long-boat in the foreground of the original composition had been partially blocked by the introduction of South Bastion, as seen in the oil sketch, Copley altered its position so that the group of figures clinging to the mast would be visible. In the forward section a variety of figures, including a Spanish monk, hang on to the foundering boat and try to attract the attention of Curtis and his men in the boat approaching on the left. In the bow of the boat a compositional descendent of the harpoonist in *Watson and the Shark* extends a grappling hook to the distressed Spaniards. Two groups pull figures from the water, one group retained from the first sketch and a new "deposition"-like group in the center. Sir Roger Curtis balances on the gunwhale of the boat, in a reverse of his stance in the earlier sketch, and points to the stricken Spanish boat in a gesture that echoes the pose of General Eliott on King's Bastion. In immediate proximity to Curtis are an oarsman, a wounded strokesman, and a helmsman, while behind and above him two figures hang from a rope attached to the battering ship. Figures above on the bow of the first battering ship, retained from the initial composition, try to unsnag the Spanish colors. Behind the bow of Curtis' boat, a second one under the command of Captain Bradshaw Smith rides almost perpendicularly to it and is involved with rescue operations down the side of the battery ship on the left, parts of which again repeat "deposition" motifs.

Very few changes were required in the right-hand section of the picture between the 1788 oil sketch and the final version. A portrait of Colonel Drinkwater was added in the upper right, "a spontaneous proposal of Mr. Copley in compliment, as he also was pleased to observe to the Historian of the Siege, & also as a return to Col. D. for the many hours *He* devoted to affording Mr. C. information." [17] The only other notable changes in the officer group are the addition of Major Lewis' boot, and the hat and fragment placed in the right foreground.

After the composition had been altered to Copley's satisfaction, the enormous physical task of completing the large canvas remained. In a letter to his mother in December 1789, John Singleton Copley, Jr., commented, "I shall ask nothing concerning the great picture, as the group is doubtless already finished." On May 1, 1790, Copley reported to the committee that the picture would be finished in about three months and that he would notify it when the members should come to George Street. But on October 20 he advised the committee that, because of "the increase of work that has presented itself in the course of finishing the Picture," he would have to extend his estimate of the date of completion. But he invited the committee to see the picture in

[17] Autograph notes at the end of Drinkwater's personal copy of *A History of Gibraltar*, National Maritime Museum.

its current state. They visited his studio on October 28, at which time he explained the picture to them and promised to complete it as soon as possible.[18]

By the spring of 1791, the mammoth *Gibraltar* (measuring almost 18 by 25 feet) was done. Eight years had passed since the commission had been given to Copley, and for several years the demands of the large picture had left him virtually no time to augment his income by portraiture. Now the time was at hand for the picture's exhibition, and Copley had high hopes of capitalizing on his labors at the rate of one shilling per visitor. To solve the physical problem of exhibiting such a large painting, Copley procured a "magnificent Oriental tent," 84 feet long, which he set up in Green Park, near the head of Arlington Street, in April. Because the Duke of Bolton and other residents of Arlington Street objected that the tent interfered with their view, Copley had to move his tent several times. Finally George III, who had seen the picture early in May, told Copley to "Push it up nearer to my Wife's house — she won't complain," and the problem was solved.[19]

Once the tent had been permanently pitched and the exhibition opened on June 8, a large number of people flocked to see the picture. Copley later told his friend Nathaniel Marchant that sixty thousand people had attended the exhibition.[20] Bartolozzi's engraved admission ticket (fig. 584), which must have imaginatively anticipated the exhibition, suggests what it may have been like. The grand scale of the picture overpowered the slim *Relief of Gibraltar* below. *The Relief* (fig. 585) had not been painted by Copley, however. He had subcontracted this part of the commission to Dominic Serres, the noted marine painter, who some years earlier had made one of the first views of the action at Gibraltar.[21] *The Relief* was flanked by Copley's medallion portraits of Admirals Howe and Barrington.[22] On the left in the Bartolozzi view, a small picture indicates that other objects, perhaps the oil sketches for *Gibraltar*, were also exhibited. At a Pembroke table in the left background, subscriptions may have been taken for the engraving. The proposal for the engraving, given to visitors as they paid their admission, also served as a catalogue, describing the action and identifying the participants.

The critical reception accorded *Gibraltar* was mild. The principal criticism was that the picture suffered from a lack of perspective in the left side, which caused figures in the distance to appear too clearly and too closely. This point was sharply put by the

---

[18] Sir Theodore Martin, A *Life of Lord Lyndhurst* (London, 1883), p. 20; "Journal, Committee on General Purposes," CRO, I, 220, 301–02, 310.

[19] Drinkwater, "Recollections," National Library of Scotland, Ms. 1836, p. 4; *Morning Chronicle*, April 30 and May 20, 1791; *Morning Post*, May 5 and 18, 1791; *World*, June 9, 1791; J. H. Anderdon, "Collectanea Biographica," Department of Prints and Drawings, British Museum, XXII [1853].

[20] "Anecdotes of Artists of the Last Fifty Years," *Library of the Fine Arts*, IV (July 1832), 25.

[21] See n. 5 above.

[22] Neither *The Relief* nor the portraits now accompany the painting, and *The Relief* is known only through the 1810 engraving. The *Relief* panel was detached from the large picture a few years later (see n. 28 below), and it is not known whether Copley ever actually turned the medallion portraits over to the Corporation.

artist Richard Collins, who went to see the painting with his fellow artists, Thomas Stothard and Ozias Humphry, the latter Copley's friend of long standing whose portrait had been incorporated into the composition.[23] Collins wrote to George Cumberland on June 18, 1791:

> The other Evening we went to Copley's Picture, which is now exhibiting in that superb Pavillion which caused you and myself not a little mirth, when we last walked in the Park. Stothard seemed pleased with many parts of it, but the feebleness of the general effect struck him, as it must everybody — probably it is very much owing to an inattention to local colouring; the foreground, which is a stone bastion, is nearly as dark as black can make it; and the flame, from the floating batteries on fire, is kept in half tint; while the sea is quite light. And I could not help observing the absurdity of making out little figures an Inch high, with the same scrupulous precision as the figures on the foreground the size of life. Mr Humphry pointing out, and extolling the likeness of his own Portrait, which Mr Copley had painted of him, at more than a mile distance, made me burst out with laughter almost in his face: — however if we compare this Picture with other modern performances, and take execution into account, it is certainly not a bad Picture.[24]

The *Morning Chronicle* on June 23, 1791, praised the likenesses in the painting, especially that of Sir Robert Boyd, "a most characteristic likeness: it is not merely a map of the face, but a picture of the mind: you see what passes in his soul at the moment." The portrait of General Eliott also pleased the reviewer, although it was not held to be the equal of Reynolds' portrait in Boydell's Shakespeare gallery. Even the small panel of *The Relief* was praised.[25]

Having waited many years for *Gibraltar* to be painted, and then waiting while Copley exhibited it to his own advantage, the committee on general purposes inquired in March 1792 when the city might expect to receive the picture. Copley replied that, since it was so large, it was necessary that a smaller copy be made from which the engraver might work. This copy had been started soon after the painting was finished, and it was expected to be completed during the summer, at which time the big picture would be delivered. By September, however, Copley saw that it would still take a while longer for Saunders, the copyist, to finish his work, so he suggested that the picture be installed in the Guildhall and that Saunders be allowed to finish his copy there.[26]

At the same time, Copley broached to the committee a delicate subject that was much on his mind. Because of the additional labor spent on *Gibraltar* beyond the first accepted plan, he hoped to receive a larger fee from the Corporation. He spoke to this

---

[23] Humphry drew a portrait of Copley's daughter Elizabeth, which may have been in return for this.

[24] Cumberland Papers, British Museum, Add. Mss. 36496, VI (May 1788–June 1791), 348.

[25] The reviewer was apparently not aware that the artist was Serres but noted, "It is equal to Brooking, and much in his manner." Charles Brooking was the leading marine painter of an earlier period whose premature death left Dominic Serres without peer in this specialty. Ellis Waterhouse, *Painting in Britain, 1530–1790* (Baltimore, 1953), pp. 112–13.

[26] "Journal, Committee for General Purposes," CRO, II, 13 (March 15, 1792), 25–26 (April 20, 1792), 52–54 (Sept. 27, 1792).

point personally at the meeting, and the committee voted to inspect the picture, which was still on exhibition in Green Park. After examining it, their primary reaction, which had nothing directly to do with Copley's request, was concern over the fact that the picture had square corners — if it were going to be placed in one of the intended windows of the new Common Council Room, it would have to be "mutilated and a material Part of the Representation cut off." [27]

Early in 1793 Copley renewed his plea for more funds. In answer to a reaction that had cast some aspersions on his deviation from the original plan, Copley explained the manner in which he had made a large sketch shortly after receiving the commission and noted that this was seen and approved by the committee, which also approved the payment to him of 500 guineas, the other half to go to him upon completion of the painting. Thus all the Corporation had a right to expect for its money was a painting in accordance with that initial plan. But the finished picture was much more extensive and superior. The changes were approved while the work was in progress, for the committee "did not wish to confine me in a Work of Genius and imagination." Copley also sent along the original sketch to make the differences obvious. On March 7, 1793, he submitted a more formal and complete request for additional funds:

> In a former Letter which I had the Honor of addressing to the Chairman of this Committee, I expressed the hope that I should receive the patronage and support of the Committee in an application for a more adequate compensation for the Picture of the Siege and Relief of Gibraltar. The reasons on which I ground this application are the following. That it was supposed when I was first honored with the Commission, that a painting of half the dimensions of the present work with Figures half the size of Life would be sufficient to do justice to the subject, that such a Work I judged would have been executed in eighteen Months, and that the Sum I thought a *reasonable* Price for it was fifteen hundred pounds. This was the opinion I delivered to the Committee when I first had the Honor to meet them. It was given without any previous consideration; I was called upon on a sudden, and was neither possessed of materials or information to enable me to form an accurate judgment. Still however, had the subject been of the ordinary kind; had there been nothing peculiar in the nature of it, which it was impossible for me as an Artist to foresee I might from experience I have had in my profession have been able with some degree of certainty to have formed an Estimate of its intricacy and extent. The opinion I had formed upon those common rules and principles by which I have been in general guided when called upon on similar occasions, I afterwards found upon frequent conversations with Lord Heathfield, Sir Robert Boyd, Sir Roger Curtis &c. &c. to be greatly defective. My Plan was too confined; the manner in which I proposed to treat the subject very inadequate to its splendor and importance. In addition to the increase in the extent

[27] *Ibid.*, II, 62, Oct. 5, 1792. Late in 1792 the picture was temporarily installed under Copley's supervision in the Great Hall of the Guildhall, since to alter one end of the new Common Council Room to accommodate the picture would cost £100. After some attempts to improve visibility in the Great Hall by changing the hanging height, and after considering a skylight that would also cost £100, it was decided early in 1793 to place the picture in a temporary location in the Common Council Room (*ibid.*, II, 69–103).

of the work itself, I found the time and attention necessary for procuring information and Materials in its prosecution to exceed everything I had before experienced, and every idea that could have been formed on the subject. Five years I have found to be little more than sufficient for producing the work, I have received five hundred Guineas from the City, Three hundred of which has been paid away for necessary expences attending the Work. I do not include in this Three hundred Guineas, my expences in going to Germany to take the Portraits of the Hanoverian officers, that expence having been paid by the late Lord Heathfield and Mr. Alderman Boydell. By the above Statement it will be clearly seen that I must have broken in very considerably on my own Property during the Progress of the work, and how great a sufferer I must be unless rescued by the liberality of the City. I will not take up more of your time, than to say, that having been desirous however of producing a Work that should be a lasting monument of that great and splendid event, I have not spared my own exertions: how far I have been successful, it becomes me not to say.

I will not touch on the merits of the Painting.[28]

The committee ignored Copley's request for additional funds and paid him the second 500 guineas in May 1793, as payment in full of the agreement. On February 13, 1794, Copley wrote a long letter to the Court of Common Council presenting once again the case that he had set before the committee, but the letter was simply referred back to that committee. Copley then met with the committee, and an agreement was reached to pay him an additional 300 pounds. The waters were quickly muddied, however, when Alderman Boydell objected that, if Copley were going to get more money, 200 guineas of it should go to him as repayment of his "advance" to Copley in 1787 for the trip to Germany. When Copley was told that he would get the extra payment only on condition that he turn 200 guineas over to Boydell, he was incensed. Since the committee also summoned him to the next meeting to explain the present state of the medallion portraits of Howe and Barrington, he sent back a stinging refusal to attend. The affair was tabled.[29]

Copley's son appeared before the committee for general purposes in July 1795 and requested the return of his father's original sketch for the painting, advising the com-

---

[28] *Ibid.*, II, 101–03 (Feb. 5, 1793); and 109–12 (March 7, 1793), letter dated Feb. 15, 1793. At this very time the committee was wrestling with the problem of where to install the behemoth. Finally a decision was made to alter one end of the Council Room. In June 1793, the committee approved a design and an expenditure of £130 to James Brewer for a frame for the picture. Copley received permission to move the picture out of the room while the room was being altered and over to the Royal Academy at Somerset House, where his copyist, Saunders, could conveniently work on it. At the end of 1794 the frame for *Gibraltar* was ready, and the room was ready, but in a comedy of errors it was found that the frame had not been changed to fit the alteration of the room. The committee therefore ordered that the small *Relief of Gibraltar* be detached, and the frame altered accordingly. *Ibid.*, II, 121–22 (March 15, 1793), 159–60 (June 27, 1793), and 450 (Dec. 18, 1794).

[29] *Ibid.*, II, 147 (May 17, 1793), 322 (May 21, 1794), and 343–47 (June 25, 1794); "Journal, Court of Common Council," CRO, XL, 62b–63b (Feb. 13, 1794), and 164b–65 (May 21, 1794), LXXIV, 164–65 (June 3, 1794); and Copley autograph manuscript account of possible case between himself and the City of London, Boston Public Library, Ch. I.3.10, printed in *More Books*, V (1930), 203–04.

mittee that his father had not yet received the 300 guineas voted to him for additions to the original design of *Gibraltar*. He was informed that, of the 300 guineas, 200 had gone to Boydell; the committee could not return the sketch until Copley had received the remaining 100 guineas due him, and he should apply for it to the Court of Common Council. Copley in his angry pride would not submit to this. The end of this affair came four years later when, in the face of severe financial difficulties, Copley wrote to the committee asking for the 100 guineas and his sketch. He was told to appear and acquiesce in the payment of 200 of the 300 guineas to Boydell. This he did and received the sketch and the 100 guineas. The *Gibraltar* commission that had begun in 1783, when Copley was at the peak of his power and reputation, concluded sadly sixteen years later, with Copley now content to pick up whatever income he could at the sacrifice of his own sensibilities.[30]

The subscription for an engraving of *The Siege of Gibraltar* had been announced early in 1788, while the painting was still in progress.[31] This subscription was repeated when the picture was exhibited in 1791. The engraving was to be executed by Bartolozzi, of a size to be a centerpiece to the almost completed engraving of *The Death of Chatham* and the projected engraving of *Charles I Demanding in the House of Commons the Five Impeached Members* (fig. 599). But Copley encountered his customary difficulties with engravers and engravings. Ten years after the exhibition of *Gibraltar*, the engraving had not yet been executed and Copley had engaged William Sharp to replace Bartolozzi.[32]

Sharp's engraving was finally published by Copley on March 27, 1810, along with a key plate to identify the figures. This was followed on May 22 by the publication of the companion print of *The Relief of Gibraltar*, painted by Serres and engraved by Pollard, flanked by Sharp's engravings of Copley's medallion portraits of Howe and Barrington. Copley's patience with Sharp, based in large measure upon his confidence in the ultimate quality of the print, was remarkable (and quite uncharacteristic). The engraving was a financial failure, and many of the original subscribers did not even think it worthwhile to pay the remainder of their subscription fee to get it. The event depicted had occurred twenty-seven years before, and now new battles and new heroes claimed the public's interest.

If Copley had held to his original plan for *Gibraltar*, he would certainly have ended up with a more cohesive and attractive picture than the one he finally created. The left-

---

[30] "Journal, Committee of General Purposes," CRO, II, 583–84 (July 21, 1795); "Journal, Court of Common Council," CRO, LXXIX, 32b–33b (Nov. 29, 1799).

[31] *World*, Jan. 7, 1788.

[32] Sharp had engraved John Trumbull's *Sortie from Gibraltar*, which was published in 1799, and this is probably why Copley engaged him when arrangements with Bartolozzi foundered. Sharp planned to complete the engraving by the winter of 1802–03, but kept extending his deadline for the first proof. It was finally produced in the middle of 1804, but then the pace slowed down again. Copley found himself "daily harassed by the impatience of some of the subscribers and rudeness of others" (Amory, p. 260, Mary Copley to Mrs. Gardiner Greene, Aug. 17, 1804). The print was finally completed in 1809, but there was further delay before it could be published (*ibid.*, pp. 210ff).

hand side of *The Siege of Gibraltar* contains some exciting and dramatic passages, and the portrait group on the right is comparable in effectiveness with *The Death of Chatham*, but the fusion of the two elements into a peculiar double composition is not at all successful. The romantic turmoil on the left is much too close to shore for factual accuracy or even probability, and yet it is too remote to capture the kind of viewer involvement that was possible with *Watson, Chatham,* or *Peirson.* In the beginning, the painting of the scene of destruction was to have been on a scale of half life size. The addition of the officers shrunk the scale of the left side of the picture in half again, and, as in *The Sitwell Family*, Copley was plagued with doll-sized figures that gave no impression of life. Copley had received the commission for *The Siege of Gibraltar* when he was at the peak of his powers, and at the height of his English career. As the years of involvement with *Gibraltar* lengthened, the sweet taste of victory in winning the commission from Benjamin West yielded to the bitterness of successive setbacks; the ending was the unsuccessful publication of the engraving when Copley was in his early seventies, only a shadow of what he had been.

Academy Affairs and *Charles I*

1792-1798   Sir Joshua Reynolds died on February 23, 1792, and the issue of his successor as president of the Royal Academy became paramount. The leading contender was Benjamin West. Since the Royal Academy was chartered by and existed under the sufferance of George III, and since Benjamin West as history painter to the king enjoyed a closer relationship with him than any other artist had, it was obviously in the best interest of the academy to elect West president.[1] But just as Copley could not accept a role second to West as a history painter, he would not acquiesce to a secondary political role. The *Argus* of March 7, 1792, jokingly noted, "Mr. *Copley* has laid *siege* to the President's Chair of the Royal Academy," his previous experience with *Gibraltar* giving him an advantage. Copley's political fences at the Royal Academy were in a state of disrepair, however. With his exhibitions of *Chatham* and *Peirson*, and *Gibraltar* just the year before, he had directly competed with academy annual exhibitions, and he had not exhibited anything at the academy since 1786. Although Copley and Cosway were considered contenders for the presidency,[2] the election swung easily to West.

With West as president, Copley seemed determined to play a prominent role in academy affairs in order not to be completely eclipsed by his rival; and during the 1790's he became increasingly active in the academy. His turn in rotation as a visitor to the academy came in 1792, and his turn as member of the council in 1793.[3] In 1793, Copley was also on the committee for hanging the exhibition and on the committee in charge of arrangements for celebrating the academy's twenty-fifth anniversary. In the latter, West and Joseph Farington were part of a dominant subgroup, which agreed to plans before meetings. As a result Copley's ideas and suggestions were consistently re-

[1] When Reynolds could not attend an assembly meeting on Nov. 10, 1791, he asked West to preside in his place ("Assembly Minutes," RA, I, 269). This may imply that West was Reynolds' own choice as his successor.

[2] "Cuttings on Art," Victoria and Albert Museum, III, 619, Feb., 1792.

[3] The council was the governing executive body of the academy, with members elected for two-year terms by the general assembly of academicians. In practice all members were elected to the council on a rotating basis.

jected.[4] This was the position in which Copley found himself with increasing frequency during subsequent years — excluded from the inner ruling circles of the academy and frequently in opposition to West and his friends.

The antipathy between Copley and West was heightened by the publication in 1793 of Robert Anthony Bromley's uneven and biased *History of the Fine Arts*. In the section in which he discussed history painting, Bromley wrote of the type of picture which records "an event which is minutely known to us . . . within our memories. Happily there is one, though only one, which comes within this predicament." [5] The picture to which he referred was West's *Death of Wolfe*. Copley's *Chatham, Peirson*, and *Gibraltar* were ignored. Bromley's book also offended other academicians in a variety of ways, and during the winter of 1793–94 Copley and several others successfully urged that Bromley's book be removed from the academy library and that the anticipated second volume not be accepted. This led to Bromley's publication in the *Morning Herald* of a series of vituperative letters, addressed individually to Fuseli and Copley, that had been privately circulated to the academicians. Bromley was a friend and admirer of West, and Copley strongly suspected that West was behind Bromley's letters, which added another burden to their strained relations.[6]

In 1796 a dispute erupted in the Royal Academy over a proposal that, in order to preserve eligibility in the pension fund, members must exhibit at the academy at least every two years. The history painters, other than the prolific West, objected to

[4] "Farington Diary," pp. 86–87, Dec. 30, 1793.

[5] Bromley, I, 56.

[6] Academicians siding with Copley in this affair included Opie, Farington, Barry (because of Bromley's plagiarism of his lectures), Fuseli (who was attacked in the book), Smirke, and Bacon ("Farington Diary," p. 59ff, Nov. 29, 1793–Feb. 20, 1794; "Assembly Minutes," RA, I, 309–328, Dec. 10, 1793–Feb. 20, 1794). Bromley in his first letter to the *Morning Herald* (May 15, 1794) pointed to Copley as the initial and most virulent leader of the attacks on his book, and cited Copley's "malicious and unwarrantable conduct" toward him in the academy as the reason for the letters. Bromley claimed that Copley's antipathy could be traced to an occurrence in 1786, when Bromley had served as one of the judges in a dispute between Copley and an unidentified party who had complained of being slandered by Copley. Although the party is not identified, the supposedly slanderous comments might have had something to do with Copley's response to Hoppner's review of *The Daughters of George III* of the previous year. The judgment was unanimously against Copley. Bromley's second letter (May 26, 1794) chided Copley for his indelicacy in criticizing West and *The Death of Wolfe* in the Royal Academy over which West presided. According to Bromley, one of Copley's outbursts in the Royal Academy went as follows: "Mr. R —, take care of what you said the other night; I remember well what you said, and you shall answer for it: you declared that Mr. West was the first Painter in the world. Yes, you shall answer for that language." R replied, "I said, that he was *one of the first* Painters in the world." "Oh! Sir, that is another matter; now I am better satisfied."

In the third letter (July 9, 1794) Bromley defended the choice of *The Death of Wolfe* in his book, getting to the ideological heart of the dispute. Bromley said that he favored history pictures that convey universal truths over those that rely on matters of fact. He did not mind artistic license if it helped to reveal the spirit of the event. Copley of course stood for a purer brand of realism. In this letter Bromley twitted Copley over a claim that his *Boy with a Squirrel* was equal to Van Dyck. Copley saw West's influence behind this attack, and he told his friend Nathaniel Marchant that the reference to the painting of the *Boy with a Squirrel* must have come originally from West ("Farington Diary," p. 222, Sept. 18, 1794). The fourth letter (Aug. 4, 1794) ridiculed Copley's attempt to secure more money from the Corporation for his *Gibraltar*, while in the final letter (Sept. 13, 1794) Bromley resumed his theoretical attack, saying that Copley's realistic history paintings were hardly a degree above portraits and had no sense of epic. Earlier English history painters had disdained this type of factual painting and "were not fond of creeping at the bottom of that class in which they exercised their pencils."

this since their type of painting involved much more time per picture than portraiture or landscape. Copley again locked horns with West and resolved to place his arguments before the king, but West got to the king first and Copley's reception was cool.[7]

Another academy affair in which Copley participated was the ouster in 1799 of James Barry from his professorship of painting and from academic status. Although he criticized Barry for "much quackery, defficient in drawing — in colouring &c." and "expressed privately his contempt for Barry, saying He considered him as a sort of Pretender in Art," Copley nonetheless argued that Barry should not be expelled without being advised of the charges against him. This proposal was defeated, and he abstained from joining in the vote against Barry. After the Barry affair, West confided to Farington that he had told the king about everything that had happened, including "Copley's long speeches."[8]

During the 1790's, cliques were calcifying within the academy, and factional points of view were becoming more divergent, foreshadowing the great dispute of 1803. Copley's relations with Joseph Farington worsened at this time as Farington moved further into West's camp.[9] Although Farington in his well-known diary tended increasingly to record stories unfavorable to Copley, he usually made some attempt to be fair. Anthony Pasquin's *Memoirs of the Royal Academicians*, published in 1796, was downright vindictive, and Copley was a prime target. Pasquin labeled Copley "a man of imitation, but not of genius," whose "professional acquisitions are a greater compliment to his assiduity than his powers of fancy." Copley, according to Pasquin, followed West in "the same hardness of execution, the same veneration for buttons and buttonholes . . . and the same apprehension of having any reliance upon the vigour of his intellects." This was his final estimation of Copley: "As an observing inveterate drudge, who is true to trifles, from a conviction that he can never be great — who attends to all the mechanism of colouring, without welcoming a thought that would be honorable to the imagination, and dear to the *poetry of canvass*, I shall not hesitate to arrange Mr. *Copley* as among the first of modern artists." Pasquin also had a word to say about one of Copley's personal flaws: "to talk of any man possessing genius, who is so immoderately fond of money, is preposterous: the warm beams of genius thaw the icy altars of avarice; and to have genius, and be ungenerous, is impossible."[10]

[7] "Farington Diary," pp. 821, 835, 872, 1087, Nov. 7, 1796–Aug. 26, 1797.

[8] *Ibid.*, p. 1791 (March 17, 1799), pp. 1524–25 (April 15, 1799), p. 1535 (April 23, 1799); "Assembly Minutes," RA, II, 51, April 15, 1799.

[9] Farington himself cited an instance of the degree of partisanship in the Royal Academy. In a debate on whether the academy should vote for only one associate (as Farington favored) or for more (as Copley favored), West's original intention was to vote for more than one, but after listening to the debate and observing who took which side he directed a vote on only one associate (*ibid.*, p. 1657, Nov. 4, 1799).

[10] Pasquin, *Memoirs*, p. 138. Anthony Pasquin was the pseudonym of John Williams (1761–1818), a rather vitriolic satirist and critic. He wrote an imaginary congratulatory letter from Copley to West on West's election to the presidency of the academy: "Rest assured, that I rejoice you are now the principal figure in the *Academic group* — though I may not be so brilliant in my colouring, I have as much *truth of expression* as those who flatter more — In any measure that may contribute

The visual representations of Copley at this period are certainly more friendly than the verbal accounts. The history painter, Henry Singleton, did a picture between 1793 and 1795 of the *Royal Academicians Gathered in Their Council Chambers, 1793, To Judge the Work of the Students* (fig. 586). In this painting Copley appears in the foreground, elegantly dressed and leaning on a walking stick, while in the upper right his diploma picture, *The Tribute Money*, is prominent. Joseph Farington stands to the right of Copley, while the seated figure wearing a hat is Benjamin West. George Dance made a drawing of Copley on March 30, 1793 (Royal Academy), which was subsequently etched by W. Daniell (fig. 588). Paul Sandby made thumbnail sketches at print sales in the margin of his catalogues (Windsor Castle), and an engraving of these, including a sketch of Copley, was published in 1798 (fig. 589).

Copley's ties with America, though attenuated over the years, had by no means been obliterated. He and his wife still had a number of friends and relatives there with whom they kept in sporadic contact. On occasion the Copleys even considered the possibility of going back to Boston. Copley's son, who took a reverse grand tour to America after his appointment as a fellow of Trinity College, wrote from America late in 1796 of "the different conversations we had in George Street in regard to the expediency of returning to America." Young Copley's own opinion of the advisability of such a move for his father and the rest of the family was in favor of a return. He wrote, "I have thought ever since I set foot in this country that it was possible you might think of returning hither. That you would find your profession more profitable than in England I have no doubt; the state of society and of government would be more congenial to your inclinations, and nothing but the difficulty of moving seems to stand in the opposite scale." Farington recorded in his diary on November 13, 1795, "It is understood that Copley would go to America but He told Marchant Mrs. Copley will not." All of the evidence suggests that Copley stayed in England primarily because his family preferred it there. It seemed likely that young Copley, with his exceptional promise, would make a career in England, and life in London was socially more agreeable to Mrs. Copley and her daughter Mary. But the older daughter, Elizabeth, married a Boston widower, Gardiner Greene, in 1800 and set off for a new and fruitful life in America at the age of thirty.[11]

---

to your dignity, or your advantage, you will always find me ready to *subscribe* my name. I have altered the design of the *Last Day*, and changed the Lawyers into Demons, and the Penitent Wenches to Angels. I have placed *Will Tell* and *Tom Paine* by the Redeemer, and have suspended Mun Burke between Heaven and Hell. — Pray, *Ben*, do you know if the Athenian Ladies wore smocks? My sister Patty improves exceedingly; she dead coloured four infants last week, and has managed another battle most delightfully. I have found a brighter varnish than was ever known to *Reynolds*: it supersedes the *Copel* and *Gum Mastic* . . . By the bye I expect all the world to see me, for I have discovered a *new lake*" (*ibid.*, pp. 63–64). The satire of a history painter's vocabulary and Copley's attitude toward West is obvious, as is the interest in accurate costume. The last portion reflects Copley's strong interest in technical matters, suggesting that he indulged in quite a bit of shop talk at the academy.

[11] Amory, p. 153; Martin, *Lyndhurst*, p. 44, letter

While in America, young Copley tried to straighten out his father's unfortunate real-estate problems in Boston. The story of Copley's land tangles is a most intricate one. After the artist and his family left Boston, their Beacon Hill "farm" was rented. Henry Pelham looked after things and, when he also left Boston, Copley's mother remained to collect rents and oversee his interests.[12] With the death of Mary Pelham in 1789, Copley's position as an absentee landlord became more difficult. Early in 1793 he sent Samuel Cabot a plan of his property with an eye to selling it. Early in 1794 he wrote again to say that Captain Scott — acting as agent for a Boston group anxious to acquire the land (William Scollay, Charles Bulfinch, Jonathan Mason, Jr., Joseph Woodward, and Harrison Gray Otis) — had offered £2500, but some friends had advised against the sale because of the development of the Beacon Hill area. He said that he would be influenced by Cabot's opinion. Subsequently Copley made Cabot his agent for one year, with power to sell the land. On the day he legally became Copley's agent, June 17, 1795, Cabot concluded the sale of the property to the group. Meanwhile Copley had decided to sell the land to General Hull and wrote to Cabot on August 29, 1795, instructing him not to communicate in any way with Scott or his principals and stating that the sale to Hull would stand, that Scott was threatening a suit in Chancery, and that he would never sign over his land to Scott's group. Although more than two months had elapsed, Cabot had evidently not yet told Copley of his action in selling the land to the Boston group.[13]

When young Copley arrived in Boston early in 1796 with power of attorney for his father's Boston property, he found that the sale was a legal reality and that he had to confirm it, although he did obtain more money. Copley himself regretted this sale from the beginning, and his discontent grew as he learned of the rise in land values on Beacon Hill and the still considerable speculative value of such holdings.[14]

---

from John Singleton Copley, Jr., Boston, to his father, London, Feb. 27, 1796; "Farington Diary," p. 412, Nov. 13, 1795. Legally Copley always tried to keep one foot on each side of the ocean. He said that he left America "in pursuit of improvement in my profession that was not attainable in America a year before the War commenced and was not influenced by political opinions as I can abundantly prove" (Society for the Preservation of New England Antiquities [SPNEA], Copley to S[amuel] Cabot, Boston, March 3, 1794). Yet when he was subsequently subpoenaed by two Americans in London, Joshua Johnson and Samuel Bayard, relevant to the squabble over his Beacon Hill property, he wrote to them that the courts of Massachusetts had no jurisdiction over him, as a resident of London, and he would not appear before them (SPNEA, March 8, 1796).

[12] Mary Pelham acted as Copley's attorney in April 1784 in a suit to collect £100 for nonpayment of rent from Samuel Gardner Jarvis, a Boston merchant (Suffolk County Courthouse, Early Court Records, file no. 95292, vol. 540, fol. 14). In December of that year she signed a one-year lease on Copley's mansion house, rented by General Henry Knox, again as Copley's attorney (Massachusetts Historical Society, Dec. 6, 1784).

[13] SPNEA, Copley to Samuel Cabot, March 2, 1793, Aug. 2, 1793, March 3, 1794 (with plan enclosed), and Aug. 29, 1795, and sales agreement between Cabot and Mason et al., June 17, 1795. At the SPNEA there is also a deposition from Samuel Cabot about the affair. Copley had obtained the plan he sent to Cabot and additional information about his Boston lands from Henry Pelham (Amory, pp. 129–31).

[14] SPNEA, document approving sale signed for Copley by his son, entered Suffolk Deeds, Lib. 182, fol. 104.; *ibid.*, power of attorney for Copley, Jr., issued Oct. 9, 1795, received Feb. 24, 1796. For a comprehensive account of the sale of Copley's Boston property, see Allen Chamberlain, *Beacon Hill: Its Ancient Pastures and Early Mansions* (Boston and New York, 1925), pp. 61–69. The

Copley submitted his first picture in seven years to the 1793 annual exhibition of the Royal Academy. As a member of the council, it was certainly fitting that he do this, and as a member of the exhibition hanging committee he probably had little trouble in securing one of the four central places in the great room of the academy (West receiving two, Thomas Lawrence one) for his *Red Cross Knight* (fig. 592). The picture, a group portrait of the younger Copleys with John as the Knight on the left, Elizabeth as Fidelia in the center, and Mary as Speranza on the right, was ignored by the critics, although the *True Briton* observed on May 1, 1793: "this, it seems is a Family Picture, which represents the Son and Daughters of the artist who painted it," and the figures are "so very light and airy" that a heavy wind would blow them away. Copley took his subject directly from Spenser's *Faerie Queene* (book I, canto 10) and adheres to the literary source closely in the color of the costumes, the iconographical details, the direction of the glances, and so on. Although the picture is unique in Copley's work as a purely literary illustration, it does bear some relation to earlier (*The Ascension*) and contemporaneous (*Hagar and Ishmael in the Wilderness*) religious subjects, and to his major history picture of *Charles I Demanding*, already in an advanced state of preparation; all of these are based on written sources. One factor in his choice of this atypical subject may have been his renewed effort to compete with West. He had done this earlier with history pictures like *Chatham* and *Peirson*. West had previously painted a number of medieval or "gothic" themes, including four Spenserian subjects, one of which was *Fidelia and Speranza* (unlocated), exhibited at the academy in 1777.

The task of painting *The Siege of Gibraltar* had prevented Copley from undertaking his usual number of portrait commissions, although in 1790 he did paint a small portrait of *William Ponsonby, Second Earl of Bessborough* (fig. 590), which presents the standing figure from *The Death of Chatham* in a seated position. However, after *Gibraltar* was finished, Copley turned out a series of strong portraits of military figures. The most impressive of these is the three-quarter-length standing portrait of *Charles*,

---

subject is also covered in the "Gleaner" articles by Nathaniel Ingersoll Bowditch, which appeared in the *Boston Evening Transcript* in the summer and autumn of 1855 and were reprinted in the *Boston Record Commissioners' Reports*, 2nd ed., V (1880), 193–203.

In 1796 Samuel Cabot was in London as a mercantile agent appointed to aid in the adjustment of claims for British spoliations. It appears that Copley met with Cabot and his brother at the London Coffee House and Copley read aloud a letter he had received from Boston containing insinuations about Cabot's conduct in managing Copley's land affairs. Cabot then offered to show Copley supporting documents to prove the legality of his actions, as well as a testimonial from prominent Bostonians to the effect that he never could have betrayed Copley's trust by selling his property below value or by having a

personal interest in the sale. Copley, however, did not want to see the testimonial, claiming that it would not change his opinion of the man who had done him irreparable damage and, recognizing his lack of a valid legal position, wanted to drop the whole matter. He did eventually read the testimonial, but returned it without further comment. In the end the Copleys signed a relinquishment of claims on April 17, 1797, on account of £4200 received. Massachusetts Historical Society, Mr. G. Cabot, Brookline, to Mr. Samuel Cabot, London, Nov. 27 and Nov. 30, 1796; *ibid.*, testimonial letter for Samuel Cabot, Dec. 30, 1796; *ibid.*, Copley to Samuel Cabot, Nov. 30, 1796, and Oct. 30, Nov. 6, Dec. 5, 1797; SPNEA, Copley relinquishment of claims, April 17, 1797, received and entered Boston, March 7, 1799, Suffolk Deeds, Lib. 191, fol. 167.

Second Earl and First Marquis Cornwallis (fig. 594), painted on commission from Alderman John Boydell who presented it to the Corporation of London in 1793. It is a bold portrait with strong contrasts of light and shadow and of red and black in the uniform. A dramatic background sky of pink, red, green, and blue-green appears to the left over an Indian scene complete with a row of elephants and mounted troops. Characteristically the figure is set low on the canvas, occupying only two thirds of it. An engraving of the picture by Benjamin Smith was published by the Boydells in 1798.[15]

The portraits of Howe and Barrington, conceived as flanking medallions to *The Relief of Gibraltar*, were probably completed at this time. The portrait of *Richard Earl Howe, Admiral of the Fleet*, was engraved by Dunkarton and published by Copley in 1794. The engraving, like the one by William Sharp published with *The Relief of Gibraltar* in 1810, seems based on the picture now in the National Maritime Museum (fig. 596). Another version in which the figure wears a sash is in the collection of Earl Howe.

The portrait of *Admiral the Honorable Samuel Barrington* was also probably painted at this time, since the uniform is of a type worn during 1787–1795. An engraving by Ridley was published on October 1, 1800, and the picture was also engraved in medallion form by Sharp for publication in 1810 with *The Relief of Gibraltar*. The portrait is owned by the Barrington family (fig. 597), and a small medallion sketch (fig. 595) may be the original study for it.

Another portrait of the same general period, engraved by A. Fogg in 1794, is that of *Henry Belasyse, Second Earl of Fauconberg* (fig. 591), who lived across from Copley on George Street. An oval portrait of *John Quincy Adams* (fig. 598) also dates from the mid-1790's. Portrait commissions were few in the 1790's, and because of general hard times they must have been particularly welcome. During this period, perhaps as a result of the paucity of commissions, Copley often made replicas of portraits, notably *Barrington, Howe, Bessborough*, and *Fauconberg*.

Copley exhibited his historical painting *Charles I Demanding in the House of Commons the Five Impeached Members* (fig. 599) to the public in May 1795, but work on the picture had begun fourteen years earlier. After he had completed *The Death of Chatham* in 1781, Copley was approached by John Boydell with a commission for a history picture for the Boydell gallery of English paintings. Ten possible subjects, all relating to the struggle between Charles I and Parliament, were considered.[16] The

[15] On June 5, 1795, Boydell paid Copley £67–14–6 for this portrait. This came on the heels of Boydell's successful attempt to divert to himself two of the three hundred pounds that the Corporation had voted to give Copley for his additional labor on *Gibraltar*. Possibly the payment for the Cornwallis picture was also involved in this affair in some way.

James Hughes Anderdon, "Royal Academy Exhibition Catalogues," British Museum, Department of Prints and Drawings (1796).

[16] The other subjects have occasionally been incorrectly recorded as works painted by Copley. Benjamin West also painted seventeenth-century historical scenes in 1782, so Copley's interest at this

subject of *Charles I Demanding* was chosen as the most suitable, both for its intrinsic drama, significance, and compactness and for the fact that this scene in the House of Commons made an admirable companion piece to the scene of *The Death of Chatham* set in the House of Lords.[17] The appearance of Charles I in Commons had marked the crisis of the developing conflict between king and Parliament. Charles I had sent a message to the House of Commons demanding the persons of five members accused of treason. Receiving an evasive reply, he went himself to Commons on January 4, 1641/2 and, repeating his demand, asked Speaker Lenthall if any of the accused were present. This demand and Lenthall's memorable response — "I have, Sir, neither eyes to see, nor tongue to speak, in this place, but as the house is pleased to direct me, whose servant I am here" — summed up admirably the confrontation that led to civil war.

Copley set to work gathering historical materials and determining a suitable composition. However, when it was decided that a modern subject, *The Death of Peirson*, would be a more appropriate commission for the Boydell gallery, *Charles I* was set aside. Copley seems to have taken the subject up again in 1785 after *The Daughters of George III* had been exhibited. Late in her life, Copley's daughter Elizabeth recalled that during that summer she and her father drove to various country seats to see old portraits of participants in the scene in Commons when Charles I appeared with his demand. The Fogg oil sketch for the picture (fig. 601) probably represents the state of the composition late in 1785, when Copley again set it aside to work on another commissioned subject, *Gibraltar*. It is even possible that the sketch can be dated as early as 1781–82, when Copley replaced the subject with *The Death of Peirson* for Boydell. Certainly when Copley turned back to *Charles I* after the completion of *Gibraltar* in 1791, the picture was well advanced, so much so that he received an offer of £900 for it from Lord Ferrers, which he declined. On January 2, 1792, Robert Bowyer, miniature painter to the king, published a prospectus for an edition of Hume's *History of England*, to be profusely illustrated with reproductions of history paintings, medals, coins, and such. Copley was listed as one of the large number of painters and engravers engaged to work on it. Copley, with *Charles I* in progress, was a natural choice but perhaps his terms were too high, for in the later exhibitions of pictures for the book that were held at the "Historic Gallery," 87 Pall Mall, Copley was not represented.[18]

---

period was not unique. At one point Copley also considered depicting "The Landing of George I at Greenwich," and jotted down information on the historical background and personages involved, but he seems to have carried it no farther. Microfilm at the Massachusetts Historical Society of manuscripts in the Library of Congress.

[17] In subsequent brochures soliciting subscriptions for his engravings, Copley suggested this picture as a pendant to *Chatham*, with *Gibraltar* as a larger centerpiece. *Chatham* also appeared with *Charles I* in the 1795 public exhibition. "Cuttings on Art,"

Victoria and Albert Museum, III, 748, May 1795.

[18] Amory, p. 98; "Cuttings on Art," III, 617, Jan. 2, 1792. Ferrers wrote to Copley on June 5, 1791: "Lord Ferrers' compliments to Mr. Copley; he cannot form any judgment of the picture; but as money is scarce, and any one may make eight per cent. of their money in the funds, and particularly in navy bills, and there is so much gaming, he hopes he'll excuse his valuing his picture in conformity to the times, and not think he depreciates in the least from Mr. Copley's just merit; but if he reckons fifty-seven figures, there are not above one-third that are

Charles I was finally exhibited publicly at Spring Gardens on May 5, 1795. On the following day the picture was closed to the public for a private viewing by the king and queen and "by a most select party of fashion and taste," who examined it for two hours. It was reported that "many compliments were bestowed upon the artist for his judgment in the choice and skill in the execution of so interesting and splendid a work." Despite the compliments, it seems unlikely that George III of all people should have been particularly pleased by the public display of a painting which celebrated parliamentary disobedience to the king. Even if *Charles I* did gain royal approval, the public response was unenthusiastic. Farington went to see the exhibition of the picture on May 30, and only four other visitors appeared while he was there. He observed, "The picture struck me as rather glaring, & as being very much injured by a frame, overcharged with mouldings, looking like gilt lace work round the picture. — Very carefully finished." That evening Farington learned from Marchant that "Copley appears much disappointed in his pursuits." [19]

The major reason for Copley's lack of public success with this picture was undoubtedly the pedantic nature of his performance. *Charles I* is a cerebral rather than a sensual painting. It is quite unlike *The Death of Peirson*, the portrait of *Midshipman Augustus Brine*, *The Daughters of George III*, or many of the oil sketches in which zestful brushwork, brilliant color harmonies, and crackling light-dark contrasts reflect the highest achievement in England of Copley as a painter, virtuoso, and craftsman. Copley had traits that compelled his art in a different direction, more difficult to appraise and to appreciate, and this other side of Copley's artistic nature dominates here.

Copley had a serious, realistic turn of mind, and a particular interest in history. In

---

capital, but are only heads or a little more; and therefore he thinks, according to the present times, if he gets nine hundred pounds for the picture with the frame, after the three other figures are put in, and it is completely finished, and he has the power of taking a copy, it is pretty near the value: that is what very few people can afford to give for a picture. However, if Mr. Copley would undertake to do a family piece for him with about six figures, about the size of the picture he has of Mr. Wright's, with frame and all, he would agree to give him a thousand guineas for the two pictures. But he imagines the emperor or some of the royal family may give him more, perhaps a great deal more, which he wishes they may, and thinks he will deserve; but if he can't make a better bargain, Lord Ferrers will stand to what he says, and give him six months to consider of it, and will not take it amiss if he sells it for ever so little more than he has mentioned, as he has stretched to the utmost of his purse, though he does not think he has come near up to Mr. Copley's merit" (Cunningham, *Eminent Painters*, IV, 154). The final picture contains only fifty-eight figures, one more than cited by Ferrers.

[19] "Cuttings on Art," III, 748, May 1795; "Farington Diary," p. 348, May 30, 1795. Another reason for the lack of enthusiasm for *Charles I* was the fact that many visual attractions were competing for the public's shillings. When Copley opened his show at Spring Gardens, charging a shilling, he again conflicted with the Royal Academy exhibition. De Loutherbourg at the Historic Gallery on Pall Mall was exhibiting *Earl Howe's Victory over the French Fleet* and the *Grand Attack on Valenciennes*, charging only one shilling for the double feature. At 28 Haymarket Mr. Hickel had on display, also for a shilling, his picture of the House of Commons with ninety-six portraits in it, begun in 1793. At the Saville Row Gallery it cost only sixpence to see the De Colonne Collection, plus some paintings by Reynolds and others offered for private sale. The current panorama represented the City of Bath, and even though that soon closed the panoramic view of London remained on exhibition. *Morning Chronicle*, May 6–7, 1795.

fact more than a realist, he can be called a factualist. In his colonial portraits, he had attempted through a careful methodical approach to translate exactly what he saw onto the canvas. Similarly, when he painted *The Siege of Gibraltar*, he literally laid siege to the rock all over again in miniature in his studio. He was a perfectionist,[20] and the large number of drawings for *Gibraltar* attests to the lengths to which he would go in order to achieve a particular result. Copley's factualism and his sense of history had combined to lead him to a new kind of history painting, the results of which we have seen in *Watson, Chatham, Peirson*, and *Gibraltar*. Using verbal, literary, and pictorial source material, with the inclusion of real portraits, he re-created for an interested audience current events that had strong dramatic, emotional, or patriotic appeal. This was a profitable extension of the boundaries of history painting, successful in part because the artist's imagination was stimulated by information from living and participating reporters, and in part because he was dealing with events in which he himself had a vital interest. Copley's problem was to balance his interest in accuracy and detail against his painterly sense of color, of chiaroscuro, of pigment itself. The balance, when properly achieved as in *The Death of Peirson*, finds Copley at the top of his form. It is notable, though, that the commission from John Boydell that resulted in *Peirson* began as *Charles I*.

After the success of *The Death of Chatham*, Copley thought he could fruitfully apply his realistic approach in the same way to the past. As in *Chatham* he had achieved authenticity by taking portraits of the participants, he now planned to do the same for an event out of the past by locating old portraits, grouping them into a historical composition, and endowing them with expressions appropriate to the central event. In other words, he intended to turn back to the standard subject matter of history painting while utilizing his newly discovered techniques. He would gather materials just as he had gathered materials for current events, but what in terms of a modern subject required a journalistic effort to uncover the facts now required a scholarly effort. Copley's belief was that, if imaginary history painting was the highest form of art, history painting that accurately re-created a significant historic moment, complete with accurate delineations of the people who had participated in the events, would not be compromised but enhanced. As he advised the public in his descriptive brochure:

> The interest Mr. Copley imagined would be . . . heightened, by the introduction of the portraits of those members of the long parliament, who were distinguished for their abilities or exertions in these disputes. He was led to suppose that the scene would thus be brought nearer to the feelings, and that he should contribute towards gratifying a desire natural to mankind, of being acquainted with representations of persons, any wise remark-

---

[20] "I sat with Copley some time and remarked upon the remarkable neatness of His Painting room. He sd. He cd not paint unless everything was in order abt. Him. He cd. not bear to see rags & other things scattered about." "Farington Diary," p. 4627, Aug. 17, 1810.

able for their virtues or their vices, for the greatness of their actions, or the extent and splendor of their talents or fortunes.

Although Copley's theory was interesting, he was very wrong in supposing that a scholar's quest for historical accuracy would heighten the appeal of his picture: the public, then as now, finds doses of history more palatable when laced with a dash of excitement and does not mind a little distortion if it makes the result more entertaining.

As a first step in his effort, Copley consulted historians. His primary source of information was the historian Edmund Malone, who sent him a long, comprehensive letter on January 4, 1782, containing historical data on the scene. Malone attached a long list of individuals whose portraits might be included, and specific information about where Copley could find likenesses of these people in old paintings, prints, and medals.[21] Copley's completed picture contains portraits of fifty-eight individuals, thirty-six of whom were among those listed by Malone. Malone may even have initially suggested the subject itself, since he began his letter of January 4 to Copley by noting that he had "turned the subject that he had mentioned to Mr. Copley in his thoughts," and strongly recommended that Copley paint it. He described the moment that would be best for depiction, with King Charles standing by the chair, the Speaker kneeling and about to reply, Prince Rupert also near the chair, and all the others standing, their attention fixed on the by-play between Charles and the Speaker. Malone also gave a few suggestions about the groupings. For example, he noted that Clarendon, then Mr. Hyde, usually sat next to Lord Falkland and was also intimate with Palmer. Copley did place these figures in the same general area, but separated Sir Edward Dering and Oliver Cromwell, even though Malone had noted that they probably sat next to each other.

Copley's achievement in gathering his historical visual material is something of a *tour de force*. With painstaking care, he collected the portraits of fifty-eight seventeenth-century dignitaries and wove these into a cohesive history picture. The difficulties involved in this were manifold, even with the help of Malone and others. In the first place, the list of possible subjects had to be limited; the availability of materials was undoubtedly helpful in restricting the selection. Then there was a chronological problem. The event depicted took place in 1642, but the available materials represented the participants at various stages in their lives. Copley had to determine how old these people were in 1642 and adjust his interpretation accordingly.[22] Equally vexing was

[21] Boston Public Library; part of this letter is printed in Amory, pp. 450–53, misdated 1785.

[22] For example, Malone told Copley that there was a good picture of Prince Rupert (see key, fig. 600) by Lely, but that unfortunately it showed him thirty-one years after the event. Sometimes Copley used an older likeness and intentionally made it look more youthful. For Geoffrey Palmer (47), Malone referred him to a painting by Lely owned by Richard Owen Cambridge in Twicken-ham. Copley stated in his brochure that he used this picture: it must have been identical with or related to one of the versions now in the Clarendon Collection or the Palmer Collection (National Portrait Gallery Photograph File), which clearly show how Copley effected his transformation, puffing out the subject's cheeks and successfully making him look younger. In using Miss Hotham's portrait of Sir John Maynard (22), he helped to disguise his conversion from age to youth by casting

the problem of pose, since frequently the figures in the available sources faced the wrong way for the projected composition; even more frequently they faced forward when a profile was needed, which, as Copley noted in his brochure, forced him "to trace the appearance of a side face from a more direct view, [which] has required some practice and much attention." [23] Still, more often than not, Copley was able to use his sources without too much change by weaving his composition around them. For the sake of expediency, Copley did not bother to identify all of his sources in the brochure. He listed only the sources for the major characters, to establish "the general authenticity and truth" of the picture. But he did affirm that "every part has demanded, and received, equal attention."

After collecting data, Copley turned to locating the objects themselves. Primarily these were in the hands of noblemen, antiquarians, and collectors. One such collector was John Thane, whose *British Autography* (1793) included likenesses of many of the individuals portrayed in the painting. Copley's personal contact with Thane suggests that these likenesses were available to the artist prior to the published appearance of *British Autography*. Another important source for Copley, visual as well as verbal, would have been the illustrated second edition of Lord Clarendon's *History of the Grand Rebellion Compleated* (1717). This includes an engraved likeness of every major figure in the narrative, with an accompanying reference to the passages in the text where the figure is discussed. Copley's other sources are greatly varied. His standard procedure is seen in the case of Sir Ralph Hopton (fig. 602). Malone recommended this picture, now in the National Portrait Gallery and then in the collection of Sir Jacob Astley, and Copley used it, acknowledging his indebtedness to the subsequent owner, Sir Edward Astley. The head, the collar, and the sash are all the same, and only the position of the eyes has been shifted to suit the action (see no. 3 in the key, fig. 600). [24] The way in which Copley was led from source to source is indicated

the face into shadow, according to versions now at Exeter College, Oxford, and Blickling Hall, Norfolk (National Portrait Gallery Photograph File). With the lord chancellor's portrait of Orlando Bridgman (35), presumably one of the several pictures by or after Pieter Borsselaer, he simplified the face almost into caricature in making it appear more youthful. For Sir Robert Harley (12) his problem was the reverse, since he seems to have based himself on the Peter Oliver miniature, making the subject look older. Occasionally, as in the case of John Selden (11), Copley had one likeness that was too old and one that was too young. Malone had told him of the picture that was in the Bodleian Library at Oxford, calling it Van Dyck instead of Lely, and noted engravings by Faber, Vertue, and White. Copley presumably used the Vertue engraving, which faces in the same direction as the figure in the painting, but he made the face younger, relying on a painting by Mytens owned by the lord chancellor, now also in the Bodleian.

[23] This was the case with Sir W. Waller (6), based on a portrait then owned by the Earl of Harcourt and still in the family; with Sir Peter Temple (7), based on a print; and with Sir Bevil Greenville (44). Malone called Copley's attention to an engraving by Vertue of Sir Henry Slingsby (30) and Copley apparently used it, but the subject is turned from right to left and his head is angled downward and his attention made to focus on Charles I. In the case of John Rushworth (57), Copley claimed to have used the painting in the Speaker's Room in the House of Commons. In that picture the upright figure stares out blankly and wide-eyed, but in his painting Copley alters the presentation to accommodate the fact pointed out by Malone that Rushworth "took down King's Speech in shorthand." The change is so great that the prototype would be unrecognizable were it not for Copley's own statement of his source.

[24] For Sir Benjamin Rudyard (17), Malone recommended a portrait owned by "Col. Soothby" in

in the case of Speaker William Lenthall (28). Malone told Copley that Lenthall should be presented "on one knee, as if about to speak to the King," but he did not know of any prints or pictures. Yet he did point out that "a lineal descendent of his died (a greatgrandson I believe) at Burford in Oxfordshire, last November." Copley followed this lead and noted that he had "consulted a picture in the possession of Mr. Lenthall of Burford." But this was not the source he relied upon. An informative letter from A. Bowles referred him to the Thomas Simon medal, engraved and published by Vertue, which was a profile facing left.[25] When Thane published the medal, he noted that it

Bloomsbury Square. This portrait by Hoskins is still in the Sotheby family, and Copley did use it, again changing the position of the eyes and making the head less square. Malone did not mention John Belasis (25), but Copley lived across the street from Henry Belasyse, Lord Fauconberg, who owned a full-size painting, probably the Van Dyck engraved by White, which has the same treatment of hair curling on the forehead as in Copley's painting, and a miniature by Cooper. Since it was convenient and politic (Copley painted a portrait of Fauconberg in the 1790's), Copley included John Belasis. Malone told Copley of engravings of Henry Vane, Jr. (27), after a painting by Lely formerly in the collection of the Earl of Orford. Copley located the Lely in the collection of the Countess Dowager Darlington and used it closely.

Copley derived his likeness of Sir John Hotham (33) from a painting in the collection of the late Sir Charles Hotham, the same source from which he got his likeness of Sir John Maynard (22). An engraving of Hotham in Thane's *Autography*, II, opp. 33, which was probably based on this painting, shows that Copley adhered quite closely to such details as the pose, skull cap, collar, and tassels. Copley probably also used a print source for Ferdinand, Lord Fairfax (39), perhaps the one reproduced in Thane, II, opp. 28, which has the same collar, form, and hairline; the strong accent of moustache and beard further suggests a print source for the likeness.

Malone told Copley about "two curious prints" of Sir Isaac Pennington (41) in Granger's *Biographical History* and also mentioned a painting, "in the possession of William Bosville, Esq. — to be heard of at the Prince of Wales's Hotel, Conduit Street." Copley could have followed up this lead easily because Conduit Street was nearby, but perhaps Malone did it for him since, at the end of the list Malone sent to Copley, is this note: "Lord Macdonalds best Compliments to Mr. Copley. Has seen Mr. Bosvill this morning who says that the Picture of Sir Isaac Pennington on wood (very capital) is at his seat at Thorpe (4 miles from Burlington) in Yorkshire — He says 'The Arts must not be impeded on his account,' on the contrary that the picture shall be delivered, or viewed or sent to Mr. Copley whenever he shall express a wish to that effect — So says the owner — and may everybody who can assist

in perpetuating a transaction so interesting, and so worthy of the Artist do the same." Whether or not Copley received this portrait, he does not seem to have used it since in his brochure he did not acknowledge the loan, and the figure of Sir Isaac Pennington seems closely based on a print that was published in Thane, II, opp. 37.

In the case of Oliver St. John (43), Copley may not have used a visual source at all, or he may have used one but doctored it according to Malone's description of St. John "in his Barristers robes. He was a man (says Clarendon) of a dark and clouded Countenance." For Sir Philip Warwick (45), Copley stated his use of a Lely prototype, and an engraving bears this out, suggesting only that the glance has been changed. For Sir Edward Nicholas (48), Malone mentioned a 1653 print after a painting by Hanneman, probably owned by a descendant of William Nicholas, Esq., who had been "one of the restorers of the Antiquarian Society in 1717." This led Copley to a miniature that he used rather than the Hanneman. For Lord Viscount Falkland (56), Malone cited the original picture at Longleat, and Copley acknowledged indebtedness to Admiral Forbes. The picture at Longleat, variously attributed to Van Dyck and Cornelius Johnson, is an exact source for Copley's figure. Malone mentioned a print by Van der Gucht for Colonel George Goring (58), but Copley went directly to the source, a Van Dyck owned by the Earl of Egremont, and borrowed the figure intact.

[25] A letter at the Massachusetts Historical Society, microfilm of manuscripts in the Library of Congress, A. Bowles, North Aston, Oxfordshire, to Copley, Aug. 19, 1785, gives historical references, and it lists possibly useful illustrations "by Simon the Medalist in his Book of Medals & Seals," referring to George Vertue, *Medals, Coins, Great-Seals, Impressions, from the Elaborate Works of Thomas Simon . . .* (London, 1753). Copley's interest in accurate historical materials is reflected in an event of 1799 when the old House of Lords building was going to be demolished. Copley expressed concern about the fate of a tapestry there, "supposed to represent with uncommon truth and accuracy, the Costume, civil, religious, and military, of the Country about the period of the fourteenth Century; a Work of incalculable use to Artists, who would otherwise be left to collect with great trouble, much loss of time,

was "in the cabinet of the Rev. C. M. Cracherode"; it is likely that Thane personally told Copley about the medal, and in his brochure Copley acknowledges his reliance on the "exquisite medal" in Cracherode's collection.

In the end, Copley had spent an enormous amount of time and effort in this task of re-creating an important moment in England's history. In his earlier paintings of scenes from contemporary history, Copley's imagination had been fired by the interpretations of living participants, by their passions, distortions, and faded memories. However, when forced to rely on pictorial and literary sources for the reconstruction of a scene from the past, Copley was not able convincingly to revivify the events portrayed. In *Charles I*, then, he reached an artistic cul-de-sac because the major emphasis of this kind of painting was nonartistic. It is perhaps because Copley grew aware of this that he never finished the large *Monmouth Before James II Refusing To Give the Names of His Accomplices* (fig. 604), a picture that is related closely to *Charles I*. A full oil sketch (fig. 605) and a drawing for one of the figures (fig. 603) are extant for this picture, both of which seem to date stylistically from the early or mid-1780's.[26] The oil sketch is very similar to the oil sketch for *Charles I* (fig. 601) of that period. The composition was undoubtedly contemplated as a pendant for *Charles I*, both pictures depicting a seventeenth-century event in which a hero refused to betray his fellows to the king. But the idea of painting *Monmouth* as a companion piece to *Charles I* was never stated publicly and, in fact, the latter picture was considered a companion to *The Death of Chatham*.

In 1796 Copley again began to exhibit at the Royal Academy. During the previous ten years he had exhibited only one picture there, *The Red Cross Knight* in 1793. Now, following the lethargic public response to *Charles I*, Copley's interest in exhibiting at the academy revived and with only one subsequent exception, *The Victory of Lord Duncan* (fig. 621), which he exhibited independently, he remained a faithful academy exhibitor throughout the remainder of his career. One of the pictures Copley exhibited in 1796 was *Abraham Offering Up His Son Isaac*, currently unlocated and known only through an engraving (fig. 606).[27] This was his first religious subject since *The Tribute Money* of 1782. Rather than reflecting the impact of his early Italian visit, so apparent in the early religious paintings, this picture seems to have been influenced by an en-

---

and in a far less perfect and satisfactory manner, from the inspection of illuminated Missals, and other Manuscripts, the necessary information upon these points." "Assembly Minutes," RA, II, 77–78, Dec. 10, 1799; also "Farington Diary," pp. 1682–83, Dec. 2, 1799.

[26] Apparently Sir Joshua Reynolds contemplated this subject at about the time that Copley began his picture. Reynolds wrote to Lord Hardwick on March 5, 1783: "The subject which your Lordship mentions of the interview between the Duke of Monmouth and James the 2ᵈ is certainly better calculated for a Picture than that of the old Duke of Bedford,

tho I think even this has scarce enough of intelligible action and perhaps the expression is too delicate for our art. But the insuperable objection to subjects of that period, is the dress. The first effect of such a picture will be allways mean and vulgar and to depart from the Costume is as bad on the other side." Hilles, *Reynolds*, pp. 101–02.

[27] Copley also exhibited two currently unidentified portraits of gentlemen, but none of the three pictures seems to have attracted much attention. The *Oracle*, April 25, 1796, merely said that they "possess the merit of a good tone of Colouring."

graving of *The Sacrifice of Isaac* by Schelte à Bolswert after Theodore Rombouts (fig. 607). The points of similarity are manifold. On the right there is the ram and the bush below, the angel above, and the diagonal accent of the tree trunk. On the left trees provide another strong accent. In both pictures Abraham looks over his shoulder at the angel, his hand resting on the head of Isaac, whose arms are tied behind his back. There is even some general relationship in the type of altar used for the sacrifice. A drawing for Copley's picture (fig. 608) indicates that his original idea was still more closely related to the engraving, with both the angel and Isaac presented in more upright positions.

In the following year Copley exhibited nothing, but he must have been very active if we are to judge by the exhibition of 1798, in which he hung five pictures. Two of these were of religious subjects, *Hagar and Ishmael in the Wilderness* (fig. 609) and *Saul Reproved by Samuel* (fig. 610). *Hagar and Ishmael* was a pendant to *Abraham Offering Up Isaac* and, like it, is unlocated. Both pictures represent a standing adult and a reclining child in similar elevated positions in a woodland setting, with angled trees left and right, foliage in the right foreground, and an angel approaching in the upper right. It seems probable that both of these pictures had been percolating in Copley's mind for a while before they finally saw the light of day at the Royal Academy, since Copley's son mentions *Hagar and Ishmael* in a 1791 letter.[28] The other religious picture exhibited was the large *Saul Reproved by Samuel* (fig. 610). In this picture the whirling, pointing figure of Samuel balances the entire group to the right, as the figure of Christ balances the rest in *The Tribute Money* (fig. 420). Several preliminary drawings are extant. In fig. 611 a nude study of Samuel on the left turns a little stiffly, with the upward angle of his hand diminishing the directive thrust of his rebuke to Saul. Saul, in the center, approximates the final stance, but the position of the head and arms will change considerably. A further sketch on the right alters the position of the head and studies the arrangement of a cape that is attached over the right shoulder. A subsequent drawing (fig. 613) contains two studies of Samuel, largely concentrating on the drapery and in neither case arriving at the ultimate arrangement.

Copley also exhibited three portraits at the academy in 1798. One was a portrait

[28] The high-spirited letter that young Copley sent home from Cambridge is dated 1791 by his biographer, Sir Theodore Martin (*Lyndhurst*, pp. 26–27; also Amory, pp. 118–19). Copley, Jr., cited two errors in the painting in its current state. First, he pointed out that the town seen five or six hundred yards in the distance really was about forty miles away, according to the biblical text. Second, he indulged in an elaborate proof to demonstrate that Hagar at the time of the event was at least fifteen years old, and not twelve or thirteen as he appeared in the painting. If the date of 1791 for this letter is correct, it seems likely that *Hagar and Ishmael* and probably *Abraham Offering Up Isaac* were among the subjects Copley first attacked on being freed from the burden of *Gibraltar*. The delay in exhibiting them could have resulted either from Copley's putting them aside until the completion of *Charles I* in 1795 or from his holding them back until the engravings were nearly ready for publication, so that the timing of the exhibition would assist the sale of prints. Both pictures were engraved by Robert Dunkarton and published by Copley within a year of each other, *Abraham* on Nov. 1, 1797, and *Hagar and Ishmael* on July 2, 1798.

of *John Andrew Graham* (fig. 617). The second was a portrait of *Henry Addington, First Viscount Sidmouth, as Speaker of the House* (fig. 614). Ozias Humphry notes in his memorandum book on October 7, 1797, that Copley "was employed in painting a whole-length portrait of the speaker." Since it was a full-length portrait of a very prominent individual, Copley wanted it to make the best possible appearance in the academy exhibition, since a good reception might bring him other such commissions. Farington notes in his diary on April 1, 1798, during the hanging of the exhibition, that "Copley [was] down yesterday to condition for situation for his picture of the Speaker." The general critical response was restrained, but stressed that the picture was a "good likeness." Copley also exhibited a portrait of Lord Sidmouth at the Royal Academy in 1809, probably the version that depicts him at three-quarter length in a plain black long coat, perhaps as prime minister (fig. 616).[29] In the full-length portrait of Sidmouth, Copley used the same table that he had included in the *Izard* double portrait painted in Rome twenty-two years earlier. Since the Izard painting was still in Copley's studio, it seems likely that he unrolled it and copied the detailing of the table. The composition of the hand on the scroll on the table, the opening to the left, the column to the right, and the drapery above is familiar, relating to the earlier portraits of *Admiral Gayton, Henry Laurens, Elkanah Watson, Lord Mansfield*, the unidentified portrait of *A Cleric* [?], *John Adams*, and *Lord Bessborough*.

Copley's third portrait in the exhibition at the Royal Academy was a portrait of *Adam Viscount Duncan* (fig. 620), commended in the *Morning Post*, May 25, 1798, as "a bold, strong, faithful likeness. The figure stands out of the canvas, and displays much good colouring." This portrait is directly related to Copley's last major history painting, *The Victory of Duncan*.

[29] British Museum, Add. Mss. 22949; "Farington Diary," p. 1231; *Morning Post*, May 25, 1798; *Sun*, April 23, 1798.

XVIII   *The Victory of Duncan*

1798-1799   ADMIRAL ADAM DUNCAN, COMMANDER-IN-CHIEF OF BRITISH NAVAL operations in the North Sea, led a British fleet in defeating the Dutch off the coast of Holland at Camperdown on October 11, 1797. He had boarded the seventy-four-gun *Venerable* in 1795 to blockade and, if possible, to destroy the Dutch fleet (Holland had become allied with France in that year to preserve her independence in the face of French arms). When the Dutch ships emerged on October 7, 1797, English patrols advised Duncan's main fleet, which had returned briefly to Yarmouth. Four days later Duncan's force intercepted the Dutch as they were returning to their sanctuary. In a vicious battle the English gained a virtually complete victory, and only a few of the damaged Dutch ships managed to escape. The *Venerable* was so badly damaged that it was ordered to be thoroughly overhauled, and Duncan, who a few days after the battle received a viscountcy from the king, was obliged to transfer his flag to the newly launched *Kent*.[1]

Shortly after the battle of Camperdown, Copley painted a splendid life sketch of *Admiral Duncan* (fig. 619). From this he composed the three-quarter-length portrait exhibited at the academy (fig. 620), which depicts Duncan on the deck of the *Venerable* with the Dutch flagship *Vryheid* burning in the left distance. Copley dashed off this painting with uncharacteristic rapidity, and published an engraving of it by Richard Earlom on March 1, 1798, well before the portrait was exhibited at the academy and in time to capitalize on the still warm public interest in Duncan's heroic victory. Perhaps because of this public enthusiasm, and perhaps because of the inherent drama of the subject, Copley decided to paint *The Victory of Lord Duncan* (*Surrender of the Dutch Admiral DeWinter to Admiral Duncan, Oct. 11, 1797*) as a full-scale history painting (fig. 621). He chose to paint the exact moment when DeWinter offered his sword to Duncan on the *Venerable*. Duncan, responding gallantly, had refused the traditional token of surrender, saying, "I would much rather take a brave man's hand than his sword."[2]

Copley's first task was to steep himself in verbal and visual accounts of the engage-

[1] Earl of Camperdown, *Admiral Duncan* (London, 1898), pp. 37, 43, 172ff.

[2] Camperdown, pp. 269–70. Copley's decision to paint *The Victory of Duncan* on a large scale was made prior to Jan. 22, 1798, when Boydell told Farington of Copley's intention ("Farington Diary," p. 1204).

ment. Shortly after the battle at Camperdown, a considerable number of reportorial prints depicting the engagement were published in Holland as well as in England; but none of these seems to bear any relationship to Copley's production other than to suggest general atmosphere and the design of the *Venerable*.[3] The few drawings that survive give only a rough idea of the picture's compositional development. One early drawing (fig. 623) explores on the left the figure of DeWinter and on the right the background figures on the poop deck raising the flag. In the final version Copley considerably curtailed the vigorous forward stride of DeWinter, presumably so that the figure would not become a dominant focus of action and, in the painting at least, win the day over Duncan. The upreaching figures on the right are ultimately reversed, although the arm positions remain the same: the figure on the left in the final arrangement faces toward the rear, but the arm holding the rope is unchanged. The same is true of the other figures. A second drawing (fig. 624) concentrates on this group alone, putting the figures in the general position they occupy in the large picture. On the right there is a figure pulling on a rope, which in the final arrangement is placed to the left of the other two. This group, considerably more advanced than in the first scheme, is squared for transfer. Similarly squared is the scaled figure of Duncan (fig. 625), based on the portrait but extended to full length with changes in the position of the right hand, the jacket, and an added medal. Another sheet develops the figure bearing the enemy colors (fig. 626) from the dull, sketchy, restrained figure on the left to the brisk, full-striding figure on the right. Whereas the treatment of the Dutch admiral becomes increasingly stiff, the treatment of this colorful but subordinate figure gains in vigor. In the finished picture the figure is still more successful, with the impression of movement enhanced by a fuller fall of the drapery.

Copley's next step was to take portraits of the key participants in the action. Admiral Duncan's portrait had already been painted, and in the large picture his appearance is based directly on the earlier portrait, with only minor changes in pose and costume. In all probability Copley did not get a life portrait of Admiral DeWinter. Shortly after his capture, DeWinter was released, and he returned to Holland at the end of November 1797. But Copley undoubtedly used some sort of source to ensure

[3] For example, *A Representation of the Glorious Victory Obtained by Admiral Duncan over the Dutch Fleet, Oct. 11, 1797* was published on Dec. 19, 1797, by G. Thompson and J. Evans, West Smithfield. It shows the *Venerable* on the right and the *Vryheid* in the center blasting away at each other at close quarters. A little more detail of the *Venerable* is presented in *A Representation of His Majesty's Ship Venerable, Adml. Duncan, at the Close of the General Engagement, Oct. 11, 1797*, which was published six months later on June 18, 1798, by John Fairburn, London, but the information it affords about the placement of the masts and rigging is minimal. An actual view of the surrender painted "on board the Venerable" by Daniel Orme was engraved and published by the artist on Aug. 20, 1800. Regardless of whether or not he was able to see the picture before it was published, the only idea Copley might have had from it would seem to be the figure in the rigging. Another interpretation of the event was painted by Henry Singleton, and an engraving of it by James Daniell was published by the engraver on March 25, 1799. It shares certain general elements with Copley's design — the cannon on the right, the relative position of the major figures, the disposition of the rigging, the burning boat in the background — but no definite lines of affinity can be drawn and, even if there is an influence, it is questionable which way it flowed.

fidelity. At least one portrait of DeWinter had been painted while he was in England, a miniature taken from life by Daniel Orme in November 1797, which DeWinter gave to Duncan. As Copley worked on the large picture, his son later recalled, a series of men who had served aboard the *Venerable* came to the George Street studio to have their portraits painted. Particularly memorable was colorful John Cresey, the boatswain, "who wore a large pigtail and insisted on being painted in such a position as to display it." Cresey, though not identified in the key that was published with the subscription for the engraving (fig. 622), is probably the figure on the right who hauls on a rope with his back to the viewer.[4]

Lieutenant John Little, whose portrait is included in the painting (7), was born in Halifax, Nova Scotia, the son of an American loyalist, Samuel Little. He entered the Royal Navy in 1795 and, fortunately for Copley, had been aboard the *Venerable* throughout the action at Camperdown. Apparently Copley, who must have known Lieutenant Little through the father, asked him to send a description or drawing of the deck of the *Venerable* as it had appeared at the time of the action. Little sent Copley a detailed drawing (fig. 627), signed by Benjamin Turner, attached to the following letter:

> Sir:
>
> Enclosed I send you a view of the Venerable's Quarter Deck & Poop, supposed to be standing near the Mainmast & having it in your left hand. The cabin is cleared for Action & the stern windows are seen. The number 1 shews the

[4] Camperdown, pp. 287, 343. Among the others in the painting who probably came to the studio to be painted was James Porteous (1), the pilot. Like many of the others who served aboard the *Venerable*, he transferred to the *Kent* with Admiral Duncan in March 1798. Captain Cleland (2) was second lieutenant aboard the *Venerable* at the time of the action at Camperdown and is correctly shown in the undress uniform of a lieutenant. Sir William George Fairfax (4), former captain of the *Repulse*, became flag captain of the *Venerable* in the autumn of 1795. Mr. Burnet (6), Admiral Duncan's secretary, was a supernumerary and later received a lucrative appointment from the first Lord of the Admiralty, Earl Spencer. John Little (7), a lieutenant aboard the *Venerable*, was transferred to the *Kent* and secured a promotion in July 1799, both at Admiral Duncan's request. Captain Thomas Trollope (8) was in charge of the detachment of sixty-seven marines aboard the *Venerable*. Captain Oswald (9) at the time of the action was a lieutenant and is so pictured with the white cuffs of the lieutenant's full-dress uniform. He was not a regular member of the crew of the *Venerable*, but had been in command of an English lugger that had run aground. Henry Thompson (10), twenty-one years old at the time of the event and from London, was on the muster roll of the *Venerable* as an able seaman awaiting promotion to midshipman, a rank

he presumably had achieved by the time Copley exhibited his picture. George Patterson (11), the master, is recorded like many of the others as being highly regarded by Duncan, a fact which indicates the possibility that Admiral Duncan may have suggested to Copley those individuals whom he thought should be included in the picture. John Crawford (12) was another twenty-one-year-old who served aboard the *Venerable* as an able seaman. The other three foreground figures at the gun (with John Cresey) and the young sailor bearing the Dutch colors are not identified. But Duncan's biographer Camperdown claims, "It is almost certain that one of the men at the gun is Archibald Moody," and suggests the probability that the others are those recommended for promotion along with Moody by Duncan in a letter to the Admiralty of May 25, 1798 (Patrick Barry and William Liddle for boatswains and George Weir, along with Moody, for gunner). Information on the individuals portrayed in the picture comes from Camperdown, pp. 245, 343–47; "*Venerable* Muster Book, March 1, 1797–March 14, 1798," Public Record Office, London, ADM 36/11649; "*Kent* Muster Book, March 10–August 30, 1799," *ibid.*, ADM 36/2415; and a letter to the author from M. S. Robinson, Keeper of Prints and Drawings, National Maritime Museum, Greenwich, March 9, 1959.

covering of Hammacoes on the Quarter Deck & Poop. The number 2 shews the sauve tete Netting. The number 3 shews part of the Wheel. The rest needs no explanation —

[If] it can be of the smallest use to you [it] will give me much satisfaction.[5]

Copley received Benjamin Turner's drawing only about two months before *The Victory of Duncan* was exhibited to the public. Therefore he did not use the drawing as a *mise en scène* for the entire action, but merely as a source of information for various details. There was no major revision of the picture to have it conform to all of the facts. Copley did not, for example, attempt to incorporate the "sauve tete" netting; nor did he try to include all of the "swifters" (temporary rigging) or "back stays" (permanent rigging) indicated by Turner. The major use of the drawing seems to have been in the treatment of those areas of the ship visible between the heads of Duncan in the center and Patterson, the master, on the right. The rail covering is shown with a suggestion of the diagonal grill pattern beneath. The steps leading up to the poop deck are similar, but lack handrails. Fire buckets marked with GR, as in the drawing, stand on floor level rather than on a supporting shelf, but a series of rails have been added above to give something of the proper effect.

The final picture Copley created is one of his best history paintings, a picture that is qualitatively only a notch below *Peirson* and may be fairly ranked with *Watson* and *Chatham*. The picture seems to divide itself in half, Duncan being associated with the left side which is strong and well executed. The burning *Vryheid* in the distance, engulfed by red and yellow flames, adds to the pictorial effect of this half of the painting. Figures like Duncan, the sailor with the enemy flag, and John Crawford in the upper left rigging can be compared with Copley's work at the peak of his career fifteen years earlier. Silhouetted against the light background, Crawford is one of the strongest accents in the picture, a kindred spirit to the figure of the harpooner in *Watson and the Shark*, holding on to the rigging much as the harpooner holds his weapon. The inclusion of Crawford in the rigging undoubtedly refers to the published story of his bravery. Going aloft to rehoist the flag that had been shot down, he nailed it in place with his pistol butt. While doing this, enemy shot struck the mast near his head and drove a wooden splinter through his cheek and into his mouth. After descending he calmly told his mates, "Never mind, that's naught."

On the right side of the picture, however, the only really successful area is the

[5] John Marshall, *Royal Naval Biography* (London, 1835), IV, part 2, 68–69; National Maritime Museum, John Little, H.M.S. *Kent*, Sheerness, to Copley, March 5, 1799. At the time of the action aboard the *Venerable* Benjamin Turner was a twenty-one-year-old landsman. He had been transferred, and at the time of Little's letter to Copley a year later he was serving aboard the *Kent* as an ordinary seaman ("*Venerable* Muster Book" and "*Kent* Muster Book"). Although Turner may have made his drawing from memory, it would not have been difficult for him to go from the *Kent's* anchorage at Sheerness a short distance up the Medway to inspect the *Venerable*, which was in the naval dockyard at Chatham ("*Venerable* Log Book," National Maritime Museum, information courtesy of Miss K. F. Lindsay-MacDougall).

pyramidal cannon group in the foreground. The portraits of Burnett, Little, Trollope, and Patterson on the quarter deck are static and dull. The flat, stiff figures on the poop deck in the upper right are a foretaste of the technical weakness that appeared with greater frequency as the years carried Copley into old age. Characteristically the painting is composed of self-contained color areas. Also characteristic is the small scale of the foreground figures in relation to the size of the canvas, a huge expanse of which looms over their heads.

Working on this large picture, Copley seems to have kindled within himself a burst of enthusiasm that infused his painting with renewed vigor and energy, and its afterglow lasted for about five years. His earlier successes had been achieved with grand historical depictions of modern events, *Watson, Chatham, Peirson*, and *Gibraltar*. But *Gibraltar* had been commissioned in 1783, and *The Victory of Duncan* was the first new history painting initiated in fifteen years. While he painted this picture for which he was so technically and temperamentally suited, England was chalking up a string of brilliant naval victories. This provided him with an ample store of subjects, and once more he saw the road to prosperity and success opening before him, as it had in the 1780's. So carried away was he that, ignoring his past humiliation at the hands of the Corporation of London, he wrote eagerly and in good humor to the man who was at the center of his earlier disagreement, Alderman John Boydell:

> Having been informed that the Corporation of the City of London intends to place in their Guildhall some memorial of the late splendid naval victories which has so much contributed to the security and glory of the nation: I have taken the liberty of addressing this letter to inform you that I am at present engaged in painting two pictures one representing Admiral De Winter surrendering to Lord Duncan on board the Venerable, the other Lord Nelson surrounded by his Officers on the quarter deck of the Vanguard the moment preceding the explosion of the french admiral's ship[.] the former picture is very advanced and will be finished early in the spring[.] for the other I have already made my arrangements and hope to complete it in a year. These pictures will contain the portraits of Lord Duncan[,] Lord Nelson[,] Admiral de Winter and the principal officers of the Venerable and Vanguard. The splendid circumstances of these victories as well as those of Lord Howe and Lord St. Vincent are well calculated to produce a striking effect on canvas: and I beg leave to offer to the consideration of the gentlemen of the common council whether historical pictures are not the most pleasing and eligible mode of perpetuating the memory of these glorious events and whether the two above mentioned which are of a size to fill the end of the Council Room opposite to the Gibraltar picture will not fully meet the intention of the corporation with respect to the victories they represent. I shall be much obliged if you will have the goodness to communicate the contents of this letter to the common council.[6]

[6] Corporation of London Record Office, Guildhall, Copley to Alderman Boydell, Jan. 25, 1799. Perhaps it was Copley's hope to clear the way for such a commission that led him in this year, 1799, to accept the hundred guineas from the corporation, closing the books on the *Gibraltar* dispute.

Thus, in addition to the almost completed *Victory of Duncan*, Copley claimed to have begun work on a victory of Lord Nelson and suggested an interest in the victories of Howe and St. Vincent. Several months later Copley had an opportunity to show *The Victory of Duncan* to the Court of Common Council,[7] but the council was not moved to acquire it for the Guildhall. Copley then proceeded with his original plan to exhibit the picture to the public, to take subscriptions for an engraving, and to lobby for the eventual sale of the picture.

It was Copley's hope to exhibit the picture in a pavilion in Green Park, as he had done with *Gibraltar* in 1791. But the noblemen again objected to this blot on their "prospect," and Copley was forced to make private arrangements. On May 22, 1799, *The Victory of Duncan* was exhibited to the public, along with *Charles I* and *Chatham*, in a great tent pitched in the garden of Lord Suffield's house on Albemarle Street. Admission was one shilling, for which the visitor also received a descriptive brochure. The brochure contained a key to the picture and a description written by Copley's son.[8] The description concluded with a clear statement of Copley's theory in painting his particular brand of history pieces:

> The introduction of portraits in works of this nature must infinitely enhance their value, as well to the present age as to posterity. And here, perhaps, posterity may be mentioned without presumption, since, whatever are the merits of the artist, a painting which records so glorious and splendid an event can never be neglected or forgotten. To feel in its full force the interest which a remote age will take in these representations, it is only necessary to reflect upon the gratification we ourselves should experience in contemplating a picture, painted by a contemporary artist, descriptive of the interview between Scipio and Hannibal, and in which the features and persons of those celebrated heroes, and of the principal officers in the Roman and Carthaginian armies, were faithfully preserved.

A note was appended to the brochure: "*The Victory of the Nile* will be painted by Mr. Copley as a companion to the above work, and he has already collected the necessary information and materials for that purpose." The description also included proposals for the publication by subscription of a print to be engraved by Anker Smith. Having had his fingers burned before by the dilatory tactics of engravers, Copley followed the proposal with this emphatic statement: "In consequence of the delay which has too frequently taken place in the execution of similar works, and which is generally, but for the most part very improperly, ascribed to the publisher, Mr. Smith has agreed to become responsible to the Public for the completion of the Engraving in two years from the delivery of the Picture," and this was followed by Anker Smith's own pledge of punctuality. Despite the published pledge, Smith for some reason did not engrave the picture. Copley hired James Ward to execute a mezzotint in his most finished manner and to keep the plate in repair until four hundred good impressions

[7] "Cuttings on Art," Victoria and Albert Museum, I, 22 (no date, but mounted between cuttings of March 10 and April 18, 1799).
[8] Camperdown, p. 343.

had been pulled, for which Ward was to receive 250 guineas in two equal installments. Copley published the excellent print on August 1, 1800, well in advance of the promised date.[9]

A review in the *Morning Chronicle* that appeared on May 24, 1799, two days after the opening of the exhibition, was very favorable. The writer speculated that it was a credit to England that she not only turned out heroes to win battles, but also artists "worthy to record" these events. This "successful attempt to treat a naval victory in a new and agreeable manner," with the "simplicity and taste of the composition" and the "skillful management of effect," was held to be "at least equal to any of the former productions of this celebrated Artist."

Despite general approval, the public did not turn out to see *The Victory of Duncan.* Commenting on this picture as "one of those elaborate productions" by which Copley "has enriched the circle of the British arts," an anonymous writer in the *British Magazine* noted that public interest in this "popular and national" subject had virtually disappeared before the painting was exhibited and the engraving published. The author, apparently presenting Copley's thoughts on the subject, noted that the artist still had not received any real payment for his labor on the picture. "The fortune attending the production of public pictures . . . of subjects the most interesting and important to the national glory, has at length opened the eyes of the artists, who have speculated on public patronage, to the infatuation that had cheated them of their time and their money, and left them a prey to chagrin and disappointment." The article noted that Copley still had *The Death of Chatham* and *Charles I* in his studio, and that the owner of *Peirson* (Boydell) had not been able to sell it. Commenting on de Loutherbourg's difficulties with *The Grand Attack on Valenciennes* and *Earl Howe's Victory,* it concluded that the only bright spot in patronage for history pictures was the City of London's commission for *The Siege of Gibraltar.*[10]

All was not lost, however. Early in 1802 Admiral Duncan's aunt, Lady Mary Duncan, became interested in the picture and concluded that it should remain in the family. She purchased the picture from Copley for 1000 guineas and presented it to her nephew, with the instruction that it remain in Lord Duncan's family forever. Today it still hangs in the Duncan home, which has been turned over to the City of Dundee.[11]

[9] Grundy, "Prints," p. 73.
[10] II (July–Dec. 1800), 334–35.
[11] British Museum, Add. Mss. 36,594, fol. 61,

Copley to Caleb Whitefoord, Feb. 10, 1802; Amory, p. 95, Mrs. Copley to [Mrs. Gardiner Greene?], 1802.

XIX *The Knatchbull Family* and the Academy Dispute

1799-1803   THE ENGRAVING OF COPLEY'S *Priam Beseeching Achilles for the Body of Hector* (fig. 340), a picture that had probably been composed some twenty-five years earlier, was published on June 4, 1799. Why was it published at this late date? And why, if Copley wanted to engrave one of his early works, did he select this picture rather than the highly praised *Ascension* (fig. 337)? The decision and choice probably resulted from economic and political factors. Copley had encountered increasing financial woes during the 1790's, caused by the paucity of portrait commissions, the limited success of his later history pictures, the demands of maintaining his George Street residence, and the general hard times that hit the lot of English artists. A possible source of income that might have relieved the situation, the sale of engravings on the Continent, was choked off by the continuing war with France and her allies. Now, suddenly, a lull in hostilities permitted some interchange. West took advantage of it to go to France and purchase pictures. And Copley published an engraving on a classical theme that would have sales appeal in republican France. His picture was directly derived from Gavin Hamilton, who had earlier influenced the young French painters in Rome and who, along with West, had continued to exert influence in France through engravings of his early paintings on classical themes.[1]

After the exhibition of *The Victory of Duncan* in 1799, Copley set to work on a welcome series of major portrait commissions that came his way. Aided by an artistic second wind that had come with the Duncan portraits, he turned out several works that rival the high quality of his earlier portraits. Among the best of these is a full-length portrait of *George John, Second Earl Spencer* (fig. 628). Earl Spencer had been Lord Duncan's superior as First Lord of the Admiralty, and Copley had astutely dedicated his print of *The Victory of Duncan* to him. He also painted a half-length portrait of Spencer with the same likeness but in plain dress (fig. 629). There is some question about whether the portrait of Spencer exhibited at the Royal Academy in 1800 was the half-length or the full-length. Although an engraving of the full-length composition

[1] Locquin, "Retour à l'antique," p. 481.

was published by Dunkarton [2] in October 1801, the painting may not have been completed by that time. The engraving could have been based on the likeness in the half-length, with the remaining details based on sketches. This theory is supported by a letter of 1803 from Copley to Alderman Boydell, in which he notes the resolution passed by the city council to put a portrait of Boydell in the Guildhall and expresses a wish to get the commission: "I am just now engaged in painting a full length portrait of the Earl of Spencer in his Robes as a peer," and he wished to show this picture as a specimen of his work.[3] Copley's letter indicates that he was still actively engaged on the full-length in 1803; furthermore, the receipt for Spencer's payment of 100 guineas to Copley for this picture is dated June 26, 1806.[4] So the picture exhibited at the Royal Academy was probably the bust portrait.

Two other portraits Copley exhibited at the academy in 1800 were listed as *Lady Dudley and Ward* and *Lord Viscount Dudley*. John, Second Viscount Dudley and Ward, was represented in *The Death of Chatham*, and Copley subsequently painted a three-quarter-length version of this figure (fig. 630). However, the portraits exhibited at the academy in 1800 were presumably the dual full-length portraits of *William and Julia, Third Viscount and Viscountess Dudley and Ward* (figs. 631 and 632). Copley's portrait of *R. Wilson, Esq.*, also exhibited at the academy in 1800, has not been located.

On July 3, 1800, Copley's eldest daughter Elizabeth married Gardiner Greene, a prosperous Boston widower. At the time Elizabeth left for Boston, Copley had started a portrait of her. This was probably undertaken as soon as it became known that she was going to be married; but only the head had been completed by the time she left. Before Copley could finish the portrait (fig. 634), which everyone seemingly admired, he was forced to set it aside for several large commissions, notably *The Knatchbull Family*. Only early in 1803, after the completion of the large Knatchbull picture, could Copley invite his wife and his other daughter, Mary, into the painting room and, with Mary modeling the drapery, complete Elizabeth's portrait.[5] The treatment of the arm with drapery folded over it is reminiscent of the 1800 *Viscountess Dudley and Ward* (fig. 632).

In August 1800 Sir Edward Knatchbull, Eighth Baronet, took Copley by post chaise

---

[2] "As to poor Dunkarton, he has exceeded slowness itself in his Lord Spencer. It is a disappointment, as usual, when anything depends upon him; but it is to be *very fine*, to console us." Amory, p. 211, Mrs. Copley to Mrs. Gardiner Greene, July 8, 1801.

[3] "Anderdon Scrapbooks," RA, XII, 1803, copy (not verbatim but close to the original) of a letter, from Copley to Alderman Boydell, 1803. Although there is room for error in Anderdon's recording of the date as 1803, it is probably correct. It is not surprising, in view of Copley's record of conflict with Boydell and the council, that he achieved the same result with this as with his bid to paint *The*

Victory of Duncan and *Lord Nelson's Victory* for the city — he did not get the job.

[4] The receipt is owned by Earl Spencer, Althorp.

[5] Chapman, *Marriages . . . St. George, Hanover Square*, p. 223; Amory, p. 238, Mrs. Copley to Mrs. Greene, Feb. 1, 1803. With Elizabeth in Boston, an extensive correspondence flowed between the Copleys and the Greenes, which is a valuable source of information concerning Copley's activities during his last years. Copley did not usually write himself, except when it was necessary to borrow money from his son-in-law or to forestall repayment during the difficult years that followed.

to his Adam mansion in Mersham le Hatch, near Ashford, Kent, so that the artist could see the projected location for the family picture he had already begun, the light for working, and other conditions. Mrs. Copley reported to Elizabeth in Boston: "The baronet is much pleased with the design for the picture as far as it is gone, but you will find that he has but little idea of the artist's application when I tell you that he expected the picture would be painted in the course of a month. A year quite alarms him." [6]

After starting on the Knatchbull group, Copley also launched a large three-figure portrait of *Colonel Fitch Saying Farewell to His Sisters, the Misses Fitch* (fig. 635). The Miss Fitch in a white dress is again reminiscent of *Viscountess Dudley and Ward*, while her arm is extended in front of her darker-clad sister like the young girl on the left in *The Knatchbull Family*. By December Copley had completed the heads of the Misses Fitch and in March was finishing the picture for the academy exhibition. Sukey wrote to her daughter of the picture, "If I dare to give an opinion before the connoisseurs, I should say it was very fine." [7]

The Knatchbull Family project (figs. 636–638) started most auspiciously. After his brief inspection of the house at Mersham in August 1800, Copley was there for most of September and October, graciously received and entertained. By the time he returned to George Street, he had made good progress in sketching the picture and taking portraits.

Sir Edward Knatchbull was a widower of forty-five, with ten children, the eldest of whom was nineteen. In April 1801, while Copley was working on the picture, Sir Edward married twenty-year-old Mary Hawkins. Although Copley had hoped to finish the picture during the summer of 1801, it was not possible. In the first place, Knatchbull's new wife had to be included in the composition, and before long room had to be made in the canvas for an anticipated infant. Second, this was the time of the unpleasant affair over *The Death of Chatham* engraving, and it was a drain not only on Copley's shaky finances but on his time and energy. [8]

The year 1802 was a particularly busy one for Copley. Mrs. Copley told her daughter, "Your father is almost always in his painting room." [9] The large *Knatchbull Family* had become complicated not only by the introduction of the new wife and child, but

[6] Amory, p. 183, Mrs. Copley to Mrs. Greene, Aug. 23, 1800.

[7] *Ibid.*, pp. 193, 202, 203, Mrs. Copley to Mrs. Gardiner Greene, Dec. 20, 1800, and March 3 and April 6, 1801. The *Oracle*, which reviewed the exhibition on May 7, 1801, called the picture "One of the finest groups of family portraits we have seen. Colonel Fitch is a graceful, manly figure, with an engaging and animated countenance. He is taking leave of his sisters, and about to mount his horse. Fraternal affection is finely expressed in the countenances." The review added the poignant observation that Colonel Fitch had since died, and this farewell was his last. Another review found fault with the picture, especially with the "wooden horse" (Whitley Papers, British Museum, p. 357).

[8] Amory, pp. 202–03, 223, 224, Mrs. Copley to Mrs. Greene, March 4, 1801, and Jan. 8 and March 18, 1802.

[9] *Ibid.*, p. 233, Mrs. Copley to Mrs. Greene, Aug. 31, 1802.

by Sir Edward's rather unusual request that his first two wives be shown in some way. Moreover, Copley undertook a considerable number of other portrait commissions that came along and was occasionally forced to set the Knatchbull group aside. He had also become intrigued with some technical problems.[10] However, by the end of 1802, Copley had finished *The Knatchbull Family* except for the general toning.

The large completed *Knatchbull Family* was cut apart sometime during the last century, probably because it was not highly prized after the many barbs directed at it and valued likenesses could thus be preserved and distributed. So it is difficult to assess the effect and quality of the original work, and we are forced to rely heavily on a sketch (fig. 639). Because this sketch differs in many ways from the evidence of the surviving parts of the original, it seems likely that a considerable amount of development took place between the sketch and the finished picture. *The Knatchbull Family* is a distant cousin of Copley's earliest ventures in group portraiture, *The Copley Family* and *The Pepperrell Family*. However, with twice as many figures to accommodate, Copley found it necessary to recess the group deeper into pictorial space, with a resultant loss of intimacy between the group and the observer. Rather than a warm family scene, the composition resembles the detail of a frieze, especially on the left where two smaller figures drain attention from the natural stop of the group of the elder sons, almost as if providing an intentional transition to something further to the left. On the right the compositional bracket of Sir Edward's figure is vitiated by the heavenly choir above.

Perhaps the best way to examine this picture is straight across from left to right, noting the development of the composition and the subsequent division of the painting into the surviving portraits. The young boy on the extreme left is known only in the oil sketch. The girl appears in a fine squared and scaled drawing at the Boston Museum of Fine Arts (fig. 641), which is closely related to the oil sketch except for the position of the left hand.[11] The surviving portion of the left side of the painting is the double portrait of Sir Edward Knatchbull, 9th Bt., with his younger brother Norton (fig. 636).

---

[10] In 1797 West and other academicians had paid fees to subscribe to certain "secrets" of Venetian painting: a newly discovered "Titian Shade" (a mixture of pigments) and a clue to the preparation of the grounds. Copley, however, did not subscribe, and the scheme turned out to be quite fraudulent. His theory was that the mastery of the Venetians resulted from the medium they used, not the pigment or the ground. In the summer of 1802 he discovered his own Venetian secret. Young Copley confided to his sister: "It is of interest not to our little group alone, but to the whole circle of the Arts; not only to the present time, but to all future generations. But what is it? Well, then, attend: My father has discovered the Venetian — 'the true Venetian,' — more precious than the philosopher's stone! Is that all? And are you already so barbarized by your transatlantic residence as to put such a question? Is that all? To have made a discovery which the artists of three generations have in vain been endeavoring to explore! What is it that has raised the Venetian artists to so high a pitch of celebrity? It is not their drawing; it is not their superior skill in composition, in the distribution of drapery, or in the management of light and shade: it is principally to be ascribed to the medium, or vehicle, of which they made use, which was peculiar to themselves, which they carefully concealed from others, and which was lost with the decline of their school. Henceforth, then, you may fairly expect that my father's pictures will transcend the productions even of Titian himself." Amory, pp. 230–31, Copley, Jr., to Mrs. Greene, Aug. 9, 1802.

[11] The pose of this figure is reminiscent of Reynolds' portrait of *Lady Jane Halliday*, a 1779 engraving of which by Valentine Green was owned by Copley. See appendix, Copley Print Sale (35).

The double portrait, clipped from the final canvas and retouched, is a dull bit of business. The best portion consists of the portrait heads which, since Copley as usual left much space above and below, stand out as the two salient details in an otherwise boring expanse of canvas. Other areas are simply poor, such as Edward's arm, which is unnaturally extended and as boneless as an elephant's trunk. Since the figure of a sister was very close to Norton with her arm passing in front of him, it was necessary for her to be painted over, largely replaced by the red chair on the left. The "ghosts" of her hand reaching in front of Norton and of her head extending above the added chair are clearly evident. In the lower right corner of the double portrait, where the cradle on a stand appears in the original sketch, a section of canvas has been snipped out and replaced by another piece depicting a globe, which sits on the same stand. In the oil sketch the young men rest their respective book and scroll on the arm of the central sofa, and in the earliest drawing (fig. 642) Norton is in scholarly regalia and stares abstractly off into space. In the double portrait the sofa is replaced by a desk complete with standish, but this change may have been part of the final picture rather than a subsequent alteration in the double portrait. Since naval service made it necessary for Norton to be away from home much of the time while the family picture was being executed, Copley painted an oil sketch of him from which to work (fig. 640). The figure of Norton was also carefully treated in a scaled drawing (fig. 643), which does indicate his hand resting on a book but does not clarify whether the book is on the end of the sofa or on a desk.

From the center of the picture only the figure of Mary Knatchbull remains (fig. 637). Quite a few drawings survive for the central grouping, but they are not too informative. Copley's earliest rough sketch (fig. 645) indicates that he considered presenting a few children crawling on the floor and planned a closer rapport between the mother and child, with the child leaning back, raising a hand to the mother's face and staring into her eyes, similar to the relationship between young Copley and his mother in *The Copley Family*. A further development on the recto of the same drawing (fig. 647) shows the pointing child standing in the mother's lap. The other half of this drawing shows another child seated on the floor in a pose similar to that finally used, except for the awkward left arm. A third child, leaning over the side of the sofa and looking out at the viewer, is placed on the sofa in the oil sketch. There are two other studies of the central group, one stressing the children and the other the mother. It is difficult to judge which came first. The one with the children (fig. 644) depicts a charming child on the floor, still with the problem of the arm unsolved, although it is further shielded by her body. The mother now holds the child away from her, and there is little rapport between the two. The other drawing of Sir Edward's wife (fig. 646) concentrates on the drapery.

The decision to salvage Mary Knatchbull (fig. 637) from the central group necessitated a considerable amount of repainting. The mother and child are eliminated on the left, as is the boy on the sofa to the right. The scene is shifted to a landscape setting, and a little dog is inserted in the lower left. Actually the result is a lovely child's portrait, more harmonious and unified than one might suspect from its origin. The gently but strongly painted head is the dominant detail, although the tambourine provides strong competition. The coloring and the composition are successful and, with the exception of the boneless arms, the whole is well painted with crisp, sure strokes. This figure bears an obvious relationship to another Mary, the princess in *The Daughters of George III.*

From the group on the right, only Sir Edward Knatchbull was preserved in a large portrait (fig. 638). Recently shot game is strewn on an elegant table to the left, and hunting dogs are introduced on the right. There is a squared drawing extant for the figure of the girl in this group, which has been painted out (fig. 648), and there is a similar drawing of Sir Edward (fig. 649). The dominant element in the portrait of Sir Edward is the head, with the hands as secondary accents. The treatment, as with the portrait of Mary, is superior to the double portrait of young Edward and Norton. The slanting lines of the gun barrel and the table edge enliven the composition. The still life and the dogs are dully painted, but the distant background is alive, and the figure stands forth clearly, the head elegantly framed by the hat. The large expanse of canvas, top and bottom, is familiar. Sir Edward stands on a stone floor with diamond-shaped insets at the joins of the large slabs of stone; the floor in the oil sketch is covered with a red carpet with two green stripes on either side; the finished figures of the younger Edward and Norton stand on a red rug with a linear-diamond design in black.

When the time came early in the spring of 1803 to send in pictures for the Royal Academy exhibition, Copley asked for an extension for his *Knatchbull Family* on the basis that the picture was seventeen or eighteen feet wide, eleven or twelve feet high, and he was concerned for its safety.[12] His real reason seems to have been that Knatchbull had not yet given permission for the picture to be exhibited and was in fact balking at the prospect. Copley's request for an extension, innocuous though it seemed, touched off a series of explosions that rocked the Royal Academy and culminated in a bitter controversy which required the intercession of the king.

The conflict within the academy began as early as January 1800: in an acrimonious meeting of the general assembly, the question arose as to whether the assembly was assuming the powers of the governing council.[13] West, with a heavy majority, asserted

[12] "Council Minutes," RA, III, 177, March 26, 1803.

[13] The question of the relative authority of the council and the general assembly essentially involved the completeness of West's power. West could usually count on majority support in the general assembly of academicians, which had elected him president. But the governing council of the academy was appointed by the assembly according to a formula whereby new academicians were elected to the council in the year following their election to the academy, and the remaining council seats were filled by others on a strict rotation basis. The council term was two years, with half of the council replaced annually. It was thus possible for an anti-West majority to exist on the council during

the rights of the assembly, while Copley and Rigaud objected. A month later Joseph Farington heard a rumor from Northcote "that Beechy, Tresham, Bourgeois, Sandby, Copley, Rigaud & Cosway have resolved to establish a Club in opposition of that of the Royal Academy, & have fixed on the Thatched House Tavern. — It is to be on the same days as the Academy Club. They say the King approves the Plan."[14]

Matters remained fairly calm throughout 1801, and during the summer the painters even joined forces on Copley's behalf in common cause against the engravers in the Delattre case. However, when Copley was elected to the council in 1802, the power struggle began in earnest. It broke out at the meeting of the general assembly held on February 10, 1802, for the purpose of electing three new academicians. Since these new members would serve with Copley on the council during his second year, 1803, they represented the balance of power. The opposition club met in advance and decided to support Bonomi for one of the academy vacancies. But the plan of West's group to defeat Bonomi with Turner, Soane, and Rossi in turn was successfully carried out. The three new academicians were duly named to the council for 1803, along with Copley's ally, Bourgeois, whose regular term came up.[15]

The basic issue of council versus assembly quickly erupted again, on the matter of whether or not a report should be received from a special committee formed in January 1803 to look into the question of a raise in salary for holders of Royal Academy posts. Turner, Soane, and Rossi, the three new council members, voted yes. Copley, Wyatt, and Bourgeois voted no on the basis that the council had the sole responsibility for running the academy and could not accept a report from a body that did not include council members. Yenn abstained, and West broke the tie in favor of the newcomers and the committee. The general assembly subsequently endorsed this vote, and at a special meeting unanimously approved a series of resolutions by Hoppner condemning the actions of Copley, Bourgeois, Yenn, and Wyatt.[16]

This was the troubled state of academy affairs in 1803 when Copley made his re-

certain years. The academician Rigaud had seemingly precipitated this particular clash by complaining to George III through William Beechey, portrait painter to the queen, of the power of the ruling cabal in the academy, referring to West and his circle. "Farington Diary," pp. 1728ff, Jan. 14, 1800.

[14] *Ibid.*, p. 1770, Feb. 16, 1800.

[15] *Ibid.*, pp. 2002ff, Feb. 10, 1802. There were many minor points of personal resentment and anger that further widened the academy schism. For Copley these included the calling to account by the council in 1801–02 of Wyatt and himself for their expenses as stewards for the 1799 king's birthday dinner (*ibid.*, p. 2103, Nov. 13, 1802). There was also his unsuccessful stand at the academy on Nov. 1, 1802, that pastels were "not to be admitted into the Class of Painting"; he challenged anyone to show him a pastel that had been admitted as quali-

fication for an academician, and was greeted, according to the prejudiced Farington, by hoots of laughter "as there was a Crayon Portrait by Cotes before him & Russells *admission* picture behind him" (*ibid.*, p. 2044, Nov. 1, 1802). A final matter was the defeat of Copley's son by Charles Burney in an election to choose the academy's "Professor in Ancient Literature to succeed Bennet Langton, deceased" ("Assembly Minutes," RA, II, 177–78, Jan. 15, 1803).

[16] The account of the 1803 dispute given here is based on "Assembly Minutes," RA, II, 181ff, March 12–Nov. 21, 1803; "Council Minutes," RA, III, 177–210, March 26–May 24, 1803; and "Farington Diary," pp. 2221, 2229, 2357–58, April 7–Aug. 13, 1803. A letter signed "Candidus" reviewed the entire affair from an anti-Copley point of view in the *True Briton*, April 27, 1803.

quest for an extension in presenting his *Knatchbull Family* for exhibition. The council unanimously approved Copley's request, but at the next meeting a letter came from West, who had been forced to miss the academy proceedings for a while because of illness, expressing his concern over the latitude allowed Copley. The council voted to endorse the permission, but noted that this was not to establish a precedent.

West also sent a long letter to the general assembly that bitterly opposed the council's resolution to grant Copley an indulgence in the form of additional time for the *Knatchbull* picture, and he decried the action of Copley, Bourgeois, Wyatt, and Yenn, attacking Copley by name. The assembly in response voted that the four had acted contrary to the interests of the Royal Academy, and Farington noted with relish that the meeting ended "happily & effectually . . . obliging Mr. Copley to comply with the General Opinion, — & asserting the authority of the General Assembly." Two days later, Copley appeared before the general assembly and informed it that his picture had been sent for exhibition. But the appearance of peace was deceptive. Copley's apparent capitulation merely enabled him to put his political house in order before lobbing a grenade at West at the next day's council meeting. West had submitted for exhibition a painting of *Hagar and Ishmael in the Wilderness*. Copley, who had recently painted the same subject himself and who had been familiar with West's work for over twenty-five years, recognized it as a picture that West had exhibited in 1776 (at the first Royal Academy exhibition in which Copley had participated). Copley called this to the attention of the council, citing the cardinal academy rule that no object could be exhibited in an annual exhibition more than once. In the course of a brief meeting from which West was absent, *Hagar and Ishmael* was rejected. West first learned about the rejection through an article published in the April 14 *Morning Post*, which said that the council had been shocked at his "deception." He was furious. At the next day's meeting of the council, with Copley in the chair, Soane submitted a moderate, conciliatory letter for council approval, which denied the tenor of the *Morning Post* article and said that the misunderstanding had resulted from West's illness. This letter, which it was hoped would undo the damage of the leaked story, was published the following day, April 16, in the *True Briton*. Unfortunately it appeased no one.

The affair was further embittered and complicated by two subsequent developments, neither of which benefited Copley. The first was the firm and final decision by Lord Knatchbull not to permit the exhibition of his family picture, despite Copley's pleas, and despite the intercession on Copley's behalf of the influential Sir Joseph Banks, who was married to the sister of Knatchbull's first wife. Knatchbull's reasons were undoubtedly mixed, but the main cause was probably the anti-Copley sentiment emanating from the academy and the reports of derision directed at the picture because of the two former wives floating in the upper right among the angels. But Knatchbull said he had so decided because his present wife had consented to sit only on the understanding that the picture would not be exhibited. Copley, after creating such a turmoil by his request for a delay, was now in the embarrassing position of having to request the withdrawal of the picture from the exhibition. He did this at a council meeting of April 17, which he chaired in West's continued absence. West made his voice heard, however, when a letter from him was introduced noting that it was not feasible to withdraw the picture since the exhibition was hung and the catalogue nearly complete. To counter this Copley read some of his correspondence with Sir Edward to exonerate himself and to demonstrate that the picture had to be recalled. After two indecisive meetings, it was finally voted on April 19 to withdraw the picture, since the catalogue had not yet been actually printed.

Copley had barely extricated himself from this tangle when a second complication developed. On the day the withdrawal of the Knatchbull picture was approved, the *True Briton* announced that not only had Copley been the one who had identified West's *Hagar and Ishmael* as an earlier exhibition piece, but he had caused the fact to be revealed in the press. Copley missed the council meeting of April 21 at which West's *Hagar and Ishmael* was definitely voted out of the exhibition, but he attended the general assembly meeting of April 25 when West returned to the fray in person. West submitted two stinging letters, one of which lashed out at the unnamed academician who caused the academy to be "deranged and embarrassed" by removing a picture from the Great Room after it had been hung for the exhibition, and by making it unlikely that the catalogue could be printed in time for the opening. The second letter recounted how he had not learned of the council's rejection of *Hagar and Ishmael* until six days after the meeting, and then only by means of a newspaper article. He called for an investigation to discover who had leaked Royal Academy business proceedings to the press.

On May 12 the council denied any leakage to the press on the matter of West's *Hagar*. Two weeks later it approved Copley's series of resolutions which set forth its primacy over the general assembly in running the academy and requested that the matter be referred to the king for adjudication. The assembly responded quickly and decisively by suspending Copley, Soane, Wyatt, Yenn, and Bourgeois from the council.

The matter now rested in the hands of George III. West saw the king regularly during this period, sometimes with others of his group, to present his version of the dispute. Copley attempted to get the king's ear as well, and on one occasion the opposing groups even met at Windsor Castle. They did not speak. The king was disgusted by the childish and malicious behavior of the academicians on both sides, but on the basis of the issues he supported Copley's position on the supremacy of the council and exonerated the five council members. He ordered that they be reinstated, that their protests and motions be entered in the minutes, and that all other entries attacking and expelling them be expunged from the minutes. Thus an uneasy peace was instituted, although the bitterness remained even after the expiration of Copley's council term at the end of 1803.[17] In 1804 Copley's son wrote and published an anonymous pamphlet, *A Concise Vindication of the Conduct of the Five Suspended Members of the Council of the Royal Academy*, which included a postscript by John Soane. This, in its own biased but well-written way, recounted the events and elicited a wordy and dull rebuttal, published anonymously in the same year, *A Concise Review of the Concise Vindication . . .* which basically protested the injustice of having a temporary minority in the council wielding more power than the permanent majority in the general assembly.

In the final analysis Copley had won the argument, but both he and West had weakened their political positions in the academy. Antipathy to West increased when it became known that George III had turned against him. This could have worked to Copley's advantage except that, as de Loutherbourg told Farington, "the King also hated Copley." Once, in a fit of exasperation, the King told Beechey in front of witnesses: "West is an American, — & Copley is an American; — and You are an Englishman, and if the devil had you all, I wd. not enquire after you!" As a result of the growing feeling against West, James Wyatt was put up as a candidate for the presidency of the academy. Copley had reservations about supporting Wyatt. He probably saw himself as the logical alternative to West and was chagrined at being ignored. He had also long opposed a prominent role for architects in academy affairs. Thus when the matter came to a vote in December 1804, Copley abstained. Others were also unenthusiastic about Wyatt, and West won the election.[18]

[17] At the king's birthday dinner in June 1804, Bourgeois arranged the place cards for members of his group at the end of the table. When Farington observed the impropriety of this, Bourgeois noted "how disagreeable it wd. be to them to be near West." "Farington Diary," p. 2680, June 4, 1804.

[18] *Ibid.*, pp. 2812, 2829, 2852, Nov. 15 and 22, and Dec. 10, 1804. A differently phrased version of the king's denunciation in *ibid.*, p. 2937, Feb. 19, 1805, includes Hoppner among the condemned artists. Farington's diary, even allowing for bias, abounds with unfavorable remarks that reveal Copley's low prestige and popularity in this period (see pp. 2388, 2544–48, 2572, 2597, 2672–73, Sept. 9, 1803–May 31, 1804). Farington noted that on meeting Sir Edward Knatchbull at Lawrence's house, the artists "agreed that [Copley] had done more injury to the Arts, & to the Character of Artists, than any man of his time." West also told Farington that, during the work on the *Knatchbull* picture, Copley came to him for an opinion and that when West "first saw the picture the figures appeared like so *many pokers*, there being nothing to *mass* and *unite them*. The Composition was too much for Copley who did not know what to do with it. [West] recommended to him to introduce the large Mass of *red* in the *Center* which gave vigor and effect to the whole. — In return for this service did this man act that illiberal part in what respected the picture of Hagar & Ishmael sent by West to the Exhibition last year."

Nollekens reported that Copley "when a member of the Committee of Arrangement . . . seldom attended the duty till 1, 2, or 3 oclock in the afternoon." Woodforde said that the Royal Academy model who usually sat for him and other artists privately for one shilling an hour "spoke of Copley's behavior to her, who would make her sit a longer time than she could well bear & would scarcely pay her half the price. She had resolved not to go to him any more." West described a meeting with the Marquis of Stafford in which he learned that Copley had asked Stafford if he would sit for a portrait, not as a commission. The marquis replied that if he sat he would pay, but that he did not wish another portrait of himself. West told Stafford that Copley's "coarse conduct" indicated an ulterior motive, perhaps a scheme concocted by Copley, Bourgeois, and Desanfans to use the sittings so that Copley could "impress on the mind of his Lordship such matter as might be conceived to suit their purpose." Finally, Marchant told Farington that Copley "was so little attached to anything in this country that He would have quitted it had not his wife opposed it." Since Mrs. Copley did mention to her daughter in Boston in July 1803 the vague possibility that they might be coming to America (Amory, p. 245), the idea was undoubtedly being considered at George Street.

Copley's disagreement with Sir Edward Knatchbull over payment for the large picture was still unresolved. No clear-cut terms had originally been set. Upon completion of the picture, the two disagreed on price, and their difference of opinion was intensified during 1803 by the unpleasantness over exhibiting the picture at the academy; matters were further exacerbated when Copley, in the hope of gaining royal approval, showed the picture to the king without Knatchbull's permission. In February and March 1804, the dispute came to a head. Although no price had been agreed upon in advance, Copley had initially received seven hundred and fifty pounds. Upon completion of the picture, Knatchbull planned to give Copley enough to bring the total up to twelve hundred pounds. Now Copley asked eighteen hundred, and Knatchbull demurred. The case was headed for court, and Knatchbull subpoenaed West, Lawrence, Shee, Hoppner and Opie, artists not generally friendly to Copley. Sir Edward paid into the court enough to bring Copley's fee up to fourteen hundred guineas. The dispute was privately arbitrated in the chambers of a lawyer on March 1 and at West's on March 2. During the first day's hearings, Caleb Whitefoord said that two thousand guineas would have been a moderate price for the Knatchbull picture, and Thomson, the print seller, said three thousand. Bourgeois testified that there "was more work & difficulty in painting the Landscape Back ground to that picture than would be to paint Back grounds to 14 separate whole length." Beechey's opinion was that, since he himself had received a thousand pounds for his picture of the king and his sons, Copley was entitled to eighteen hundred pounds for the Knatchbull group. Most of the artists, with a decided interest in favoring high fees, took Copley's side, with added support coming from a few nonartists.

In rebuttal Sir Edward relied on himself, West, and Lawrence. He said that he had merely wanted to have portraits of his two former wives in the background of the picture, but that Copley had insisted on putting them in the sky. He also complained that the picture had been submitted for the academy exhibition and shown to the king without his permission. Copley had spent ten days at Mersham before deciding whether a particular location in the house would suit the planned picture, and during his more than three months in Kent "seldom began to paint before 11 or 12 oClock, appearing to be a very long time in setting the pallet." West testified that he felt twelve hundred guineas to be a "handsome price" for the Knatchbull picture, and "1400 guineas a princely price." He stated that he could have painted the Knatchbull picture in six months, to which Copley replied that it would be impossible in three times that long. West also testified that he could have finished a sketch for the picture in ten days, and that Rubens frequently did sketches in forty-eight hours. He felt that a fair basis of reckoning would be to take Copley's current price for a full-length, one hundred and twenty guineas, and calculate on that basis; it would come to twelve hundred guineas for the picture.

At these hearings young Copley appeared on his father's behalf, and his sharp questioning annoyed West, especially when he asked if the standard of prices West was quoting had been used in charging George III twenty-nine thousand pounds for pictures. The arbitrator threw out the line of questioning, but afterwards West noted that Copley, Jr., was "a chip off the Old Block" and that he "appeared to be His Father's *double refined*, a pretty promise as a lawyer." Shee noted that "young Copley seemed to be worse than his Father, — very pert &c."

Farington does not record the final result of the arbitration, which suggests that it may have been determined in Copley's favor. The quantitative weight of testimony was on his side, and Farington's later notation, that Knatchbull said he would have come to trial with Copley in open court if it had not been contrary to the wishes of his wife, perhaps reflected Sir Edward's feeling that he would have fared better in a court trial. However, even if Copley received the fee he wanted, he was not yet done with the Knatchbull picture. It apparently remained in his studio until August 1807 when, having finally altered the picture by painting out the angels in the sky, he delivered it to Sir Edward.[19]

[19] *Ibid.*, pp. 2245, 2547–48, 2556–61, 2572, 2596, 2635, 3944, May 5, 1803–Jan. 10, 1808; Amory, p. 288, Aug. 20, 1807.

The Final Years

Forced to withdraw *The Knatchbull Family* from the academy exhibition in 1803, Copley had to rely on his double portrait of *Charles, First Marquis of Northampton, and His Son Spencer, Lord Compton* (fig. 650) to represent him in the exhibition. The *Northampton* double portrait is a straightforward, unexciting picture, much less vigorous and resplendent than the *Earl Spencer* full-length (fig. 628). The treatment reflects some of the flat, dull quality that first appeared in Copley's work in 1795 with *Charles I*, and became increasingly characteristic of his later style. No longer does Copley's flying brush toss up ridges of rich and glistening impasto. The lack of lively textural effect renders his method of painting in complete color areas disturbingly apparent. This segmentation almost to the point of unrelatedness of parts is an enduring Copley characteristic, even in the drawings, but in his periods of greatest power the crispness of the design, the fluidity of the brushwork, and the sparkling contrasts of lights and darks convert it into a pictorial asset. After his picture-making capacities had diminished, however, and the effectiveness of the paintings had come to rest on the re-creation of visual reality, then the unrealistic articulation of parts works against the success of the picture. The erosion of Copley's style is evident here in the loose composition, the flat surface, the poverty of the value contrasts, and the soft figures, their arms like rubber tubes, posed statically as on a stage. Copley's customary device of leaving a considerable amount of space above and below his figures, which adds to the effect when like Gainsborough or Romney he creates a picture rather than a copy of externals, here becomes another factor contributing to dullness. Only the portrait heads are at all successful.[1]

[1] The *Morning Post*, April 30, 1803, called the *Northampton* picture "a truly chaste and classical performance," and the reviewer innocently noted in reference to *The Knatchbull Family* that he had "looked in vain for a large family group" by Copley on which he had heard favorable comments. The equally placid *Morning Herald* review on May 3 praised the Northampton likeness and called it "a very fine picture, beautifully colored in all its parts." The *True Briton* critic said on May 6 that he had not seen *The Knatchbull Family* but that, if it were no better than the *Northampton* double portrait, Copley should have no regrets about the refusal to have it exhibited. Lord Northampton looked like "a Dancing Master, going to give a lesson to his pupil," he wrote, and the figure of the boy was so awkward that he seemed to need the lesson. The attack continued: "The colouring is raw and glaring, in our opinion, and although the artist has contrived to purloin one of Raphael's *Pillars*, yet it by no means tends to give a classical air to the Picture, but, on the contrary, being introduced so little in conformity with modern objects, is an egregious violation of taste." The *British Press* review of May 14, a particularly vicious one, congratulated the artist, the Knatchbull family, and the public on the absence of the large picture if it "was equally crude and inharmonious." The critic noted that the figures are

The year 1803 was Copley's time of greatest controversy, yet he was able to accomplish a considerable amount of painting, particularly portraits. After *The Knatchbull Family* and the double *Northampton* picture were done, Copley completed the portrait of his daughter Elizabeth (fig. 634).[2] In July 1803 he was working on a portrait of *Mrs. Richard Crowninshield Derby as St. Cecilia* (fig. 651), and Mary Copley thought "she makes a most beautiful picture."[3] The composition of the picture is a close repetition of Joshua Reynolds' 1775 portrait of *Mrs. Sheridan as St. Cecilia*. At this time the Copleys formed a friendship with another family named Copley, which led to a commission to paint the family's children. The daughter, who had a family of her own, was the wife of Rear Admiral Montague. In the resulting portrait (fig. 652), she is painted with her younger brother Robert Copley.

At the exhibition of 1804 Copley exhibited four portraits: *Mrs. Derby as St. Cecilia* (fig. 651); *Mrs. Montague and Her Brother* (fig. 652); *The Right Honorable Viscount Dudley and Ward* (probably fig. 630); and *Sir Robert Graham* (fig. 653). This was a relatively strong showing for Copley, who had not often played a major role as an exhibitor, and the *Daily Advertiser* noted on April 30 that "Mr. Copley's contribution to the general display reflects honour on his industry and talents."[4] The reviewers

so unrelated by the action that they could be framed separately, "without any detriment to the Artist, unless he fears, that by cutting off some of his red curtains, large columns, sky, &c. he would take away some of the *best parts* of the picture," and in a cruel final thrust, "If Mr. C. was a *young ingenious* man, we might hope to see improvement, but veteran arrogance seldom profits by good council, or corrects long-established errors." Lord Northampton must have felt in retrospect that he should have followed the example of Knatchbull and withdrawn his picture from the exhibition. The suggestion that the picture could be cut up and the figures framed separately was strangely prophetic of the actual fate of *The Knatchbull Family*. The reviewer in the *British Press* had clearly chosen sides when on May 9 he took the part of West and his circle against the "guilty few" who disrupted the academy through their "nefarious, clandestine, and illiberal conduct." He accused Copley and Bourgeois of using positions on the hanging committee to secure "a conspicuous and favorable location" for their pictures in the Great Room, noting that it was lucky for some exhibitors that the still larger *Knatchbull* picture had been withdrawn, since the space used for many other pictures would have been pre-empted.

[2] Having this portrait to keep as a remembrance in London, the Copleys decided to send the oil sketch for the 1776 *Copley Family* (fig. 346) to their daughter in America. This involved getting it back from Mrs. Thew, the widow of the engraver who had been working on a print from the picture when he died (Amory, pp. 79–80, 240, Mrs. Copley to Mrs. Greene, March 1, 1803). It took a year to get the sketch, but they sent it to Boston the following summer and Mrs. Copley told her daughter, "Should it ever be thought worth while to finish the plate, you must let the sketch cross the Atlantic again; in the mean time, we shall be happy in the pleasure it affords you and the rest of our dear friends in America. It contains the best likeness of my departed and dearly valued father" (*ibid.*, p. 263, Aug. 31, 1804; this letter is also printed in part in *ibid.*, p. 80, and misdated Dec. 1802). Copley also decided at this point to make a portrait copy of a drawing of his brother-in-law, Charles Startin, then in New York, but if he did make one it is still unlocated (*ibid.*, p. 240, Mrs. Copley to Mrs. Greene, March 1, 1803).

[3] *Ibid.*, p. 246, Mary Copley to Mrs. Greene, July 31, 1803.

[4] The exhibition was hung by Farington and de Loutherburg. Turner gave them some difficulty because he "was very anxious about his Sea Piece being under Copley's White Drapery," which presumably was *Mrs. Derby* but perhaps *Mrs. Montague and Her Brother* ("Farington Diary," p. 2624, April 20, 1804). Animosities in the academy persisted, with an argument over the issue of whether or not artists could take their families to the exhibition opening. It was ruled, to the annoyance of Copley, Beechey, and Hoppner, that only one guest could be taken. Feeling ran so high the day before the opening that, when West arrived at the academy and learned from Farington that Copley and Beechey were upstairs, "He wd. not go up" (*ibid.*, p. 2632, April 26, 1804). Copley was so piqued at not being able to have his family at the opening that he stayed home (*ibid.*, p. 2633, April 27, 1804).

were generally kind to Copley, although they did not say much. There was some disagreement over the "likeness" of *Graham*, but *Mrs. Montague* was considered "graceful and elegant; and the general effect is extremely rich and harmonious." *Mrs. Derby* was also thought elegant, "and the countenance extremely beautiful." But West said "that Copley's whole length of a Lady as St. Cecilia . . . appeared to have been painted piece by piece; there was no whole in it, — no union." [5]

The portrait of *Sir Robert Graham* (fig. 653) is similar in character to the series of seated male portraits related to the *Earl of Mansfield* (fig. 429). It is perhaps a little drier and more rigid than the earlier efforts and the face has a pinched quality, but the total effect is pleasing. In the *Montague* double portrait (fig. 652), a vase on a pedestal on the right is a familiar compositional element, and Robert Copley's pose, with a foot on a stool, echoes *Henry Laurens* (fig. 416), of twenty years earlier. The picture is a prettily posed and sweetly charming confection, but the figures are listless dolls that lack strength and character. The portrait of *Mrs. Derby* seems better, but the figure is small for the canvas, and the presence of the putti in the upper left indicates that Copley had only learned a partial lesson from his *Knatchbull* experience — at least he did not turn the putti into departed relatives.

After the exhibition, Copley, who was not often ill, "was seized with a numbness in his hand, which likewise affected his legs and feet." It did not prove serious. He took some "bark," and after a few weeks young Copley could write to his sister in Boston that their father was "again well and cheerful, and as industrious and indefatigable as ever." He added, "He is at present employed in painting an equestrian picture of the Prince of Wales, which is to rival the Charles of Vandyck and the Ferdinand of Rubens." Copley had undertaken this equestrian portrait of the Prince of Wales in 1804 on his own initiative. After completing a sketch of it, he took it to the prince, who was pleased and promised "to sit for the likeness when he returns to town." Although Copley worked on the picture throughout the fall and presumably much of the winter, he was not able to complete it in time for the exhibition of 1805 and had to content himself with exhibiting a currently unlocated portrait bust of *Mr. Cawthorne*.[6]

Instead of achieving security, tranquillity, and honors in the last years of his career, Copley encountered strife, rebuffs, and a constant economic struggle to maintain himself and his family on George Street. The bickering in the Royal Academy did not stop. Copley as a member of the council in 1802–03 had enjoyed a position of some strength from which to do battle with his foes, but throughout 1804 he was on the outside and the council was packed with West's supporters. The council had its way to such an extent that in the middle of 1805 Copley found himself one of seventeen academicians calling for a meeting of the general assembly, "to enquire into certain alledged irregu-

[5] The *Daily Advertiser*, May 5, 1804, called *Graham* an "indifferent likeness," but the *Times* of April 28, 1804, called it a "strong likeness." *Morning Post*, April 28, 1804; "Farington Diary," p. 2621, April 19, 1804.

[6] Amory, pp. 258–59, Mrs. Copley to Mrs. Greene, July 28, 1804; p. 265, Copley, Jr., to Mrs. Greene, Sept. 3, 1804; p. 266, Mrs. Copley to Mrs. Greene, Oct. 29, 1804.

larities of Council & to examine into the state of the Academy." Farington, finding himself on the council and defending its authority against Copley, who was now calling for an assembly investigation, could not resist twitting Copley on this reversal of their positions.[7]

In December 1805 West resigned as president of the Royal Academy. Wyatt was elected in his place for the coming year, and Copley was made a visitor.[8] But the insurgents were only in power for a year, and by 1807 West was back in office. Copley, nursing his wounds, planned not to go to the academy again as a result of the "disrespect shown to a man of his reputation." But actually, nearing seventy, the battles and disputes for Copley were now more a matter of habit than conviction. He was a beaten old man with a head and heart full of bitterness, disillusionment, and disappointment. He could not triumph over West and his party in the academy, and even when minor victories were scored his fellows in the opposition did not accept or honor him as their leader. Mrs. Copley confided to her daughter in Boston on February 20, 1807: "Your father often regrets that he did not [return to America] many years since, but these retrospects are vain." [9]

Copley had many problems. He could not get the Prince of Wales to sit so that he could finish the large equestrian portrait. He could not get Sharp to finish the *Gibraltar* engraving, which he felt certain would help him out of his financial difficulties. He received a humiliating rebuff from George III in the middle of 1806. The king in general was disgusted with artists, their squabbles and their impositions upon his generosity. He had made up his mind never to sit for a portrait again and, according to Northcote who related the narrative to Farington, vowed that "if any person shd. ask him twice [to sit for a portrait] He would turn Him out of the House." Unaware of the king's frame of mind, Copley went to the palace and placed himself in a room through which he knew the king would pass. When King George appeared, Copley asked him if he could speak to him in private. "Whatever you have to say you may speak here," the king replied. "Copley then humbly requested that His Majesty would sit to Him for a Portrait. To which the King hastily replied, '*Sit to you for a Portrait. What do you want to make a Show of me*'. — and went off indignantly." All of this could not help but weaken the aging Copley's spirit. One day in December 1807 Copley astonished Farington by coming up to him and conversing "civilly" for "the first time in several years." Farington observed that Copley "appeared to me to have suffered much in His faculties: His mind seemed to be incapable of comprehending what was going forward." [10]

But there were occasional bright spots. One of these was a commission reported in

[7] "Farington Diary," pp. 3000, 3005–06, May 31 and June 6, 1805. Shortly afterwards an attack on Farington appeared in the press. Shee maintained that Copley and his son were responsible. Farington also blamed Soane, Tresham, and Bourgeois, finally narrowing it down to Copley and Soane, but he decided not to honor the attack with a reply (pp. 3050–51, 3062, Aug. 5 and Sept. 3, 1805).

[8] One of Copley's standing complaints was that his opponents for many years had prevented him from serving as a visitor to the academy. "Farington Diary," p. 3005, June 6, 1805.
[9] *Ibid.*, pp. 3558–59, Jan. 13, 1807; Amory, p. 284.
[10] "Farington Diary," pp. 3321–22, 3913, June 17, 1806, and Dec. 22, 1807.

January 1806 from "Thomson, the Print seller — of Newport Street" to paint *The Death of Lord Nelson* for twelve hundred pounds or guineas. Thomson intended to have the picture engraved and sold by subscription. But this bright hope faded quickly: Mrs. Copley reported to her daughter in August of this year that the artist had sprained his arm in a fall, which "prevented him from using his brush, and interfered with his finishing the picture of Lord Nelson." Since the time factor in producing reportorial engravings was of critical importance if the public's interest was to be captured, Copley's unfortunate accident presumably voided the agreement with Thomson. Benjamin West's version of the Nelson subject was completed before mid-1806, including a number of portraits of participants, and other versions were executed while Copley was inactive. As with the planned "Installation of the Order of St. Patrick" twenty-four years earlier, the project was apparently abandoned. Copley's picture was not engraved, and it is possible that he did not finish it.[11]

One happy event was the successful sale by lottery for two thousand guineas of *The Death of Chatham* on June 27, 1806. Alexander Davison, who drew the winning lot, in that year initiated a program of commissioning history paintings from English artists. The central provision of each commission was that the subject be drawn from English history, but the actual choice of subject was left to the artist. Copley received one of the first commissions from Davison, and during the late part of 1806 and the early part of 1807 painted for him *The Offer of the Crown to Lady Jane Gray* (fig. 654), later described in the Davison sale catalogue as follows:

> The composition of this subject represents, to the left, Lady Jane as having arisen from her seat, supported by her husband Lord Guilford Dudley, whose importunities are said to have principally prevailed upon her to receive the Crown, which is offered to her by his father the Duke of Northumberland, who with the Duke of Suffolk, her own father, are seen kneeling before her, and soliciting her acceptance of it. Behind them the Earl of Pembroke appears, joining his entreaties also with theirs; and Cranmer, Archbishop of Canterbury, with others assisting on the occasion, fill up the group to the right, in which the Portrait of the Artist is introduced. The scene lies in a state apartment of Sion House, as supposed to have formed a part of that ancient religious structure.[12]

The sale of *Chatham* and the Davison commission for *Lady Jane Gray* temporarily alleviated Copley's financial problems (and even enabled him to repurchase his masterpiece, *The Death of Peirson*, at the Boydell sale), but by no means solved them. He found it continually necessary to borrow money from relatives and friends.[13]

---

[11] *Ibid.*, p. 3144, Jan. 13, 1806; Amory, p. 281, Mrs. Copley to Mrs. Greene, Aug. 23, 1806.

[12] *A Catalogue . . . Subjects taken from English History: Painted expressly for Alexander Davison, Esq.*, Stanley's, June 28, 1823. The picture was not ready to be delivered in time for Davison's banquet on April 4, 1807, but was hanging in the dining room of his home on St. James's Square when

the Copley family visited there on June 22, 1807. "Farington Diary," p. 2645, April 5, 1807; Amory, p. 286, Mary Copley to Mrs. Greene.

[13] Copley had been in financial straits for more than ten years. While his son was still at Cambridge, Copley had found it necessary to write an engraver, to whom he owed forty pounds, requesting an extension so as not to interrupt his son's "honourable

Copley exhibited a larger version of *Lady Jane Gray* at the Royal Academy in 1808 (fig. 655). He felt so strongly about making a good showing that he stunned West by calling upon him to see about obtaining a favorable position for the picture "over the Chimney." [14] The painting was featured in the exhibition and was listed first in the catalogue. Although the *Morning Post* review of May 7 objected to the high coloring of the picture, it declared that "the drapery, the ornaments of the apartments, and the general management of the back ground, are all highly creditable to the conception and taste of the Artist; nor is he less entitled to commendation for the ability he displays in the prospective [*sic*] both lineal and aerial." In addition to *Lady Jane Gray*, Copley also exhibited a portrait, *Reverend John Codman* (fig. 660). This was the fourth Codman family portrait Copley had painted, preceded by *Richard Codman* (fig. 657), and two older generations of *John Codmans* (fig. 658 is said to be a copy after a painting by Thomas Johnston, taken to England from Boston by the sitter's son, the John Codman in fig. 659).

The Offer of the Crown to Lady Jane Gray is reminiscent compositionally of a predecessor scene from English history, *Charles I Demanding the Five Impeached Members* (fig. 599). There is a similar gothic interior with a large glazed opening on the right. In both pictures figures on the right are placed in relationship to a prominent standing royal (or potentially royal) figure on the left. The key individuals in the right-hand group are kneeling, while standing figures in the right foreground close the

career at the University, and its promise of future success" (Martin, p. 523). In 1800 he had a bill for one hundred pounds fall due to the firm of Williams and Brooks (British Museum, Department of Manuscripts, Copley to Messrs. Williams and Brooks, Jan. 10, 1800). During the time of his 1803 conflicts in the Royal Academy, he borrowed money from his ally, the architect John Soane (Soane Museum, Copley to Soane, n.d. [1803 watermark]), and this debt had not been discharged by the time of his death. In November 1803 Copley asked Gardiner Greene for a loan of a thousand pounds in order to help young Copley get his start at the bar; Greene obliged and received the thanks of both father and son (Amory, pp. 249–51, 255, 257). In subsequent years Copley found it continuously necessary to borrow money from his family and friends (Amory, pp. 293–94, 303–04; "Farington Diary," p. 4142; Soane Museum, Copley to Soane, Dec. 29, 1809, March 24, 1814, and Copley, Jr., to Soane, May 30, 1814). During this period Copley attributed his inability to repay his debts primarily to Sharp's delay in producing the engraving of *Gibraltar*. He anticipated that the *Gibraltar* engraving would bring in £8–10,000 when completed (Amory, p. 294, Copley to Gardiner Greene, June 19, 1809). Sharp was slow, perhaps interrupting his work on *Gibraltar* to undertake more immediately lucrative jobs. He complained to Marchant that, although he was to get £2000 from Copley for the engraving, none of it

was paid in advance ("Farington Diary," p. 4142, Feb. 10, 1808). When the engraving was finally completed in 1810, according to a report Farington heard, Sharp stationed a man in Copley's house to take the money received as subscribers called for their prints (*ibid.*, p. 4576, June 26, 1810). By the following summer the financial failure of the *Gibraltar* engraving was apparent. Many of the original subscribers could not be located, some were dead, and some no longer wanted the engraving sufficiently to pay the remainder of the subscription price. Opportunities for overseas sale were closed. Sharp took two thirds of the money received, reported at £600, in mid-1811. Copley had anticipated a much higher increment and had borrowed accordingly. For a while the possibility loomed that the George Street house would have to be abandoned (*ibid.*, p. 1813, May 20, 1811).

[14] "Farington Diary," p. 4024, March 30, 1808. Mary Copley described the original picture, while it was being painted for Davison, as four and one half feet high and four feet wide (Amory, p. 283, Mary Copley to Mrs. Greene, Jan. 28, 1807). But the picture exhibited at the Royal Academy was much larger than that and is almost certainly the version that was offered for sale unsuccessfully the following year at the British Institution, later sold at the Lyndhurst Sale and now hanging in the Somerset Club, Boston.

composition. Both pictures seem to owe a general debt to an engraving after Rubens by Schelte à Bolswert that Copley owned, *Salome Before Herod with the Head of John the Baptist* (fig. 656).[15] There is a similar large architectural opening on the right, with a group of figures on the right arrayed around a royal figure on the left. Herod is thus akin to Lady Jane Gray or, more closely, to Charles I with matching throne and rakish hat, his left leg extended like that of Prince Rupert in Copley's picture. Salome offering the head of John the Baptist is akin to Speaker Lenthall or to the kneeling figures offering the crown to Lady Jane Gray, and the print source has similar figures in the right foreground facing into the composition. The small group of figures in the background of *Charles I Demanding* echoes a similarly placed statuary group in the engraving. However, it is also like similar figures raised up in the right background of *The Death of Chatham.*

Copley exhibited a second portrait of *Viscount Sidmouth* (probably fig. 616) at the academy in 1809, but nothing else. The following year he was at last able to complete and exhibit the large equestrian portrait of *George IV (as Prince of Wales)* (fig. 661), which he had initially planned to exhibit five years earlier. The project had become more ambitious than originally planned, with the addition of attending officers and an encampment in the distance. The composition is heavily indebted to Van Dyck's portrait of *The Duke of Arenburg* (fig. 662), probably through the engraving by Pieter de Bailliu, which Copley owned,[16] with the same device of mounted figures visible in the middle distance beneath the rearing horse, and use of the same kind of foliage in the lower left and the tree arrangement in the upper right. For a long time after beginning the painting, Copley had found it very difficult to induce the prince to sit, and not until the middle of 1808 was he back at work on the picture in earnest. Hoping to finish it in time for the academy exhibition of 1809, he requested an extension of time from the council in the name of the Prince of Wales, but this was denied.[17] Copley did not actually finish the large picture until August 1809, when the prince at last agreed to a final sitting.[18]

The equestrian portrait was prominently displayed in the 1810 exhibition. Copley optimistically hoped that it would be well received, but, as Mrs. Copley told Elizabeth, they knew from experience to expect adverse criticism.[19] Thus they were perhaps able to accept with equanimity this descriptive review:

A very large canvas, covered with what is not very likely to mislead the public taste. The

[15] See appendix, Copley Print Sale (74).

[16] See appendix, Copley Print Sale (98).

[17] According to Farington, Copley went to West's house at 9.00 A.M. on the day of the council meeting and, on being told that West was engaged, entered anyway and demanded an extension in the name of the prince. West demurred and said it had to go through the council. The council turned down the request, and West so informed the prince and Copley. Copley wrote back that the prince said that in 1807 his portrait by Hoppner had been allowed an extension, but the council refused to alter its stand. "Farington Diary," pp. 4191–92, April 2, 1809; "Council Minutes," IV, 115–20, April 1 and April 5, 1809.

[18] Amory, pp. 270–71, Mrs. Copley to Mrs. Greene, June 4, 1805; p. 291, Mary Copley to Mrs. Greene, Aug. 9, 1809; p. 295, Mrs. Copley to Mrs. Greene, Aug. 23, 1809.

[19] *Ibid.*, p. 298, April 10, 1810.

officers in the back-ground are too diminutive, and make the Prince look like a Brobdignag general at a Lilliputian review. The colouring offends, from the large daubs of deep blue, plastered on in profusion, and relieved by the black hide of the charger that carries his Royal Highness; between whose legs, and in the distance, are seen a host of little figures, seemingly cut out of pasteboard or tin. The Prince looks like an apparition of the old exploded taste of Hyacinthe Rigaud, so happily ridiculed by Hogarth, in the back-ground of his first picture in "Marriage a la Mode." [20]

The equestrian portrait is in no sense a successful picture, although it is not as poor in its parts as it is in the whole. For example, the color is bold and strong, and the portraits on the right are well studied and effective in themselves. But Copley attempted to pack a quantity of additional details into a standard equestrian portrait. The portraits on the right are unassimilated, and the antlike procession seen in the distance through the legs of the prince's black charger is even more distressing. This skimpy group is quite different from the massed distant cavalry in the Van Dyck source. Drawings for the large picture (figs. 663–666) also clearly reveal the decline in Copley's powers, particularly fig. 664, with the stiff rider as large as his misshapen mount, and fig. 666, in which there is no feeling of life in either the poorly drawn and crudely outlined horse or the rider.

The two events that Copley had counted on for financial relief, the publication of the *Gibraltar* engraving and the exhibition of *George IV*, took place in 1810. Copley had been frustrated over a period of years in his attempts to complete these projects by the dilatoriness of the central figures, the engraver Sharp and the Prince of Wales. Now when the print was published, the proceeds were disappointing; and when the equestrian portrait was exhibited, the critical response was unfriendly. Whatever prospects existed for selling the portrait, notably to the prince if it had been well received, passed. Possible income from an engraving of it awaited completion of the plate. Hard times were earnestly felt at George Street, and among other economies the family had to give up a country house in Fulham, which they had enjoyed since 1804. [21]

While Copley was in such financial straits he had reason to envy West, who had retained all of his prestige as president of the Royal Academy and could still turn out

[20] "Exhibition of Paintings, Somerset House," *Repository of Arts, Literature, Commerce, Manufactures, Fashions, and Politics*, III (June 1810), 366. A more restrained reviewer merely noted, "Mr. Copley has furnished another colossal production, the Prince of Wales on horseback, — certainly not good" ([Louis Simond], *Journal of a Tour and Residence in Great Britain During the Years 1810 and 1811, by a French Traveller* [Edinburgh, 1815], I, 128). A wordy review written in the tone of a tolerant rebuke for the poor performance pointed out that Copley was a republican, the son of "an exemplary Parish Clerk at Salem," according to the governor of Massachusetts, and was not an aristocrat or courtier as his flattering brush might suggest (the picture flattered the Prince of Wales by making him appear much younger than he really was). The other figures were "accurately drawn as to resemblances," although the horse, with legs going in all directions, was not graceful (*Morning Herald*, May 29, 1810).

[21] The house, called Walnut Tree Cottage, was on the east side of North End Road, north of the intersection of Lillie Road and very close to Cambridge Lodge, which Bartolozzi the engraver occupied in 1780–1802 and which was occupied by another engraver, John Vendramini, until 1809. "Fulham Poor Rate and Overseers' Acts," Fulham Public Library; Charles James Fèret, *Fulham Old and New* (London, 1900), pp. 268–74.

mammoth canvases that sold for handsome prices; Copley's own works lined the walls of his studio. Mrs. Copley wrote in September 1811 to her daughter of West's great success with *Christ Healing the Sick*, which he had sold for three thousand guineas. Copley by that time had almost completed his own picture on a religious theme, *The Resurrection*, now unlocated, which he exhibited at the academy the following year.[22] Copley could only emulate West in the formula, not in the results. The picture, the last he was to exhibit at the academy, passed virtually unnoticed. The hopeful subject matter found no counterpart in Copley's personal fortunes, which remained as depressed as before.

Four unidentified drawings (figs. 667–670) probably date from this general period. They apparently are intended for a history painting depicting the death of a military figure, perhaps the death of Sir John Moore at Corunna, an event of 1809. The cannon crew in figs. 667 and 668 is a feeble compositional echo of the vigorous and colorful group hauling on the recalcitrant cannon in *The Victory of Duncan*.

Copley's last years of serious activity at the Royal Academy were 1810–11 when he served on the council. West was frequently absent and ailing, and Copley as senior council member usually chaired the meetings. Council minutes for this period frequently begin: "The President in the Gout, Mr. Copley in the Chair." Copley involved himself in very little controversy, and most of his functions were social or honorary. He helped to hang the 1810 exhibition, customarily chaired events in West's absence, attended the academy banquet, and so on. Copley chaired his last council meeting on December 28, 1811.[23]

In the face of the financial worries that harrassed him to the day of his death, Copley was haunted by the bitter memory of the sale of his Boston property. When Farington spoke with West about Copley's "dejected appearance," West related how Copley told him that he had originally paid seven hundred pounds for the land and sold it for seven thousand pounds. After the high ground of Beacon Hill had been selected by the wealthy as a residential area, the land was worth a hundred thousand pounds. Farington wrote, "upon this He ruminates, & with other reflections founded upon disappointment, Passes these His latter days unhappily." [24]

---

[22] Amory, p. 302, Sept. 23, 1811.

[23] "Council Minutes," RA, IV, 319. One bit of dissension in the council occurred early in 1811 when it was proposed that John Soane be removed from his professorship of architecture for failure to present his lectures. Copley had been Soane's ally in the past and, further, was in his debt. Since he was presiding, Copley refused to consider the question, quit the chair, and the meeting broke up. A few nights later the council met again, put Nollekens in the chair, and passed the motion over the vote of Copley and Yenn; the vote was later rescinded (*ibid.*, IV, 277–79, Feb. 15 and 18, 1811).

Anthony Pasquin published a satire on the Royal Academy dinner of 1810 in the *Morning Herald*, April 30, 1810. One of the satirical jabs stressed West's and Copley's orientation toward money, not touching at all on their highly disparate abilities to earn it. In Pasquin's imaginary scene the American minister asks West and Copley to sing a duet (to the tune of *Yankee Doodle*). After the first stanza by West, Copley sings two: "From Massachusetts rebel state, / When loyalty was crying, / I ran on shipboard here to paint / Lord *Chatham*, who was dying. / Then I hung up the House of Peers / (Though some were quite unwilling) / And gave the groupe to public view, / And showed them for — a shilling!" The chorus after each stanza, for West and Copley, goes: "Let *David* paint for hungry fame; / And *Wilkie* subjects funny; / Let *Turner* sit and study storms, / But we will paint for money!"

[24] "Farington Diary," p. 5973, Nov. 30, 1811.

As Copley attended the academy in his final term as a council member, Farington and West noted his decline. Farington commented, "His mind seemed to be clear, but I saw in Copley's look the appearance of age and imbecility, a weakness." A year later he noted to West, who agreed, that Copley's appearance had changed greatly, "having a look of imbecility, and a sort of absent, bewildered manner." The young American artist, Samuel F. B. Morse, wrote to friends on September 17, 1811:

> I visited Mr. Copley a few days since. He is very old and infirm. I think his age is upward of seventy, nearly the age of Mr. West. His powers of mind have almost entirely left him; his late paintings are miserable; it is really a lamentable thing that a man should outlive his faculties. He has been a first-rate painter, as you well know. I saw at his room some exquisite pieces which he painted twenty or thirty years ago, but his paintings of the last four or five years are very bad. He was very pleasant, however, and agreeable in his manners.[25]

In his old age Copley gave up his customary walks but continued to paint, which he enjoyed. On August 16, 1813, Mrs. Copley wrote to Elizabeth that her father was "painting some portraits," but that "he finds that he cannot apply as closely as he used to do." Among the portraits he was working on may have been the half-lengths of the *Prince of Orange*, later William VII, King of Holland (figs. 671 and 672), a mezzotint of which was published in 1813. This figure also appears, with a scroll instead of a sword, in the large canvas of *The Battle of the Pyrenees* (fig. 673), to the left of the Duke of Wellington. Copley undertook the large painting with the idea — never fulfilled — of exhibiting it at the academy in 1814. In that year he managed to obtain a sitting from the Duke of Wellington. A drawing of a mounted figure (fig. 674), with a curving sword similar to that held by the Prince of Orange in the large pictures, may be an early project for it.[26]

Copley apparently felt that not all of the Beacon Hill estate had been sold to the Mason-Otis group, and in 1805 he fought a claim to a small piece of land by one Bill Vose (Amory, p. 272ff). The land issue came up again in 1809 when litigation in Boston required a clarification of the land title and Copley was asked for the original deed. When he could not produce it, he was asked for a deposition to the effect that his title was good. Since in his opinion the land had been taken from him unjustly, he felt that these people had no right to ask him for favors, especially when it involved rendering them secure in their title to the land. The legal attempts to get Copley to sign an affidavit about the deed, even with the assistance of young Copley and Copley's nephew, Henry Bromfield, Jr., brought out all of the stubbornness in Copley's nature. The lawyers found him mulish and impossible to deal with. When they asked him to sign, he would often mutter something about being busy with his painting and unable to spare any daylight (Amory, p. 300, Mrs. Copley to Mrs. Greene, Dec. 11, 1810;

Massachusetts Historical Society, Michael Joy, London, to Benjamin Joy, Boston, Dec. 1810 and Jan. 1811). Finally Copley signed the deposition on Jan 22, 1812, affirming the legality of his purchase of the Boston land in 1769 from Chardon and the successful defense of the title against a suit by Bannister (SPNEA).

[25] "Farington Diary," pp. 4627, 5963–64, Aug. 17, 1810, and Nov. 21, 1811; Edward L. Morse, ed., *Samuel F. B. Morse: His Letters and Journals* (Boston and New York, 1914), I, 47.

[26] Amory, p. 308, Aug. 16, 1813; "Varieties, Literary and Philosophical," *Monthly Magazine: or, British Register*, XXXVI (Dec. 1813), 432–33. Thomas Lawrence told Farington on July 15, 1814, that when he painted the Duke of Wellington, the "Duke had sat at home in mrng. to Copley for prepared picture" ("Farington Diary," p. 6568). This must have happened not long before, since the duke sat to Lawrence in 1814 (Kenneth Garlick, *Sir Thomas Lawrence* [London, 1954], p. 62).

The large canvas of the *Pyrenees* is alarmingly poor in concept and design, clearly reflecting the extent of Copley's artistic disintegration. The portrait of the *Prince of Orange* is not nearly so bad, but is a feeble effort compared to Copley's earlier works. Although Copley's courage as a colorist is still reflected in the play of red and black, the vitality that once characterized his style is gone. The pigment seems flat, dry, and in certain areas muted to the point of muddiness. The value contrasts are fairly strong, but lack the flickering energy of the earlier works. The pose is stiff, and, although there is still clarity in the delineation of details, the effect is static. Mrs. Copley wrote to her daughter on April 7, 1814, that despite increasing feebleness Copley had undertaken still another new painting,[27] possibly the depressingly inept *Siege of Dunkirk* (fig. 678), the sole distinction of which is that it may be Copley's last history painting. In July 1815, Copley apparently went for a vacation to Stapleton, then a small rural hamlet outside of Bristol. There he wrote a poem, "Lines for a Garden-Seat at Stapleton." Its last stanza suggests the serenity he now sought and perhaps also indicates the feelings of a seventy-seven-year-old painter, steeped in eighteenth-century classicism and rationalism, in response to a newer way of looking at the world.

> Some may the wilder prospects hail,
>   Where torrents foam, and mountains rise;
> But Stapleton's Delightful Vale
>   Will charm the pensive and the wise.[28]

Copley was felled by a stroke at dinner on August 11, 1815. His mind remained clear, but his left side was paralyzed and he could not speak so as to be understood. The doctors held out hope for a partial recovery, but on September 9 he died, peacefully.[29]

The Copleys continued at George Street. Young John Copley, who had long been the apple of his family's eye and who was obviously destined for success in law and politics, became the support of his mother and spinster sister, Mary. At first times were

[27] Amory, p. 309.
[28] Boston Public Library, Ch. J.5.72.
[29] Amory, pp. 310–13, Mary Copley to Mrs. Greene, Aug. 18 and 29, Sept. 1 and 9, 1815. Copley died intestate, and the estate was valued at £1500, with administration granted to Mrs. Copley (Principal Probate Registry, Somerset House, Administration Acts, July 3, 1817). This £1500 was the valuation of pictures left in the studio, according to a list Mrs. Copley enclosed in her letter to Mrs. Greene, received on June 23, 1821 (Boston Public Library, Ch. F.6.4). *Charles I* was valued most highly at £500. The equestrian portrait of *George IV*, *The Death of Peirson*, and the collection of prints were each rated at £250. *Lady Jane Gray* and *Saul and Samuel* were valued at £125 apiece. A version of *Watson and the Shark*, *Samuel and Eli*, *The Resurrection*, and a copy of *Gibraltar*, as well as a group of old-master copies, were not assigned any value. After his father's death Copley, Jr., wrote to John Soane of the heavy claims upon the estate held by Gardiner Greene and Isaac Winslow Clarke, and noted that he himself had "advanced upwards of 2000£ upon my late father's acc^t and I am *still* under very considerable engagements for him." He regretted not being able to settle his father's debts immediately, but thought that the property, if "prudently managed," would satisfy all claims. He noted that all details "respecting my late fathers debts and assets are in the hands of Messrs Lambert and Son, Bedford Row, my mothers solicitors" (Soane Museum, Feb. 28, 1816). This firm's successor lost all of its early records during the last war (letter to the author from Andrew, Purves, Sutton & Creery, Feb. 4, 1959).

hard because of Copley's debts. There was virtually no market for the paintings left in the studio, and an auction of Copley's collection of prints in 1820 was disappointing in the proceeds it yielded. But eventually the home on George Street again became a focal point for creative activity as the brilliant career of another Copley unfolded. John Singleton Copley, Jr. (fig. 677), at the time of his father's death, had already enjoyed marked success as a lawyer and had shown great promise for the future.[30] He was elected to Parliament in 1818, knighted and made solicitor general the following year, and in April 1827 was created Baron Lyndhurst and became lord chancellor, the first holder of that office to have been born outside Great Britain. He served as lord chancellor twice more during a long and distinguished career of public service. His mother witnessed his rise to eminence before her death at the age of ninety on January 11, 1830.

Copley the artist had begun his professional career in 1753 as a boy of fifteen in the American colonies. During the next twenty-one years he distinguished himself as an American artist who would remain without peer until the advent of Winslow Homer and Thomas Eakins a century later. Following his departure from America he set out upon a new career in England, primarily as a history painter. There, in company with his fellow American Benjamin West, he carried that branch of art to new levels of effectiveness.

The broadest characteristic of Copley's art is realism, whether in the accurate delineation of colonial Americans or in the painstaking re-creation of historic scenes. But the elements that give his best works lasting quality go deeper than this. Although Copley possessed a strong and clear intelligence, his greatest gifts as an artist were sensual rather than intellectual. He loved to paint, and took a craftsman's delight in the materials of his trade and the process of applying paint to canvas. His picture surfaces are vibrant, reflecting his facility with the brush and belying the great care he took to achieve desired results. He was more at ease in handling problems of color and light than those of draughtsmanship and composition, but it was all of these formal aspects of art, and the techniques that contributed to their successful realization, that interested him. The more ideational possibilities of art he left to colleagues like Benjamin West and Joshua Reynolds. He was no theoretician, and his few pronouncements tended to be pragmatic rather than abstract.

Looking back over Copley's long and productive career, one finds that the question of the relative merit of his English and American work lacks pertinence. The fascination that this question has held for many writers on American art, and the rather consistent conclusion that the American pictures are better than the English ones,

[30] As early as May 1809, Farington recorded the opinion expressed by a Mr. Reynolds, who had been on the Midland circuit with young Copley, that he was "a vain young man of extraordinary abilities" and that there was "no one more likely to become Lord Chancellor." "Farington Diary," p. 4216, May 3, 1809.

seems based more on nationalistic than on artistic considerations. The temptation to split Copley into two artists — good in America and poor in England — has done him a disservice. Indeed there were times in Copley's career when his achievements were below par aesthetically, but these periods occur where one might expect to find them: at the very beginning, when he struggled to shape his style and to transcend the limitations of contemporary colonial art, and at the very end, when age, hard times, and disillusionment combined to deprive his mind of acuity and his hand of skill. But for over thirty years in between, divided between America and England with an Italian journey in the middle, Copley's achievements were notable. It hardly seems possible to say whether Copley was a better artist as a successful portraitist in Boston in 1769 or as a triumphant history painter in London in 1783. But it is possible to recognize that Copley successfully applied his special artistic gifts to a variety of problems. His versatility and, above all, the quality of his best pictures produced both in America and in England constitute the true index of his artistic power and his final achievement.

Appendices

Pictures Exhibited by Copley

The Copley Print Sale

The Lyndhurst Library Sale

The Lyndhurst Sale

Pictures Exhibited by Copley

The following items are transcriptions of entries in exhibition catalogues of pictures exhibited by Copley during his lifetime. Minor changes in capitalization and punctuation have been made. Titles and numbers in brackets at the end of entries refer to figures shown in this book, whenever it has been possible to identify the objects. Otherwise the picture remains unidentified or unlocated.

SOCIETY OF ARTISTS

1766

24. A boy with a flying squirrel. [*Henry Pelham*, 163; exhibited as by "Mr. William Copeley, Boston, New England"]

1767

28. Portrait of a young lady, with a bird and dog; full length. [*Mary Warner(?)*, 164; exhibited as by "Mr. William Copeley, Boston, New England"]

1768

23. Portrait of a gentleman; half length. [*Mr. Rogers*, 217?]
24. Portrait of a lady; in crayons.

1768 (special)

19. A boy playing with a squirrel. [163]

1771

22. A lady; half length. [*Mrs. Humphrey Devereux*, 283]

1772

50. A lady; half length. [*Mrs. Thomas Gage*, 284]

ROYAL ACADEMY

1776

62. A conversation. [*Mr. and Mrs. Ralph Izard*, 342]

1777

61. A family; whole length. [*Copley Family*, 344]
62. A portrait of a gentleman; whole length.
63. A portrait of a gentleman; three quarters.
64. The Nativity. [347]

1778

63. A family; whole length. [*Pepperrell Family*, 356]
64. Portrait of a lady; three quarters.
65. A boy attacked by a shark, and rescued by some seamen in a boat; founded on a fact which happened in the harbour of the Havannah. [*Watson and the Shark*; 371]

1780

97. Portrait of a lady.
172. Portrait of an Highland officer. [*Major Montgomerie*, 389]
195. Portrait of a gentleman. [*George Boone Roupell*, 388]
211. Portrait of a naval officer. [*Joshua Loring*]

1783

5. Portrait of a nobleman. [*Earl of Mansfield*, 429]
227. Portraits of two young gentlemen. [*Western Brothers*, 436]

1785

80. Their Royal Highnesses Princess Mary, Princess Sophia, and Princess Amelia. [468]

1786

230. Portrait of a lady; half length.

423. Portraits of a young lady and her three brothers. [*Sitwell Family*, 477]

1793
75. The Red Cross Knight, Fidelia, and Speranza; *vide* Spenser's *Fairy Queen*, book I, canto 10. [592]

1796
46. Abraham offering up Isaac. [606]
91. Portrait of a gentleman.
287. Portrait of a gentleman. [*John Adams*, 438]

1798
73. Portrait of J. A. Graham, Esq., L.L.D. [617]
101. Portrait of the Speaker of the House of Commons. [*Viscount Sidmouth*, 614]
107. An historical picture, representing Hagar and Ishmael in the wilderness. "Arise, lift up the Lad. — Gen. c. 21. v. 18." [609]
111. Portrait of Lord Viscount Duncan. [620]
235. An historical picture, representing Saul reproved by Samuel. "The Lord hath sent the Kingdom of Israel from thee this day. — First Book of Samuel, ch. 15, ver. 28." [610]

1800
24. Portrait of Earl Spencer. [629]
72. Portrait of Lady Dudley and Ward. [632]
108. Portrait of Lord Viscount Dudley. [631]
556. Portrait of R. Wilson, Esq.

1801
21. Portraits of the late Col. Fitch and the Miss Fitches. [635]

163. Portrait of R. Richards, Esq., of Lincoln's-inn.

1803
70. Portrait of Earl of Northampton. [650]

1804
21. Portrait of Baron Graham. [653]
31. Portrait of Mrs. Montague, lady of Rear Admiral Montague, and her brother. [652]
96. Portrait of the Right Honorable Lord Viscount Dudley and Ward. [probably 630]
184. St. Cecilia, a portrait. [Ten-line quotation from Dryden's *Ode*, from "at last divine Cecilia came" to "She drew an angel down."] [651]

1805
183. Portrait of Mr. Cawthorne.

1808
1. The offer of the Crown to Lady Jane Gray, by the Dukes of Northumberland and Suffolk, and other Lords, deputies of the Privy Council. [Quotation from Hume's *History of England*, vol. IV, ch. 36.] [655]
146. Portrait of the Rev. Mr. J. Codman, of Boston, New England. [660]

1809
201. Portrait of Lord Sidmouth. [616]

1810
58. Portrait of His R. H. the Prince of Wales at a review, attended by Lord Heathfield, General Turner, Col. Bloomfield, and Baron Eben; Col. Quintin in the distance. [661]

1812
188. The Resurrection. [Quotation from Matthew, 28.2.]

BRITISH INSTITUTION

1806
16. The death of the Earl of Chatham. [392]
45. Hagar and Ishmael in the wilderness. [609]
51. Abraham offering up his son Isaac. [606]
63. Saul reproved by Samuel, for not obeying the commandments of the Lord. — I *Samuel*, xv, 28. [610]

1807
62. King Charles I demanding in the House of Commons the five impeached members. 11. 3 x 8. 9. [599]
110. A youth rescued from a shark in the Harbour of the Havanna. 7. 0 x 8. 7. [372]

1809
130. The offer of the crown to Lady Jane Gray, by the Dukes of Northumberland, Suffolk, and other Lords, deputies of the Privy Council. *Vide* Hume's *History of England*, vol. IV, ch. 36. 8. 6 x 7. 10 [including frame]. [655]

1811
76. Samuel relating to Eli the judgments of God upon Eli's house. 8. 0 x 6. 6 [probably including frame]. "Then Eli called Samuel, and said, What is the thing that the Lord hath said unto thee? And Samuel told him every whit, and hid nothing from him, and he said, it is the Lord: Let him do what seemeth him good. — one Sam. ch. iii, ver. 16, 17, 18." [destroyed replica of 391]

The Copley Print Sale

A Catalogue of the Genuine Collection of Prints and Copper Plates,
The Property of the late John Singleton Copley, Esq., RA. & F.S.A.
Mr. Sotheby, Feb. 15 & 17, 1820

This transcript is from a priced copy of the sale catalogue at the British Museum. There is another copy at the Victoria and Albert Museum, dated Jan. 26–27, 1820. The original spellings, italics, and capitals in the catalogue are retained. The number at the end of each entry refers to the number of items in the lot; the purchase price for Copley items is given in parentheses (when available).

The sale contained, in addition to a large number of engravings after paintings by Copley, approximately 1125 prints and 16 bound volumes, as well as several miscellaneous portfolios. The entire sale realized a total of only £373.7.6. John Singleton Copley, Jr., purchased lots 29, 75, 76, 89, and 94.

PRINTS

1. Miscellaneous, *a large parcel.*
2. Mezzotintos by Various Masters — 33.
3. English and Foreign Portraits — 30.
4. Landscapes and Huntings *by Kirkall,* Vases *by Tournier,* Ornaments *by Chastillon* & — 32.
5. History of King Charles the first, *after Vanderbank by Baron,* &c. — 15.
6. Landscapes after Teniers, Claude, Berchem, &c. — 20.

BRITISH PORTRAITS

7. Queen Elizabeth, Procession to Hunsdon House, &c. *by Vertue,* and Henry 8th granting the Charter to the Surgeons Company *by Baron* — 7.
8. Archbishop Tenison *by R. White,* and various *by Vertue, Houbraken,* &c. — 20.
9. Captain Cook by Sherwin, Richard Brothers *by Sharp,* &c. — 15.
10. Theodore de Mayerne *by Simon,* Duke of Montagu *by Faber,* &c. — 10.
11. William Duke of Gloucester, &c. w.l. portraits, *all by J. Smith* — 15.
12. Bishop Willis by Simon, Judges Fortescue and Willis *by Faber,* &c. — 9.
13. Lady Byron, w.l. *by Faber,* Mrs. Knight (Comedian) *by Ditto,* &c. — 7.
14. Sir John Chicheley, *after Lely by Browne, scarce,* and various Ladies *after Ditto, all counter proofs* — 5.
15. Countess of Exeter *by Tompson,* Elinor Gwynne *by Ditto,* &c. — 4.
16. WILLIAM FIELDING EARL OF DENBIGH BY VOERST, 1631, *oval large 4to. very fine and rare* — 1.
17. Philip Herbert Earl of Pembroke *by* DITTO, *ditto* — 1.
18. Robert Bertie Earl of Lindsey *by* DITTO, *rare* — 1.
19. James Stewart Duke of Lenox *by* DITTO, *ditto* — 1.

20. Thomas Scott, *Obiit 1626*, several English verses under the oval, *by W. Marshall*, fine and scarce
— 1.
21. George Withers in a hat *by F. Delaram, 1622. oval 4to ditto* — 1.
22. Duchess of Ancaster, and Lady Mary Campbell, w ls. *by McArdell*, &c. — 8.
23. Sir Vicary Gibbs *by Reynolds*, James Townley Esq. *by Say*, General Washington, w l. *by V. Green, proof*, &c. — 6.
24. Princesses Mary, Sophia and Amelia *by Bartolozzi, proof and letters*, Family of Mr. West P.R.A. *by Facius*, &c.
25. Earl of Besberough *after Copley, by Dunkarton, proof and letters*, The Prince Regent (Equestrian) *after Ditto, by C. Turner*, &c. — 4.
26. Lords Spencer, w.l. in his robes of the Garter, and Lord Sidmouth, w.l. *after Copley by Dunkarton* — 2.
27. Lord Duncan, w.l. *by Earlom*, and Victory of Ditto *by J. Ward, proof and letters* — 3.

SIR JOSHUA REYNOLDS

28. His own Portrait *by J. K. Sherwin, proof*, R. B. Sheridan *by Hall, Ditto*, &c. — 3.
29. Lord Camden *by Basire*, w.l. and Lords Thurlow and Mansfield *by Bartolozzi, the latter a proof* — 3.
30. Lord Thurlow *by Bartolozzi*, FINE PROOF — 1.
31. Lord Thurlow *by Ditto*, PROOF *before the Coat of Arms* — 1.
32. Duke of Cumberland *by T. Watson*, Marquis of Rockingham, w.l. PROOFS, &c. — 2 [changed by pencil to 3].
33. Duchesses of Rutland and Devonshire, w.ls. *by Val Green, fine* — 2.
34. Lady Sarah Bunbury sacrificing to the Graces, w.l. *by Fisher, proof* — 1.
35. Lady Betty Delme, and Lady Jane Halliday, w.ls. *by V. Green* — 2.
36. Viscountess Townshend, Lady Louisa Manners, and the Countess of Harrington, w.ls. *by Ditto* — 3.
37. Viscountess Crosbie, and Mrs. Matthews, w.ls. *both by Dickinson, fine* — 2.
38. Ladies Beresford, Townend and Gardiner, w.ls. *by T. Watson*, Proof — 1.
39. Lord Lifford, w.l. PROOF, Garrick between Tragedy and Comedy *by Fisher*, and Perceval Pott, F.R.S. *by C. Townley, p.p.* — 3.
40. Charles Duke of Marlborough, *By Houston*, Laurence Stern *by Fisher*, &c. — 7.
41. Lord Hardwicke's Daughters *by Fisher*, Lady Caroline Howard *by V. Green*, Miss Kitty Fisher, with the pearl *by Houston*, &c. — 6.
42. Mrs. Cockburn and her Children *by C. Wilkin*, Infantine Academy *by F. Howard*, PROOFS, &c. — 4.
43. Cardinal Vertues (from the Paintings at New College Oxford) *by Facius* — 7.
44. Death of Cardinal Beaufort *by Car. Watson*, and Witch Scene in Macbeth *by Shew* — 2.
45. Holy Family *by W. Sharp*, CHOICE PROOF — 1.
46. Infant Hercules *by Hodges*, and Count Ugolino *by Dixon, fine* — 2.
47. Susanna and the Elders *after Rembrandt, by Earlom*, Render to Caesar, *after Ditto by McArdell, proofs*, &c.
48. Air Pump and Orrery *after Wright of Derby*, Iron Forge and Blacksmith's Shop, *after Ditto, by Earlom*, &c. — 5.
49. Quack Doctor, *after G. Douw by C. Hess*, Susanna *after Dominichino*, &c — 4.
50. Pool of Bethesda and Good Samaritan, *after Hogarth*, Cockpit *by Ditto*, &c — 5.
51. Christ bearing his Cross, and Christ appearing to Mary Magdalen *by Sherwin*, PROOFS — 2.
[52. Omitted from catalogue.]
53. Profile Medallion of Sir Robert Strange, *by himself, fine*, and ditto *an unfinished proof, rare* — 2.
54. Danae, and Venus and Adonis *by Ditto, fine* — 2.

55. Charles the first, w.l. and Queen Henrietta Maria, with her Children, *after Vandyck by Ditto, very fine* — 2.
56. SORTIE MADE BY THE GARRISON OF GIBRALTAR BY SHARP, PROOF — 1.
57. BATTLES OF LA HOGUE AND BOYNE, After WEST by WOOLLETT, &c. PROOFS — 2.
58. Cromwell dissolving the Long Parliament *by Hall, proof etching,* Copies of the Death of Wolfe and Battle of La Hogue *by Guttenberg* and Voysard, *proofs, &c* — 5.
59. Hundred Guilder, *after Rembrandt by Capt. Baillie, very fine, on india paper, &c.* — 4.
60. Scriptural and Historical Subjects, published by Boydell, &c. *several proofs* — 10.
61. Prospects of the Falls of Nigara (aquatintas) *by Lewis, &c.* — 3.
62. Fancy Subjects *by modern Masters,* and the Holy Family *after A. del Sarto, by Bartolozzi* — 8.
63. Busts from the Antique and Fancy Subjects *by Bartolozzi proofs,* &c. Etchings of Views in Rome *by D. Allan, &c.* — 22.

WORKS OF RUBENS

64. His Own Portrait, with his Wife and Child *by McArdell,* &c. and Ruben's Wife *by Sailliar and Earlom* — 4.
65. St. Michael overcoming the Dragon *by Vorsterman and Suyderhoef,* Last Judgment *by C. Visscher, &c.* — 4.
66. Melchisedec blessing Araham *by Witdouc,* Meeting of Jacob and Esau *by De Bailliu, &c.* — 5.
67. Lot and his Daughters *by Swanenberg,* and the Brazen Serpent *by Bolswert* — 2.
68. Defeat of Senaccherib *by Soutman, fine, and the larger* Judith and Holofernes *by C. Galle* — 2.
69. Visitation *by De Jode,* and Presentation in the Temple *by Pontius, fine* — 2.
70. Visitation and Presentation in the Temple, the Four Penitents and Descent from the Cross *all by Val: Green, ditto* — 4.
71. Nativity *by Bolswert and Vorsterman,* Adoration of the Wise Men *by Witdouc, &c.* — 5.
72. Massacre of the Innocents (on two sheets) by Pontius, *very fine,* and the same subject *by P. Martenasie, &c.* — 3.
73. Miraculous Draught of Fishes (on three sheets) by S. a. Bolswert, *very fine* — 1.
74. Herodias with the head of John Baptist *by Ditto, (two different)* Mary Magdalen washing the Saviour's feet *by Earlom, fine, &c.* — 4.
75. Raising of Lazarus and the Last Supper *by B. a. Bolswert, &c.* — 4.
76. Ecce Homo *by Lauwers,* and the large Crucifixion (on three sheets) *by Witdouc* — 2.
77. Bearing the Cross *by Pontius,* Crucifixion between two thieves *by Bolswert, fine, &c.* — 3.
78. Entombing of Christ *by Galle and Witdouc,* Resurrection *by Bolswert, &c* — 6.
79. Day of Pentecost *by Pontius,* Holy Family *by Bolswert, fine,* Ditto (in chiaro scuro) *by Jegher, scarce, &c* — 4.
80. Marriage of the Virgin, and St. Anne instructing the Madona *by S. a. Bolswert,* Glorification of the Virgin *by C. Visscher, &c. fine* — 4.
81. Assumption of the Virgin *by Bolswert, Pontius and Witdouc, ditto* — 3.
82. St. Ildephonsus *by Witdouc,* Ignatius Loyola and Francis Xavier *by Marinus, &c.* — 5.
83. St. Roche *by Pontius,* St. Thomas *by Neefs,* Martyrdom of St. Laurence *by Vorsterman, &c.* — 4.
84. Dispute of Transubstantiation *by Snyers,* Triumphs of the Gospel (on two sheets) *by Lauwers, &c.* — 4.
85. Historical Roman Subjects, *by Muller and Schmuzer* — 5.
86. Thomyris Queen of Scythia, ordering the head of Cyrus to be plunged into a bason of blood *by Pontius, fine,* and a copy of the same *by Duchange* — 2.
87. Discovery of Achilles by Ulysses *by C. Visscher, fine,* Three Graces *by P. de Jode, &c.* — 5.
88. Judgment of Paris *by Lommelin,* Garden of Love, (*two plates in wood*) by C. Jegher, *scarce, &c.* — 5.
89. Saul's Conversion, and the Grand Lion Hunt, *both by S. a. Bolswert, fine* — 2.
90. Hunting the Wild Boar *by Soutman, &c.* — 4.

91. Landscapes *by Bolswert*, (two large and eight of the smaller) — 10.
92. Watering Place *by Browne*, and Heads of Count Olivarez *by Pontius*, &c. — 4.
93. LUXEMBURG GALLERY, *fine uniform set* — 25.

VAN DYCK

94. Crucifixion *by J. Falck*, Virgin with the Infant Jesus and St. John *by V. Green, proof*, &c. — 5.
95. Duke of Richmond *by Earlom*, Duke of Buckingham and his Brother *by McArdell*, &c. w.ls. *fine* — 6.
96. Set of w.l. Portraits *by Gunst* — 10.
97. ———— Beauties *by Lombart*, &c. — 17.
98. Pembroke and Nassau Families, &c. *by Baron*, and Count Aremberg *by De Bailliu* — 5.
99. Charles I. and his Queen *by Voerst*, Ditto *by Baron*, &c — 6.
100. Varia *by C. Schut, C. Visscher*, &c. — 13.

SECOND DAY'S SALE: ETCHINGS BY REMBRANDT, &c.

101. Angel appearing to the Shepherds, Taking down from the Cross, Disciples at Emaus, &c — 7.
102. Good Samaritan, Peter and John at the beautiful gate of the Temple, &c. — 7.
103. Small Scripture Subjects, Joseph, Death of Eli, &c. *fine* — 8.
104. Christ and the Samaritan Woman, Flight into Egypt, &c. — 10.
105. Heads of Rembrandt, the large Jew Bride, &c. — 7.
106. Doctor Faustus, Manasseh Ben Israel, &c — 7.
107. Janus Sylvius, and various heads *by and after Rembrandt* — 15.
108. Beggars, Rat-catcher, Little Goldsmith, &c — 9.
109. Blind Bagpipers, &c. *by Rembrandt*, St. Jerome *by Lievens*, and Holy Family *by F. Bol* — 15.
110. Landscape, &c. *by and after Rembrandt* — 12.
111. Dutch Boors *by Ostade*, Landscapes *by Waterloo*, &c. — 15.
112. Etchings of Animals *by Ridinger*, and the large Hunting of the Wild Boar *by Hondius, scarce* — 18.
113. Varia *by Callot, Hollar*, &c. — 22.
114. Etchings *by Flamen, Sarbot, Wyek*, &c. — 17.
115. St. John in the Island of Patmos, surrounded by small ovals of Saints and Emblematical figures, 1466, *rare and curious* — 1.
116. Various Engravings and Wood cuts, *by A. Durer and Lucas van Leyden* — 48.
117. Little German Masters, *Aldegrever, Altdorffer*, &c. — 30.
118. Miscellaneous *by Goltzius, Muller, Sadeler*, &c. — 18.
119. Drawings by Old Masters, &c. — 11.

FRENCH AND ITALIAN MASTERS

120. Holy Family, *after Poussin by Natalis*, Brazen Serpent *by Audran*, &c — 7.
121. Holy Families and Madonas *by Boulangér, Poilly*, &c. — 9.
122. Historical *after N. Poussin, S. Bourdon*, &c. — 11.
123. Sacraments, *after Poussin by Pesne* — 6.
124. Large Scriptural Subjects *by Audran, Stella*, &c. — 8.
125. Etchings *by Parmegiano, Caracci, Schiamanossi*, &c. — 18.
126. Transfiguration *by Procacini*, and Various *after Titian*, &c — 11.
127. Etchings *by and after Castiglione, Bolognese, Carlo Maratti*, &c. — 21.
128. Set of the Apostles, *after Raphael*, and three ditto by *M. da Ravenna* — 17.
129. Combat of the Centaurs *by A. Mantegna*, Mount Parnassus *by Marc. Antonio*, &c. — 7.
130. Historical *after M. Angelo, Julio Romano*, &c. — 18.
131. The Cartoons, *after Raphael by Dorigny* — 7.

132. Ditto (small set) *by Tardieu*, &c. and two studies of heads (*drawings*) *by Dorigny* — 9.
133. Historical *after Raphael*, from Pictures in the Vatican, *by F. Aquila, and published by Rossi, 1722* — 22.
134. Opera di Polidoro da Caravaggio, Disegno della Loggia di San Pietro in Vaticano, &c. — 60.
135. Varia, *after Corregio, Caracci, Guercino*, &c. — 18.
136. Large Historical etchings *after Raphael, Paul Varonese*, &c. — 10.
137. Aurora and Companion, *after Guido by Jac. Frey*, Descent from the Cross *by Dorigny*, &c. — 4.
138. Battle of the Standard, *after L. da Vinci by Edelinck*, and Holy Family, *after Ditto by Anker Smith*.
139. Holy Family, *after And. del Sarto by Bartolozzi, proof and letters*, and Poetry *after Raphael by Morghen* — 3 [changed by pencil to 4].
140. TRANSFIGURATION, after RAPHAEL by MORGHEN *very fine* — 1.
141. Ditto, *ditto*, BEAUTIFUL PROOF — 1.

BOOKS OF PRINTS

142. Adam Mantuanus's Engravings from Michael Angelo's Paintings in the Vatican, *Roma 1773*, and Palladio's Architecture, *Paris 1650*.
143. Tempesta's Battles and Huntings, and a Volume containing Miscellaneous Prints and Drawings.
144. A Volume containing **thirty-two Etchings** of Landscapes *by and after Claude Lorraine* ["&c" added in pencil].
145. Holland's Heroologia Anglicana, *portraits by Crispin de Passe, wants title*, &c.
146. Plans, Elevations and Sections of Houghton in Norfolk, 1760.
147. Bellorii Picturae Antiquae Cryptarum Romanarum, *plates, Romae, 1750*.
148. ———— Veteris Arcus Augustorum Triumphis Insignes *plates, Romae, 1690*.
149. Bartoli Virgiliani Codicis Fragmenta et Picturae ex Biblitheca Vaticana, *plates, Romae, 1742*.
150. ———— Etchings after the Paintings of Raphael in the Vatican.
151. ———— Admiranda Romanarum Antiquitatum, *plates, Romae, 1693*.
152. ———— Columna M. Aurelio — Antonino, *Ditto*, 1704.
153. ———— Colona Trajana, *Ditto*.
154. Imagine Veteriss ac Novi Testamenti a Raphaele in Vaticano, *plates*, 1675.
155. Loves of Cupid and Psyche, after the designs of Raphael *by Marc. Antonio*, Romae, 1774.
156. Michael Angelo's Last Judgement, on Ten Plates *by George Mantuanus*, and Loves of Cupid and Psyche, *from Raphael by Dorigny*, Romae, 1693.
157. Schola Italica Picturae a Gavini Hamilton Pictoris, *Romae, 1773, half bound, russia back*.

PORTFOLIOS

158. Four portfolios, *without leaves*.
159. Four ditto.
160. Two larger ditto.
161. Three very large ditto, *blue covers*.
162. One ditto, marble cover, russia back and corners.

COPPER PLATES, WITH IMPRESSIONS

163. Three, Military Costume (*etchings*).
164. Catherine Countess of Desmond — 1.
165. Right Honble Wm. Pitt, *after Copley by Bartolozzi*, 80 PROOFS, 294 *lettered impressions* — 374. (2.10.0)
166. The Princesses Mary, Sophia and Amelia, *after Ditto by Ditto*, 73 PROOFS, 388 letters, 16 *in colours and 3 etchings* — 480. (1.15.0)
167. Admiral Earl Howe, *after Ditto by Dunkarton*, 46 PROOFS and 17 *letters* — 63. (1.4.0)
168. Admiral Lord Duncan, *after Ditto by Earlom*, 21 PROOFS and 63 *letters* — 84. (1.10.0)

169. William Ponsonby, Lord Besborough, *after Ditto by Dunkarton*, 9 PROOFS *and* 15 *letters* — 24. (1.3.0)

170. GEORGE JOHN EARL SPENCER, W.L. in his Robes of the Garter, *after Ditto by Ditto*, 34 PROOFS — 34 (*only thirty Prints were taken off after the Proofs*). (5.5.0)

171. Right Honble. Henry Addington (VISCOUNT SIDMOUTH) when Chancellor, w.l. in his Robes, *after Ditto by Ditto*, 26 PROOFS and 52 *letters* — 78 (very few impressions were taken off). (5.10.0)

172. HIS ROYAL HIGHNESS THE PRINCE REGENT, Equestrian Portrait, *after Ditto by C. Turner*, 117 PROOFS, 136 *letters*, 13 *in colours* and 20 *etchings* — 286. (9.15.0)

173. Priam supplicating Achilles for the Body of Hector, *after Ditto by Fogg*, 10 PROOFS, 54 *prints and* 15 *in colours* — 79. (1.2.0)

174. Abraham offering up his Son Isaac, *after Ditto by Dunkarton*, 77 PROOFS, 170 prints, 79 *in colours, and* 16 *finished ditto* — 342. (2.5.0)

175. Hagar and Ishmael in the Wilderness, *after Ditto by Ditto*, 12 PROOFS, 213 *prints and* 22 *in colours* — 247. (2.2.0)

176. VICTORY OF LORD DUNCAN, after DITTO by J. WARD, 46 PROOFS, 84 *prints and* 10 *etchings* — 140. (4.0.0)

177. DEATH OF LORD CHATHAM, after DITTO by DELATTRE (*unpublished plate*), PROOFS — 50. (35.12.0)

178. DEATH OF LORD CHATHAM, After COPLEY by BARTOLOZZI, R.A.
     PROOFS — 70
     DITTO, *on India paper* — 49
     DITTO, *during the progress of the plate* — 96
     PROOF Etchings — 40
     PRINTS, 1st *month* — 37
     DITTO, 2d, 3d, and 5th *ditto* — 50
     DITTO, 4th *ditto* — 56
     DITTO, 6th and 7th *ditto* — 27
     DITTO, 8th and 9th *ditto* — 29
     PROOFS (*imperfect*) — 90
     PROOFS (*ditto*) — 180
     [total] 724

179. SIEGE & RELIEF OF GIBRALTAR, After J. S. COPLEY by W. SHARP.
     PROOFS, *with the letters etched in* — 130
     DITTO *before the Inscription* — 25
     DITTO *on India paper* — 19
     PRINTS, first hundred — 59
     DITTO, second ditto — 38
     DITTO, third ditto — 21
     DITTO, fourth ditto — 34
     DITTO, fifth ditto — 4
     DITTO, sixth ditto — 17
     DITTO, seventh ditto — 55
     DITTO, eighth ditto, *and to the end of the printing* — 155.
     PROOF, Etchings — 18
     PROOFS *during the progress of the plate* 29
     DITTO *in an unfinished state* — 12
     PRINTS received in the course of printing to repair by — 10
     [total] 626
     Vignette plate, representing the British Fleet off Gibraltar, by *Pollard*, with portraits of Earl Howe and Admiral Barrington by *Sharp*, 141 *plain* and 19 *on India paper*, and a quantity of keys for explanation — 160.

The Lyndhurst Library Sale

Catalogue of the Valuable Library of the Rt. Hon. Lord Lyndhurst, Deceased:
also, a few Engravings and Sketches by J. S. Copley, R.A., Christie, Feb. 26–27, 1864

This listing (copied exactly) is selected from a priced copy of the sale catalogue at Christie, Manson & Woods. The number of items in each lot is given in parentheses. The sale of Lord Lyndhurst's library contained several categories of materials of possible relevance to a study of John Singleton Copley. The most important of these consisted of fourteen lots of drawings by Copley (660–672, plus 669 *), containing a total of 243 drawings and an untabulated parcel. The name of the purchaser and the price is given here in parentheses for these items. The sale also included a number of engravings after Copley's paintings and engravings of other than Copley's work, which could conceivably have belonged to Copley himself and have been retained by Lyndhurst. Any of these engravings, however, could have been acquired by Lyndhurst after Copley's death. The same is true of the final category of material of possible interest, books published before or during Copley's lifetime, which could have been in his own library and then passed on after his death to Lyndhurst.

When James Hughes Anderdon was looking through folios in advance of the library sale, he discovered Copley's diploma as an associate of the Royal Academy, signed by Sir Joshua Reynolds, and his diploma as an academician. But these two items, lots 654 and 655 in the catalogue, were withdrawn from the sale by order of Lady Lyndhurst (Anderdon, Royal Academy, II, 1776 and 1778).

The library sale was preceded by a sale of other Lyndhurst property, which began on Feb. 22, 1864. The first two days of this sale were held at Christie's and were devoted to disposing of silver, ceramics, decorative furniture, and other objects. On Feb. 24 the sale moved to George Street. Obviously the house was commodious and contained an enormous amount of elegant material. It is noteworthy that Copley as an artist had lived in sufficiently high style for the house to be worthy of a lord chancellor. It is virtually impossible to identify any of the objects as having survived from Copley's furnishing of the house in the eighteenth century, but the sale did contain a "box of mathmatical instruments & a camera lucida" (206), a "mahogany picture easel" (330), and a "mahogany box, with two drawers enclosing paints and other artist's materials" (420).

SKETCHES BY J. S. COPLEY, R.A., IN CHALK, FOR PARTS OF PICTURES

660. The long boat; and three others for the Siege of Gibraltar (4). (Redgrave [for the Victoria and Albert Museum], 0.15.0)
661. Studies of sailors, for the same (51). (Jupp, 1.5.0)
662. Groups of officers, for the same (24). (Redgrave [for the Victoria and Albert Musem], 2.0.0)
663. Various portions of the same picture (15). (Kimpton, 0.17.0)
664. Life size heads and other sketches for the Death of Chatham (16). (Jupp, 1.2.0)
665. Figures and groups for Charles I. and Lady Jane Grey (18). (Kimpton, 1.8.0)
666. Death of Major Peirson (10). (Graves, 2.8.0)
667. Duncan's Victory (10). (Graves, 1.10.0)
668. Boy saved from a shark, &c. (14). (Clark, 1.2.0)
669. Sacred Subjects, &c. (39). (Dr. H, 1.5.0)
669*. A parcel — various. (Waller, 1.7.0)
670. Studies for men's portraits (22). (Jupp, 1.8.0)
671. Ditto of ladies (8). (Jupp, 0.14.0)
672. Ditto family groups (12). (Clark, 3.3.0)

ENGRAVINGS AFTER PAINTINGS BY COPLEY

629. Pitt, Bartolozzi &c (7).
630. Duncan, Earlom — proof &c (3).
631. Spencer, Duncarton &c. — proof (5).
642. Addington, Dunkarton (3).
643. Ponsonby, Dunkarton &c (6).
647. Chatham, Bartolozzi (18).
648. Chatham — small plate proofs. One with Artist's signature (3).
649. Prince Regent, Turner — proofs &c (5).
650. Gibraltar, Sharpe (27).
656. Abraham, Dunkarton (7).
657. Samuel and Eli, V. Green, &c (6).
658. Duncan's Victory, Ward, &c. (6).
659. Lord Howe's Victory, after Serres, by Pollard (32).

ENGRAVINGS AFTER ARTISTS OTHER THAN COPLEY

622. Various Topography and Maps.
623. Piranesi's Views in Rome (10).
624. Views on the Rhine, &c. (40).
625. Diez's Portraits of the Royal Family, &c. (18).
633. St Geneviève, after Van Loo, by Balechon.
634. La Poesia, after C. Dolce, by Morghen.
635. Hagar and Ishmael, after Raffaelle, by Garavaglia, &c. (3).
636. After Raffaelle, by Bettelini, &c. (3).
637. Pulcra, after Raffaelle, by R. Morghen, &c. (2).
638. St. Catharine, after Raffaelle, by Desnoyers — proof, &c. (3)
639. After Raffaelle, by Ingouf — proofs, &c. (4).
640. La Vierge au Poisson, after Raffaelle, by Desnoyers, proof.
641. Holy Family, after Poussin, by Anderloni — proof, &c.
651. Parce Somnum Rumpere, after Titian, by Morghen — proofs.
652. The Virgin and Child, by Sharp, &c. (4).
653. Cromwell dissolving the Long Parliament, by Hall, &c. (5).

SELECTED BOOKS PUBLISHED BEFORE OR DURING COPLEY'S LIFETIME

1. Addison's (Jos.), Remarks on several Parts of Italy. Tonson, 1705.
8. America, The History of the Bucaniers of. 2 Vols. 1774.
11. Annual Register. 25 vols. — wanting the years 1767, 1771, 1778, 1780.
22. Beaumont and Fletcher's Works. *Portraits.* 10 vols. — vol. 3 wanting. *Tonson,* 1750.
23. Beaumont and Fletcher, Dramatic Works. *Plates.* 10 vols. 1778.
35. Brantome (Seigneur de), Oeuvres, 15 vols. *La Haye,* 1740.
36. Bridge (Rev. B.) A Treatise on Algebra. 1836; Atwood's (G.), Treatise on the Rectilinear Motion. 1784; and 7 others: 9 vols.
37. British Poets, with Prefaces by Dr. Johnson. 68 vols. in 67. 1780.
50. Buffon, Histoire Naturelle Générale et Particulière. *Colored plates.* 52 vols. (*The Duke of York's copy*) 1785.
60. Bury, Histoire de la Vie de Louis XIII. 4 vols. *Paris,* 1768.
66. Camoen's Lusiad, translated by W. J. Mickle. 2 vols. 1798.
71. Cazotte, Oeuvres Choisies et Badines. 6 vols. *Paris,* 1798.
75. Cervantes (M. de), The History and Adventures of Don Quixote, with a Life of the author by T. Smollett. 4 vols. 1793.
77. Chatterton's Works with Life by Dr. Gregory. *Plates.* 3 vols. 1803.
78. Cheseldon (W.), The Anatomy of the Human Body. 1773; Lipscomb on Hydrophobia. 1809; and four others: 6 vols.
79. Chesterfield (Lord), Letters to his Son. 4 vols. 1776; and 4 others: 8 vols.
81. Chubb (T.), The True Gospel of Jesus Christ Asserted. 1738; Clarke (S.), Discourses on the Attributes of God. 1728; and 11 others.
82. Cibber (Colley). The Dramatic Works of. 4 vols. 1760; Cibber's Apology. 6 vols. 1740.
84. Clarendon's (Earl of), History of the Rebellion and Civil Wars in England. 6 vols. *Oxford,* 1705.
85. ———— History of the Rebellion completed; *containing 85 portraits after Van Dyck,* &c. 1715.
90. Comines (Philippe), Mémoires. *Portraits.* 5 vols. 1723.
92. Congreve's Works. 3 vols. 1753.
113. D'Anville (M.), Géographie Ancienne abrégée. 2 vols. 1768; and 14 others: 16 vols.
114. De Bussi-Rabutin (Le Comte), Histoire Amoureuse des Gaules. 2 vols. 1754; Memoires sur la Vie de Madlle. de l'Enclos. *Amsterdam,* 1754; and 3 others: 5 vols.
116. De Piles (M.), The Art of Painting; Webb's Inquiry into the Beauties of Painting; and 2 others. 4 vols. 1760.
120. Diderot (M.), Oeuvres de Théâtre. 2 vols. *Paris,* 1771; and 22 others: 24 vols.
135. Dryden's Dramatic Works. *Portraits & plates.* 6 vols. 1735.
136. ———— Poetical Works. 4 vols. 1760.
137. ———— Prose Works, with Notes by Malone. 4 vols. 1800.
139. Du Halde's Description of China. *Plates.* 4 vols. 1741.
164. Frazer (James), The History of Nadir Shah. 1742; India, Ancient Accounts of, translated from the Arabic, by Renaudot. 1733; and 9 others: 11 vols.
165. Frédéric II, Oeuvres Posthumes. 15 vols. *Berlin,* 1789.
168. Gibbon's History of the Decline and Fall of the Roman Empire, 12 vols. 1783; Miscellaneous Works, edited by Lord Sheffield. 5 vols. 1814: together 17 vols.
197. Herodotus, translated by Beloe. 4 vols. 1791.
204. Homer's Iliad and Odyssey, translated by Pope. 9 vols. 1771.
205. Home's (H.), Elements of Criticism. 2 vols. 1769; Burke (E), On the Sublime. 1824; and 6 others: 9 vols.
208. Horace, Les Poésies d', traduites en François [*sic*] par R. Sanadon. *Amsterdam,* 1766.
210. Hume's (D.), Essays and Treatises. 4 vols. 1770.

212. Hutchinson's (Lucy), Memoirs of Colonel Hutchinson. *Plates*. 2 vols. 1810.
218. Johnson and Stevens' Annotations on Shakespeare. 12 vols. — wanting vols. 9 & 10. *Bell's* edition, 1788.
222. Josephus's Works, translated by Whiston. Plates. 5 vols. *Dublin* 1741.
227. LaHarpe, Lycée, ou Cours de Littérature Ancienne et Moderne. 14 vols. 1799.
239. Le Sage (M.), Histoire de Gil Blas. 5 vols. *Paris*, 1769; and 3 others: 8 vols.
241. Lettere Caro. 3 vols. *Venezia*, 1756; Lettere di Jacopo Ortis. *London*, 1817; and 16 others: 20 vols.
246. Livii Opera cura Drakenborchii. 8 vols. 1794.
252. Machiavel's Works, translated by Farneworth. 4 vols. 1775.

[*quartos begin*]

258. British Museum; Description of the Ancient Terra-Cottas in the British Museum. 1810; Description of the Ancient Marbles in the British Museum, parts 1, 3, 4, 5, 9, 10. 7 vols. Plates. 1812–45.
263. Copley's (J. *Seminarie Priest*), Doctrinall and Moral Observations concerning Religion. 1612.
272. Jeffery's Collection of the Dresses of different Nations, Ancient and Modern, particularly old English Dresses, after Holbein, Vandyke, Hollar, &c. 480 *plates*. 4 vols. 1757.
276. Martyn and Lettice's Antiquities of Herculaneum. *Plates*. 1773.
282. Smith's System of Optics. 1778; and 4 others: 5 vols.
284. Tarranton (Andrew), England's Improvement by Sea and Land. 1677.
286. Walpole's Anecdotes of Painting. 2 vols. *Strawberry Hill*, 1762.

[*folios begin*]

289. Adam's Ruins of Spalatro. 1764.
291. Barrow's (Isaac), Works. 1700.
292. Bayle, Dictionnaire Historique et Critique. 4 vols. *Rotterdam*, 1720.
293. Bayle's Dictionary, by Gale. 3 vols. 1734.
296. Chardin's Travels. 2 vols. in 1. 1686.
298. Lactantii Opera. *Basil*, 1532.
299. Le Brun's Battles, &c. 5 vols. — *strained and rolled*.
302. Palladio's Architecture. 1738.
304. Percier et Fontaine, Recueil de Décorations Intérieures. Paris, 1812.
305. Perry's View of the Levant. *Plates*. 1743.
306. Raffaelle's Plates to the Bible; and Reliefs in the Vatican, by Bartoli.
307. *Rossini's Views in Rome*. 100 *plates*. 3 vols.
311. Selden (J.), Titles of Honour. *Portrait*. 1672.
314. Spelmanni Glossarium Archaiologicum. 1664.
316. Thuani Historiae. 1733.
317. Turnbull (Geo.), A Curious Collection of Ancient Paintings. 1744.
318. Views in Venice, after Canaletti, by Vincentini. 36 *plates*.
319. Whitelock's Memorials of English Affairs. 1682.

[*second day's sale starts with octavos*]

361. Milton's (J.), Paradise Lost, with notes by Bishop Newton. 2 vols. 1778.
363. Molière, Oeuvres. 8 vols. *Paris*, 1799; Rousseau, Oeuvres. 9 vols.; Boileau, Oeuvres. 2 vols.: together 19 vols.
367. Montaigne, Essais, avec les Notes de Coste. 10 vols. *Portrait*. 1771.
390. Ockley (Simon), The History of the Saracens. 2 vols. 1718.

406. Perefixe, Histoire du Roy Henri le Grand. *Amsterdam,* 1661.
417. Pope (Alexander), Works of. 12 vols. 1764.
420. Potter's (J.), Antiquities of Greece. 2 vols. 1697; Pliny's Letters. 2 vols. 1752; and four others: 8 vols.
431. Rapin's History of England. *Plates.* 28 vols. 1726.
434. Richardson's (W.) Essays on Shakespeare's Dramatic Characters. 1812; Upton's (J.), Critical Observations on Shakespeare. 1746; and four others: 6 vols.
435. Richelieu (Cardinal), La Vie de, par M. Le Clerc. 3 vols. *Amsterdam,* 1724; and 8 others: 11 vols.
441. Rollin's Ancient History. 8 vols.; and 4 others: 12 vols. *Edinburgh,* 1789.
446. Rousseau (J.), La Nouvelle Héloise. 4 vols. *Paris* 1764; and 20 others: 24 vols.
447. Rowe (Nicholas), The Works of. 2 vols. 1792.
453. Saint Simon, Oeuvres complètes. 13 vols. in 7. *Strasbourg,* 1791.
471. Shaftesbury's (Earl), Characteristics of Men, Manners, Opinions, Times. 3 vols. *Portrait.* 1732.
472. Shakespeare's Plays. *Portraits, and Scene and Character. Plates.* 20 vols. *Bell's Edition,* 1788.
478. Smith's (Capt. E.), History of the Lives and Robberies of Highwaymen, Footpads, Shoplifts, and Cheats of both Sexes; with the Thieves New Canting Dictionary. *Plates.* 2 vols. 1719.
483. Sophocles' Tragedies, translated by the Rev. T. Francklin. 2 vols. 1766; and 4 others: 6 vols.
486. Spectator — *plates by Hayman.* 9 vols. 1765.
488. Spenser's Poetical Works, edited by Dr. Aikin. *Portrait and plates after Stothard.* 6 vols. 1802.
489. Stael (Madame de), Oeuvres de. 4 vols. *Londres,* 1765; Histoire de Timur Bee. 4 vols. 1722; and 12 others: 20 vols.
496. Sterne (L.), The Life and Opinions of Tristram Shandy. 3 vols. 1794.
497. Sully (Duc de), Memoires. *Portraits.* 6 vols. Paris, 1788.
498. Swift's (Dean), Works, with Notes by Hawkesworth. *Plates.* 20 vols. 1765.
508. Thomson's Poetical Works. *Plates.* 3 vols. 1804.
509. Thucydides' History, translated by W. Smith. 2 vols. 1805.
511. Trial of the Twenty-nine Regicides. 1679.
513. Tryals. 2 vols. 1690; and 8 others: 10 vols.
514. Voltaire, Oeuvres complètes. 70 vols. 1785.
515. Ferguson's Mechanical Experiments, 1778.
516. Vertot (Abbé), Histoire des Chevaliers Hospitaliers de S. Jean de Jérusalem. 5 vols. *Paris,* 1726; and 16 others: 21 vols.
517. Virgil's Works, translated by Dryden. *Portrait and plates.* 3 vols. 1748.
518. Voltaire, Le Henriade. *Plates.* Dresden, 1748.
519. ———— Théâtre de. 5 vols. *Paris,* 1803; and 5 others: 10 vols.
538. World (The), by Adam Fitz Adam. 4 vols. Dodsley, 1682.
539. Wycherley's Plays. 1735.

The Lyndhurst Sale

*Catalogue of the Very Valuable Collection of Pictures
of the Rt. Hon. Lord Lyndhurst, Deceased;
Including Most of the Important Works of His Lordship's Father,
That distinguished Historical Painter,
John Singleton Copley, R.A., Christie, March 5, 1864*

There are several important annotated copies of the catalogue for the Lyndhurst picture sale (which was held a few days after the library sale). One at the Boston Athenaeum, the gift of Mrs. Gordon Dexter, apparently belonged to one of the American members of the family who acquired objects at the sale, perhaps Martha Babcock Amory, the artist's granddaughter and subsequent biographer. This copy is coded to indicate the American purchasers: MBA (Martha Babcock Amory), FGD (F. Gordon Dexter), and JSA (James Sullivan Amory). It also gives the names of the official purchasers, often agents for the real purchasers, and the prices paid. Among the other penciled notations in the catalogue are "Cox's 57 and 58 Pall Mall" (Cox bought a number of items for Martha Babcock Amory) and "Lady Lyndhurst Hampdon Court Palace."

A second annotated copy at the Royal Academy contains notations by James Hughes Anderdon. A third, at the National Portrait Gallery, belonged to Sir George Scharf, then director of the National Portrait Gallery, which in addition to notations contains thumbnail sketches of some of the items in the sale. The annotations in these catalogues that relate to Copley items, including purchaser and price, are added in parentheses here. Figure numbers are given in brackets for pictures illustrated in this book. All else is a direct transcription of the sale catalogue.

The *Times*, March 7, 1864, noted that the total realized by the sale was £5147.9.6. The sale of the plate and ornamental objects had netted £3360.0.0, and the sale of the furniture and library £1472.0.0.

ENGRAVINGS. FRAMED AND GLAZED.

1. General Sir G. Murray, after Pickergsill, by Fox.
2. The Transfiguration, after Raffaelle.
3. The Prince Regent reviewing the Troops, after Copley. (Radclyffe)
4. The Temple of Jupiter, after Turner, by Pye — *proof*.
5. La Madonna della Scala, after Correggio, by Ravenet.
6. La Maitresse du Titien, after Titian, by Forster.

7. The Virgin and Child and St. John, after Van Dyck, by V. Green — *mezzotint*.
8. La Madonna della Scodella, after Correggio, by Ravenet.
9. La Vierge de la Maison d'Albe, after Raffaelle, by Desnoyers.
10. "Verbum caro factum," after C. Maratti, by Garavaglia.
11. Jupiter and Antiope, after Correggio, by Audouin.
12. The Conversion of Saul, after Rubens, by Bolswert.
13. The Assumption of the Virgin, after Poussin, by Logier.
14. The Annunciation, after Correggio, by Ravenet — and the companion.
15. The Holy Family, after Sir J. Reynolds, by Sharp.
16. La Madonna del Sacco, after A. del Sarto, by R. Morghen — *proof*.
17. Carthage, after Turner, by D. Wilson — *proof before letters*.
18. Portrait of Sir W. Grant, by Golding; and Earl of Durham, after Sir T. Lawrence, by Turner.
19. Modesty and Vanity, after L. Da Vinci, by Scotto.
20. A Literary Party at Sir J. Reynolds's, after Doyle, by Walker.
21. Portrait of Lord Eldon; and the Princess Royal, after Sir W. Ross.
22. H.M. the Queen, after Winterhalter, by Forster.
23. The Prince of Wales, after Winterhalter, by Noel.
24. The Death of the Earl of Chatham, after Copley, by Heath. (Graves)
25. Portrait of a gentleman; and a photograph of Lord Brougham.
26. Sir William Follett, after Ray; the Queen, after Sir W. Ross; and the Siege of Gibraltar, after Copley. (Harner)
27. The Visitation, after Raffaelle, by Desnoyers.
28. The Temple of Jupiter, after Turner, by Pye.
29. Duncan's Victory, after Copley. (Duncan)
30. The Siege of Gibraltar, after ditto. — (G. Earl)
31. The Death of Major Peirson, after ditto. (G. Earl)
32. The Dance of the Seasons, by R. Morghen.
33. The Repose of the Holy Family, by ditto.
34. The Return from Hawking, etching after Landseer; and one after Rubens.
35. THE TRANSFIGURATION, after Raffaelle, by R. Morghen — *proof before letters*.

DRAWINGS. FRAMED AND GLAZED

36. View of Guy's Cliff, near Leamington.
38. View of the village of Turville, a lake scene, and two coast scenes.

F. TAYLER

39. A group of beggars.
40. Interior of a gamekeeper's cottage — *in bistre*.

PROUT, AFTER

41. Old buildings — *in pencil*.

F. TAYLER

42. A trumpeter of the Guards.
43. An illustration to 'Waverley.'
44. A street scene, with a carriage.
45. An interior, with two figures at breakfast.
46. A street scene, with a church and other buildings.
47. Post-boys — *a pair in one frame*.

COUNT D'ORSAY

48. Portrait of a lady, seated — *in pencil.*

K. HARTMAN

49. A mother and child.

F. BARTOLOZZI

50. Studies from Copley's picture of the death of the Earl of Chatham; heads of the Marquis of Stafford, Earls of Sandwich, Radnor, and Leicester. (Graves, 5.0.0)

51. Studies from Copley's picture of the Death of the Earl of Chatham, of the heads of Lord Mansfield, the Bishop of St. Asaph, Lord Harcourt, Lord Dudley and Ward, and Lord Coventry. (Waters, 6.15.0)

52. Studies from Copley's picture of the Death of the Earl of Chatham, of the heads of the Archbishop of York, Duke of Manchester, Dr. Brocklesby, the Earl of Effingham and Coventry — *unframed.* (Waters, 1.1.0)

PICTURES BY J. S. COPLEY, R.A.

53. PORTRAIT OF LORD HOWE [596] — small circle. *Engraved.* (Anthony, 17.17.0)

54. PORTRAIT OF ADMIRAL BARRINGTON [595] — small circle. *Engraved.* (Anthony, 11.11.0)

55. PORTRAIT OF ADMIRAL VISCOUNT DUNCAN, afterwards Lord Camperdown [620]. *Engraved. Exhibited at the Royal Academy, 1798.* (Hon. H. Duncan, 246.15.0)

56. ANOTHER PORTRAIT OF ADMIRAL DUNCAN [619] — *rolled.* (King, 7.17.6; "good head but hard," Anderdon)

57. HEAD OF LORD HEATHFIELD: a study for the 'Siege of Gibraltar' [495]. (Scharf, 39.18.0, MBA [incorrect])

58. HEAD OF AN OFFICER — *rolled.* (Anderdon, 8.10.0; "a handsome young officer Sketch," Anderdon)

59. CUPID CARESSING VENUS [386]. (Cox, 10.10.0, MBA; "a work of considerable originality & power," Anderdon)

60. PORTRAIT OF A LADY [*Mrs. Richard Skinner*, 315]. *Signed, and dated Boston, 1772.* (Timmins, 56.14.0)

61. A YOUTH RESCUED FROM A SHARK. *Engraved by V. Green.* (Cox, 11.11.0), MBA]

62. THE NATIVITY [347]. *Engraved.* (Colonel Hawkesley, 10.10.0; "a sketch," Anderdon)

63. Charles I. demanding the arrest of the five Members. *A sketch for the celebrated picture in the Gallery at Boston, U.S.* [601]. (Waters, 13.13.0)

64. MONMOUTH BEFORE JAMES II., refusing to give the names of his accomplices [604]. (Waters, 8.18.0)

X. (Cox, 9.9.0) [An object not listed in the catalogue must have been sold at this point.]

65. THE SIEGE OF GIBRALTAR [499]. *A sketch for the celebrated picture at the Guildhall. Painted for the Common Council of the City.* (Gregory, 16.16.0)

66. PORTRAITS OF COLONELS HUGO AND SCHLEPPEGRELL [498]. *Fine studies for the picture of 'The Siege of Gibraltar.'* (Clarke, 10.10.0, MBA)

67. PORTRAIT OF MAJOR-GENERAL DE LA MOTTE [496]. *A fine study for the same picture.* (Clarke, 10.10.0, MBA)

68. PORTRAIT OF COLONEL DACHENHAUSEN [497]. *A fine study for the same picture.* (Clarke, 10.10.0, MBA)

69. HEAD OF A FAVOURITE NEGRO [381]. *Very fine. Introduced in the picture of 'The Boy saved from the Shark.'* (Isaac, 11.11.0)

70. THE DEATH OF THE EARL OF CHATHAM [403]. *The first sketch for the picture in the National Gallery.* (Anderdon, 4.14.6, MBA)

71. THE DEATH OF MAJOR PEIRSON [450]. *The first sketch for the large picture.* (Cox, 1.1.0)
72. CHARLES I. DEMANDING THE ARREST OF THE FIVE MEMBERS. *An early sketch for the picture at Boston, U. S.* (Rutley, 15.5.6)
73. HEAD OF AN AMERICAN LADY. (Goldsmith, 21.0.0; "a clever sketch very powerful for an ugly head," Anderdon)
74. PORTRAIT OF ONE OF THE MISS COPLEYS, in a hat [476]. (Timmins, 10.0.0)
75. PORTRAIT OF THE ARTIST [350?]. (Cox, 26.5.0, MBA, "destroyed in the fire 1872" [in a later hand]; "this is hard & unpleasing, dark, ugly," Anderdon)
76. PORTRAIT OF MR. BRANSDON. (Stuart, 19.0.0)
77. ABRAHAM'S SACRIFICE [606]. *Exhibited at the Royal Academy, 1796. Engraved by R. Dunkarton.* (Goldsmith, 25.4.0)
78. HAGAR AND ISHMAEL IN THE WILDERNESS [609] — the companion. *Exhibited at the Royal Academy, 1798.* (Goldsmith, 33.12.0; "this was pleasing," Anderdon)
79. T.R.H. PRINCESS MARY, PRINCESS SOPHIA, AND PRINCESS AMELIA, the Children of George III., in the garden at Windsor — engraved [after 468]. *A highly finished sketch for the well-known picture at Buckingham Palace. Exhibited at the Royal Academy in 1785.* (Whitehead, 257.5.0)
80. SAMUEL AND ELI [destroyed replica of 391]. *The well-known picture, engraved by Valentine Green for Macklin's Bible.* (Cole, 105.0.0; "marked J. S. Copley 1810," Anderdon)
81. PORTRAIT OF LORD MANSFIELD, seated, in his robes [429]. *The well-known engraved picture.* (Scharf, 241.10.0)
82. THE ST. JEROME, AFTER CORREGGIO. *A fine copy of the celebrated picture at Parma, the size of the original, painted at Parma about 1774 or 1775.* (Anthony, 53.11.0)
83. THE VIRGIN AND CHILD, ST. CATHERINE, AND AN ANGEL. *A beautiful study for a portion of the preceding picture, painted at Parma about 1774 or 1775.* (Rich, 25.4.0)
84. SAUL REPROVED BY SAMUEL [610]. "The Lord hath rent the kingdom of Israel from thee this day." — 1 Sam.xv. 28. *Exhibited at the Royal Academy, 1798.* (Cox, 28.7.0, MBA; pleasing & well coloured," Anderdon)
85. A BOY WITH A SQUIRREL [163]. *Painted in 1760. The well-known picture, exhibited anonymously at the Royal Academy, and which was the cause of Mr. Copley's coming to England in 1764; he went to Rome the same year. Exhibited at the International Exhibition.* (Bentley, 241.10.0, JSA, "Owned by Frederic Amory — 1932" [later hand])
86. THE RED CROSS KNIGHT: portraits of Lord Lyndhurst and his two sisters (Mrs. Green, of Boston, U. S., and Miss Copley) [592]. (Clarke, 73.10.0, FGD [later hand])
87. THE BATTLE OF THE PYRENEES, with portraits of the Duke of Wellington, the Prince of Orange, and Lord March [673] *A grand work, unfinished.* (Radclyffe, 5.15.6, MBA; "this was an enormously ugly [sic] & enormous in size," Anderdon)
88. GEORGE IV., WHEN PRINCE OF WALES, at a review, attended by Lord Heathfield, General Turner, Colonel Bloomfield, and Baron Eben: Colonel Quintin in the distance [661] — engraved. *Exhibited at the Royal Academy in 1810.* (Cox, 5.0.0., MBA; "enormous & most ugly!" Anderdon)
89. THE OFFER OF THE CROWN TO LADY JANE GREY, by the Dukes of Northumberland and Suffolk, and other Lords — deputies of the Privy Council [655]. *Exhibited at the Royal Academy, 1808.* (Cox, 23.2.0, MBA; "a very ill drawn & tame affair," Anderdon)
90. THE DEATH OF MAJOR PEIRSON [442]. *The celebrated chef-d'oeuvre. Engraved by Heath. Painted for Alderman Boydell, and afterwards repurchased by Mr. Copley. Exhibited at the International Exhibition.* (National Gallery, 1600.0.0; "This grand gallery picture was the great attraction of the room," *Times*, March 7, 1864)
91. THE WELL-KNOWN FAMILY PICTURE [344]: portraits of John Singleton Copley, R.A., with his wife caressing the infant (Lord Lyndhurst) and his three other infant children, in a

landscape; the gentleman seated is Mr. Clarke, the father of Mrs. Copley. *Engraved by R. Thew. Exhibited at the International Exhibition.* (Clarke, 1050.0.0, MBA; Anderdon noted of lots 90 and 91 that there was "quite around of applause as the Hammer fell to each of these last")

PICTURES BY OLD MASTERS

SIR P. LELY

92. PORTRAIT OF GEOFFREY PALMER, Speaker of the House of Commons, *temp.* Charles I., seated in an armchair, holding a letter. *This portrait is introduced by Mr. Copley in his celebrated picture of Charles I. demanding the five impeached Members.*

93. PORTRAIT OF JAMES II., in armour and white scarf.

BERGHEM

94. A landscape, with two peasants driving cows through a stream, and two figures, with a mule.

TITIAN

95. THE VIRGIN AND CHILD, AND ST. JOHN.

BOUCHER

96. "LA COURTISANE AMOUREUSE" — *engraved.*

BASSANO

97. WINTER.

MODERN

98. Portrait of a lady.

ROTENHAEMER

99. St. Jerome — on copper — small — oval.

PETERS

101. Vessels in a storm.

VAN DYCK

102. PORTRAIT OF ARCHBISHOP LAUD, in his robes.

UNKNOWN

103. PORTRAIT OF SIR ISAAC NEWTON, seated at a table, holding a pen in his hand. *Admirably painted.*

TITIAN

104. DANAË. *A capitol old replica.*

VAN DYCK

105. CUPID AND PSYCHE, in a landscape.

A. SACCHI

106. THE VISION OF MOSES.

WOUVERMANS

107. A HAWKING PARTY, in a landscape, near the entrance to a château.

M. RICCI

108. CHRIST AND THE CENTURION.

BERGHEM

109. A RIVER SCENE, with cattle in a stream of water, under a rocky height, and a peasant with a dog.

VAN DYCK

110. PORTRAIT OF LADY MIDDLETON, in a black dress lined with pink satin, pearl necklace and earrings, holding flowers in her hands.

CORREGGIO, AFTER

111. THE NOTTE. *A capital replica of the celebrated work*, at Dresden, by Carlo Maratti.

LOCATELLI

112. A LANDSCAPE: view near the coast, with a horse and figures on a road.

RUYSDAEL SCHOOL

113. A WOODY RIVER-SCENE, with a waterfall.

P. POTTER

114. A LANDSCAPE, with a bull and two cows.

TINTORETTO

115. IL MIRACOLO DEL SERVO. A fine sketch for the celebrated picture.

MANGLARD

116. THE DELUGE.

LOCATELLI

117. AN UPRIGHT WOODY LANDSCAPE, with buildings and figures.

CHARDIN

118. PORTRAIT OF MADAME GEOFFRIN, seated at a table, taking chocolate. *Admirably painted.*

ALBANO

119. DIANA AND ACTAEON.

DOMENICHINO

120. THE MAGDALENE, in a landscape.

TINTORETTO

121. PORTRAIT OF A VENETIAN SENATOR, in a crimson robe, lined with ermine.

CANALETTI

122. THE GRAND CANAL, VENICE, with the church of Sta. Maria della Salute, and the Dogana in front, looking towards St. Mark's Quay, with numerous gondolas and figures.

CANALETTI

123. VIEW OF ST. MARK'S PLACE, with numerous figures — the companion. *These fine works were bequeathed to Lord Lyndhurst by the Baron Bolland.*

Catalogue of English Pictures

Catalogue of English Pictures

The purpose of this catalogue is to record authentic English Copleys.[1] To keep the catalogue free from possibly erroneous attributions, a rigorous policy of not including problematical pictures has been followed. Although it is likely that some English Copleys have thereby been excluded from the catalogue, it seemed more prudent to leave out problematical pictures until further information or an opportunity for more thorough stylistic analysis is available. The exclusion of a work here, then, should not be regarded as necessarily implying that it is not a Copley.

The number of English pictures attributed to Copley during the past fifty years is quite large. I have encountered over two hundred and fifty such pictures, the majority of them examined in person or seen in photograph, which I have not included here. Because there has been no definitive study of Copley's English work, a temptation has long existed to fit provincial English portraits, especially those of military figures and children, into an imaginary period of transition between his realistic American style and his more flamboyant and elegant English manner. A few initial misattributions provided the platform for others, and a snowballing effect resulted in more and freer attributions, often accompanied by certificates of authenticity.

The present study attempts to clarify the situation by restricting the catalogue to pictures that the author believes to be demonstrably and unquestionably by Copley. It can, in turn, provide a firm base for further attributions. In a few instances objects examined only in photograph, usually those related in some way to incontestably authentic objects listed, have been allowed to remain in the catalogue even though the photograph did not convey a clear enough impression of the picture to permit a firm judgment of its authenticity. In these cases the reservation has been noted by an observation that the object has been examined only in photograph.

The catalogue is arranged alphabetically, with the pictures listed by the sitter's name in the portrait section and by subject (title) in the section devoted to historical, religious, and mythological pictures. Titled sitters are listed according to title rather than family name: thus Henry Belasyse, Second Earl of Fauconberg, appears under *Fauconberg* rather than *Belasyse*.

The first section of each entry presents the title, the life years for sitters (in parentheses), medium, size, date, present ownership, and figure number in this volume [in brackets]. The subsequent categories of information are:

[1] The handful of surviving paintings and drawings done in Italy in 1774–75 (figs. 335–342) are also included here.

Provenance: I have stressed the primary ownerships, without attempting to trace all commercial ownerships. When a picture has descended in a single family, that fact is given rather than separate citations for succeeding owners. For pictures or drawings that passed through one of the Lyndhurst sales, the purchaser's name is given unless the specific lot number is questionable or unless the purchaser appears as the next regular owner of the picture. For the full citation of an object as listed in one of the Lyndhurst sale catalogues, see that catalogue in the appendices. Information on art sales has been compiled from a variety of sources, including the Frick Art Reference Library, New York; the Witt Library, Courtauld Institute, London; the Copley photograph files, National Portrait Gallery, London; and such auction records as *Art Prices Current*, Graves's *Art Sales*, and special art-sale records kept by the Witt Library, M. Knoedler & Co. (London), and Thomas Agnew & Sons (London), which I have been able to consult. The following abbreviations are used to identify recurrent ownerships:

Amory-Dexter: Mrs. Charles Amory (Martha Babcock), Boston; her daughter, Mrs. F. Gordon Dexter (Susan Greene Amory), Boston; her son, Gordon Dexter; his wife, Mrs. Gordon Dexter.

CDC-OPS: Charles D. Childs Gallery, Boston, and The Old Print Shop, New York.

Jupp-Amory: Edward Basil Jupp, London; Amory family, Boston; Linzee Amory, Boston. Most of the Amory-Dexter pictures were acquired by Martha Babcock Amory, granddaughter (and biographer) of Copley and daughter of Mrs. Gardiner Greene (Elizabeth Copley), at the Lyndhurst sale. Sir Edward Jupp acquired a number of drawings at the Lyndhurst library sale, and in some undocumented transaction many of these drawings were acquired by the Amory family in Boston, specifically though perhaps not initially by Linzee Amory; after his death, they were left to a servant whose family eventually sold them to CDC-OPS.

Exhibited: Only the record of pictures exhibited during Copley's lifetime is included here (for the full titles of pictures as exhibited, see appendix, Pictures Exhibited by Copley). Subsequent exhibition records are sometimes included in *Provenance* or *Bibliography* if they contribute relevant information. Further data on nineteenth- and early twentieth-century exhibitions can be found in Algernon Graves, *A Century of Loan Exhibitions, 1813–1912*, 5 vols. (London, 1913). Later exhibitions are frequent and often not important. References to these can often be found through reviews and articles listed in *Art Index*. Numbers in parentheses are listed numbers in the exhibition catalogues.

Engraved: Only engravings made during Copley's lifetime are listed.

Bibliography: This is a selection of references from the basic writings on Copley, especially those containing a listing of works, and of other sources that contribute relevant data about the picture. A few abbreviations are used for recurrent sources. In addition to such obvious short titles as Amory, Perkins, Perkins' *Supplement*, Bayley

(1915 ed.), *Copley-Pelham Letters,* and Parker-Wheeler (see my bibliography for full citations), there are the following:

BMFA '38: *John Singleton Copley, 1738–1815,* Loan Exhibition, Boston Museum of Fine Arts, Feb. 1–March 15, 1938.

Bolton: Theodore Bolton and Harry Lorin Binsse, "John Singleton Copley," *Antiquarian,* XV (Dec. 1930), 76–83, 116, 118.

Charles I brochure: *Mr. Copley's Picture of King Charles the First, Demanding in the House of Commons the Five Impeached Members, A.D. MDCXLI–II, Now Exhibiting in Spring Gardens* (London, [1795]).

Copley Exhib. '65: *John Singleton Copley, 1738–1815,* National Gallery of Art, Metropolitan Museum of Art, and Boston Museum of Fine Arts, Sept. 18, 1965–March 6, 1966. Text by Jules David Prown.

Hipkiss: Edwin J. Hipkiss, *Eighteenth Century American Arts: The M. and M. Karolik Collection* (Boston, 1941).

Met '37: *An Exhibition of Paintings by John Singleton Copley,* Metropolitan Museum of Art, Dec. 22, 1936–Feb. 14, 1937. Text by Harry B. Wehle.

Panorama: Helen Comstock, "Drawings by John Singleton Copley," *Panorama,* Harry Shaw Newman Gallery, II (May 1947).

Copies: Information, where available, is given to prevent possible confusion in future compilations.

Other relevant data or observations not given in the text are added at the conclusion of the entry. In sum, the catalogue is selective, aiming to identify firmly and present basic data for each object, but not to record exhaustively each reference, reproduction, and exhibition.

Portraits

ADAMS, ABIGAIL (Mrs. William Stephens Smith; 1765–1818). Oil on canvas, before 1794. Destroyed. [Engraving, 440]
   Provenance: John Quincy Adams, brother of the sitter; given by him to Mrs. Caroline Amelia de Windt, Fishkill, N.Y., the sitter's only daughter; destroyed by fire.
   Bibliography: Perkins, pp. 108–09; Perkins, *Supplement,* p. 7; Bayley, p. 230; TBA Journal, Oct. 24, 1794, Adams Papers, Massachusetts Historical Society, Boston.
   Copies: Miniature; owned by Charles Francis Adams, 1915.
ADAMS, JOHN (1735–1826). Oil on canvas, 93¾″ x 57¹⁵⁄₁₆″, 1783. Harvard University, Cambridge, Mass. [438]
   Provenance: Adams family; gift of Ward Nicholas Boylston, 1828.
   Exhibited: Royal Academy, 1796 (287).
   Bibliography: Perkins, p. 27; Bayley, pp. 32, 38; *Copley-Pelham Letters,* p. 374; Bolton, p. 116; Met '37 (41).
   Copies: Adams Memorial, Quincy, Mass.
——— STUDY FOR (recto of Study of the Duke of Richmond for *Death of Chatham* [407]).

411

Black and white chalk on gray-blue paper, 18¾″ x 14¼″, 1783. Metropolitan Museum of Art, New York (Harris Brisbane Dick Fund, 1960). [439]

Provenance: Lyndhurst Library Sale (670); Jupp-Amory; CDC-OPS.

ADAMS, JOHN QUINCY (1767–1848). Oil on canvas, 30″ x 25″, 1796. Museum of Fine Arts, Boston. [598]

Provenance: Adams family; gift of Charles Francis Adams, 1917.

Bibliography: Perkins, p. 27; Bayley, p. 39; Bolton, p. 116; Marie (Healy) Bigot, *Life of George P. A. Healy* (n.p., n.d.), p. 53; BMFA '38, p. 19 (1); Copley Exhib. '65, pp. 113, 141–42 (92).

AMHERST, LORD. In *Death of Chatham.*

ASAPH, BISHOP OF ST. See *St. Asaph.*

BALFOUR, MRS. LETITIA (daughter of Francis Leigh, Esq.). Oil on canvas, 29″ x 24″, 1782. Max Safran, New York.

Inscribed: Signed and dated lower right, "J. S. Copley, R.A. / 1782" (signature apparently by a later hand, perhaps replacing lost original).

Provenance: David Chrichton Collection Sale, Christie, Oct. 25, 1957 (56).

BARNARDISTON, SIR NATHANIEL (1588–1653). In *Charles I Demanding.*

BARRINGTON, ADMIRAL THE HONORABLE SAMUEL (1729–1800). Oil on canvas, 30″ x 25″, 1791–95. Viscount Barrington, Berwick Place, Essex. [597]

Provenance: Barrington family.

Exhibited: South Kensington [Victoria and Albert] Museum, London, 1867 (739).

Engraved: W. Ridley, stipple, 4⅛″ x 3⅜″, published by Bunney and Gold, October 1, 1800; W. Sharp, line engraving, 5″ x 3¾″, published by Copley, May 22, 1810.

Bibliography: Met '37 (45).

———— Oil on canvas, 7⅝″ x 5⅞″, 1787–95. Mr. and Mrs. Leo L. Pollock, New York. [595]

Provenance: Lyndhurst Sale (54), to Anthony; Dr. Joseph P. Eidson, New York; M. Knoedler & Co., New York.

Bibliography: Perkins, p. 131; Bayley, pp. 34, 57.

BATHURST, HENRY, SECOND EARL (1714–1794; Lord Chancellor). In *Death of Chatham.*

BELASYSE, JOHN, BARON (1614–1689; created Baron Bellasis of Worlaby). In *Charles I Demanding.*

"A picture, in the possession of Earl Fauconberg, and an excellent miniature by Cooper, at a more advanced age, in the possession of the same Nobleman, were sufficient materials" (*Charles I* brochure).

BERNARD, SIR FRANCIS, BT. (1712–1779). Oil on canvas, 29″ x 24″, 1776–79. Christ Church, Oxford. [352]

Provenance: "Mr. Bernard late Student of this House made a present to the Chapter of a Picture of his late Father Sir Francis Bernard" (Nov. 16, 1789, Chapter Minute Book [copy], Christ Church Library).

Bibliography: Mrs. Reginald Lane Poole, comp., *Catalogue of Portraits in the Possession of the University, Colleges, City and County of Oxford*, III (Oxford, 1912–26), 72 (186); List of Oxford Portraits compiled by John Gutch, 1790, I, opp. p. 293 (Christ Church Library).

BERTIE, LORD ROBERT. In *Death of Chatham.*

BESSBOROUGH, WILLIAM PONSONBY, SECOND EARL OF (1704–1793). In *Death of Chatham.*

———— Oil on canvas, 23″ x 18¾″ (sight), 1790. Fogg Art Museum, Harvard University, Cambridge, Mass. (Grenville L. Winthrop Collection). [590]

Inscribed: Signed and dated lower right, "J. S. Copley RA / 1790."

Provenance: Property of Claude A. C. Ponsonby, Christie, March 28, 1908 (12), to Sabin; Grenville L. Winthrop.

The guilloche design on the apron of the table and the vase against the open sky in the upper left are reminiscent of *The Izard Family*, which Copley had in his studio at the time this portrait was painted.

────── Oil on canvas, 27″ x 21″, c. 1790. Earl Fitzwilliam, Milton, Peterborough.

Provenance: Earl of Clanbrassil.

Engraved: R. Dunkarton, mezzotint, 17⅝″ x 13⅞″, published by Copley, May 12, 1794 (from an original portrait in the possession of the Earl of Clanbrassil).

Bibliography: Perkins, p. 128; Bayley, pp. 59, 199.

BLACKBURN, JOHN, ESQ. Oil on canvas, 30″ x 25″, 1785–90. Unlocated.

Provenance: Spink and Sons, London.

A photograph suggests that the head is by Copley, but the remainder of the picture seems to have been overpainted by another hand.

BLOOMFIELD, COLONEL BENJAMIN (1768–1846). In *George IV (as Prince of Wales)*.

BOYD, LIEUT. GEN. SIR ROBERT (1710–1794). In *Siege of Gibraltar*.

BRANSDON, MR. Unlocated.

Provenance: Lyndhurst Sale (76), to Stuart.

BRIDGEMAN, ORLANDO (1606?–1674). In *Charles I Demanding*.

"From a portrait, in the possession of the Lord Chancellor; it was necessary to give a younger appearance than he bears in the Lord Chancellor's portrait" (*Charles I* brochure).

BRINE, MIDSHIPMAN AUGUSTUS (1770–1840). Oil on canvas, 49½″ x 39½″, 1782. Metropolitan Museum of Art, New York. [423]

Inscribed: Signed and dated lower left, "J. S. Copley Pin . . . /1782."

Provenance: Brine family, Boldre Hill, Lymington, Hampshire; Mrs. Knapton, Stanwell House, Lymington; Lord Duveen, London; Brewerton Sale, Christie, December 12, 1924 (111), to F. Sabin, London; bequest of Richard De Wolfe Brixey, 1943.

Bibliography: Josephine L. Allen, "An English Copley," *Metropolitan Museum Bulletin* (1944), pp. 260–62; Albert TenEyck Gardner and Stuart P. Feld, *American Paintings: A Catalogue of the Collection of the Metropolitan Museum of Art*, I (New York, 1965), 48–49; Copley Exhib. '65, pp. 100, 140 (75).

BROCKLESBY, RICHARD (1722–1797). In *Death of Chatham*.

────── Oil on canvas, before 1798. Unlocated. [Engraving, 618]

Provenance: According to William Curran, a Brocklesby scholar, the Copley portrait was last owned by a descendant of Thomas Young, the famous physician and Egyptologist, in Bristol, and was destroyed in 1940 during the bombings.

Engraved: W. Ridley, stipple, 3⅞″ x 3″, published by J. Sewall, June 1, 1798, plate in *European Magazine*.

Bibliography: Bayley, p. 66.

The engraving represents Brocklesby as considerably older than he had appeared in *The Death of Chatham*, and, unlike the Pitt or Bessborough engravings, this is not based on *Chatham*. But the costume suggests that the portrait was painted long before the engraving was produced.

────── See Study for *Death of Chatham* [405].

BROWN, MAJOR GENERAL RICHARD (d. 1669). In *Charles I Demanding*.

"From a beautiful medal in Dr. Hunter's museum" (*Charles I* brochure).

BROWN, MAJOR. In *Siege of Gibraltar*.

BUCHANAN, LIEUT. In *Death of Peirson*.

BUCKHURST, RICHARD LORD (1622–1677). In *Charles I Demanding*.

"From a fine miniature by Mr. Humphrey, after an original picture, in the collection of his Grace the Duke of Dorset" (*Charles I* brochure).

BURGWYN, JOHN (1731–1803). Oil on canvas, 30¼″ x 25″, 1788. Hall of History, Raleigh, North Carolina. [486]

Inscribed: Signed and dated lower right, "J. S. Copley pint 1788."

Bibliography: Perkins, *Supplement*, pp. 1–2; Bayley, p. 70.

Burgwyn paid Copley 83 guineas for this half-length portrait.

BURNET, MR. In *Victory of Duncan*.

CAMDEN, CHARLES PRATT, EARL OF (1713–1793). In *Death of Chatham*.

CARDIFF, LORD. In *Death of Chatham*.

CAWTHORNE, MR. Oil on canvas, 1805. Unlocated.

    Exhibited: Royal Academy, 1805 (183).

    Bibliography: Amory, p. 270; Bayley, p. 75.

Mary Copley, London, writing to her sister, Mrs. Gardiner Greene, Boston, May 2, 1805, about the Royal Academy exhibition that had just opened, noted, "My father has only a head in it" (Amory, p. 270).

CHARLES I (1600–1649). In *Charles I Demanding*.

"A bust by Bernini supplied the forms of the side face; for the tinting, recourse was had to a genuine portrait by Vandyck, in the possession of Lady Fermanagh" (*Charles I* brochure).

CHATHAM, WILLIAM PITT, FIRST EARL OF (1708–1778). In *Death of Chatham*.

CHATHAM, JOHN PITT, SECOND EARL OF (1756–1835). In *Death of Chatham*.

CHOLMONDELEY, GEORGE JAMES, FOURTH EARL OF (1749–1827). In *Death of Chatham*.

CLARKE, RICHARD (1711–1795). In *Copley Family*.

CLELAND, CAPTAIN. In *Victory of Duncan*.

CLEPHANE, CAPTAIN. In *Death of Peirson*.

CODMAN, JOHN (1719/20–1792). Oil on canvas, 36¼″ x 28″, c. 1800. Museum of Fine Arts, Boston. [658]

    Provenance: Codman family; Mrs. Maxim Karolik (Martha Codman); gift of Maxim Karolik, 1938.

    Bibliography: Perkins, p. 45; Bayley, pp. 33, 79–80; Bolton, p. 116; BMFA '38, p. 21 (18); Hipkiss, pp. 12–13 (6).

This portrait was painted after an earlier American portrait by Thomas Johnston.

CODMAN, JOHN (1755–1803). Oil on canvas, 36″ x 28″, c. 1800. Private collection. [659]

    Provenance: Capt. John Codman, Boston, 1875 [?]; Gertrude, Lady Carter, Bahama Islands.

    Bibliography: Perkins, *Supplement*, p. 2 [?]; Bayley, pp. 79–80.

    Copies: Two copies of this picture, including one by Bass Otis, are said to exist.

Bayley notes that this sitter was painted in Torquay, England.

CODMAN, REVEREND JOHN (1782–1848). Oil on canvas, 36″ x 28″, 1808. Mrs. Robert Codman, Boston. [660]

    Provenance: Bishop Robert Codman, Portland, Maine, 1915.

    Exhibited: Royal Academy, 1808 (146).

    Bibliography: Bayley, pp. 79–80.

CODMAN, RICHARD (1762–1806). Oil on canvas, c. 1790. Private collection. [657]

    Bibliography: Perkins, p. 45; Bayley, pp. 80–81; Bolton, p. 116.

COKE, SIR JOHN (1563–1644). In *Charles I Demanding*.

COLCHESTER, CHARLES ABBOTT, FIRST BARON (1757–1829). Oil on canvas. Unlocated.

    Bibliography: Bayley, p. 82; Thomas Frognall Dibdin, *Reminiscences of a Literary Life*, II (London, 1836), 152n. Dibdin refers to this picture as among Copley's more notable portraits, along with those of Lords Spencer and Sidmouth, and Richard Heber.

COPLEY FAMILY, THE. Oil on canvas, 72½″ x 90⅜″, 1776–77. National Gallery of Art, Washington D.C. (Andrew Mellon Fund, 1961). [344]

    Provenance: Lyndhurst Sale (91), to Clarke; Amory family.

    Exhibited: Royal Academy, 1777 (61).

    Engraved: R. Thew, stipple, 22″ x 26″, unfinished.

    Bibliography: Perkins, pp. 20, 48–49, 134; Bayley, pp. 35–36, 101–02; Bolton, p. 116; BMFA '38, pp. 11–12, 21 (22); Copley Exhib. '65, pp. 83, 89, 139 (61).

Copies: *Head of Richard Clarke*. Oil on canvas. Marguerite Kumm, Fairfax, Va.

Included in the family picture are the artist, young Susanna Copley, Richard Clarke, Elizabeth Clarke Copley, John Singleton Copley, Jr., Mrs. Copley (Susanna Clarke), and Mary Copley.

———— SKETCH FOR. Oil on canvas, 20¾″ x 26½″, 1776. Private collection. [346]
Provenance: Greene and Amory families.
Bibliography: Perkins, p. 48; Bayley, p. 102; BMFA '38, p. 21 (23); Copley Exhib. '65, pp. 83, 89, 139 (62).
Copies: Owned by Frederic Amory, 1915. *Bibliography*: Bayley, p. 102.

———— SKETCH FOR. Oil on canvas, 15¾″ x 13½″, 1776. Mrs. Gordon Sweet, Mt. Carmel, Conn. [345]
Provenance: Greene family.
Bibliography: Perkins, p. 48, Bayley, pp. 85, 102; Bolton, p. 116; BMFA '38, p. 22 (24).

COPLEY, ELIZABETH (1770–1866). In *Red Cross Knight*.
———— In *Copley Family*
———— See *Greene, Mrs. Gardiner*.

COPLEY, JOHN SINGLETON (1738–1815). Oil on canvas, 18⅛″ diameter, 1776–80. Private collection. [350]
Provenance: Probably Lyndhurst Sale (75), to Cox, although Augustus Thorndike Perkins, "Sketch of Some of the Losses to the Departments of Literature and the Fine Arts, Occasioned by the Great Fire in Boston of 1872," *New England Historical and Genealogical Register* XXVII (Oct. 1873), 370, notes that a Copley self-portrait in the collection of Charles Amory (Cox purchased pictures for Mrs. Amory at the Lyndhurst Sale) was said to have been destroyed in the 1872 Boston fire; Mrs. Gardiner Greene Hammond (Esther Fiske).
Bibliography: Perkins, p. 132; Bayley, p. 84; Bolton, p. 116; Met '37 (frontis.); BMFA '38, p. 21 (19); Copley Exhib. '65, pp. 89, 139 (64).
———— In *Copley Family*.
————[?]. Oil on canvas, 21″ x 15″, 1776–78. Mrs. Douglas B. Smith, Sarasota, Florida. [351]
Provenance: Amory family
Bibliography: Bayley, p. 84; Bolton, p. 116.

Since this sitter does not resemble Copley but does have a striking resemblance to the older figure of Richard Clarke in *The Copley Family* (fig. 344), the portrait may represent one of Copley's brothers-in-law, Jonathan or Isaac Winslow Clarke.

COPLEY, MRS. JOHN SINGLETON (Susanna Farnham Clarke; 1745–1836). In *Copley Family*.

COPLEY, JOHN SINGLETON, JR. (1772–1863). Oil on canvas, 29″ x 24½″, c. 1813. Unlocated. [677]
Provenance: Lord Lyndhurst; Lady Lyndhurst; Mrs. Sophia Clarence Beckett; Lord Aberdare; Aberdare Sale, Christie, June 3, 1932 (83), to Dunnottar.
Bibliography: Perkins, pp. 82–83; Bayley, pp. 169–70; Allan Cunningham, *The Lives of the Most Eminent British Painters and Sculptors*, IV (New York, 1834), 156.
———— In *Red Cross Knight*.
———— In *Copley Family*

COPLEY, MARY (1773–1868). In *Red Cross Knight*.
———— In *Copley Family*

COPLEY, SUSANNA (1776–1785). Oil on canvas, 25¼″ x 20¼″, 1785. Commander Peter Du Cane, Haselbech Grange, Northampton. [475]
Provenance: Lyndhurst–Du Cane family.
Bibliography: Amory, p. 107; Bayley, pp. 85, 267.
Copies: Amory and Bayley refer to a pastel of this subject in Boston, presumably a copy since there are no English pastels currently known.

———— In *Copley Family*

CORBETT, CAPTAIN. In *Death of Peirson.*

CORNWALLIS, CHARLES, SECOND EARL AND FIRST MARQUIS (1738–1805). Oil on canvas, 57″ x 45″, before 1793. Guildhall Art Gallery, London. [594]

   Provenance: Gift of Alderman Boydell to the Corporation of the City of London, 1793.

   Engraved: Benjamin Smith, stipple, 16½″ x 13⅛″, published by J. and J. Boydell, Sept. 1, 1798.

   Bibliography: Perkins, p. 128; Bayley, pp. 85–86; Bolton, p. 116.

   Copies: Lancelot Speed, Clare College, Cambridge.

   Copley's receipt to Boydell for £67.14.6, dated June 5, 1795, is in the British Museum, Department of Prints and Drawings, "Anderdon, Royal Academy, 1796."

COURTENAY, WILLIAM VISCOUNT (1742–1788). In *Death of Chatham.*

COVENTRY, GEORGE WILLIAM, SIXTH EARL OF (1722–1809). In *Death of Chatham.*

CRAIG, COLONEL. In *Siege of Gibraltar.*

CRAWFORD, JOHN. In *Victory of Duncan.*

CROMWELL, OLIVER (1599–1658). In *Charles I Demanding.*

   "In the portrait of Cromwell, the difficulty was not to procure, but to select materials. A picture in the possession of Mr. Thane, and an accurate drawing by Cipriani, from a third picture by Walker, which a direct descent from the Protector has given to Mr. Cromwell of Gray's Inn, were sufficient and excellent authorities; and a mask taken from the face, in the possession of Mr. Richards, deserved, and obtained, a careful inspection" (*Charles I* brochure).

CUMBERLAND, HENRY FREDERICK, DUKE OF (1745–1790). In *Death of Chatham.*

CURTIS, SIR ROGER (1746–1816). In *Siege of Gibraltar.*

DACHENHAUSEN, COLONEL GUSTAV FRIEDRICH VON. Study for *Siege of Gibraltar.* Oil on canvas, 21″ x 17″, 1787. Fogg Art Museum, Harvard University, Cambridge, Mass. [497]

   Provenance: Lyndhurst Sale (68), to Clarke; Amory-Dexter; gift of Mrs. Gordon Dexter, 1942.

   Bibliography: Perkins, p. 132; Bayley, pp. 34, 36, 97, 225; Bolton, p. 116.

———— In *Siege of Gibraltar.*

DARTMOUTH, WILLIAM LEGGE, SECOND EARL OF (1731–1801). In *Death of Chatham.*

DAUGHTERS OF KING GEORGE III, THE THREE YOUNGEST (Mary, Sophia, and Amelia). Oil on canvas, 104½″ x 73″, 1785. Her Majesty Queen Elizabeth II, Buckingham Palace. [468]

   Inscribed: Signed and dated lower left, "J. S. Copley R.A. 1785."

   Provenance: Royal family

   Engraved: F. Bartolozzi, stipple, 19″ x 14¼″, published by Copley, Feb. 1, 1792.

   Exhibited: Royal Academy, 1785 (80).

   Bibliography: Perkins, pp. 22, 128, 133; Bayley, pp. 16, 31, 202; Met '37 (42); Sacheverell Sitwell, *Conversation Pieces* (New York and London, 1937), frontis. and p. 89; Copley Exhib. '65, pp. 106–09, 140–41 (80).

   Copies:

      1. Oil on canvas, 20½″ x 15½″, Mrs. Alan Cunningham, Brookline, Mass. *Provenance*: Lyndhurst Sale (79), to Whitehead; Sir John Pender; Christie, May 29, 1897, sold to Hodgkins; Mrs. Robert Treat Paine II, Chestnut Hill, Mass. *Bibliography*: Bayley, pp. 35, 36, 202; Bolton, p. 83; BMFA '38 (17); James Thomas Flexner, *John Singleton Copley* (Boston, 1948), plate 29. This appears to be a contemporary copy of the picture, probably made for the engraving. It is a highly finished version that follows the original closely in color and detail, except for the signature, which is omitted.

      2. Pen and gray wash over pencil, 9¾″ x 7⅝″. Her Majesty Queen Elizabeth II, Windsor Castle. *Bibliography*: A. P. Oppé, *English Drawings, Stuart and Georgian Periods . . . at Windsor Castle* (London, 1950), p. 35, n. 136. This is a drawing made after the picture by another hand, and not a study for it.

———— SKETCH OF PRINCESSES SOPHIA AND AMELIA. Oil on canvas, 49½″ x 39½″, 1785. Formerly Max Safran, New York.

Provenance: Lt. Col. C. B. Steuart, Westwood, Longniddry, East Lothian.

Bibliography: "Collectors' Questions," *Country Life*, CXII (Aug. 29, 1952), 608.

This sketch has been examined only in photograph.

———— STUDY FOR. Black and white chalk on blue-gray grounded paper, 8⅝″ x 11½″, 1784–85. Museum of Fine Arts, Boston (M. and M. Karolik Collection). [469]

Provenance: Lyndhurst Library Sale (672), to Clark; Weyhe Galleries, New York.

Bibliography: Hipkiss, p. 328 (259); BMFA '38, p. 34 (127).

———— STUDY FOR. Black and white chalk on grounded white paper, 17″ x 12⅜″, 1784–85. Worcester Art Museum, Worcester, Mass. [470]

Inscribed: Upper right, "Daughters of George 3ʳᵈ"; on back, "E. B. Jupp".

Provenance: Lyndhurst Library Sale (probably 671); E. B. Jupp; gift of Mr. and Mrs. Arthur L. Williston, Dedham, Mass., 1952.

———— STUDY FOR (recto of *Unknown Subject, studies from the antique* [335]). Black and white chalk on blue paper, 11″ x 13⅜″, 1784–85. Museum of Fine Arts, Boston (M. and M. Karolik Collection). [471]

Provenance: Lyndhurst Library Sale (672), to Clark; Weyhe Galleries, New York.

Bibliography: Hipkiss, p. 326 (258); BMFA '38, p. 31 (97).

———— STUDY FOR. Black chalk on blue-gray paper, 14¼″ x 23″, 1784–85. Victoria and Albert Museum, London. [472]

Provenance: Lyndhurst Library Sale (perhaps 660, 662, or 672); Redgrave.

The drawing is covered with measurements in inches.

DeBLOIS, GILBERT (1725–1791). Oil on canvas, 36¼″ x 27⅞″, 1777–80. Dr. Elizabeth DeBlois, Boston. [383]

Provenance: To his son Lewis; to his daughter Charlotte; sold after her death to Mrs. Augustus Thorndike Perkins; Mrs. C. H. Parker; George L. DeBlois, Boston.

Exhibited: Boston Athenaeum, 1871 (248).

Bibliography: Perkins, p. 51; Bayley, p. 93; Bolton, p. 116; *New England Historical and Genealogical Register*, LXVII (Jan. 1913), 10–11.

Copies: An early copy was owned by Dr. Thomas Amory DeBlois, Boston, 1913.

DEERING, SIR EDWARD. In *Charles I Demanding*.

DE LA MOTTE, MAJOR GENERAL AUGUST. Study for *Siege of Gibraltar*. Oil on canvas, 21″ x 17″, 1787. Fogg Art Museum, Harvard University, Cambridge, Mass. [496]

Provenance: Lyndhurst Sale (67), to Clarke; Amory-Dexter; gift of Mrs. Gordon Dexter, 1942.

Bibliography: Perkins, p. 132; Bayley, pp. 34, 36, 94, 225.

———— Oil on canvas, 23¾″ x 20″, after 1787. Mrs. Norman B. Woolworth, New York.

Provenance: Lt. Col. C. B. Steuart, Westwood, Longniddry, East Lothian; Hirschl & Adler, New York; Atlanta Art Asociation, Atlanta, Georgia; M. Knoedler & Co., New York.

Bibliography: "Collectors' Questions," *Country Life*, CXII (Aug. 29, 1952), 608.

Copies: Oil on canvas, 30½″ x 24½″, Fogg Art Museum, Harvard University, Cambridge, Mass. *Provenance*: Gift of Mrs. Gordon Dexter, 1942. *Bibliography*: *Fogg Art Museum Bulletin*, X (Nov. 1942), 3; Bolton, p. 116 [as by Copley].

This replica has been examined only in photograph.

———— In *Siege of Gibraltar*.

DERBY, MRS. RICHARD CROWNINSHIELD, AS ST. CECILIA (1783–1832). Oil on canvas, 94½″ x 58″, 1803–04. Mrs. Daniel M. Coxe, Drifton, Pa. [651]

Inscribed: Signed and dated center right, "J S Copley Pinx 1806."

Provenance: Purchased by the Boston Athenaeum, 1837; sold in 1853 to Nathan Appleton; William Sumner Appleton; to his niece, Mrs. Coxe, 1947.

Exhibited: Royal Academy, 1804 (184).

Bibliography: Amory, p. 246; Perkins, pp. 50–51; Bayley, pp. 33, 95, 234 [Mrs. Copley as St. Cecilia]; Bolton, p. 116.

Copies: E. C. A. Winslow, oil on canvas, 96″ x 60″, 1919. Kenneth Harper, Stamford, Conn.

DEVONSHIRE, WILLIAM, FIFTH DUKE OF (1748–1811). In *Death of Chatham*.

DeWINTER, ADMIRAL JAN WILLEM (1750–1812). In *Victory of Duncan*.

DRINKWATER, CAPT. JOHN (1762–1844). In *Siege of Gibraltar*.

DRYSDALE, LIEUTENANT. In *Death of Peirson*.

DUDLEY AND WARD, JOHN, SECOND VISCOUNT (1724/5–1788). In *Death of Chatham*.

———— Oil on canvas, 56″ x 46¾″, before 1804. Earl of Dudley, Great Westwood, King's Langley, Herts. [630]

Provenance: Dudley family.

Exhibited: Royal Academy, 1804 (96) [probably]; Birmingham, 1934 (443), as by Sir Thomas Lawrence.

Bibliography: Perkins, p. 129 [?]; Bayley, pp. 33, 97.

The figure is taken directly from *The Death of Chatham*.

DUDLEY AND WARD, WILLIAM, THIRD VISCOUNT (1750–1823). Oil on canvas, 1800. Earl of Dudley, Great Westwood, King's Langley, Herts. [631]

Provenance: Dudley family.

Exhibited: Royal Academy, 1800 (108).

Engraved: Freeman O'Donoghue, *Catalogue of Engraved British Portraits . . . in the British Museum*, VI (London, 1908–25), 139, cites an engraving of this portrait, but the illustration is taken from a painting and there is no further evidence that an engraving exists.

Bibliography: Bayley, pp. 32, 97; Algernon Graves and W. D. Cronin, *A History of the Works of Sir Joshua Reynolds* (London, 1899–1901), p. 264 (erroneously as a portrait by Reynolds of John, First Viscount Dudley and Ward).

DUDLEY AND WARD, JULIA, THIRD VISCOUNTESS (1754–1833). Oil on canvas, 1800. Earl of Dudley, Great Westwood, King's Langley, Herts. [632]

Provenance: Dudley family.

Exhibited: Royal Academy, 1800 (72).

Engraved: Freeman O'Donoghue, *Catalogue of Engraved British Portraits . . . in the British Museum*, VI (London, 1908–25), 140, cites an engraving of this portrait, but the illustration is taken from a painting and there is no further evidence that an engraving exists.

Bibliography: Bayley, pp. 32, 97; Algernon Graves and W. D. Cronin, *A History of the Works of Sir Joshua Reynolds* (London, 1899–1901), p. 264 (erroneously as a portrait by Reynolds of Mary, First Viscountess Dudley and Ward).

———— STUDY FOR. Black, red, and white chalk on blue-gray paper, 14¾″ x 12″, 1799–1800. Boston Athenaeum. [633]

Provenance: Lyndhurst Library Sale (671); Edward Basil Jupp; purchased 1883 from the Jupp Collection, London.

Exhibited: Museum of Fine Arts, Boston, 1883 (522).

DUNCAN, ADAM, VISCOUNT, ADMIRAL OF THE WHITE (1731–1804). Oil on canvas, 22½″ x 19⅜″, 1797. Yale University Art Gallery, New Haven, Conn. [619]

Provenance: Lyndhurst Sale (56), to King; M. Bernard, London.

Bibliography: Perkins, pp. 128[?], 131; Bayley, pp. 34, 73; Copley Exhib. '65, pp. 125, 142 (97).

There is a thumbnail sketch of this picture in Sir George Scharf's copy of the Lyndhurst Sale Catalogue at the National Portrait Gallery, London.

———— Oil on canvas, 50″ x 40″, 1798. Thomas Ewan Farrar, on loan to the National Maritime Museum, Greenwich. [620]

Provenance: Lyndhurst Sale (55), to Hon. H. Duncan.

Exhibited: Royal Academy, 1798 (111).

Engraved: Richard Earlom, published by Copley, March 1, 1798; W. Ridley, stipple, 4¼" x 3⅜", published by Bunney and Gold, Sept. 1, 1800.

Bibliography: Perkins, pp. 128, 131; Bayley, pp. 32, 34–35, 73, 99.

Copies: Oil on canvas, 50" x 40", loaned to the National Maritime Museum along with the original.

———— In *Victory of Duncan.*

EBEN, BARON. In *George IV* (*as Prince of Wales*).

EDGECUMBE, HON. MR. RICHARD (1764–1839). In *Death of Chatham.*

EFFINGHAM, EARL OF. In *Death of Chatham.*

EGLINTON, ARCHIBALD MONTGOMERIE, ELEVENTH EARL OF (1726–1796). In *Death of Chatham.*

EGLINTON, HUGH MONTGOMERIE, TWELFTH EARL OF. See *Montgomerie.*

ELIOTT, GENERAL GEORGE AUGUSTUS (1717–1790; later Lord Heathfield). Study for *Siege of Gibraltar.* Oil on canvas, 26½" x 23", 1787. National Portrait Gallery, London. [495]

Provenance: Lyndhurst Sale (57), to Scharf [National Portrait Gallery].

Exhibited: South Kensington [Victoria and Albert] Museum, London, 1867 (486).

Bibliography: Bayley, pp. 34, 36, 140.

Bayley refers to a study of this figure owned by Mrs. F. Gordon Dexter, Boston, and a study 26" x 23" at the Guildhall, London. Both references seem erroneous. The first study has not been located, and the second is probably confused with the National Portrait Gallery picture.

———— In *Siege of Gibraltar.*

FAIRFAX, FERDINANDO, SECOND BARON (1584–1648). In *Charles I Demanding.*

FAIRFAX, CAPTAIN SIR WILLIAM. In *Victory of Duncan.*

FALKLAND, LUCIUS CARY, SECOND VISCOUNT (1610?–1643). In *Charles I Demanding.*

"A Vandyck, in the possession of Admiral Forbes" (*Charles I* brochure).

FANSHAWE, SIR THOMAS (1596–1665; created Viscount Fanshawe of Dromore in Ireland). In *Charles I Demanding.*

"From a picture, procurred by Mr. Turner, to whose general assistance and attention in the progress of the work, Mr. Copley has been much indebted" (*Charles I* brochure).

FAUCONBERG, HENRY BELASYSE, SECOND EARL OF (1743–1802). Oil on canvas, 31½" x 26½", before 1794. Museum of Fine Arts, Boston. [591]

Provenance: Amory-Dexter; gift of Mrs. F. Gordon Dexter in memory of Charles and Martha Babcock Amory.

Engraved: A. Fogg, stipple, 10⅜" x 8¾", 1794.

Bibliography: Perkins, p. 53; Bayley, p. 103.

———— Oil on canvas, 30" x 25", probably before 1794. Mrs. Robert Dickey, New York.

Provenance: Scott & Fowles, New York.

———— In *Death of Chatham.*

FERRERS, GEORGE TOWNSHEND, LORD (1753–1811; later Earl of Leicester). In *Death of Chatham.*

FIENNES, NATHANIEL (1608?–1669). In *Charles I Demanding.*

"A medal by Simon, from the collection of Mr. Tysson" (*Charles I* brochure).

FITCH, COLONEL, SAYING FAREWELL TO HIS SISTERS, THE MISSES FITCH. Oil on canvas, 102" x 134", 1800–01. National Gallery of Art, Washington, D.C. [635]

Provenance: Fitch was killed soon after the picture was finished, and the painting was sent to an uncle in Boston, Mr. Lloyd, for whom it was painted; gift of Mrs. Eleanor Lathrop, Gordon Abbott, and Mrs. Katherine A. Batchelder, 1960.

Exhibited: Royal Academy, 1801 (21).

Bibliography: Amory, pp. 195–96; Perkins, p. 54; Bayley, pp. 32, 104.

The three-figure composition is reminiscent of *The Red Cross Knight* (fig. 592). The vase in the upper left-hand corner of the picture echoes the *Izard* portrait (fig. 342), the small *Bessborough* portrait (fig. 590), and the similar placement of the statue in the *John Adams* portrait (fig. 438).

—————— SKETCH FOR. Oil on canvas, 30⅛″ x 25⅛″, 1801. R. Hatfield Ellsworth, New York.

Inscribed: Signed and dated lower right, "J S Copley/1801."

This study is badly rubbed, and most of the original surface is gone.

FITZWILLIAM, WILLIAM WENTWORTH, SECOND EARL (1748–1833). In *Death of Chatham*.

FORT, MRS. SEYMOUR [?]. Oil on canvas, 49½″ x 39⅝″, c. 1778. Wadsworth Atheneum, Hartford, Conn. [363]

Bibliography: Bayley, p. 108; Bolton, p. 83; Met '37 (37); BMFA '38, p. 22 (30); *The Hudson-Fulton Celebration*, Metropolitan Museum of Art, Sept.–Nov. 1909, p. 8 (13).

Copies: Oil on canvas, 36″ x 28″. *Provenance*: Christie, July 17, 1931 (83), as a portrait of Mrs. Jesse Foot by J. Opie; Seligman Sale, Parke-Bernet, Jan. 23–24, 1947 (278); Paul W. Cooley, Simsbury, Conn.

There is no positive identification of the sitter as either Mrs. Fort or Mrs. Foot [see *Copies*], and the identity of the subject is an open question.

GAYTON, CLARK, ADMIRAL OF THE BLUE (1720?–1787?). Oil on canvas, 50½″ x 40½″, 1779. National Maritime Museum, Greenwich. [385]

Inscribed: Signed and dated lower left, "J S Copley P./1779."

Provenance: Mrs. Dockray, a descendant of the sitter; purchased 1949 (Caird Collection).

GAYTON, MRS. CLARK (afterwards Mrs. Pigott). Oil on canvas, 50″ x 40″, 1779. Detroit Institute of Arts, Detroit, Mich. [384]

Inscribed: Signed and dated center right, "J S Copley. Fec. 1779."

Provenance: Mrs. Pigott died in 1809; her husband, Rev. Pigott, 1812; Lydia, second daughter of Rev. Pigott by first wife who married William Thresher, Fareham, Hampshire; Thresher family to Captain W. Thresher, R.N.; O'Hagan Sale, Christie, November 24, 1922 (106); M. Knoedler, London; Woolworth Sale, American Art Association, January 5–6, 1927 (87); Metropolitan Galleries, New York; gift of D. J. Healy, 1927.

Bibliography: Bolton, p. 116.

GEORGE IV (AS PRINCE OF WALES) [1762–1830]. Oil on canvas, 147½″ x 125½″, 1804–10. Museum of Fine Arts, Boston. [661]

Provenance: Lyndhurst Sale (88), to Cox; Amory-Dexter; gift, 1925, in memory of Charles and Martha Babcock Amory.

Exhibited: Royal Academy, 1810 (58).

Engraved: C. Turner, mezzotint, 26″ x 22″, published by Copley and Messrs. Colnaghi, 1813.

Bibliography: Perkins, pp. 129, 134; Bayley, pp. 33, 35–36, 114; Bolton, p. 116; Copley Exhib. '65, pp. 130, 142 (103).

Listed in the 1810 Royal Academy exhibition as "Portrait of His R. H. the Prince of Wales at a review, attended by Lord Heathfield, General Turner, Col. Bloomfield, and Baron Eben: Colonel Quinton in the distance."

—————— Oil on canvas, 39″ x 33½″, c. 1810. Her Majesty Queen Elizabeth II, Royal Lodge.

Provenance: Bowyer-Smith heirlooms, Ruffer Sale, Christie, April 29, 1932 (78); royal family.

This replica has been examined only in photograph.

—————— STUDY FOR GEORGE IV. Black and white chalk, 1804–06. Unlocated. [664]

Provenance: Lyndhurst Library Sale; CDC-OPS; John M. Schenck, Flemington, New Jersey.

—————— STUDY FOR THE HEAD OF GEORGE IV. Black and white chalk on blue paper, 25¼″ x 20¾″, 1804–09. Museum of Fine Arts, Boston (M. and M. Karolik Collection). [663]

Provenance: Lyndhurst Library Sale; Linzee Amory; M. and M. Karolik.

Bibliography: Hipkiss, pp. 332–33 (264).

—————— STUDY FOR LORD HEATHFIELD. Black and white chalk on blue paper, 17¼″ x 11⅝″, 1804–06. Museum of Fine Arts, Boston (M. and M. Karolik Collection). [665]

Provenance: Lyndhurst Library Sale; Linzee Amory; M. and M. Karolik.

Bibliography: Hipkiss, pp. 334–35 (265).

———— STUDY FOR. Black and white chalk on blue paper, 13¼″ x 17⅜″, 1804–09. William B. O'Neal, Charlottesville, Virginia. [666]

Provenance: Lyndhurst Library Sale; CDC-OPS.

GERMAIN, LORD GEORGE (1716–1785). In *Death of Chatham*.

GLYNNE, SERJEANT (1603–1666). In *Charles I Demanding*.

GODOLPHIN, SYDNEY (1610–1643). In *Charles I Demanding*.

GOODWIN, ARTHUR (1593?–1643). In *Charles I Demanding*.

GORING, COLONEL GEORGE (1608–1657). In *Charles I Demanding*.

"From a fine Vandyck, in the collection of the Earl of Egremont" (*Charles I* brochure).

GOWER, GRANVILLE, EARL (1721–1805; later Marquis of Stafford). In *Death of Chatham*.

GRAFTON, AUGUSTUS HENRY FITZROY, THIRD DUKE OF (1735–1804). In *Death of Chatham*.

GRAHAM, JOHN ANDREW (b.1764). Oil on canvas, 31″ x 25″, 1798. Phoenix Art Museum, Phoenix, Arizona. [617]

Provenance: Hirschl & Adler, New York.

Exhibited: Royal Academy, 1798 (73).

Bibliography: Bayley, pp. 32, 122.

GRAHAM, SIR ROBERT (1744–1836). Oil on canvas, 57¼″ x 46⅞″, 1804. National Gallery of Art, Washington, D.C. [653]

Inscribed: Signed center left, "J S Copley. R.A. pinx."

Provenance: Thomas George Graham White; Christie, March 23, 1878, to Graves; Amory-Dexter; gift of Mrs. F. Gordon Dexter.

Exhibited: Royal Academy, 1804 (21), listed as "Portrait of Baron Graham."

Bibliography: Amory, pp. 239, 241, 244; Perkins, p. 129; Perkins, *Supplement*, pp. 18–19; Bayley, pp. 33, 122; Bolton, p. 116; Copley Exhib. '65, pp. 130, 142 (102).

GREEN, MAJOR GENERAL SIR WILLIAM (1725–1811). In *Siege of Gibraltar*.

GREENE, MRS. GARDINER (Elizabeth Copley; 1770–1866). Oil on canvas, 30¾″ x 25¾″, 1800–03. Mrs. Copley Amory, Cambridge, Mass. [634]

Provenance: Greene and Amory families.

Bibliography: Amory, p. 238; Perkins, p. 64; Bayley, p. 128; Bolton, p. 116; Copley Exhib. '65, pp. 125, 142 (99)

GREENVILLE, SIR BEVIL. In *Charles I Demanding*.

"The assistance of medals failing, a profile was again deduced from a more full face with considerable attention and study. Two pictures in the collection of the Earl of Egremont, and an original miniature, for the use of which Mr. Copley was indebted to Mr. Wavel, were the faithful guides in this transformation" (*Charles I* brochure).

GREY, THOMAS LORD (1623?–1657). In *Charles I Demanding*.

"An original picture, in the collection of Mr. Knightley" (*Charles I* brochure).

GRIMSTON, SIR HARBOTTLE (1603–1685). In *Charles I Demanding*.

HARCOURT, GEORGE SIMON, SECOND EARL OF (1736–1809). In *Death of Chatham*.

HARDY, LIEUT. COL. In *Siege of Gibraltar*.

HARLEY, SIR ROBERT (1579–1656). In *Charles I Demanding*.

HARRISON, ADJUTANT. In *Death of Peirson*.

HARRISON, SIR JOHN. In *Charles I Demanding*.

"The collection of the Earl of Leicester supplied another excellent Cooper, and the age and view of the face happily corresponded with the present subject and design" (*Charles I* brochure).

HARRISON, WILLIAM. In *Charles I Demanding*.

"From a picture in the collection of the Earl of Leicester" (*Charles I* brochure).

HAY, MRS. JOHN (Catherine Farnham). Oil on canvas, 29½″ x 25½″, 1780. Unlocated. [387]

Provenance: Louisa Farnham Cobb, Boston.

Exhibited: Boston Athenaeum, 1871 (246).

Bibliography: Perkins, pp. 70–71; Bayley, pp. 139–40; Bolton, p. 116; "Fine Arts," *Old and New* (Dec. 1871), p. 735; George Atkinson Ward, *Journal and Letters of the Late Samuel Curwen* (New York and Boston, 1842), p. 296.

Samuel Curwen, after visiting Copley's studio on Dec. 19, 1780, records that "Mrs. Hay appeared in view so very like, that the first glance announced for whom it was intended."

HEATHFIELD, FRANCIS AUGUSTUS ELIOTT, SECOND BARON, LIEUTENANT GENERAL (d. 1813). In *George IV (as Prince of Wales)*.

———— See Study for *George IV* [665].

HEATHFIELD, GEORGE AUGUSTUS ELIOTT, LORD. See *Eliott*.

HEBER, RICHARD (1773–1833). Oil on canvas, 65½″ x 51¼″, 1782. Charles C. Cholmondeley, Yeovil, Somerset. [424]

Provenance: Charles Cholmondeley is a direct descendant of Richard Heber, and the painting has come down in the family.

Exhibited: British Institution, 1865 (122); Leeds, 1868 (3188); Wrexham, 1876 (224).

Bibliography: Bayley, pp. 140–41; R. H. Cholmondeley, *The Heber Letters, 1783–1832* (London, 1950), frontis.

———— STUDY FOR. Black and white chalk on blue-gray paper, 11¼″ x 14⅛″, 1782. Henry Francis du Pont Winterthur Museum, Winterthur, Delaware. [425]

Provenance: Lyndhurst Library Sale (670); Jupp-Amory; CDC-OPS.

HEMERY, CAPTAIN. In *Death of Peirson*.

HERBERT, PHILIP LORD (1584–1650). In *Charles I Demanding*.

"Recourse was had to a print" (*Charles I* brochure).

HILL, ROGER (1605–1667). In *Charles I Demanding*.

"A picture, in the possession of Mr. Way" (*Charles I* brochure).

HINCHCLIFFE, DR. JOHN, BISHOP OF PETERBOROUGH. See *Peterborough*.

HOLLOWAY, LIEUTENANT. In *Siege of Gibraltar*.

HOOPER, MRS. THOMAS (Mary Heron; 1757–1820). Oil on canvas, 30″ x 25″, c. 1783. Mrs. Richard K. Anderson, Sumter, South Carolina. [427]

Inscribed: Signed lower left [illegible].

Provenance: The sitter's niece and adopted daughter, Mrs. William Wallace Anderson (Mary Jane Mackenzie Hooper); Anderson family.

Bibliography: Bolton, p. 118.

HOPTON, SIR RALPH (1598–1652). In *Charles I Demanding*.

"From a picture by Vandyck, for the assistance of which Mr. Copley has been indebted to Sir Edward Astley" (*Charles I* brochure).

HOTHAM, JOHN. In *Charles I Demanding*.

HOTHAM, SIR JOHN (d. 1645). In *Charles I Demanding*.

"The collection of the late Sir Charles Hotham supplied a good portrait of the Governour of Hull" (*Charles I* brochure).

HOWE, RICHARD EARL, ADMIRAL OF THE FLEET (1725/6–1799). Oil on canvas, 30″ diameter, before 1794. National Maritime Museum, Greenwich. [596]

Provenance: Lyndhurst Sale (53), to Anthony; Marquis of Sligo.

Engraved: R. Dunkarton, mezzotint, 16⅞″ x 13⅞″, published by Copley, 1794; W. Sharp, line engraving, 5″ x 3¾″, published by Copley, May 22, 1810.

Bibliography: Perkins, pp. 128, 131; Bayley, pp. 34, 149; Copley Exhib. '65, pp. 111, 141 (85).

———— Oil on canvas, 28¾″ diameter, probably before 1794. Earl Howe, Penn House, Amersham, Bucks.

Provenance: Howe family.

Exhibited: South Kensington [Victoria and Albert] Museum, 1867 (730).

———— Oil on canvas, 29″ diameter (sight), probably before 1794. Empire Trust Co., New York.

Provenance: Mitchell, London; Childs, Boston; Old Print Shop, New York.

Bibliography: Connoisseur, LXIV (Nov.–Dec. 1922), 136, 187, 245.

HUGO, COLONEL ERNST AUGUST VON. In *Siege of Gibraltar.*

———— AND LIEUT. COLONEL VON SCHLEPEGRELL. Study for *Siege of Gibraltar.* Oil on canvas, 26″ x 22″, 1787. Fogg Art Museum, Harvard University, Cambridge, Mass. [498]

Provenance: Lyndhurst Sale (66), to Clarke; Amory-Dexter; gift of Mrs. Gordon Dexter, 1942.

Bibliography: Perkins, p. 132; Bayley, pp. 34, 36, 151, 225; Bolton, p. 83; Copley Exhib. '65, pp. 111, 141 (86).

Copies: A copy, oil on canvas, was made by Robert Cumming, Dorchester, Mass., 1947.

HYDE, EDWARD (1607–1659). In *Charles I Demanding.*

"A very fine medal was lent by Sir Lucius O'Brien; and the likeness was further indebted to a picture by Lely, in the possession of Mr. Willett" (*Charles I* brochure).

HYDE, ROBERT, SQUIRE OF HYDE. Oil on canvas, 29¾″ x 24¾″, 1778. Chicago Art Institute, Chicago, Ill. [354]

Inscribed: Signed and dated lower left, "J. S. Copley Pinx/1778."

Provenance: Hyde family to F. Colville Hyde of Hampsthwaite, Harrogate, Yorkshire; Ellis and Smith, London, 1937; E. and A. Silberman & Co., New York, 1942.

Bibliography: Copley Exhib. '65, pp. 90, 139 (65).

HYDE, MRS. ROBERT. Oil on canvas, 29½″ x 24¾″, 1778. Viscount Mackintosh of Halifax, Hethersett, Norfolk. [355]

Inscribed: Signed and dated upper left, "J. S. Copley Pinx/1778."

Provenance: Same as above to Ellis and Smith, London; Lady Kent Sale, Sotheby, Dec. 17, 1947 (114); Thos. Agnew, & Son, London.

HYDE, SQUIRE HYDE OF. Oil on canvas, 30½″ x 25¼″, 1777. Krannert Art Museum, University of Illinois, Urbana. [353]

Inscribed: Signed and dated lower left, "J S Copley/1777."

Provenance: Hyde family; probably with Ellis and Smith, London; Newhouse Galleries, New York, 1936; Art Institute of Chicago; exchanged with E. and A. Silberman Galleries, New York; Merle J. Trees, Chicago; gift to University of Illinois.

Bibliography: Connoisseur, XCVI (Oct. 1935), 233–34; *Art News,* XXXV (Dec. 26, 1936), 21.

IZARD, MR. [1742–1804] AND MRS. RALPH (d. 1832). Oil on canvas, 69″ x 88½″, 1775. Museum of Fine Arts, Boston. [342]

Provenance: Sold by Copley's widow to Dr. Gabriel Manigault, grandson of the sitter, 1825; in Manigault family until 1903, when sold to the Boston museum.

Exhibited: Royal Academy, 1776 (62) [probably].

Bibliography: Perkins, pp. 78, 126; Bayley, p. 156; Bolton, p. 118; *Copley-Pelham Letters,* pp. 295; 300, 308, 340; BMFA '38, pp. 11, 16, 25 (49); Copley Exhib. '65, pp. 80, 89, 139 (60).

JACKSON, JONATHAN (1743–1810). Oil on canvas, 22″ x 18″, c. 1785. Mrs. James Jackson, Sr., Westwood, Mass. [474]

Provenance: Jackson family.

Bibliography: Perkins, p. 79; Bayley, p. 157.

JEPHSON, MRS. Unlocated.

"The picture of Mrs Jephson at Copleys was not compleatly finished as he intended she should have set once more — it is a fine painting & a pretty good likeness, a good miniature will cost five Guineas" (Mrs. Urquhart to Mrs. Henry Knox, Oct. 11, 1788, Massachusetts Historical Society).

Bibliography: Perkins, p. 79; Bayley, pp. 159–60.

JERMYN, HENRY (created Earl of St. Albans; d. 1684). In *Charles I Demanding.*

JERSEY, GEORGE BUSSY, FOURTH EARL OF (1735–1805). In *Death of Chatham.*

KNATCHBULL FAMILY, THE. Oil on canvas. [636–638]

The large painting was cut apart, and three sections survive as separate portraits: Edward, 8th Bt. [638], his sons Edward (later 9th Bt.) and Norton [636], and his daughter Mary [637].

Bibliography: Bayley, p. 160.

———— SKETCH FOR. Oil on canvas, 25½″ x 37½″, 1800–02. Lord Brabourne, Mersham le Hatch, Ashford, Kent. [639]

Provenance: Probably the group of portraits (monochrome), 24″ x 36½″, owned by John Cleland and exhibited at Grosvenor Gallery, 1888 (260); and the group, 24″ x 36″, owned by G. T. Taylor, exhibited Birmingham, 1903 (5); purchased in the United States, 1922.

Bibliography: Bayley, pp. 160, 271–72; Met '37 (46); Copley Exhib. '65, pp. 125, 130, 142 (100).

Bolton, p. 118, refers to a sketch for *The Knatchbull Family* owned by Ehrich Galleries in 1930.

———— SIR EDWARD KNATCHBULL, 8TH BT. (1781–1849). Oil on canvas, 95″ x 58″ (sight), 1800–03. Lord Brabourne, Mersham le Hatch, Ashford, Kent. [638]

———— EDWARD (9TH BT.) AND NORTON KNATCHBULL. Oil on canvas, 90″ x 58″ (sight), 1800–03. Lord Brabourne, Mersham le Hatch, Ashford, Kent. [636]

———— MARY KNATCHBULL. Oil on canvas, 52″ x 34″ (sight), 1800–03. Lord Brabourne, Mersham le Hatch, Ashford, Kent. [637]

———— SKETCH FOR NORTON KNATCHBULL. Oil on canvas, 21″ x 17″ (sight), 1800–03, probably 1800–01. Lord Brabourne, Mersham le Hatch, Ashford, Kent. [640]

———— STUDY FOR SIR EDWARD KNATCHBULL, 8TH BT. Black and white chalk, pencil, on dark gray-blue paper, 13⅞″ x 11⅝″, 1800–02. Metropolitan Museum of Art, New York (Harris Brisbane Dick Fund, 1960). [649]

Provenance: Lyndhurst Library Sale (670); Jupp-Amory; CDC-OPS.

———— STUDY FOR EDWARD (9TH BT.) AND NORTON KNATCHBULL. Pencil and white chalk on blue-gray paper, 13⅜″ x 11″, 1800–02. University of Nebraska Art Galleries, Lincoln (Frank M. Hall Collection). [642]

Provenance: Lyndhurst Library Sale (probably 670 or 672); Victor Spark, New York.

Bibliography: Copley Exhib. '65, pp. 125, 130, 142 (101).

———— STUDY FOR NORTON KNATCHBULL. Black and white chalk on dark gray-blue paper, 13⅞″ x 11⅝″, 1800–02. Metropolitan Museum of Art, New York (Harris Brisbane Dick Fund, 1960). [643]

Provenance: Lyndhurst Library Sale (670); Jupp-Amory; CDC-OPS.

———— STUDY FOR A DAUGHTER. Black, red, and white chalk, pencil, on blue paper, 13⅞″ x 11½″, 1801–02. Museum of Fine Arts, Boston. [641]

Inscribed: Upper left, "Daughters of George 3rd."

Provenance: Lyndhurst Library Sale (672), to Clark; Greene family; gift of Henry Copley Greene, 1941.

Bibliography: BMFA '38, p. 33 (118).

———— STUDY FOR LADY KNATCHBULL AND CHILDREN (recto of next item [645]). Black and white chalk on gray-blue paper, 12¼″ x 19⅜″, 1801–02. Museum of Fine Arts, Boston (M. and M. Karolik Collection). [647]

Provenance: Lyndhurst Library Sale (probably 672); Weyhe Galleries, New York; Maxim Karolik.

Bibliography: Hipkiss, p. 332 (263); BMFA '38, p. 33 (116).

———— STUDY FOR LADY KNATCHBULL AND CHILDREN (verso of previous item [647]). Black chalk on gray-blue paper, 12¼″ x 19⅜″, 1800–02. Museum of Fine Arts, Boston (M. and M. Karolik Collection). [645]

Provenance: same as previous item.

Bibliography: same as previous item.

———— STUDY FOR LADY KNATCHBULL AND CHILDREN. Black and white chalk on blue paper, 13⅞″ x 11½″, 1800–02. Museum of Fine Arts, Boston (M. and M. Karolik Collection). [644]

Provenance: Lyndhurst Library Sale (probably 672); Weyhe Galleries, New York; Maxim Karolik.

Bibliography: Hipkiss, p. 331 (261); BMFA '38, p. 32 (113).

——— STUDY FOR LADY KNATCHBULL AND CHILD. Black and white chalk on blue paper, 13⅞″ x 11½″, 1800–02. Museum of Fine Arts, Boston (M. and M. Karolik Collection). [646]

Provenance: Lyndhurst Library Sale (probably 672); Weyhe Galleries, New York; Maxim Karolik.

Bibliography: Hipkiss, p. 331 (262); BMFA '38, p. 32 (115).

——— STUDY FOR A DAUGHTER. Black, white, and red chalk on blue paper, 14″ x 11½″, 1800–02. Museum of Fine Arts, Boston. [648]

Provenance: Probably Lyndhurst Library Sale (672), to Clark; gift of Thomas Inglis, 1883.

Bibliography: BMFA '38, p. 33 (117).

LANE, THOMAS, AND HIS SISTER HARRIOT. Oil on canvas, 47″ x 59″, c. 1783–88. Museum of Fine Arts, Boston. [484]

Provenance: Leger Galleries, London, 1953; Hirschl & Adler, New York, 1953.

LAURENS, HENRY (1724–1792). Oil on canvas, 54⅛″ x 40⅝″, 1782. National Portrait Gallery, Washington D.C. (Mellon Collection). [416]

Inscribed: Signed and dated lower right, "J S Copley. R.A. pinx 1782."

Provenance: Thomas B. Clarke.

Engraved: Valentine Green, published by J. Stockdale, Oct. 1, 1782.

Bibliography: Perkins, p. 80; Bayley, p. 162; Bolton, p. 118; "That Copley 'Laurens,'" *American Art News*, XVIII (April 3, 1920), 1, 4.

Copies: Frontis., David R. Wallace, *Life of Laurens* (1915), attributed to Charles Fraser.
   Provenance: Henry Laurens, New Orleans, Louisiana.

There is some question about whether this painting is the original portrait or a replica. Bayley records that the original portrait of Henry Laurens burned in Charleston, South Carolina, in 1861 when it was owned by John Laurens, a descendant of the sitter.

LENTHALL, WILLIAM (1591–1662). In *Charles I Demanding*.

"Mr. Copley consulted a picture in the possession of Mr. Lenthall of Burford; but followed a most exquisite medal, in the collection of the Revd. Mr. Cracherode" (*Charles I* brochure).

LEWIS, COLONEL. In *Siege of Gibraltar*.

LINDSAY, HON. LIEUT. COL. In *Siege of Gibraltar*.

LISLE, JOHN (1610?–1664). In *Charles I Demanding*.

"A medal, in the collection of Mr. Tysson" (*Charles I* brochure).

LITTLE, LIEUTENANT JOHN. In *Victory of Duncan*.

LORING, JOSHUA. Oil on canvas, 1780. Unlocated.

Provenance: British and Foreign Bible Society, London; sold c. 1926.

Exhibited: Royal Academy, 1780 (211).

Bibliography: E. Alfred Jones, *Loyalists of Massachusetts* (London, 1930), plate 32, opp. p. 193; William T. Whitley, *Artists and Their Friends in England, 1700–1799*, II (London, 1928), 376.

Whitley, presumably drawing information from a contemporary newspaper review, identifies (211) exhibited at the Royal Academy in 1780, "Portrait of a Naval Officer," as "Mr. Loring, Lieutenant in the Navy, from Boston; a spirited sketch."

LOUGHBOROUGH, LORD (1733–1805; Solicitor General). In *Death of Chatham*.

LYSTER, SIR MARTIN. In *Charles I Demanding*.

LYTTELTON FAMILY, THE. Oil on canvas, 59⅛″ x 64⅞″, 1786–88. Destroyed by fire, December 1925. [478]

Provenance: Lyttelton Family.

Exhibited: Manchester, 1857 (255).

Bibliography: Bayley, p. 166; *Catalogue of the Pictures at Hagley Hall*, privately printed, 1900 (72); Arthur T. Bolton, "Hagley Park, Worcestershire, the Seat of Viscount Cobham," *Country Life*, XXXVIII (Oct. 16, 1915), 521.

The portrait represents William Henry Lyttelton, Lord Westcote, afterwards Lord Lyttelton (1724–1808), with Catherine Bristow, his second wife, and Caroline Anne Lyttelton, their daughter.

———— STUDY FOR. Black chalk on white paper, 8¼" x 8", 1785–88. Courtauld Institute of Art, London. [480]

Provenance: Lyndhurst Library Sale (672), to Clark; Parsons, London, before 1932; Sir Robert Witt.

Bibliography: BMFA '38, p. 34 (128).

———— STUDY FOR. Black and white chalk on gray-blue paper, 11¹³⁄₁₆" x 9⁷⁄₁₆", 1785–88. British Museum, London. [479]

Provenance: Lyndhurst Library Sale (661–64, according to British Museum records).

———— STUDY FOR [?]. Black and white chalk on buff paper, 13½" x 9¾", 1785–88. Mrs. Francis Minot Weld, Manchester, Mass. [481]

Provenance: Lyndhurst Library Sale (672), to Clark; Charles Amory, Boston, 1873; his daughter, Mrs. F. Gordon Dexter (Susannah Amory); Mrs. Theodore Phillips Burgess (Elizabeth Slade); her daughter, Mrs. Francis Minot Weld (Elizabeth Burgess).

There is a possibility that this drawing might be for *The Daughters of George III*.

———— STUDY FOR [?]. Black and white chalk on buff paper, 15¼" x 8", 1785–88. William P. Wadsworth, Geneseo, N.Y. [482]

Provenance: Lyndhurst Library Sale (672), to Clark; Mrs. W. Austin Wadsworth.

There is a possibility that this drawing might be for *The Daughters of George III*.

MACNEIL CAPTAIN. In *Death of Peirson*.

MAHON, CHARLES STANHOPE, LORD VISCOUNT (1753–1816; later Earl of Stanhope). In *Death of Chatham*.

MANCHESTER, GEORGE MONTAGU, FOURTH DUKE OF (1737–1788). In *Death of Chatham*.

MANSFIELD, WILLIAM MURRAY, FIRST EARL OF (1705–1793). Oil on canvas, 88" x 57½", 1783. National Portrait Gallery, London. [429]

Inscribed: Signed lower right, "J. S. Copley. pinx."

Provenance: Lyndhurst Sale (81), to Scharf [National Portrait Gallery].

Exhibited: Royal Academy, 1783 (5).

Bibliography: Perkins, pp. 22, 127, 133; Bayley, pp. 31, 35, 171; Bolton, p. 118; Met '37 (39); Copley Exhib. '65, pp. 100–01, 140 (76).

Copies: Oil on canvas, 72" x 50", Inworth Hall Sale, Phillipson and Neale, London, Sept. 19–20, 1951 (26), to Mrs. Waller.

———— Black and white chalk on blue-green paper, 11⁵⁄₁₆" x 14⅜", 1782–83. Yale University Art Gallery, New Haven, Conn. [430]

Provenance: Lyndhurst Library Sale (670); Jupp-Amory; CDC-OPS.

———— Black and white chalk on gray-blue paper, 12¼" x 19½", 1782–83. Bayou Bend Collection of Americana, Museum of Fine Arts, Houston, Texas. [431]

Provenance: Lyndhurst Library Sale (670); Jupp-Amory; CDC-OPS.

———— Black and white chalk on gray-blue paper, 11⅛" x 14⅛", 1782–83. Amherst College, Amherst, Mass. [432]

Provenance: Lyndhurst Library Sale (664 or 670); Jupp-Amory; CDC-OPS.

———— Black and white chalk on gray-blue paper, 10½" x 8¾", 1782–83. Unlocated. [433]

Provenance: Lyndhurst Library Sale (670); Jupp-Amory; CDC-OPS, 1959.

———— Black chalk heightened with white on gray paper, 12⅛" x 9¹³⁄₁₆", 1782–83. Cleveland Museum of Art, Cleveland, Ohio (Norman O. Stone and Ella A. Stone Memorial Fund). [434]

Provenance: Lyndhurst Library Sale (670); Jupp-Amory; CDC-OPS.

——— Black and white chalk on blue paper, 10⅛″ x 10½″, 1782–83. British Museum, London. [435]

Provenance: Lyndhurst Library Sale (661–64, according to British Museum records).

Bibliography: Oskar Hagen, *The Birth of the American Tradition in Art* (New York, 1940), fig. 113.

——— See Study for *Death of Chatham* [406].

——— In *Death of Chatham*.

MARKHAM, DR. WILLIAM. See *York*.

MAYNARD, SERJEANT SIR JOHN (1592–1658). In *Charles I Demanding*.

"Mr. Copley was favoured by Miss Hotham, daughter of the late Sir Charles Hotham, with a portrait of Maynard. Though much too old for this period, it was of essential service" (*Charles I* brochure).

MONTAGUE, MRS. [Mary Wilmot Copley], WIFE OF REAR ADMIRAL MONTAGUE, AND HER BROTHER ROBERT. Oil on canvas, 104¼″ x 74½″, 1804. W. Averell Harriman, New York. [652]

Provenance: Montague family; Christie, July 23, 1903, as "Mrs. Mary Montagu (Mary Wilmot Copley) on Terrace with her Son," dimensions given as 89″ x 60″, to Marshall; Mrs. Edward H. Harriman.

Exhibited: Royal Academy, 1804 (31).

Bibliography: Bayley, pp. 33, 179; Bolton, p. 118.

MONTAGUE, DUKE OF. In *Death of Chatham*.

MONTGOMERIE, MAJOR HUGH (1739–1819; later Twelfth Earl of Eglinton). 1780. Unlocated. [Copy, 389]

Exhibited: Royal Academy, 1780 (172).

Bibliography: Bayley, p. 179.

Copies:

1. Oil on canvas, 87″ x 56½″. National Portrait Gallery of Scotland, Edinburgh [389]. *Provenance*: Eglinton family; Eglinton Collection Sale, Christie, 1922 [as by Henry Raeburn]; Col. M. A. W. Swinfen Brown Collection Sale, Christie, Dec. 10, 1948 (104) [as by David Martin], purchased by Spink.

2. Oil on canvas, by Henry Raeburn, Town Hall, Ayr, Scotland. This copy was made in 1821 when the original was owned by the Montgomerie family, Coilsfield, Ayrshire.

3. A small copy, attributed to Angelica Kauffmann; loaned in 1936 by Captain R. A. G. Murphy, First Gordon Highlanders, to the Scottish United Services Museum, Edinburgh. The picture was subsequently returned to the owner and is unlocated.

4. A large portrait of Major Montgomerie, approximately the same size as the copy in the National Portrait Gallery of Scotland, is reported to be privately owned in Scotland. Efforts to secure a photograph of this picture and further information have been unsuccessful.

——— STUDY FOR. Black and white chalk on pink-buff paper, 12″ x 17″, 1779–80. Mr. and Mrs. Herbert C. Lee, Belmont, Mass. [390]

Provenance: Lyndhurst Library Sale (670); Jupp-Amory; CDC-OPS.

——— STUDY FOR. Black and white chalk on blue-gray paper, 12″ x 23⅜″, 1779–80. University of Virginia Museum of Fine Arts, Charlottesville. [390a]

Provenance: Lyndhurst Library Sale (670); Jupp-Amory; CDC-OPS.

MONTRESOR, MRS. JOHN (Frances Tucker; 1744–1826). Oil on canvas, 30⅜″ x 25⅛″, 1776–80. Mr. and Mrs. Richard I. Robinson, Greenwich, Conn. [426]

Inscribed: Signed and dated center right, "J S Copley. . 7 . .".

Provenance: Howard Young Galleries, New York, 1934.

Bibliography: Copley Exhib. '65, pp. 109, 141 (82).

MOTTE, GENERAL DE LA. See *De La Motte*.

MOUNT-EDGECUMBE, GEORGE, FIRST VISCOUNT (d. 1795). In *Death of Chatham*.

MURRAY, WILLIAM. See *Mansfield, Earl of.*

NICHOLAS, SIR EDWARD (1593–1669). In *Charles I Demanding.*
"From an original miniature, now in the possession of Mr. Nicholas" (*Charles I* brochure).

NORTH, SIR DUDLEY (1581–1666). In *Charles I Demanding.*
"A fine drawing, formerly belonging to the Earl of Orford, was obtained from the valuable and extensive collection of Mr. Bull" (*Charles I* brochure).

NORTH, LORD (1732–1792; later Earl of Guildford). In *Death of Chatham.*

NORTHAMPTON, CHARLES, FIRST MARQUIS OF [1760–1828], AND HIS SON, SPENCER, LORD COMPTON (1790–1851; later Second Marquis). Oil on canvas, 120″ x 84″, 1803. Marquis of Northampton, Castle Ashby, near Northampton. [650]
Inscribed: Lower right, "Charles 1st Marquis and His Son Spencer/afterwards second Marquis of Northampton/By Copley."
Exhibited: Royal Academy, 1803 (70).
Bibliography: Amory, pp. 238–39; Perkins, p. 129; Bayley, pp. 32, 186; William Bingham Compton, *History of the Comptons of Compton Wynyates* (London, 1930), p. 234.

ONSLOW, GEORGE, FOURTH BARON (1731–1814; later First Earl). In *Death of Chatham.*

ORANGE, PRINCE OF (1792–1848; later William VII, King of Holland). Oil on canvas, 36⅜″ x 27⅛″, c. 1812–13. Wellington Museum, Apsley House, London. [672]
Provenance: "There is reason to believe that this portrait was painted for presentation to Princess Charlotte, to whom the Prince was then affianced, but who was dissatisfied with it" (Wellington Museum records). The picture then apparently went to the Duke of Wellington when the engagement was broken off. The picture has been at Apsley House since at least 1850.
Engraved: C. Turner, mezzotint, 1813.
The Prince of Orange was aide-de-camp to the Duke of Wellington in Spain, 1811–14, and this portrait is based directly on the same figure in Copley's *Battle of the Pyrenees.*
——— Oil on canvas, 50″ x 40″, c. 1812–13. Her Majesty Queen Elizabeth II, Buckingham Palace. [671]

OSWALD, CAPTAIN. In *Victory of Duncan.*

PALMER, GEOFFREY (1598–1670). In *Charles I Demanding.*
"From a fine picture by Lely, for the use of which Mr. Copley was obliged to Mr. Cambridge" (*Charles I* brochure).

PATTERSON, MR. In *Victory of Duncan.*

PEIRSON, MAJOR FRANCIS (1757–1781). In *Death of Peirson.*

PENN, JOHN (1760–1834). Oil on canvas, c. 1782. Formerly M. Knoedler & Co., New York. [487]
Bibliography: Charles Merrill Mount, "A Hidden Treasure in Britain, Part II: John Singleton Copley," *Art Quarterly* (Spring 1961), fig. 6.
This painting was formerly attributed to George Romney.

PENNINGTON, ISAAC (1587?–1660). In *Charles I Demanding.*

PEPPERRELL, SIR WILLIAM [1746–1816], AND HIS FAMILY. Oil on canvas, 90″ x 108″, 1778. North Carolina Museum of Art, Raleigh. [356]
Inscribed: Signed and dated lower left, "J. S. Copley P. 1778."
Provenance: Sir William Pepperrell, Bt.; his daughter, wife of Sir Charles Thomas Palmer, 2nd Bt., of Wanlip Hall, Leicestershire; in Palmer family until purchased by William Randolph Hearst, St. Donats, Wales, 1933; J. Rochelle Thomas, Georgian Galleries, London, 1934; Scott & Fowles, New York, 1952.
Exhibited: Royal Academy, 1778 (63).
Bibliography: Amory, p. 206; Bayley, p. 194; Copley Exhib. '65, pp. 90, 139 (66).
——— STUDY FOR. Black and white chalk on blue-gray grounded paper, 11¼″ x 17⅛″, 1777. Museum of Fine Arts, Boston (M. and M. Karolik Collection). [359]
Provenance: Lyndhurst Library Sale (probably 672); Weyhe Galleries, New York.

Bibliography: Hipkiss, p. 314 (247) [as for *The Copley Family*]; BMFA '38, p. 34 (126).

This drawing could be for *The Copley Family*, but the child with her right arm raised, the oldest daughter with her arm around another figure, the general pose of the mother, the pose of a large dog in the finished picture, and the similarity of the child on the floor with the one on the table in the Aberdare drawing suggest *The Pepperrell Family*.

———— STUDY FOR. Black, white, and red chalk on white paper, 17″ x 21½″ (sight), 1777–78. Commander Peter Du Cane, Haselbech Grange, Northampton. [357]

Provenance: Commander Du Cane is a direct descendant of Copley and Lord Lyndhurst, and the drawing has come down in the family.

———— STUDY FOR. Black and white chalk on white paper, 17″ x 21″ (sight), 1777–78. Baron Aberdare, London. [358]

Provenance: Baron Aberdare is a direct descendant of Copley and Lord Lyndhurst, and the drawing has come down in the family.

Bibliography: Anna Wells Rutledge, "American Loyalists — A Drawing for a Noted Copley Group," *Art Quarterly*, XX (Summer 1957), 195–203.

———— STUDY FOR. Black and white on pinkish buff paper, 17¼″ x 13¼″, 1777–78. Museum of Fine Arts, Boston (M. and M. Karolik Collection). [360]

Provenance: Lyndhurst Library Sale (probably 672); Weyhe Galleries, New York.

Bibliography: Hipkiss, pp. 314–15 (246); BMFA '38, p. 32 (114).

———— STUDY FOR (recto of Study for *The Ascension* [337]). Black and white chalk on buff paper, 17¾″ x 10⅞″, 1777–78. Victoria and Albert Museum, London. [361]

Provenance: Lyndhurst Library Sale (probably 672); W. E. Frost and Other Collections Sale, Christie, May 12, 1869 (45), to Hogarth; F. Rathbone, 1898; purchased with Study for *Siege of Gibraltar* (fig. 510).

Bibliography: Copley Exhib. '65, pp. 90, 139 (67).

PERRYN, MAJOR. In *Siege of Gibraltar*.

PETERBOROUGH, DR. JOHN HINCHCLIFFE, BISHOP OF (1731–1794). See Study for *Death of Chatham* [412].

———— In *Death of Chatham*.

PICTON, MAJOR GENERAL THOMAS (1758–1815). In *Siege of Gibraltar*.

PITT, HON. MR. JAMES. In *Death of Chatham*.

PITT, WILLIAM, THE YOUNGER (1759–1806). In *Death of Chatham*.

———— STUDY FOR DEATH OF CHATHAM? Black and red chalk, 5⅛″ x 3¾″ (sight), 1782–89. Chevening, Kent. [488]

Engraved: F. Bartolozzi, published by W. Dickinson, 1789 (specifically identified as "From drawing at Chevening"); I. Neidl, 1798.

Bibliography: Bayley, p. 199; Scharf Sketchbooks, National Portrait Gallery, CIX (1884), 31.

Neither the drawing nor a photograph has been examined.

PORTEOUS, MR. In *Victory of Duncan*.

PORTER, ENDIMION (1587–1649). In *Charles I Demanding*.

"A very capital medallion from Dr. Hunter's museum was attentively perused, and the resemblance was farther aided by the use of a portrait in the possession of Mr. Thane" (*Charles I* brochure).

PORTLAND, WILLIAM HENRY CAVENDISH, THIRD DUKE OF (1738–1809). In *Death of Chatham*.

QUINTON, COLONEL. In *George IV* (*as Prince of Wales*).

RADNER, JACOB, SECOND EARL OF (1750–1828). In *Death of Chatham*.

RICHARDS, R., ESQ. (of Lincoln's Inn). Unlocated.

Exhibited: Royal Academy, 1801 (163).

Bibliography: Bayley, pp. 32, 208.

RICHMOND, CHARLES, DUKE OF (1735–1806). In *Death of Chatham*.

ROCKINGHAM, CHARLES, SECOND MARQUIS OF (1730–1782). In *Death of Chatham*.

ROE, SIR THOMAS (1581?–1644). In *Charles I Demanding*.

ROGERS, MRS. DANIEL DENISON (Abigail Bromfield; 1753–1791). Oil on canvas, 50″ x 40″, c. 1784. Paul Cabot, Needham, Mass. [428]

> *Provenance*: Mrs. D. D. Rogers; her son, Henry B. Rogers; descended in the family to Mrs. W. C. Cabot (1915); Miss A. P. Rogers; Henry B. Cabot; Mrs. Henry B. Cabot.
>
> *Exhibited*: Boston Athenaeum, 1828 (9).
>
> *Bibliography*: Perkins, pp. 99–100; Bayley, p. 209; Bolton, p. 118; BMFA '38, pp. 12, 27 (66); Copley Exhib. '65, pp. 109, 141 (81).
>
> *Copies*: Miniature. Mrs. Francis Minot Weld, Manchester, Mass.
>
> The sitter was Copley's stepniece. Mrs. Copley's sister Hannah was the second wife of Colonel Henry Bromfield of Harvard, Mass. Abigail Bromfield, his daughter by a previous marriage, married Daniel Denison Rogers. After her early death, Rogers then married her half sister, Elizabeth, daughter of Colonel Henry and Hannah Clarke Bromfield.

———— Watercolor on ivory, 2⅞″ x 2⅜″, oval, c. 1784. Paul C. Cabot, Needham, Mass.

> *Provenance*: same as previous item.
>
> This miniature is stylistically consistent with Copley's American miniatures and seems to be the only currently known English miniature by Copley. That Copley did paint miniatures in England is suggested by Mrs. Urquhart's observation in 1788, after visiting Copley's studio, that "a good miniature will cost five Guineas" (see *Jephson, Mrs.*).

ROUPELL, GEORGE BOONE (1762–1838). Oil on canvas, 78″ x 52″, 1780. Brigadier George R. P. Roupell, Little Chartham, Shalford, Surrey. [388]

> *Provenance*: Gift of Lord Lyndhurst to be Roupell family.
>
> *Exhibited*: Royal Academy, 1780 (195).
>
> *Bibliography*: Anna Wells Rutledge, "Paintings of American Interest in British Collections," *Connoisseur*, CXLI (June 1958), 269–70; William T. Whitley, *Artists and Their Friends in England, 1700–1799*, II (London, 1928), 376.
>
> Whitley, presumably drawing information from a contemporary newspaper review, identifies (195) exhibited at the Royal Academy in 1780, "Portrait of a Gentleman," as "a fine whole-length of Mr. Roupel, native of South Carolina. He stands in a graceful, easy attitude and the whole is well painted."

ROWAN, ENSIGN. In *Death of Peirson*.

ROWSE, FRANCIS. In *Charles I Demanding*.

ROYALL, MRS. ISAAC (Elizabeth MacIntosh; d. 1770). Oil on canvas, 50″ x 40″, 1769–80. Virginia Museum of Fine Arts, Richmond (Mrs. A. D. Williams, 1949). [364]

> *Bibliography*: Parker-Wheeler, p. 168.
>
> This portrait was begun in America and completed in England. See also Volume One.

RUDYERD, SIR BENJAMIN (1572–1658). In *Charles I Demanding*.

RUPERT, PRINCE (1619–1682). In *Charles I Demanding*.

> "A medal from Dr. Hunter's museum, and a picture, from the Earl of Egremont's collection, by Verelst, were ample authorities for the portrait of Prince Rupert" (*Charles I* brochure).

RUSHWORTH, JOHN (1612?–1690). In *Charles I Demanding*.

> "A picture in the speaker's room, adjoining the House of Commons, was lent to Mr. Copley by the Speaker" (*Charles I* brochure).

ST. JOHN, OLIVER (1598?–1673). In *Charles I Demanding*.

SANDWICH, JOHN, FOURTH EARL OF (1718–1792). In *Death of Chatham*.

SCARSDALE, NATHANIEL, FIRST BARON (1726–1804). In *Death of Chatham*.

SCHLEPEGRELL, LIEUT. COLONEL. See *Hugo*.

———— In *Siege of Gibraltar*.

SELDEN, JOHN (1584–1654). In *Charles I Demanding*.

> "The picture by Mytens, in the collection of the Lord Chancellor, was at too early a period of

life for the present subject; it became necessary therefore to conform to the portrait by Lely, in the Bodleian Library; and though this latter represents Seldon at too advanced an age, yet by abating somewhat from the asperities induced by years, in which considerable use was made of the former portrait by Mytens, Mr. Copley has been able to deduce, what he thinks, a true resemblance of Selden at the period required" (*Charles I* brochure).

SHELBURNE, WILLIAM, EARL OF (1737–1805; later Marquis of Lansdowne). In *Death of Chatham.*

SHIRLEY, HON. MR. ROBERT (1756–1827; later Earl of Ferrers). In *Death of Chatham.*

SIDMOUTH, HENRY ADDINGTON, FIRST VISCOUNT (1757–1844; Speaker of the House). Oil on canvas, 93½″ x 64″, 1797–98. City Art Museum, St. Louis, Missouri. [614]

Inscribed: Signed and dated center left (on edge of table), "J.Copley r.a. Pinx 179[?]."

Provenance: Rt. Hon. T. H. S. Sotheron-Estcourt, 1868; G. Sotheron-Estcourt, 1891, New Gallery Exhibition; Capt. T. E. Sotheron-Estcourt, Estcourt, Tetbury, Gloucester; Estcourt Sale, Christie, Nov. 9, 1934 (7), to Nicholson; Ehrich Galleries, New York.

Exhibited: Royal Academy, 1798 (101); National Portrait Exhibition, South Kensington [Victoria and Albert] Museum, 1868 (7).

Engraved: R. Dunkarton, mezzotint, 26″ x 18¼″, published by Copley, July 1799. Another version of the Dunkarton engraving shows Sidmouth without a wig as Chancellor of the Exchequer.

Bibliography: Perkins, p. 128; Bayley, pp. 32, 33, 224–25; Met '37 (44).

———— Oil on canvas, half-length, c. 1797–98. Viscount Sidmouth, Highway Manor, Calne, Wilts. [615]

Bibliography: Hon. G. Pellew, *Life of Sidmouth* (1847), frontis. (engraved by E. Finden); Bayley, p. 224.

This picture was taken to India in 1797 by Lord Mornington (later Marquis Wellesley) when he was made viceroy and governor general of India. He returned to England five years later and presumably gave the portrait back to the Sidmouth family (letter to the author from Viscount Sidmouth, Feb. 7, 1965).

———— Oil on canvas, three-quarter length, 1809. Viscount Sidmouth, on loan to Brasenose College, Oxford. [616]

Exhibited: Royal Academy, 1809 (201).

SITWELL FAMILY, THE. Oil on canvas, 61½″ x 71″, 1786. Sir Osbert Sitwell, Bt., Renishaw Hall, Renishaw near Sheffield. [477]

Provenance: Sitwell family.

Exhibited: Royal Academy, 1786 (423).

Engraved: W. Ward, mezzotint, 19⅞″ x 23¾″, published by R. Wilkinson, August 1, 1788.

Bibliography: Bayley, pp. 32, 226; Bolton, p. 118; BMFA '38, pp. 12–13; Sacheverell Sitwell, *Conversation Pieces* (New York and London, 1937), pp. 18, 76, 107, and fig. 98.

The subjects are the children of Francis (Hurt) Sitwell. There is a record in the Sitwell family papers of a payment to Copley of £100 (letter to the author from Sir Osbert Sitwell, April 15, 1964). For the boy in the front center, Copley used the reverse pose of a projected figure for *The Siege of Gibraltar*, fig. 511.

SKINNER, SIR JOHN, LORD CHIEF BARON (1724?–1805). In *Death of Chatham.*

SLINGSBY, SIR HENRY (1602–1658). In *Charles I Demanding.*

"Application was made to Sir Henry Slingsby, Bart., of Scriven in Yorkshire, but the portrait procured proving to be an ancestor of the Slingsby of the long Parliament, and no other being discoverable, the authority of a print was again resorted to" (*Charles I* brochure).

SMITH, CAPTAIN BRADSHAW. In *Siege of Gibraltar.*

SMITH, ENSIGN. In *Death of Major Peirson.*

SMITH, MRS. WILLIAM STEPHENS. See *Adams, Abigail.*

SPENCER, JOHN, FIRST EARL (1734–1783). In *Death of Chatham.*

SPENCER, GEORGE JOHN, SECOND EARL (1758–1834). Oil on canvas, 104″ x 67″, 1799–
 1806. Earl Spencer, Althorp, Harlestone, Northampton. [628]
 Provenance: Spencer family.
 Exhibited: National Portrait Exhibition, South Kensington [Victoria and Albert] Museum, 1867
  (729).
 Engraved: R. Dunkarton, mezzotint, 26⅛″ x 18″, published by Copley, October 1801.
 Bibliography: Perkins, p. 128; Bayley, pp. 32, 232; Bolton, p. 118.
 Copley's receipt for £105, dated June 26, 1806, is at Althorp.
 ——— Oil on canvas, 29″ x 24″, c. 1800. National Portrait Gallery, London. [629]
 Provenance: Lord Willoughby; at Spencer House (1854); Admiral Sir Watkin O. Pell (1854);
  Christie, Nov. 23, 1907 (86), to Moore and Sons; Leggatt Bros., London; purchased 1908.
 Exhibited: Royal Academy, 1800 (24).
 Bibliography: Bolton, p. 118.
 This portrait of Lord Spencer as First Lord of the Admiralty was painted by Copley for Lord
  Willoughby. In February 1854 the painting was at Spencer House. Admiral Pell examined
  it there on February 3 and authorized Appleyard to purchase it for him. On the following
  day he went again to London and called at Spencer House with Lady Pell, and the picture
  was purchased. It was brought home with him a week later (manuscript pocket diary of
  Admiral Sir Watkin O. Pell [National Maritime Museum, 36 MS 0683], under the dates
  Feb. 3, 4, and 11, 1854, and the transcript of the private diary of Sir Watkin O. Pell by his
  daughter, Mrs. S. M. Maude [National Maritime Museum, 36 MS 0681], under the dates
  Feb. 3, 4, and 10, 1854).
STAPYLTON, SIR PHILIP (1603–1647). In *Charles I Demanding*.
STARTIN, MRS. CHARLES (Sarah Clarke; 1750–1802). Oil on canvas, 23¾″ x 19¾″, c. 1783.
 William P. Wadsworth, Geneseo, N. Y. [476]
 Provenance: Lyndhurst Sale (74), to George Henry Timmins, great-nephew of Lord Lyndhurst;
  descended in the Wadsworth family.
 Bibliography: Perkins, pp. 109, 132; Bayley, pp. 35–36, 233; Parker-Wheeler, p. 188; Copley
  Exhib. '65, pp. 109, 141 (83).
 The identification of this painting as Lyndhurst Sale (74) is verified by a thumbnail sketch in
  Sir George Scharf's copy of the Lyndhurst Sale Catalogue at the National Portrait Gallery,
  London.
STRANGWAYES, GILES. In *Charles I Demanding*.
 "For this portrait, Mr. Copley has consulted and studied a finely executed medal, in the collection
  of Mr. Tysson, and a picture, by Dobson, in the possession of Mr. Thane" (*Charles I*
  brochure).
TEMPLE, RICHARD, EARL OF (1711–1779). In *Death of Chatham*.
TEMPLE, SIR PETER (1600–1663). In *Charles I Demanding*.
 "From the subordinate, but only authority of a print" (*Charles I* brochure).
THOMPSON, MR. In *Victory of Duncan*.
THREE YOUNGEST DAUGHTERS OF GEORGE III. See *Daughters*.
THURLOW, EDWARD, LORD CHANCELLOR (1731–1806; then Attorney General). In *Death of
 Chatham*.
TRIGGE, COLONEL. In *Siege of Gibraltar*.
TROLLOPE, CAPTAIN. In *Victory of Duncan*.
TURNER, SIR TOMKYNS HILGROVE (1766?–1843). In *George IV* (*as Prince of Wales*).
UNIDENTIFIED SUBJECT, A CLERIC[?]. Oil on canvas, 35″ x 28″, 1780–85. Victor Spark, New
 York. [441]
 The subject wears an Oxford academic robe over clerical garb.
 ——— A GENTLEMAN. Oil on canvas, whole length. Unlocated.
 Exhibited: Royal Academy, 1777 (62).
 Bibliography: Bayley, p. 31.

———— A GENTLEMAN. Oil on canvas, three-quarter length. Unlocated.

Exhibited: Royal Academy, 1777 (63).

Bibliography: Bayley, p. 31.

———— A GENTLEMAN. Oil on canvas. Unlocated or unidentified.

Exhibited: Royal Academy, 1780 (195).

Bibliography: Bayley, p. 31.

———— A GENTLEMAN. Oil on canvas. Unlocated or unidentified.

Exhibited: Royal Academy, 1796 (91).

Bibliography: Bayley, p. 32.

———— A GENTLEMAN. Black and white chalk on gray-green grounded paper, 16½″ x 10⅝″, 1776–80. John Davis Hatch, Lenox, Mass. [362].

Inscribed: Lower left, "By Copley/From E. B. Jupp./to G. Richmond/11 May 1870."

Provenance: Lyndhurst Library Sale (670); E. B. Jupp; George Richmond, R.A.; A. W. Richmond; Colnaghi, London, 1953; Mrs. Eliot Hodgkin; Frank Galleries, London; F. Kleinberger & Co., New York.

———— HEAD OF A NEGRO. Study for *Watson and the Shark*? Oil on canvas, 21″ x 16¼″, 1777–83. Detroit Institute of Arts, Detroit, Michigan. [381]

Provenance: Lyndhurst Sale (69), to Isaac; J. W. Burnett Sale, Christie, May 23–24, 1938 (217), to Mann; Christie, Feb. 24, 1951 (102), to Mason; M. Knoedler & Co., New York, 1951.

Bibliography: Perkins, p. 132; Bayley, pp. 34, 36, 184; Edgar P. Richardson, " 'Head of a Negro' by John Singleton Copley," *Art Quarterly*, XV (Winter 1952), 351–52, taken from *idem*, in *Detroit Institute of Arts Bulletin*, XXXII (1952–53), 68–70; Copley Exhib. '65, pp. 96, 140 (69).

———— A LADY. Oil on canvas, three-quarter length. Unlocated or unidentified.

Exhibited: Royal Academy, 1778 (64).

Bibliography: Bayley, p. 31.

———— A LADY. Oil on canvas. Unlocated or unidentified.

Exhibited: Royal Academy, 1780 (97).

Bibliography: Bayley, p. 31.

———— A LADY. Oil on canvas, half-length. Unlocated or unidentified.

Exhibited: Royal Academy, 1786 (230).

Bibliography: Bayley, p. 32.

———— MAJOR PEIRSON'S BLACK SERVANT. In *Death of Peirson*.

———— A NAVAL OFFICER. Oil on canvas. Unlocated or unidentified.

Exhibited: Royal Academy, 1780 (211).

Bibliography: Bayley, p. 31.

———— AN OFFICER. Unlocated or unidentified.

Provenance: Lyndhurst Sale (58), to Anderdon.

———— SEATED BOY AND GIRL IN A LANDSCAPE. Pencil, black and white chalk on blue paper, 11¼″ x 14″, 1783–88, probably 1785–87. Museum of Fine Arts, Boston (M. and M. Karolik Collection). [483]

Provenance: Lyndhurst Library Sale (probably 672); Weyhe Galleries, New York.

Bibliography: Hipkiss, pp. 328–29 (260); BMFA '38, p. 34 (133).

VALLOTTON, MAJOR. In *Siege of Gibraltar*.

VANE, SIR HENRY, SR. (1589–1655). In *Charles I Demanding*.

"A fine picture by Lely, in the possession of the Countess Dowager of Darlington" (*Charles I* brochure).

VANE, SIR HENRY, JR. (1613–1662). In *Charles I Demanding*.

"An interesting portrait by Lely, in the possession of the Countess Dowager of Darlington" (*Charles I* brochure).

VAUGHAN, LIEUT. COL. In *Siege of Gibraltar*.

VERNEY, SIR EDMUND (1590–1642). In *Charles I Demanding*.

"From a very excellent picture by Vandyck, in the possession of Lady Fermanagh" (*Charles I* brochure).

WALDEGRAVE, JOHN, THIRD EARL (d. 1784). In *Death of Chatham.*

WALES, PRINCE OF. See *George IV.*

WALLER, EDMUND (1606–1687). In *Charles I Demanding.*
 "From a picture procured for Mr. Copley, by Mr. Waller, a descendant" (*Charles I* brochure).

WALLER, SIR WILLIAM (1597?–1668). In *Charles I Demanding.*
 "From an accurate copy of the picture at the Earl of Harcourt's" (*Charles I* brochure).

WARREN, WINSLOW, JR. (1759–1791). Oil on canvas, 30″ x 25″, 1785. Museum of Fine Arts, Boston. [473]
 Provenance: Warren family; bequeathed by Winslow Warren, Walpole, Mass., 1957.
 Bibliography: Perkins, p. 117; Bayley, p. 253; Bolton, p. 118; BMFA '38, p. 28 (78).
 Copies: By Emeline H. Gordon. Winslow Warren, Walpole, Mass., 1939.

WARWICK, SIR PHILIP (1609–1683). In *Charles I Demanding.*
 "A picture by Lely, in the possession of the hon. John Byng" (*Charles I* brochure).

WATSON, ELKANAH (1758–1842). Oil on canvas, 58⅝″ x 47⅝″, 1782. The Art Museum, Princeton University, Princeton, New Jersey. [419]
 Inscribed: On papers, lower left, "John Brown Esq/President" and "Messr's Watson & Copland [?], Nant[e]s."
 Provenance: Elkanah Watson; his daughter, Mrs. Aaron (Mary Lucia) Ward; her daughter, Mrs. John R. (Josephine) Thomson; estate of Josephine Thomson Swann.
 Bibliography: Perkins, pp. 21, 118–19; Bayley, p. 254; *Franklin and His Circle*, Metropolitan Museum of Art (New York, 1936), pp. 60–61 (97); Copley Exhib. '65, pp. 100, 140 (73).
 ———— STUDY FOR (verso of Study for *The Tribute Money* [422]). Pencil, black and white chalk on blue-gray paper, 12¼″ x 19¾″, 1782. Metropolitan Museum of Art, New York (Harris Brisbane Dick Fund, 1960). [418]
 Provenance: Lyndhurst Library Sale (perhaps 669); CDC-OPS.

WEST, BENJAMIN (1738–1820). Oil on canvas, 30″ x 25″, 1776–80. Fogg Art Museum, Harvard University, Cambridge, Mass. (Grenville L. Winthrop Collection). [382]
 Provenance: A. Meeker, Chicago; Scott & Fowles, New York; M. Knoedler & Co., New York, 1939; Grenville L. Winthrop.
 Bibliography: Bolton, p. 118.

WESTCOTE, WILLIAM HENRY, FIRST BARON (1724–1808). In *Death of Chatham* and *Lyttelton Family.*

WESTERN, CHARLES CALLIS [1767–1844; later Baron Western of Rivenhall] AND HIS BROTHER [later Rev.] SHIRLEY WESTERN (1769–1824). Oil on canvas, 49″ x 61″, 1783. Henry E. Huntington Library and Art Gallery, San Marino, California. [436]
 Provenance: Western family, Felix Hall, Kelvedon, Essex; sale of the property of Sir Thomas Charles Callis Western, Bt., Christie, June 13, 1913 (102), to Agnew.
 Exhibited: Royal Academy, 1783 (227); National Portrait Exhibition, South Kensington [Victoria and Albert] Museum, 1868 (880).
 Bibliography: Perkins, p. 128; Bayley, pp. 31, 262 [as two pictures]; C. H. Collins Baker, *Catalogue of British Paintings in the Henry E. Huntington Library and Art Gallery* (San Marino, California, 1936), pp. 35–36 and plate 2.

WESTMORLAND, JOHN, TENTH EARL OF (1759–1841). In *Death of Chatham.*

WHITE, HENRY (1732–1786). Oil on canvas, 30″ x 25″, 1782–86. Museum of the City of New York. [485]
 Provenance: Given to the museum in 1955 by Augustus Van Cortlandt, a direct descendant of the sitter.
 Bibliography: Perkins, *Supplement*, p. 23.
 Copies: By Henry Peters Gray, 1867, reproduced in *Catalogue of Portraits in the Chamber of*

Commerce in the State of New York (1924), p. 11. Besides the copy in the Chamber of Commerce two others are known to exist, one belonging to Augustus Van Cortlandt and another belonging to his sister, Charlotte Van Cortlandt (Museum of the City of New York Records). The latter picture is probably the portrait, oil on canvas, 30″ x 25″, subsequently owned by Norman Jay Bruen, Wading River, Long Island, N.Y.

WHITLOCKE, BULSTRODE (1605–1675). In *Charles I Demanding*.
"For the character of Whitlocke, it was with some regret that recourse was necessarily had to a print; but a scarce and accurate print, engraved at the time, was furnished by the collection of Mr. Bindley" (*Charles I* brochure).

WIDDRINGTON, SIR WILLIAM (1610–1651). In *Charles I Demanding*.
"A picture in the collection of Mr. Townley" (*Charles I* brochure).

WILLIAM VII. See *Orange, Prince of*.

WILSON, R., ESQ. Oil on canvas, 1800. Unlocated.
Exhibited: Royal Academy, 1800 (556).
Bibliography: Bayley, pp. 32, 258.

YORK, DR. WILLIAM MARKHAM, ARCHBISHOP OF (1719–1807). In *Death of Chatham*.

Historical and Other Subjects

ABRAHAM OFFERING UP HIS SON ISAAC. Oil on canvas, before 1796. Unlocated. [Engraving, 606]
Provenance: Lyndhurst Sale (77), to Goldsmith.
Exhibited: Royal Academy, 1796 (46); British Institution, 1806–07 (51).
Engraved: Robert Dunkarton, mezzotint, published by Copley, Nov. 1, 1797.
Bibliography: Perkins, pp. 127, 132; Bayley, pp. 32, 35, 36, 38.
———— STUDY FOR. Black chalk on white paper, 16⅜″ x 12½″, 1791–96. Addison Gallery of American Art, Phillips Academy, Andover, Mass. [608]
Provenance: Probably Lyndhurst Library Sale (669), to Dr. H.; Albert Rosenthal, Philadelphia, 1935 (as study for *Hagar and Ishmael*, according to receipt at Andover, dated Oct. 3, 1935).
Bibliography: Copley Exhib. '65, pp. 125, 142 (96).

ASCENSION, THE. Oil on canvas, 32″ x 29″, 1775. Museum of Fine Arts, Boston. [337]
Provenance: Lord Lyndhurst; M. Grist, Hackney; Martha Babcock Amory, Boston; her daughter, Susan Greene Dexter (Mrs. F. Gordon Dexter); bequest of Susan Greene Dexter in memory of Charles and Martha Babcock Amory, 1925.
Bibliography: Bayley, pp. 46–47; *Copley-Pelham Letters*, pp. 295–301; BMFA '38, pp. 16, 19 (6); Copley Exhib. '65, pp. 80, 139 (58).
———— STUDY FOR. Sepia wash and pencil on buff paper, 15⅛″ x 20½″, 1774–75. Metropolitan Museum of Art, New York (Harris Brisbane Dick Fund, 1960). [339]
Provenance: Probably Lyndhurst Library Sale (669?); Jupp-Amory; CDC-OPS.
Bibliography: Amory, p. 41; Copley Exhib. '65, pp. 80, 139 (59).
———— STUDY FOR (verso of Study for *Pepperrell Family* [361]). Black chalk on light brown paper, 10⅞″ x 17¾″, 1774–75. Victoria and Albert Museum, London. [338]
Provenance: Lyndhurst Library Sale (probably 672); W. E. Frost and Other Collections Sale, Christie, May 12, 1869 (45), to Hogarth; F. Rathbone, 1898; purchased with Study for *Siege of Gibraltar* (fig. 510).
———— STUDY FOR. A cursory drawing included in a letter from Copley in Rome to Henry Pelham, Boston, March 14, 1775. Public Record Office, London, C.O. 5/39, part 2, p. 290b.

BATTLE OF THE PYRENEES. Oil on canvas, 78″ x 85″, 1812–15. Museum of Fine Arts, Boston. [673]

Provenance: Lyndhurst Sale (87), to Radclyffe; M. Grist, Hackney; Martha Babcock Amory, Boston; her daughter, Susan Greene Dexter (Mrs. F. Gordon Dexter); bequest of Susan Greene Dexter in memory of Charles and Martha Babcock Amory, 1925.

Bibliography: Perkins, pp. 127, 133–34; Bayley, pp. 35, 36, 57; BMFA '38, pp. 14, 20 (8).

———— STUDY FOR. Possibly study for *George IV* (*as Prince of Wales*). Black and white chalk on light blue paper, 10¹³⁄₁₆″ x 8¹¹⁄₁₆″, 1805–13. Cleveland Museum of Art, Cleveland, Ohio (Norman O. Stone and Ella A. Stone Memorial Fund). [674]

Provenance: Probably Lyndhurst Library Sale (670); Jupp-Amory; CDC-OPS.

Bibliography: Panorama, p. 108.

———— STUDY FOR. Possibly study for *George IV* (*as Prince of Wales*). Black and white chalk on blue paper, 11½″ x 16½″, 1805–13. Mr. and Mrs. Vincent Price, Beverly Hills, California. [675]

Provenance: Probably Lyndhurst Library Sale (670); Jupp-Amory; CDC-OPS.

———— STUDY FOR [?]. Black and white chalk on blue paper, 11½″ x 18″, 1805–13. Metropolitan Museum of Art, New York (Harris Brisbane Dick Fund, 1960). [676]

Provenance: Probably Lyndhurst Library Sale (670); Jupp-Amory; CDC-OPS.

BATTLE OF TRAFALGAR (or THE DEATH OF LORD NELSON).

Bibliography: Amory, p. 281; Bayley, pp. 57, 184; Allan Cunningham, *The Lives of the Most Eminent British Painters*, IV (New York, 1834), 155.

Copley began to paint this picture in 1806, but was prevented from finishing it when he sprained his arm in a fall. No drawings or oil sketches for the picture are known, but several paintings that might be related to it have passed through auction:

1. *Provenance*: Auction, 1913. *Bibliography*: Bayley, p. 184.
2. *Provenance*: Lord Aberdare and Other Collections Sale, Christie, June 3, 1932, to Browne [probably Leicester Galleries].
3. Watercolor sketch, 24″ x 16″. *Provenance*: Property of the Rev. W. T. Saward, Thomas Way Sale, Sotheby, July 25, 1916 (123), to Post.

CHARLES I DEMANDING IN THE HOUSE OF COMMONS THE FIVE IMPEACHED MEMBERS. Oil on canvas, 92″ x 123″, 1782–95. City of Boston, in the custody of Boston Public Library. [599]

Provenance: Lord Lyndhurst, sold to the City of Boston in 1859.

Exhibited: British Institution, 1807 (62), 1820 (21), and 1843 (165).

Bibliography: Perkins, pp. 22, 110; Bayley, pp. 16, 76.

———— SKETCH FOR. Oil on canvas, 24¼″ x 29″, 1782–94. Fogg Art Museum, Harvard University, Cambridge, Mass. [601]

Provenance: Lyndhurst Sale (63), to Waters; property of Lady DuCane (25″ x 30″), Christie, 1902, to Bregg; Baron Aberdare, 1908 (Whitechapel Art Gallery Spring Exhibition); Lord Aberdare and Other Collections Sale, Christie, June 3, 1932 (85), to Chance; gift of Copley Amory, Jr., 1957.

Bibliography: Perkins, pp. 110, 132; Bayley, pp. 34, 36, 76; Algernon Graves, *A Century of Loan Exhibitions, 1813–1912*, IV (London, 1913), 1846; Copley Exhib. '65, pp. 122, 142 (93).

———— SKETCH FOR. Monochrome, squared for transfer. Oil on canvas, 20″ x 26″, 1782–94. Unlocated.

Provenance: Lyndhurst Sale (72), to Rutley; property of Rt. Hon. Viscount Ullswater, W. H. Jervis Wegg Sale, Sotheby, April 23, 1941 (152), to Waters; Aberdare Collection Sale, Christie, Aug. 1, 1952 (23), to Stewart.

Bibliography: Perkins, p. 132; Bayley, pp. 35–36, 76.

It is possible that the Lyndhurst Sale record for this item and the previous one should be reversed. But (63) in the Lyndhurst Sale sold for slightly more than twice as much as (72), and Sir George Scharf in his annotated copy of the catalogue noted that (72) was "very slight." Since (63) appears to have been a more important picture than (72), it was probably the previous item, which is a quite advanced sketch.

——— STUDY FOR [?]. Black chalk on white paper, 19⅞" x 15¾", 1782–94. British Museum, London.

Inscribed: Lower left, by another hand, "Drawing by/J. S. Copeley R.A."

Provenance: Purchased from Daniells, 1864 (the year of the Lyndhurst Library Sale, in which the British Museum also acquired the Copley Anatomy Book from Daniells).

Bibliography: Laurence Binyon, *Catalogue of Drawings by British Artists . . . [in the British Museum]*, I (London, 1898–1907), 247.

This drawing does not relate to any identifiable figure in the large painting. There are presumably a number of drawings for *Charles I Demanding* still unlocated, since Lyndhurst Library Sale (665), "Figures in groups for Charles I and Lady Jane Gray, to Kimpton," contained eighteen items.

DEATH OF THE EARL OF CHATHAM, THE. Oil on canvas, 90" x 121", 1779–81. Tate Gallery, London. [392, 394–398]

Provenance: Sale, Christie, April 8, 1788 (93): "7'5½" x 10'0" without frame. Mr. Bartolozzi having now finished the engraving of this picture, Mr. Copley is come to a determination of disposing of it, the width of the frame is 7½"," bought in (Algernon Graves, *Art Sales*, I [London, 1918], 149); Alexander Davison, 1806; Earl of Liverpool, 1823; gift to the British nation, 1828.

Exhibited: British Institution, 1806–07 (16), 1817 (36), and 1820 (52).

Engraved: Francesco Bartolozzi, line engraving, 22¼" x 30½", published by Copley, 1794; Jean Delattre, line engraving, 15" x 20¼", published by William Johnstone White, March 1, 1820.

Bibliography: Perkins, p. 127; Bayley, pp. 16–17, 76; Met '37 (38); Catalogue, Tate Gallery, *British School*, 23rd ed. (London, 1924), p. 71 (100); Copley Exhib. '65, pp. 96–100, 140 (70).

Copies:

1. Oil on canvas, 42" x 58". Fogg Art Museum, Harvard University, Cambridge, Mass. *Provenance*: Copley Amory, Cambridge, Mass. *Bibliography*: Bayley, p, 76. This careful copy of the heads from the picture was perhaps used in the preparation of Bartolozzi's engraving.

2. Watercolor. M. Knoedler & Co., New York. This is the same size as the Bartolozzi engraving and is perhaps another study for it.

3. Oil on canvas, 32½" x 44". Amherst College, Amherst, Mass. *Provenance*: Bequest of Herbert L. Pratt. *Bibliography*: Charles H. Morgan and Margaret C. Toole, "Benjamin West: His Times and His Influence," *Art in America*, XXXVIII (Dec. 1950), 239–40.

4. Oil on canvas. *Provenance*: Mrs. Alexander Baring, Santa Barbara, California.

5. Heads of the Earl of Mansfield; Frederick, Lord North; Charles Pratt, Baron Camden; Richard Brocklesby; William Henry Cavendish-Bentinck, Duke of Portland; John, Viscount Dudley and Ward; Thomas Howard, Earl of Effingham; John Hinchcliffe, Bishop of Peterborough; and in one drawing the Earl of Coventry, the Earl of Devon (late Lord Viscount Courtenay), and the Duke of Manchester. Nine oval drawings, black and red crayon on three sheets of buff paper, each c. 5¼" x 4⅛". Metropolitan Museum of Art, New York. *Provenance*: Baron Aberdare; Lord Aberdare and Other Collections Sale, Christie, June 3, 1932 (67); Copley Amory, Jr. *Bibliography*: Josephine L. Allen, "Portrait Drawings by Copley," *Bulletin of the Metropolitan Museum of Art*, XIV (Jan. 1956), 122–23, 126. These rather delicate drawings are copied exactly after the original and are not studies for it. Perhaps these were studies for the engravings executed by

Bartolozzi or one of the men associated with him. Although there is very little correlation, these drawings may have something to do with lots 50–52 in the Lyndhurst Sale, listed as drawings by F. Bartolozzi (see appendix, Lyndhurst Sale). Sir George Scharf records his having seen, at Lord Lyndhurst's house on Nov. 26, 1863, "Tracings by Bartolozzi of small heads in *Death of Chatham* signed J. C." (National Portrait Gallery, London, Scharf Notebooks, T.S.B. VII, 2).

——— SKETCH FOR. Oil on canvas, 25″ x 30¼″, 1779. Tate Gallery, London. [402]

Provenance: H. Scott Trimmer Sale, Christie, March 17, 1860 (31), "A sketch, in grisaille," to James H. Anderdon; J. H. Anderdon Sale, Christie, May 30, 1879 (113), to McLean; purchased by National Gallery, 1879; transferred to Tate Gallery, 1919.

Exhibited: British Institution, 1863 (179); Royal Academy, 1877 (274).

Bibliography: Catalogue, Tate Gallery, *British School*, 23rd ed. (London, 1924), p. 72 (1072).

Anderdon described this as a sketch in "Guazzo . . . without color, but worked up with much spirit" (Anderdon, "Annotated Royal Academy Exhibition Catalogues," 1778, British Museum.

——— SKETCH FOR. Oil on canvas, 28″ x 40½″, 1779. Tate Gallery, London. [403]

Provenance: Lyndhurst Sale (70), to Anderdon; Christie, May 23, 1865 (130), to James H. Anderdon; J. H. Anderdon Sale, Christie, May 30, 1879 (115), to McLean; purchased by National Gallery, 1879; transferred to Tate Gallery, 1919.

Bibliography: Perkins, p. 132; Bayley, p. 34; Catalogue, Tate Gallery, *British School*, 23rd ed. (London, 1924), p. 72 (1073).

There is a possibility that the provenance of this item and that of the preceding one [402] should be reversed. Anderdon noted that the picture that he bought at the Lyndhurst Sale, also done in a neutral tint, was larger than the one he got at the Trimmer Sale. It no longer had the crutches shown on the floor, and it was a more advanced sketch with many changes in the groupings (Anderdon, "Annotated Royal Academy Exhibition Catalogues," 1778, British Museum; Anderdon, "Collectanea," p. 22). But the Anderdon Sale Catalogue, 1879, lists (113) as the item from the Lyndhurst Sale, and item (115) as the item from the Trimmer Sale. Still this appears to be an erroneous notation, since (115) sold for about twice as much in the Anderdon Sale and presumably was the larger and more advanced study. Perhaps acting on this assumption, the 1924 Tate Catalogue lists the smaller picture (1072) as having been (113) in the Anderdon Sale, and the larger picture (1073) as having been (115) there. This is probably correct.

——— SKETCH FOR. Oil on canvas, 20¾″ x 25⅜″, 1779. National Gallery of Art, Washington, D.C. [404]

Inscribed: Signed and dated lower right, "J S Copley/1779."

Provenance: Amory-Dexter; gift of Mrs. Gordon Dexter, 1947.

Bibliography: Bayley, pp. 34, 76; Copley Exhib. '65, pp. 98–100, 140 (71).

——— SKETCH FOR, COPY, OR REPLICA. Unlocated.

Provenance: Lyman H. Tasker, Greenwood, Mass., 1915.

Bibliography: Perkins, *Supplement*, p. 15; Bayley, p. 76; *Art in America*, XXXVIII (Dec. 1950), 240.

——— STUDY FOR. Black and white chalk on light olive-green paper, 20″ x 26¾″, 1779. British Museum, London. [400]

Provenance: Probably Lyndhurst Library Sale (664), to Jupp; Jupp Sale (114), to Noseda; purchased 1901 from Leggatt Bros., London.

Bibliography: Oskar Hagen, *The Birth of the American Tradition in Art* (New York, 1940), fig. 111. The Lyndhurst Library Sale (664) contained sixteen "Life size heads & other sketches for Chatham." These were bought by Jupp, and most of them went from him to Linzee Amory in Boston and then to CDC-OPS. But a few were sold in the Jupp Sale, bought by Noseda, a dealer, and subsequently dispersed.

———— STUDY FOR. Black chalk on gray paper, 12″ x 19¼″, 1779. John Davis Hatch, Lenox, Mass. [399]

Provenance: Probably Lyndhurst Library Sale (664), to Jupp; Jupp Sale (114), to Noseda; Sir Robert Witt, London.

———— STUDY FOR THE CENTRAL GROUP. Black and white chalk on gray-blue paper, 10¼″ x 12⁷⁄₁₆″, 1779. British Museum, London. [401]

Provenance: Lyndhurst Library Sale (probably 664), to Jupp (661–64 in British Museum Records); Jupp Sale (114), to Noseda.

Bibliography: Oskar Hagen, *The Birth of the American Tradition in Art* (New York, 1940), fig. 112.

———— STUDY FOR THE CANOPY. Black and white chalk touched with red, yellow, and blue on blue-gray paper, 22½″ x 10½″, 1779–80. Munson-Williams-Proctor Institute, Utica, N.Y. [417]

Provenance: Probably Lyndhurst Library Sale (664), to Jupp; Linzee Amory; CDC-OPS.

Bibliography: *Panorama*, p. 103.

———— STUDY FOR THE EARL OF STANHOPE (formerly called Lord Abingdon). Pencil, black and white chalk on blue-gray paper, 22¾″ x 14″, 1779–80. Munson-Williams-Proctor Institute, Utica, N.Y. [414]

Inscribed: Center right, "Scale of 2 feet for Lord Abbingdon."

Provenance: Probably Lyndhurst Library Sale (664), to Jupp; Linzee Amory; CDC-OPS.

Bibliography: *Panorama*, p. 102.

———— STUDY FOR HENRY, EARL OF BATHURST. Black and white chalk on gray-blue paper, 26″ x 19½″, 1779. Museum of Fine Arts, Boston (M. and M. Karolik Collection). [413]

Provenance: Probably Lyndhurst Library Sale (664), to Jupp; Linzee Amory; CDC-OPS; Maxim Karolik.

Bibliography: Hipkiss, pp. 316–17 (248); Charles E. Slatkin and Regina Shoolman, *Treasury of American Drawings* (New York, 1947), p. xii and plate 8.

———— STUDY FOR RICHARD BROCKLESBY. Black and white chalk on gray paper, 27½″ x 21½″, 1779–80. Boston Athenaeum. [405]

Inscribed: Center left, "Height of . . . / figure 5 feet = 9 i — "; scaled on right center, "Top of Forehead, Eye, Nose, Mouth, Chin"; lower left, on shoulder, "Inch/8½″" [line from shoulder to center of jacket measures 8½″ on drawing].

Provenance: Lyndhurst Library Sale (664), to Jupp; purchased from Jupp Collection, London, 1883.

Bibliography: BMFA '38, p. 33 (121); *Franklin and His Circle*, Metropolitan Museum of Art (New York, 1936), p. 56 (88); *Athenaeum Items* (Jan. 1936), pp. 1–2; Copley Exhib. '65, pp. 100, 140 (72).

This drawing was incorrectly identified previously as Lord North.

———— STUDY FOR LORD MANSFIELD. Black and white chalk on gray paper, 24⅞″ x 18⅞″, 1779–80. Boston Athenaeum. [406]

Inscribed: Upper center, "Lord Mansfield"; scaled on left, "Top of the forehead, Eye, Nose, Mouth, Chin"; lower center, "Scale of 2 feet — Lord Mansfield."

Provenance: Lyndhurst Library Sale (664), to Jupp; purchased from Jupp Collection, London, 1883.

Bibliography: BMFA '38, p. 33 (119); *Franklin and His Circle*, Metropolitan Museum of Art (New York, 1936), p. 56 (87).

———— STUDY FOR THE BISHOP OF PETERBOROUGH. Pencil, black and white chalk on gray-blue paper, 12½″ x 22″, 1779–80. Wadsworth Atheneum, Hartford, Conn. [412]

Inscribed: Upper left, "B.P. . . ?"; "To the corner of yᵉ Eye 5 feet 2½ Inches"; "To the Eye —."

Provenance: Lyndhurst Library Sale (664); Jupp-Amory; CDC-OPS.

Bibliography: *Panorama*, p. 100 (as the Bishop of St. Asaph).

This picture, when acquired by the Wadsworth Atheneum, had been previously identified incorrectly as the Bishop of St. Asaph.

————— STUDY FOR WILLIAM PITT [?]. See Portrait Catalogue, *Pitt* [488].

————— STUDY FOR THE DUKE OF RICHMOND (verso of Study for *John Adams* [439]). Pencil, black and white chalk on gray-blue paper, 14¼″ x 18¾″, 1779. Metropolitan Museum of Art, New York (Harris Brisbane Dick Fund, 1960). [407]

Provenance: Lyndhurst Library Sale (664); Jupp-Amory; CDC-OPS.

————— ————— Black and white chalk on blue-gray paper, 11½″ x 8¼″, 1779. Boston Public Library (Chamberlain Collection). [408]

Provenance: Lyndhurst Library Sale (664); Jupp-Amory.

————— ————— Black and white chalk on blue-gray paper, 11½″ x 8¾″, 1779. Boston Public Library (Chamberlain Collection). [409]

Provenance: Lyndhurst Library Sale (664); Jupp-Amory.

————— ————— Black charcoal and white chalk on blue-gray paper, 14″ x 11¼″, 1779, Munson-Williams-Proctor Institute, Utica, N.Y. [410]

Provenance: Lyndhurst Library Sale (664); Jupp-Amory; OPS-CDC.

Bibliography: *Panorama*, p. 101.

————— ————— (recto of Study for *Watson and the Shark?* [374]). Pencil and white chalk on gray-blue paper, 14¾₆″ x 22⅜₆″, 1779. Museum of Fine Arts, Boston. [411]

Provenance: Probably Lyndhurst Library Sale (664); gift of Thomas Inglis, April 1883.

Bibliography: BMFA '38, p. 31 (99).

————— STUDY FOR [?]. See Portrait Catalogue, *Mansfield* [432]

The right side of the drawing may be a study for *Chatham*.

————— STUDY FOR [?] (recto of two studies of figure with flag for *Death of Peirson* [459]). Black chalk heightened with white on blue-gray paper, 11⅞″ x 13½″ (sight), c. 1779–80. Amherst College, Amherst, Mass. [415]

Provenance: Lyndhurst Library Sale; Jupp-Amory; CDC-OPS.

This unusually soft and incomplete drawing does not relate to any identifiable figure in *Chatham* or in any of the other history paintings or portraits.

————— STUDY FOR [?], DRAPERY. Black and white chalk on buff paper, 9¾″ x 15″, 1776–80. John Davis Hatch, Lenox, Mass.

Provenance: Sir Robert Witt, London, 1946 or 1947.

Bibliography: BMFA '38, p. 31 (98); Catalogue, Winter Exhibition, Burlington Fine Arts Club, London, 1924–25 (207).

This drawing has long been identified as a study of drapery for *Chatham*, but it does not relate to any recognizable area of that painting. It seems more like a study for the drapery in a female portrait, and stylistically would appear to date early in Copley's English career, 1776–81. Because of the limited range of the subject, and the absence of a direct relationship with any specific painting, the attribution of this excellent drawing to Copley remains an attribution only.

DEATH OF MAJOR PEIRSON, THE. Oil on canvas, 97″ x 144″, 1782–84. Tate Gallery, London. [442, 444–446]

Provenance: John Boydell; Boydell Sale, Christie, March 8, 1805 (98), bought in; John Singleton Copley; Lord Lyndhurst; Lyndhurst Sale (90), to National Gallery.

Exhibited: Manchester Art Treasures, 1857 (112); International Exhibition, 1862 (128).

Engraved: James Heath, line engraving, 22⅜″ x 30½″, published by J. and J. Boydell, 1796.

Bibliography: Perkins, pp. 127, 134; Bayley, pp. 16–17, 35, 92–93; Met '37 (40); BMFA '38, pp. 11, 12, 14, 16; Catalogue, Tate Gallery, *British School*, 23rd ed. (London, 1924), p. 71 (733); Copley Exhib. '65, pp. 103–06, 140 (77).

Copies:

1. By Holyoake. Courthouse, St. Helier, Isle of Jersey. *Bibliography: Proceedings of the*

Colonial Society of Massachusetts, Transactions, 1897, 1898, V (Boston, 1902), 214–15.
2. Oil on canvas, 47″ x 61″. Mrs. K. H. N. Berryman, Ward, Marlboro, New Zealand.
3. Oil on wood panel, small. John Woodward, Birmingham.
———— SKETCH FOR. Oil on canvas, 27¼″ x 35¼″, 1782–83. Yale University Art Gallery, New Haven, Conn. [450]
Provenance: Lyndhurst Sale (71), to Cox; Christie, Jan. 14, 1888 (51) [probably]; Horace Buttery, exhibited Military Exhibition, 1890, "Death of Major Pierson (sketch)" [probably]; C. Newton Robinson; Leggatt Bros., London; bequest of John Hill Morgan, Farmington, Conn.
Bibliography: Perkins, p. 132; Bayley, p. 35; Bolton, p. 76; BMFA '38, p. 22 (28).
Graves, *Art Sales*, I, 149, records, "Death of Major Pierson. Study," owned by B. West, P.R.A., Christie, July 1, 1820 (48). I have been unable to locate this sales catalogue.
———— STUDY FOR CENTRAL GROUP. Black and white chalk on gray-green paper, 14″ x 22⅝″, 1782–83. Tate Gallery, London. [447]
Inscribed: Figures labeled left to right, "Captain Macneil, Captⁿ Christie's Black Servᵗ, Mr. Hemer, Captⁿ Clephene, Lieutᵗ Drysdale, Enⁿ Rowan/bearing the Colours, Adjutant Harrison"; lower left, scaled, "2 feet 11½ inches" with marks of "16" and "20½"; upper left, "Highᵈ [?]."
Provenance: Lyndhurst Library Sale[?]; purchased 1939 from Mrs. Jessie Colin Campbell.
The drawing does not include the figure furthest to the left in the central group in the painting, the figure with the sword above his head, Captain Clephane (1; see key, fig. 443), but it has Clephane's name written in to suggest a position for him in the center background above the head of Peirson, probably about where Captain Corbett (4) appears in the final version. The next figure to the right in the painting, with the sword held in his right hand, is Captain Macneil (2). He is identified in the same position in the drawing, although the stance is reversed. The next figure to the right in the painting is Peirson's servant (3), identified in the drawing as Captain Christie's black servant. Adjutant Harrison (10) in the painting is the figure supporting Peirson's head. In the drawing this figure is not identified, although included, and Harrison is placed as the furthest figure to the right, the figure that becomes Lieutenant Buchanan (9) in the final version. The figure in the center supporting the body of Peirson, Lieutenant Drysdale (4), is in the same position in the drawing. The drawing identifies the general location of Ensign Rowan bearing the colors, but does not include the figure (16). The figure of Ensign Smith (7) is omitted, and the figure that becomes Captain Hemery (8) is not identified by name. This drawing is compositionally very close to the Yale oil sketch, which it probably immediately prefigures.
———— STUDY FOR CENTRAL GROUP (recto of next item [452]). Pencil on white paper, 7⅞″ x 12⅞″, 1782–83. Museum of Fine Arts, Boston (M. and M. Karolik Collection). [448]
Provenance: Probably Lyndhurst Library Sale (666), to Graves; Lord Aberdare, London, 1915; Weyhe Galleries, New York, c. 1929; Maxim Karolik.
Bibliography: Bayley, p. 93; Hipkiss, pp. 318–19 (249); BMFA '38, p. 32 (106).
Although the verso of this drawing is perhaps the earliest notation for the composition of the painting, this study of the center group is considerably later. It appears to fall after the Courtauld drawing (fig. 451), with the figure firing the musket placed in its final position. The figure to his left who points toward the target carries a musket in his left hand and points with his right.
———— STUDY FOR (verso of previous item [448]). Pencil on white paper, 7⅞″ x 12⅞″, 1782–83. Museum of Fine Arts, Boston (M. and M. Karolik Collection). [452]
Provenance: Same as previous item.
Bibliography: Same as previous item.
———— STUDY FOR (recto of next item [461]). Pencil and pen on white paper, 8″ x 12¾″, 1782–83. Museum of Fine Arts, Boston (M. and M. Karolik Collection). [449]

Provenance: Lyndhurst Library Sale (666), to Graves; Weyhe Galleries, New York, c. 1929; Maxim Karolik.

Bibliography: Hipkiss, pp. 320–21 (251); BMFA '38, p. 32 (105).

———— STUDY FOR FLEEING WOMAN AND CHILD (verso of previous item [449]). Pencil on white paper, 8″ x 12¾″, 1782–83. Museum of Fine Arts, Boston (M. and M. Karolik Collection). [461]

Provenance: Same as previous item.

Bibliography: Same as previous item.

———— STUDY FOR CENTRAL GROUP. Black and white chalk on blue-gray paper, 11″ x 14″, 1782–83. Courtauld Institute of Art, London. [451]

Provenance: Lyndhurst Library Sale (666), to Graves [?]; F. Sabin, London, c. 1924; Sir Robert Witt.

Bibliography: BMFA '38, p. 32 (111).

This appears to be the first drawing developing the central group, coming right after the two Boston drawings (figs. 448 and 449), and well before the Yale oil sketch (fig. 450). The figure with the musket is here placed to the right of the central group.

———— STUDY FOR CENTRAL GROUP AND FLEEING WOMAN AND CHILD. Black and white chalk on gray-blue paper, 13¾″ x 12¼″, 1782–83. Museum of Fine Arts, Boston (M. and M. Karolik Collection). [453]

Provenance: Lyndhurst Library Sale (666), to Graves; Weyhe Galleries, New York, c. 1929; Maxim Karolik.

Bibliography: Hipkiss, pp. 320–21 (252); BMFA '38, p. 32 (107); Charles E. Slatkin and Regina Shoolman, *Treasury of American Drawings* (New York, 1947), p. xii.

In this drawing the figure on the left points with his left hand and holds a sword in his right, as in the final picture.

———— STUDY FOR OFFICER AND WOUNDED DRUMMER. Black and white chalk on gray-blue paper, 13⅞″ x 22½″, 1782–83. Museum of Fine Arts, Boston (M. and M. Karolik Collection). [454]

Provenance: Lyndhurst Library Sale (666), to Graves; Weyhe Galleries, New York, c. 1929; Maxim Karolik.

Bibliography: Hipkiss, pp. 322–23 (253); BMFA '38, p. 31 (100).

This drawing contains an early study of the figure brandishing the sword, eventually Captain Clephane, with the sword not apparent in the sketch's central study and held aloft and forward in the more finished figure on the left. On the right are two studies of the dying drummer. This figure is developed differently in three studies on the verso of the next item (fig. 456), but none of these represents the final composition used.

———— STUDY FOR FLEEING WOMAN AND CHILD (recto of next item [456]). Black and white chalk on gray-blue paper, 13¾″ x 22¼″, 1782–83. Museum of Fine Arts, Boston (M. and M. Karolik Collection). [462]

Provenance: Lyndhurst Library Sale (666), to Graves; Weyhe Galleries, New York, c. 1929; Maxim Karolik.

Bibliography: Hipkiss, p. 326 (257); BMFA '38, p. 31 (103).

———— STUDY FOR WOUNDED SOLDIER (verso of previous item [462]). Black and white chalk on gray-blue paper, 13¾″ x 22¼″, 1782–83. Museum of Fine Arts, Boston (M. and M. Karolik Collection). [456]

Provenance: Same as previous item.

Bibliography: Same as previous item.

———— DYING FRENCH OFFICER GROUP AND OTHER FIGURES. Black and white chalk on gray-blue paper, 13⅝″ x 22⅜″, 1782–83. Museum of Fine Arts, Boston (M. and M. Karolik Collection). [455]

Inscribed: Upper right, "There were five Regaments Colour of the lappels were White Blew

Green Buff & Orange"; upper center, "some of the french were dressed in dirty Read almost Orange, *faced with dirty Yellow* / so of Militia with round hats with white border & do round y[e] crown & black Feather like the black Short Coats tacked back at the lower Button lined with White"; left, "x green coat [on dying figure], O White [on vest], Read [crossed out] White [cuff], Lapels Read [crossed out] White, Blew Coats White Do, White Coats Read Do . . . alet round . . . / colour of the facing"; lower left, "Cockcade/Read/ . . . White"; lower center, "French Lapels/Inch to be . . ."; lower right, "Scale of feet for the Battle."

Provenance: Lyndhurst Library Sale (666), to Graves; Weyhe Galleries, New York, c. 1929; Maxim Karolik.

Bibliography: Hipkiss, pp. 322–23 (254); BMFA '38, p. 32 (108); Copley Exhib. '65, pp. 106, 140 (79).

———— STUDY FOR DEAD FIGURES (recto of next item [458]). Black and white on blue-gray paper, 14⅛″ x 23″, 1782–83. Metropolitan Museum of Art, New York (Harris Brisbane Dick Fund, 1960). [457]

Provenance: Lyndhurst Library Sale (666), to Graves [?]; CDC-OPS.

Working on the distances of Captain Macneil and the Negro from Major Peirson, Copley here reduces the scale of the projected dead soldier group from five feet to four.

———— STUDY FOR DYING FRENCH OFFICER GROUP (verso of previous item [457]). Pencil on blue-gray paper, 14⅛″ x 23″, 1782–83. Metropolitan Museum of Art, New York (Harris Brisbane Dick Fund, 1960). [458]

Provenance: Same as previous item.

Bibliography: Same as previous item.

———— STUDY OF FIGURE WITH FLAG (ENSIGN ROWAN) (verso of Study for *The Death of Chatham*[?] [415]). Black and white chalk on blue-gray paper, 13⅞″ x 12¾″ (sight), 1782–83. Amherst College, Amherst, Mass. [459]

Provenance: Lyndhurst Library Sale; Jupp-Amory; CDC-OPS.

———— STUDY FOR FLEEING WOMAN AND CHILD. Black and white chalk on gray-blue paper, 13¾″ x 22″, 1782–83. Museum of Fine Arts, Boston (M. and M. Karolik Collection). [460]

Provenance: Lyndhurst Library Sale (666), to Graves; Weyhe Galleries, New York, c. 1929; Maxim Karolik.

Bibliography: Hipkiss, p. 318 (250); BMFA '38, p. 31 (104).

———— STUDY FOR FLEEING WOMAN AND CHILD AND BOY WITH HAT (John Singleton Copley, Jr.). Black and white chalk on gray-blue paper, 13⅞″ x 22¼″, 1782–83. Museum of Fine Arts, Boston (M. and M. Karolik Collection). [463]

Provenance: Lyndhurst Library Sale (666), to Graves; Weyhe Galleries, New York, c. 1929; Maxim Karolik.

Bibliography: Hipkiss, pp. 324–25 (256); BMFA '38, p. 31 (102); Copley Exhib. '65, pp. 106, 140 (78).

HAGAR AND ISHMAEL IN THE WILDERNESS. Oil on canvas, before 1791–1798. Unlocated. [Engraving, 609]

Provenance: Lyndhurst Sale (78), to Goldsmith.

Exhibited: Royal Academy, 1798 (107); British Institution, 1806–07 (45).

Engraved: R. Dunkarton, mezzotint, published by Copley, July 2, 1798.

Bibliography: Perkins, pp. 127, 133; Bayley, pp. 32, 35, 135.

HOLY FAMILY WITH ST. JEROME, THE (after Correggio). Oil on canvas, 1775. Unlocated.

Provenance: Commissioned by Lord Grosvenor (Bayley, p. 235) or Lord Cremorne (Martin, *Lyndhurst*, p. 12); Lyndhurst Sale (82), to Anthony; Wentworth B. Beaumont, 1864.

Exhibited: British Institution, 1864 (129).

Bibliography: Perkins, p. 133; Bayley, pp. 35, 145, 235; *Copley-Pelham Letters*, pp. 328–29,

332, 343, 353–54; Allan Cunningham, *The Lives of the Most Eminent British Painters*, IV (New York, 1834), 145.

Bayley's statement that the picture was exhibited at the British Institution by Beaumont in 1817 seems erroneous.

—— SKETCH FOR (Virgin and Child, St. Catherine, and an Angel). 1775. Unlocated.

Provenance: Lyndhurst Sale (83), to Rich.

Bibliography: Perkins, p. 133; Bayley, p. 35.

MONMOUTH BEFORE JAMES II REFUSING TO GIVE THE NAMES OF HIS ACCOMPLICES. Oil on canvas, 66½″ x 88″ (sight), c. 1795. Fogg Art Museum, Harvard University, Cambridge, Mass. [604]

Provenance: Lyndhurst Sale (64), to Waters; E. C. Hodgkins, New York; Mrs. Louise E. Bettens.

Bibliography: Perkins, pp. 128, 132; Bayley, pp. 34, 178.

Sir George Scharf noted in his copy of the Lyndhurst Sale Catalogue (National Portrait Gallery, London) that this item was a "large unstrained canvas — with other subjects." This suggests that Copley may have begun to paint over the canvas for another picture, but that this overpainting was cleaned off sometime after the Lyndhurst Sale.

—— SKETCH FOR. Oil on canvas, 24¾″ x 29⅝″, 1782–94. Fogg Art Museum, Harvard University, Cambridge, Mass. [605]

Provenance: Property of Lady DuCane, Christie, [Feb.?] 17, 1902, to Bregg; Baron Aberdare, 1908; Rt. Hon. Lord Aberdare and Other Collections Sale, Christie, June 3, 1932 (85); Copley Amory, Jr., Cambridge, Mass.

Bibliography: Bayley, pp. 178–79 (incorrectly considered as two separate pictures, since *The Arrest of a Conspirator* in watercolor, p. 179, is the same as the sketch recorded on p. 178); Algernon Graves, *A Century of Loan Exhibitions, 1813–1912*, IV (London, 1913), 1846; Copley Exhib. '65, pp. 122, 142 (94).

—— STUDY FOR. Pencil and white chalk on blue paper, 13¾″ x 11¼″, 1782–94. Fogg Art Museum, Harvard University, Cambridge, Mass. [603]

Inscribed: Signed lower left, "J. S. Copley."

Provenance: Probably Lyndhurst Library Sale, possibly (665) to Kempton; Victor Winthrop Newman.

Bibliography: Charles E. Slatkin and Regina Shoolman, *Treasury of American Drawings* (New York, 1947), p. xii and plate 6; *Fogg Art Museum Handbook* (1927), p. 58; Copley Exhib. '65, pp. 122, 142 (95).

NATIVITY, THE. Oil on canvas, 1776–77. Unlocated. [Engraving, 347]

Provenance: Lyndhurst Sale (62), to Colonel Hawkesley.

Exhibited: Royal Academy, 1777 (64).

Engraved: Henry Kingsbury, mezzotint, published June 1, 1779; Jacob Hurd, mezzotint, published by R. Wilkinson, Boston, Aug. 1, 1785; Thouvenin, mezzotint, published by Tessari, Paris, n.d.

Bibliography: Perkins, pp. 129, 132; Bayley, pp. 10, 31, 34, 183.

—— STUDY FOR. Black and white chalk on buff paper, 8⅞″ x 10⅞″, 1776. Museum of Fine Arts, Boston (M. and M. Karolik Collection). [348]

Provenance: Probably Lyndhurst Library Sale; Weyhe Galleries, New York, c. 1929; Maxim Karolik.

Bibliography: Hipkiss, p. 314 (245); BMFA '38, p. 33 (120).

—— STUDY FOR. Black, white, and red chalk on blue-gray grounded white paper, 10⅝″ x 15⅜″, 1776. Jules David Prown, Orange, Conn. [349]

Provenance: Probably Lyndhurst Library Sale; A. A. Weston (inscription on back of drawing); Alister Mathews, Bournemouth, England; Charles Hamilton, New York.

Bibliography: Copley Exhib. '65, pp. 89, 139 (63).

444

OFFER OF THE CROWN TO LADY JANE GRAY, THE. Oil on canvas, 76″ x 68″, 1806–07. Unlocated. [654]

Provenance: Mr. Alexander Davison; property of Mr. Alexander Davison, Stanley, June 28, 1823 (23); Frederick Treasure, Preston, England, 1928.

Exhibited: Royal Academy, 1808 (1).

Bibliography: Connoisseur, LXXXI (July 1928), lix.

———— Oil on canvas, 87″ x 80″, 1807–09. Somerset Club, Boston, through the generosity of Mrs. Gordon Dexter. [655]

Provenance: Lyndhurst Sale (89), to Cox; Amory-Dexter.

Exhibited: British Institution, 1809 (130).

Bibliography: Perkins, pp. 128, 134; Bayley, pp. 33, 35, 186.

There are presumably a number of unlocated drawings for this painting that were dispersed in the Lyndhurst Library Sale (665).

PRIAM BESEECHING ACHILLES FOR THE BODY OF HECTOR. 1775 or 1797–99. Unlocated. [Engraving, 340]

Engraved: A. Fogg, published June 4, 1799.

There are many points of similarity between Copley's composition and Gavin Hamilton's *Priam Redeeming the Dead Body of Hector*, engraved by Domenico Cunego, 1778 (reproduced in Robert Rosenblum, "The Origin of Painting: A Problem in the Iconography of Romantic Classicism," *Art Bulletin*, XXXIX [Dec. 1957], 279–90, fig. 6). The Copley composition is reversed, but it shares such common elements as the old, white-bearded Priam kneeling before the seated Achilles and kissing the hand held in both of his. In both pictures there is an urn on the table in the center, a female figure playing a prominent pictorial role, and a moonlit landscape seen through the raised canopy of the tent at the side. Copley's thinking in regard to this painting, despite the late date of the engraving, may have been formed when he was in Rome, and exposed to the influence of Hamilton. After he completed *The Ascension* he wrote to Henry Pelham, "I could wish to accompany it [*The Ascension*] with one of another kind, one of a Clasick subject, that of the Reconciliation of Achilles and Agamemnon, a very sublime Subject" (Rome, March 14, 1775, *Copley-Pelham Letters*, p. 300).

———— STUDY FOR FOREGROUND FIGURE. Black and white chalk, 1775 or 1797–99. Unlocated. [341]

Provenance: Probably Lyndhurst Library Sale; CDC-OPS.

RED CROSS KNIGHT, THE. Oil on canvas, 84″ x 107½″, 1793. National Gallery of Art, Washington, D.C., gift of Mrs. Gordon Dexter. [592]

Provenance: Lyndhurst Sale (86), to Clarke; Amory-Dexter.

Exhibited: Royal Academy, 1793 (75); Boston Athenaeum, 1871 (242).

Bibliography: Perkins, pp. 98–99, 133; Bayley, pp. 32, 35, 36, 170, 205–06; Bolton, p. 116; Copley Exhib. '65, pp. 113, 141 (90).

The painting is a group portrait of Copley's children, John, Elizabeth, and Mary, but the subject is taken from Spenser's *Faerie Queene*, book I, canto X.

———— SKETCH FOR. Oil on canvas, 17″ x 21″, 1792–93. Mr. and Mrs. Paul Mellon, Upperville, Virginia. [593]

Provenance: Baron Aberdare, London; Michael Harvard, London, 1961.

Bibliography: Bayley, p. 206; *Painting in England, 1700–1850*, Virginia Museum of Fine Arts, Richmond, 1963 (373); Copley Exhib. '65, pp. 113, 141 (91).

RESURRECTION, THE. Unlocated.

Exhibited: Royal Academy, 1812 (188).

Bibliography: Perkins, p. 129; Bayley, p. 17, 33 and 206; BMFA '38, p. 17.

ROMAN CONQUEST. See *Unknown Subject* [336].

SAMUEL RELATING TO ELI THE JUDGEMENTS OF GOD UPON ELI'S HOUSE. Oil on canvas, 77½" x 59⅞", 1780. Wadsworth Atheneum, Hartford, Conn. [391]

Inscribed: Signed and dated lower left, "J S Copley Pinx./1780."

Provenance: Legar Galleries, London, 1936; Sidney Clark, London; G. M. Cherry, London.

Engraved: Valentine Green, published Sept. 21, 1780; James Daniell, mezzotint, published by Daniell, Jan. 1, 1805.

Bibliography: Perkins, p. 127; Bayley, pp. 35, 36, 213.

The Times, March 7, 1864, noted that the picture of *Samuel and Eli* sold in the Lyndhurst Sale (80) [next item] was "engraved by Valentine Green for Macklin's Bible." But the *Catalogue of the Sixth Exhibition of Pictures Painted for T. Macklin by the Artists of Britain Illustrative of The British Poets and The Bible* (London, 1793) does not list any paintings by Copley, and Copley is not recorded in the list of painters for the projected series (p. 60).

———— Oil on canvas, 1810. Destroyed.

Inscribed: Anderdon noted in his catalogue of the Lyndhurst Sale (Royal Academy) that this picture was marked "J. S. Copley 1810."

Provenance: Lyndhurst Sale (80), to Cole; Mr. Ashton of Mold, near Liverpool; Henry Graves, London, in whose possession it was destroyed by fire in 1867.

Exhibited: British Institution, 1811 (76).

Bibliography: Amory, pp. 173–74; Perkins, p. 133; Bayley, pp. 35–36, 213.

Copies: Milan, Cathedral (a stained glass window).

Bayley implies that a second replica was destroyed by fire while in a shop being repaired for the purchaser who bought it at the Lyndhurst Sale. But it seems probable that there was only one painting destroyed.

SAUL REPROVED BY SAMUEL FOR NOT OBEYING THE COMMANDMENTS OF THE LORD. Oil on canvas, 67" x 85½", 1798. Museum of Fine Arts, Boston. [610]

Provenance: Property of J. S. Copley, Christie, May 18, 1811 (41), bought in; Lyndhurst Sale (84), to Cox; Martha Babcock Amory; bequest of her daughter, Susan Greene Dexter, 1925, in memory of Charles and Martha Babcock Amory.

Exhibited: Royal Academy, 1798 (235); British Institution, 1806 (63).

Bibliography: Bayley, pp. 32, 35; BMFA '38, pp. 13–14, 17, 27 (71).

———— STUDY FOR. Pencil and white chalk on blue-gray paper, 14½" x 13", 1797–98. Unlocated. [611]

Provenance: Probably Lyndhurst Library Sale (669), to Dr. H; Albert Rosenthal, Philadelphia, 1935.

———— STUDY FOR. Black and white chalk on blue-gray paper, 13¼" x 11½", 1797–98. Addison Gallery of American Art, Phillips Academy, Andover, Mass. [612]

Provenance: Lyndhurst Library Sale (661 or 663); Albert Rosenthal, Philadelphia, 1935; Macbeth Gallery, New York, 1935.

———— STUDY FOR. Pencil and white chalk on blue-gray paper, 14½" x 13", 1797–98. Unlocated. [613]

Provenance: Probably Lyndhurst Library Sale (669), to Dr. H; Albert Rosenthal, Philadelphia, 1935.

SIEGE OF DUNKIRK, THE. Oil on canvas, 58" x 94", 1814–15. College of William and Mary, Williamsburg, Virginia. [678]

Provenance: Lord Lyndhurst; Property of the Rt. Hon. the Earl of Derby and Different Properties Sale, Christie, May 27, 1909 (96), to Parsons; Vose Galleries, Boston.

Bibliography: Bayley, p. 237.

This picture was apparently in Lord Lyndhurst's estate, even though it was not included in the sale. In his annotated copy of the Lyndhurst Sale Catalogue, Sir George Scharf mentions "The Retreat from Dunkirk" on p. 12, the last page, as "a picture hung on the staircase at Christie's some days previously" (National Portrait Gallery, London).

SIEGE OF GIBRALTAR, THE (The Defeat of the Floating Batteries on September 13, 1782).
Oil on canvas, 214″ x 297″, 1783–91. Guildhall Art Gallery, London. [489]
Engraved: William Sharp, line engraving, 22⅞″ x 32½″, published by Copley, March 27, 1810.
Sharp also engraved the accompanying key plate.
Bibliography: Perkins, p. 128; Bayley, pp. 16, 225; James L. Howgego, "Copley and the Corporation of London," *The Guildhall Miscellany*, IX (July 1958), 34–43.
Copies:

    1. Oil on canvas, 52″ x 74″. Tate Gallery, London. Possibly the copy made by Mr. Saunders for use by the engraver. *Provenance*: William Grist; National Gallery, 1868; transferred to Tate Gallery, 1919. *Bibliography*: Catalogue, Tate Gallery, *British School*, 23rd ed. (London, 1924), p. 72 (787). This may have been the item in the Copley estate recorded as "Copy of Gibraltar," which was valued at $250 and which Mrs. Copley mentioned in the list of paintings sent to her daughter Elizabeth in Boston, June 23, 1821 (Boston Public Library).

    2. By G. V. Shepton, 1906 (on commission from the Kaiser). Bomann Museum, Celle, West Germany.

The Relief of Gibraltar, the companion event to *The Siege* that was to have been commemorated by Copley in the same canvas, was painted separately by Dominic Serres. An engraving of this by R. Pollard was published by Copley on May 22, 1810, along with flanking engraved medallion portraits of Admirals Howe and Barrington by W. Sharp, after paintings by Copley (fig. 585).

———— [?]. Unlocated.
Provenance: W. C. Alexander.
Exhibited: Whitechapel Art Galley, 1908 (274), "Taking of Spanish lines by Lord Heathfield."

———— SKETCH FOR. Oil on canvas, 36″ x 50½″, 1788. Thomas Coram Foundation for Children, London. [499]
Provenance: Lyndhurst Sale (65), to Gregory; George Burrow Gregory, M.P. (died 1892); his son, Sir Robert Gregory, who presented it to the Thomas Coram Foundation (then the Foundling Hospital), 1925.
Bibliography: Amory, p. 94; Perkins, p. 132; Bayley, pp. 34, 36, 225; Oskar Hagen, *The Birth of the American Tradition in Art* (New York, 1940), fig. 115; Met '37 (43); Copley Exhib. '65, pp. 110–13, 141 (84).

———— SKETCH FOR [?]. A note in Anderdon, Royal Academy, III, probably made in the 1860's or 70's, mentions the large *Siege of Gibraltar* at the Guildhall and notes, "at General Woods at Littleton Chertsey is a glorious Sketch for it in 'Guazzo.'"

———— STUDY FOR[?]. Pencil and black chalk on white paper, 14⅞″ x 22⅝″. Herbert Ward, New York.

———— STUDY FOR THE WRECKED LONGBOAT (recto of next item [503]). Sepia ink on buff paper, 10⅝″ x 20¾″, 1785–86. Metropolitan Museum of Art, New York (Harris Brisbane Dick Fund, 1960). [500]
Provenance: Lyndhurst Library Sale (661); Jupp-Amory; CDC-OPS.

On the right side of the drawing is a project of figures clinging to a mast in the sinking Spanish longboat in the foreground, a group also studied in a more finished fashion in fig. 501. This group was blocked out of the composition when the South Bastion was introduced as a vehicle for the English officer group. These two drawings also develop the two sprawling figures in the center of the boat, as does the next drawing, fig. 503.

———— STUDY FOR VARIOUS SPRAWLING FIGURES (verso of previous item [500]). Sepia ink, pencil on buff paper, 10⅝″ x 20¾″, 1785–86. Metropolitan Museum of Art, New York (Harris Brisbane Dick Fund, 1960). [503]
Provenance: Same as previous item.

———— STUDY FOR FIGURES IN WRECKED LONGBOAT. Black and white chalk on gray-blue paper, 14″ x 22⁵⁄₁₆″, 1785–86. Victoria and Albert Museum, London. [501]

Inscribed: Lower left figure marked "2 = 5"; drawing scaled and squared for enlargement.

Provenance: Lyndhurst Library Sale (660 or 662).

———— STUDY FOR SPRAWLING FIGURES IN WRECKED LONGBOAT. Black and white chalk on gray-blue paper, 21⁹⁄₁₆″ x 14 ⅞″ 1785–86. Victoria and Albert Museum, London. [502]

Inscribed: Upper center marked "1–3"; partially squared for enlargement.

Provenance: Lyndhurst Library Sale (660 or 662).

———— STUDY FOR FIGURES ON BOWSPRIT OF WRECKED LONGBOAT. Black and white chalk on blue-gray paper, 13″ x 21″, 1785–86. Victoria and Albert Museum, London. [504]

Inscribed: Upper center, "Two feet from the front"; Victoria and Albert inscription, lower right, "No 617/1′9″ x 1′1″."

Provenance: Lyndhurst Library Sale (660 or 662).

These figures on the bowsprit of the foreground boat turn to the left, and one figure grasps a rope pulled by two standing figures in the English gunboat, figs. 505, 506, and 553.

———— STUDY FOR FIGURES PULLING ON ROPE. Black and white chalk on gray-blue paper, 14″ x 22¼″, 1785–86. Bayou Bend Collection of Americana, Museum of Fine Arts, Houston, Texas. [505]

Provenance: Lyndhurst Library (661); Jupp-Amory; CDC-OPS.

Bibliography: *Panorama*, p. 104.

———— STUDY FOR FIGURES PULLING ON ROPE. Black chalk on gray-blue paper, 22½″ x 13¾″, 1785–86. Franklin L. Mewshaw, New York. [506]

Provenance: Lyndhurst Library Sale (661); Jupp-Amory; CDC-OPS.

———— STUDY FOR ENGLISH SAILORS IN GUNBOAT PULLING FIGURES FROM WATER. Pencil and white chalk on blue paper, 17″ x 22″, 1785–86. Unlocated. [507]

Provenance: Lyndhurst Library Sale (661); Jupp-Amory; CDC-OPS; Lyman Allyn Museum, New London, Conn.; Charles D. Childs, Boston.

A bending figure in the gunboat pulls a victim out of the water. The preliminary pose on the left is altered considerably on the right.

———— STUDY FOR KNEELING FIGURE AND FIGURE ASTRIDE CANNON PULLING DOWN SPANISH COLORS. Black and white chalk on blue-gray paper, 14″ x 22⁵⁄₁₆″, 1785–86. Cleveland Museum of Art, Cleveland, Ohio (Norman O. Stone and Ella A. Stone Memorial Fund). [508]

Provenance: Lyndhurst Library Sale (661); Jupp-Amory; CDC-OPS.

Bibliography: *Panorama*, p. 107.

On the right a figure in the bow of the gunboat sits astride the cannon (also in fig. 509), although in an early drawing, fig. 510, he kneels on it and with a boat hook tries to help his comrades aloft pull down the Spanish colors. In the middle of the boat a group of English tars cheers the seizure of the flag. Fig. 522 contains a cursive sketch in the upper right for these figures as well as a reaching figure in the upper left, which may be an early study for the figure furthest to the left in the bow of the large battering ship who reaches up to catch one of the lines securing the flag.

———— STUDY FOR FIGURE ASTRIDE CANNON PULLING DOWN SPANISH COLORS. Pencil, black and white chalk on gray-blue paper, 14″ x 7½″, 1785–86. Metropolitan Museum of Art, New York (Harris Brisbane Dick Fund, 1960). [509]

Provenance: Lyndhurst Library Sale (661); Jupp-Amory; CDC-OPS.

———— ————. Black and white chalk on gray-blue paper, 14″ x 8¹¹⁄₁₆″, 1785–86. Victoria and Albert Museum, London. [510]

Inscribed: On the back, "J. S. Copley R.A. Christies 12 May 1869.," and numbered "45" and "5559."

Provenance: Lyndhurst Library Sale (660 and 662); W. E. Frost and Other Collections Sale, Christie, May 12, 1869 (45), to Hogarth; F. Rathbone, 1898; purchased with *Study for Pepperrell Family* (fig. 361).

Bibliography: Copley Exhib. '65, pp. 112, 141 (87).

————STUDY FOR FIGURE ON CANNON IN LONGBOAT. Black and white chalk on blue paper, 13¾″ x 20¾″, 1785–86. Museum of Fine Arts, Boston (M. and M. Karolik Collection). [511]

Provenance: Lyndhurst Library Sale; Weyhe Galleries, New York, c. 1929; Maxim Karolik.

Bibliography: Hipkiss, pp. 324–25 (255); BMFA '38, p. 31 (101); Copley Exhib. '65, pp. 112, 141 (88).

On the breach of the cannon this dramatic figure, who perhaps is treated in a less developed fashion in fig. 512, waves his hat to urge his companions aloft, fig. 513, to tug even harder at the Spanish colors.

———— ————. Black and white chalk on blue-gray paper, 23⅛″ x 14¼″, 1785–86. Bayou Bend Collection of Americana, Museum of Fine Arts, Houston, Texas. [512]

Provenance: Lyndhurst Library Sale (661); Jupp-Amory; CDC-OPS.

Bibliography: *Panorama*, p. 107.

————THREE FIGURES PULLING ON SPANISH COLORS. Black and white chalk on blue paper, 15″ x 22½″, 1785–86. Corcoran Gallery of Art, Washington, D.C. [513]

Inscribed: Lower right (later hand), "This is Siege of Gibraltar"; squared for enlargement.

Provenance: Lyndhurst Library Sale (661); Jupp-Amory; CDC-OPS.

Bibliography: *Panorama*, p. 98.

————STUDY FOR FIGURE ASTRIDE SPAR. Black and white chalk on blue paper, 20¾″ x 26¾″, 1785–86. Unlocated. [514]

Provenance: Lyndhurst Library Sale (661); Jupp-Amory; CDC-OPS; Lyman Allyn Museum, New London, Conn.; Charles D. Childs, Boston.

This drawing and fig. 515 may be very early studies for the broken mainmast, which slants obliquely down to the water with one seaman astride it in front of the shattered floating battery in the middle distance. The remainder of the mast above is also covered with sailors, fig. 516. Figs. 517 and 519 are early projects for this group.

————STUDY FOR FIGURES ASTRIDE SPAR. Black and white chalk on gray-green paper, 14⅛″ x 22¹⁵⁄₁₆″, 1785–86. Victoria and Albert Museum, London. [515]

Provenance: Lyndhurst Library Sale (660 or 662).

————STUDY FOR THREE MEN ALOFT ON A SPAR. Black and white chalk on gray-green paper, 24¾″ x 20″, 1785–86. Victoria and Albert Museum, London. [516]

Inscribed: Lower right, "Scale of feet for the Lyons"; "Scale of Feet"; "nº1"; scaled and squared for enlargement.

Provenance: Lyndhurst Library Sale (660 or 662).

————STUDY FOR FIGURES CLINGING TO WRECKAGE. Ink and pencil on gray paper, 8⅛″ x 12⅞″, 1785–86. Corcoran Gallery of Art, Washington, D.C. [517]

Provenance: Lyndhurst Library Sale (661); Jupp-Amory; CDC-OPS.

————FIGURES ASTRIDE SPAR. Black, white, and red chalk on gray paper, 22½″ x 20⅝″, 1785–86. Metropolitan Museum of Art, New York (Harris Brisbane Dick Fund, 1960). [519]

Provenance: Lyndhurst Library Sale (661); Jupp-Amory; CDC-OPS.

————STUDY FOR SIR ROGER CURTIS AND OTHER FIGURES IN HIS LONGBOAT. Black, white, and red chalk on gray paper, 14⅛″ x 23¼″, 1785–86. Lyman Allyn Museum, New London, Conn. [520]

Provenance: Lyndhurst Library Sale (661); Jupp-Amory; CDC-OPS.

Bibliography: *Panorama*, p. 106.

In the lower right distance another gunboat appears in which the standing figure of Curtis, the central figure in this drawing, urges his men on. In the bow of Sir Roger's boat a figure reaches down with a boat hook to pull in a distressed Spanish seaman, while further to the right several figures on a drifting spar reach for help. The figure with the hook is posed in reverse on the left of this drawing and the next one, and is also facing rearward on the right side of the latter drawing. The twisting seated figure studied on the right of this drawing, and the group with the wounded sailor in the center of the next, may also have been intended for Sir Roger's boat.

———— [?], STUDY FOR FIGURE PULLING ON ROPE AND DEATH GROUP. Black and white chalk on blue-gray paper, 13½" x 22½", 1785–86. Boston Athenaeum. [521]

Inscribed: Incorrectly inscribed, upper center, "Death of Major Pierson."

Provenance: Lyndhurst Library Sale (661); purchased 1883 from Jupp Collection.

———— STUDY FOR FIGURE ASTRIDE CANNON, SPRAWLING FIGURE, AND CHEERING GROUP. Black and white chalk on blue-gray paper, 14¼" x 22⅞", 1785–86. Metropolitan Museum of Art, New York (Harris Brisbane Dick Fund, 1960). [522]

Provenance: Lyndhurst Library Sale (661); Jupp-Amory; CDC-OPS.

The lower left portion of this drawing and the next two drawings study the figures on the drifting spar. In the first two drawings the action is to the right, just as in the previous two drawings the figure with the boat hook reaches to the left, suggesting that Copley originally had a reversed composition in mind for this area of the picture. The group in the lower right of fig. 522 may be a study for the tumbling figures in the boat between the English gunboats. For a discussion of the upper part of this drawing, see fig. 508.

———— STUDY FOR SPRAWLING GROUP. Black and white chalk on gray-green paper, 13⅝" x 21", 1785–86. Victoria and Albert Museum, London. [523]

Provenance: Lyndhurst Library Sale (660 or 662).

———— ———— Black and red chalk on blue-gray paper, 14⅜" x 23", 1785–86. Metropolitan Museum of Art, New York (Harris Brisbane Dick Fund, 1960). [525]

Provenance: Lyndhurst Library Sale (661); Jupp-Amory; CDC-OPS.

———— STUDY FOR FIGURES ON SINKING HULK. Ink on white paper, 12⅞" x 8", 1785–86. Unlocated. [526]

Provenance: Lyndhurst Library Sale (661); Jupp-Amory; CDC-OPS; Marshall L. Carder, St. Joseph, Missouri.

Figs. 526–528 seem to be the earliest drawings for *The Siege of Gibraltar* and set down general ideas that do not seem to relate directly to the oil sketch.

———— STUDY FOR FIGURES ON BOWSPRIT AND SINKING HULK (recto of next two items [518 and 524]). Ink on white paper, 13" x 21¼", 1785–86. Henry Francis du Pont Winterthur Museum, Winterthur, Delaware. [527]

Provenance: Lyndhurst Library Sale (661); Jupp-Amory; CDC-OPS.

———— STUDY FOR BOAT, WRECKAGE, AND BOWSPRIT GROUPS (verso of previous item [527]). Ink on white paper, 13" x 21¼", 1785–86. Henry Francis du Pont Winterthur Museum, Winterthur, Delaware. [518, 524]

Provenance: Same as previous item.

———— STUDY FOR FIGURES ON SINKING HULK. Black and white chalk on blue paper, 18⅞" x 22⅞", 1785–86. Lyman Allyn Museum, New London, Conn. [528]

Provenance: Lyndhurst Library Sale (661); Jupp-Amory; CDC-OPS.

Bibliography: *Panorama*, p. 104.

———— STUDY FOR SEVERAL FIGURES. Black and white chalk on gray-blue paper, 14" x 15⅜", 1785–86. Private Collection. [530]

Provenance: Lyndhurst Library Sale (661); Jupp-Amory; CDC-OPS.

This drawing and two others, figs. 531 and 532, seem to represent discarded ideas. The figures cannot be found in either the sketch or the final version of the painting.

———— STUDY FOR FORTIFICATIONS. Pencil on blue-gray paper, 12⅝" x 11¼", 1783–86. The Art Museum, Princeton University, Princeton, N.J. [529]

Inscribed: Lower center, "feet/250/350"; lower left, "Siege of Gibraltar."

Provenance: Lyndhurst Library Sale (661) [?]; Jupp-Amory; CDC-OPS.

This is a scaled drawing of the fortifications at Gibraltar. Similar detailing of the defenses is apparent in a 1785 aquatint by C. Tomkins and F. Jukes, "Approach of the Floating Batteries before Gibraltar on the Morning of the 13th of Sepr 1782," published by Tomkins, Feb. 9, 1785, after a painting by J. Clevely. But this drawing is probably not based on a published secondary source, since in 1787 Copley had advised the committee on general purposes "that he had been at considerable expense in sending persons abroad to take an exact view of the Rock of Gibraltar, etc." This drawing could have been made by another hand. But it does not differ in general from Copley's style, although there is little basis for comparison because of its sketchy and nonfigurative nature. Whatever Copley's original source and whatever his intended use for this view, it was not incorporated into the final picture.

—————— STUDY FOR REACHING FIGURE WITH LEG RAISED. Pencil and white chalk on blue paper, 11½″ x 11¼″, 1785–86. Lyman Allyn Museum, New London, Conn. [531]

Provenance: Lyndhurst Library Sale (661); Jupp-Amory; CDC-OPS.

—————— STUDY FOR RESCUED FIGURE AND TWO FIGURES PULLING ON OAR. Black and white chalk on gray-green paper, 14¼″ x 23″, 1785–86. Bayou Bend Collection of Americana, Museum of Fine Arts, Houston, Texas. [532]

Provenance: Lyndhurst Library Sale (661); Jupp-Amory; CDC-OPS.

—————— STUDY FOR OFFICER GROUP. Black and white chalk on blue paper, 17³⁄₁₆″ x 11″, 1786–87. Victoria and Albert Museum, London. [533]

Provenance: Lyndhurst Library Sale (662).

This rough study indicates that Copley may have had from the start a concept of General Eliott on his horse above the other officers pointing toward the harbor scene at the left. But details here are unclear and, in the case of the figure at the right, obviously unsatisfactory. Copley surely knew the view of Eliott on King's Bastion by Lieutenant Koehler, fig. 494, and may have been influenced to some extent by it in his selection of a pose.

—————— STUDY FOR FIGURES LOADING CANNON. Black and white chalk on blue-gray paper, 13″ x 19½″ (sight), 1786–87. Chester County Art Association, West Chester, Pa. [534]

Provenance: Lyndhurst Library Sale (661); Jupp-Amory; CDC-OPS.

The introduction of a cannon group representing the source of the destruction in the harbor that would be shown on the other side of the painting seems to have been an early thought. In this drawing the light flows from the left, whereas in all other drawings for the right half of the composition, even the earliest, the light flows from the right.

—————— STUDY OF FIGURE FOR CANNON GROUP. Pencil and white chalk on blue-gray paper, 12″ x 23⅜″, 1786–87. J. Welles Henderson, Gladwyne, Pa. [535]

Provenance: Lyndhurst Library Sale (661); Jupp-Amory; CDC-OPS.

—————— STUDY FOR CANNON GROUP AND OFFICER. Black and white chalk on gray-green paper, 14⅛″ x 23⅛″, 1786–87. Victoria and Albert Museum, London. [536]

Inscribed: Scaled.

Provenance: Lyndhurst Library Sale (662).

This drawing for the cannon group introduces a figure holding his sword by the blade while observing the action through a telescope. This seems to have given birth to two separate groups of drawings. In the first group, figs. 537–541, an attempt is made to define a pose for this officer either by himself or as part of a group. Figs. 537, 539, and 541 also contain studies for Major Perryn (13; see key, fig. 490), usually viewing the action through binoculars but holding a baton in fig. 539, and for Lieutenant Holloway (14). The second group of drawings, figs. 542–547, transfers the telescope to an officer of lesser rank, Major Vallotton (22), who turns to report what he has seen. An early sketch for this kneeling figure may be on the left side of fig. 508. In fig. 542, he holds the telescope in his hands in one study and rests it on his right forearm in the other. This leads to the idea of resting the telescope on the cannon, which Copley wished to introduce anyway. In the first of the drawings in which the figure leans the telescope on the cannon, fig. 543, his back is to the viewer. In the next drawing, fig. 544, he turns forward again and a group of officers is introduced on the right. The horse, which had been introduced behind the kneeling figure in the first drawing of this group, is now brought into position behind the mouth of the cannon. Several of the figures are in the general positions they will occupy in the final version, notably Major Vallotton, Lieutenant Colonel Vaughan (20) leaning on the other side of the cannon, and Lieutenant Colonel Hardy (18) with one arm resting on the cannon. The figures on the right, particularly the one with the baton under his arm, apparently represent an unsuccessful attempt to introduce figures from the other officer grouping. More successful is the insertion in the next drawing, fig. 545, of the seated figure of Colonel Lewis (21) between the two established figures before the cannon. The next drawing, fig. 546, reverses the kneeling position of Major Vallotton, giving a more dramatic contrapposto to his body. In the right-hand study an unsuccessful attempt is made to put another figure between Lewis and Vallotton, but this idea is abandoned. Behind the kneeling figure on the other side of the cannon in the more finished study on the left is sketched an officer leaning on his sword. This figure is more fully studied in the final drawing, fig. 547, which also measures the completed kneeling figure of Vallotton to scale. Copley is on his way to solving the problem of the first group of officers by introducing them in a row behind Major Vallotton, with the cannon as a transition to the majestic, looming figure of Eliott.

————— STUDY FOR OFFICER GROUP. Black and white chalk on blue paper, 17⅛″ x 11¹⁄₁₆″, 1786–87. Victoria and Albert Museum, London. [537]

Provenance: Lyndhurst Library Sale (662).

————— STUDY FOR OFFICER GROUP. Black and white chalk on gray-blue paper, 17″ x 11¹⁄₁₆″, 1786–87. Victoria and Albert Museum, London. [540]

Provenance: Lyndhurst Library Sale (662).

————— STUDY FOR OFFICER GROUP. Black and white chalk on gray-green paper, 14⅞″ x 22⅜″, 1786–89. Victoria and Albert Museum, London. [541]

Inscribed: On the center figure, "17½"; on the right figure, "15½"; on the first of the three right-hand figures, "1 8″ "; partially squared for enlargement.

Provenance: Lyndhurst Library Sale (662).

In order to experiment with adding the figure of Colonel Drinkwater (15) in the upper right corner of the painting, Copley went back later to this sketch for Major Perryn (with the binoculars) and Lieutenant Holloway, and added the figure of Drinkwater behind them. Since the position of Perryn effectively blocked Drinkwater from a view of the action, it was necessary to alter it for the final painting.

————— STUDY FOR OFFICER GROUP (FIGURE WITH TELESCOPE). Black and white chalk on blue paper, 14⅜″ x 22½″, 1786–87. Victoria and Albert Museum, London. [542]

Provenance: Lyndhurst Library Sale (662).

————— ————— Black and white chalk on blue paper, 14¼″ x 22½″, 1786–87 Victoria and Albert Museum, London. [543]

Provenance: Lyndhurst Library Sale (662).

————— STUDY FOR OFFICER GROUP. Black and white chalk on blue paper, 14″ x 22″, 1786–87. Victoria and Albert Museum, London. [544]

Inscribed: Scaled; at bottom, "No 1."

Provenance: Lyndhurst Library Sale (662).

————— ————— Black and white chalk on blue paper, 14″ x 19″, 1786–87. Victoria and Albert Museum, London. [545]

Inscribed: Squared for enlargement.

Provenance: Lyndhurst Library Sale (662).

————— ————— (FIGURE WITH TELESCOPE). Pencil, black and white chalk on gray-blue paper, 14″ x 22″, 1786–87. Victoria and Albert Museum, London. [546]
Inscribed: Victoria and Albert inscription, lower right, "No 621–1–10 x 1foot 2inches."
Provenance: Lyndhurst Library Sale (662).

————— ————— (recto of next item [538]). Black and white chalk on gray-blue paper, 14⅛″ x 22¾″, 1786–87. Metropolitan Museum of Art, New York (Harris Brisbane Dick Fund, 1960). [547]
Provenance: Lyndhurst Library Sale (662); Jupp-Amory; CDC-OPS.

————— ————— (verso of previous item [547]). Pencil on gray-blue paper, 14⅛″ x 22¾″, 1786–87. Metropolitan Museum of Art, New York (Harris Brisbane Dick Fund, 1960). [538]
Provenance: Same as previous item.

————— STUDY FOR EQUESTRIAN FIGURE OF GENERAL ELIOTT. Black chalk on white paper, 25″ x 19⅞″, 1786–87. Wilmington Society of the Fine Arts, Wilmington, Delaware (The Samuel and Mary R. Bancroft Collection). [548]
Provenance: Lyndhurst Library Sale (661 or 663); purchased by Fairfax Murray, London 1898, at sale of "The last relics of the abode of Sir Benjamin West"; purchased from Murray by Samuel Bancroft, Wilmington, 1898.

————— STUDY FOR GENERAL ELIOTT. Black and white chalk on blue paper, 14½″ x 13¼″, 1786–87. British Museum, London. [549]
Provenance: Lyndhurst Library Sale (661 or 663); purchased in 1909 from Dr. J. Law Adam.
There is an inconclusive group of drawings for the equestrian group, figs. 549–552. Copley at one point seems to have considered the possibility of facing the horse and rider toward the action at the left.

————— STUDY FOR GENERAL ELIOTT'S HORSE. Black, white, and red chalk on gray-blue paper, 16¾″ x 11″, 1786–87. Deerfield Academy, Deerfield, Mass. [552]
Provenance: Lyndhurst Library Sale (661 or 663); Albert Rosenthal, Philadelphia, 1935; Mrs. Lucius D. Potter, Greenfield, Mass., who bequeathed it to Deerfield Academy.

————— STUDY FOR GENERAL ELIOTT. Black and white chalk on blue paper, 21⅞″ x 17⅛″, 1786–87. Victoria and Albert Museum, London. [550]
Provenance: Lyndhurst Library Sale (662).

————— STUDY FOR GENERAL ELIOTT'S HORSE. Black and white chalk on gray-blue paper, 13″ x 11⅛″, 1786–87. Addison Gallery of American Art, Phillips Academy, Andover, Mass. [551]
Provenance: Lyndhurst Library Sale (661 or 663); Albert Rosenthal, Philadelphia, 1935; Macbeth Gallery, New York, 1935.

————— STUDY FOR SCOTTISH OFFICER AND FIGURES PULLING ON ROPE. Pencil, black and white chalk on gray-blue paper, 14¼″ x 22½″, 1786–87. Bayou Bend Collection of Americana, Museum of Fine Arts, Houston, Texas. [553]
Provenance: Lyndhurst Library Sale (661); Jupp-Amory; CDC-OPS.
Bibliography: *Panorama* (February 1949).
This drawing and the next one trace the compositional development of the dramatic figure of the kilted Scottish officer, Lindsay (17).

————— STUDY FOR SCOTTISH OFFICER. Black and white chalk on blue paper, 14¼″ x 22½″, 1786–87. Victoria and Albert Museum, London. [554]
Inscribed: Lower left [illegible].
Provenance: Lyndhurst Library Sale (662).

————— [?] STUDY FOR CLOAKED FIGURE (recto of next item [556]). Black and white chalk on blue-gray paper, 14¼″ x 23″, 1786–87? Munson-Williams-Proctor Institute, Utica, N. Y. [555]
Provenance: Lyndhurst Library Sale (661); Jupp-Amory; CDC-OPS.

453

————[?] ———— (verso of previous item [555]). Black and white chalk on blue-gray paper, 14¼"
x 23", 1786–87? Munson-Williams-Proctor Institute, Utica, N. Y. [556]
Provenance: Same as previous item.

———— STUDY FOR FIGURES CLINGING TO MAST OF SINKING LONGBOAT. Black and
white chalk on green-gray paper, 14" x 20½", 1788–89. Victoria and Albert Museum,
London. [557]
Inscribed: Squared for enlargement and scaled.
Provenance: Lyndhurst Library Sale (660 or 662).

The recomposition of the left side of the picture allowed new groups to be introduced, including
the group of figures clinging to the mast of the Spanish longboat in the foreground, which
had been blocked out of the original composition. This group is developed here, and the
next drawing, fig. 558, contains a preliminary sketch in the lower right for the unconscious
figure. This figure, especially here, bears an interesting similarity to the figure of Brook
Watson in *Watson and the Shark*. The reaching sailor in the upper right of fig. 558 is found
in the painting in the foreground of Curtis' gunboat, stretching an arm toward the distressed group gathered at the mast of the sinking boat. The drapery study may be for the
robe of the Spanish monk nearer the front of this boat.

———— STUDY FOR FIGURES ON BOWSPRIT OF LONGBOAT. Black and white chalk on blue-
gray paper, 15⅛" x 26⅝", 1788–89. James W. Barco, Washington, D.C. [559]
Provenance: Lyndhurst Library Sale (661); Jupp-Amory; CDC-OPS.

There is a large number of drawings for the Spanish-boat bow group. This drawing is probably
a transitional study, although the figures on the right could have been initially drawn for
the Coram Foundation sketch, to which they are closely related. The figure on the left with
clasped hands introduces a new pose for the frontmost figure. This figure is placed in a
straddling position in fig. 560, and a supplicating figure with up-raised arms is introduced.
The figure bending down in an attempt to grasp a comrade in the water is still retained
from the Coram sketch. The group is further developed in fig. 561 with the middle figure
recumbent and the up-raised arm motif carried by a figure further to the right. A monk is
introduced for the first time. Fig. 562 is a detail study of the two tortured figures inserted
between the figure with clasped hands in the bow and the monk on the right, replacing the
single recumbent figure.

———— ———— Black and white chalk on blue-green-gray paper, 15¾" x 18⅞", 1788–89. Victoria and
Albert Museum, London. [560]
Inscribed: Scaled.
Provenance: Lyndhurst Library Sale (660 or 662).

———— ———— (recto of next item [558]). Black and white chalk on blue paper, 22⁹⁄₁₆" x 13⅞",
1788–89. Victoria and Albert Museum, London. [561]
Provenance: Lyndhurst Library Sale (660 or 662).

———— STUDY FOR BOWSPRIT AND FALLING FIGURES IN LONGBOAT, AND DRAPERY
(verso of previous item [561]). Black, red, and white chalk on blue paper, 22⁹⁄₁₆" x 13⅞",
1788–89. Victoria and Albert Museum, London. [558]
Provenance: Same as previous item.

———— STUDY FOR FALLING FIGURES IN LONGBOAT. Black, white, and red chalk on blue
paper, 13⅛" x 10", 1788–89. British Museum, London. [562]
Provenance: Lyndhurst Library Sale (661, recorded as lots 661–64 in British Museum records).

———— STUDY FOR FIGURE CLINGING TO BOWSPRIT OF SPANISH LONGBOAT. Black and
white chalk on gray-blue paper, 9¹¹⁄₁₆" x 12¹⁄₁₆", 1788–89. British Museum, London. [563]
Inscribed: Lower center, "Siege of Gibraltar"; "2 Inches to the foot."
Provenance: Lyndhurst Library Sale (661, recorded as lots 661–64 in British Museum records).

To complete the longboat composition, a new figure is introduced in the water, clinging to the
bowsprit in figs. 563 and 564. The pose in the drawings is more closely adhered to in the

final painting by a figure in the middle distance who clings to the fallen mainmast of the battering ship. This figure first seems to develop in fig. 517, clinging to a rope hanging from the large mainmast.

————— ————— AND ENGLISH SAILORS PULLING FIGURES FROM WATER. Black and white chalk on gray-blue paper, 13⅞″ x 22½″, 1788–89. Victoria and Albert Museum, London. [564]

Inscribed: Partially squared.

Provenance: Lyndhurst Library Sale (660 or 662).

This drawing also studies the rescue scene in the English gunboat. The figure on the left in the boat and the two figures in the water are present in the Coram Foundation sketch. The possibility arises here, as in the case of fig. 559 above, that Copley took one of his preliminary drawings for the early oil sketch and used it again, in this case to superimpose the bowsprit of the Spanish longboat and to explore the relation between the two boats. The thesis is more insistent in this case since the rescue group is squared. The other possibility is that Copley simply restudied the group here.

————— STUDY FOR VARIOUS FIGURES. Pencil, black, white, and red chalk on blue-gray paper, 14″ x 23⅛″, 1788–89. Smith College Museum of Art, Northampton, Mass. [565]

Provenance: Lyndhurst Library Sale (661); Jupp-Amory; CDC-OPS.

The final composition for this rescue group seems not to have been solved until other figures in the gunboat had been worked out. This drawing appears to be a very early sketch of various figures for this general area of the painting. On the left and in the center are exploratory studies for the man at the tiller. The other figures could either be for the sketch or the final painting, but are not used in these poses. The reaching figure is almost certainly the English sailor in the upper left who tries to disengage the rope from which the Spanish ensign flies. The sketch in the upper right also appears to be for a figure trying to grasp the ropes or the flag. The toppling figures on the right remain unidentified.

————— STUDY FOR THE WOUNDED STROKESMAN AND OARSMAN. Black and white chalk on blue paper, 14⅜″ x 22⅛″, 1788–89. Victoria and Albert Museum, London. [568]

Inscribed: Partially squared for transfer.

Provenance: Lyndhurst Library Sale (660 or 662).

The strokesman is more fully treated in this drawing, which also introduces the oarsman, than in figs. 566 and 567. Although the right-hand portion of this drawing is more finished and was done later, the actual spacing of the oarsman and the wounded strokesman in the final painting is more as in the study on the left, where the lower part of the striding figure of Curtis is sketched behind the wounded strokesman.

————— STUDY FOR HELMSMAN AND RESCUING FIGURE. Black and white chalk on gray-blue paper, 22½″ x 19″, 1788–89. Henry E. Huntington Library and Art Gallery, San Marino, California. [569]

Provenance: Lyndhurst Library Sale (661 or 663); Sir Bruce Ingram, London.

Here Curtis is in the reverse of his position in the background of the oil sketch and is close to his final appearance, except that the up-raised arm will be lowered into a pointing position echoing General Eliott's gesture. The figures of the rescue group on the left are still in the same general position of the oil sketch, only slightly shifted. In the background are preliminary studies for the helmsman, who is further advanced in the split double drawing (figs. 570 and 571).

————— STUDY FOR HELMSMAN (recto of next item [567]). Black and white chalk on gray-blue paper, 14¼″ x 7¼″, 1788–89. Addison Gallery of American Art, Phillips Academy, Andover, Mass. [570]

Inscribed: Lower left, "Siege of Gibraltar."

Provenance: Lyndhurst Library Sale (661); Jupp-Amory; CDC-OPS.

————— STUDY FOR WOUNDED STROKESMAN (verso of previous item [570]). Black and white chalk on gray-blue paper, 10¾″ x 9″, 1788–89. Addison Gallery of American Art, Phillips Academy, Andover, Mass. [567]

Provenance: Same as previous item.

—————— STUDY FOR HELMSMAN (recto of next item [566]). Black and white chalk on gray-blue paper, 10¾″ x 9″, 1788–89. The Art Museum, Princeton University, Princeton, N.J. [571]

Provenance: Lyndhurst Library Sale (661); Jupp-Amory; CDC-OPS.

Bibliography: *Panorama*, cover and p. 108.

—————— STUDY FOR WOUNDED STROKESMAN (verso of previous item [571]). Black chalk on gray-blue paper, 14¼″ x 7¼″, 1788–89. The Art Museum, Princeton University, Princeton, N.J. [566]

Provenance: Same as previous item.

The previous four studies of the helmsman and the wounded strokesman are the fronts and backs of a drawing that has been cut in half. In the original drawing, the Princeton helmsman would have been on the right and the Andover helmsman on the left side of the recto; the Princeton strokesman would have been on the left and the Andover strokesman on the right side of the verso.

—————— STUDY FOR SIR ROGER CURTIS IN HIS LONGBOAT, THE HELMSMAN, AND A RESCUING FIGURE. Black and white chalk on blue paper, 14⅜″ x 22⁵⁄₁₆″, 1788–89. Victoria and Albert Museum, London. [572]

Inscribed: On figures on the right, "2 = ½In" "2–10½"; partially squared.

Provenance: Lyndhurst Library Sale (660 [probably] or 662).

This drawing establishes the relationship between the helmsman and Curtis, and introduces a new pose for the left-hand figure of the rescue group.

—————— STUDY FOR SAILORS IN SIR ROGER CURTIS' LONGBOAT PULLING FIGURES FROM WATER (recto of next item [539]). Black and white chalk on gray-blue paper, 13¾″ x 22¹⁄₁₆″, 1788–89. Victoria and Albert Museum, London. [573]

Inscribed: Upper right center, "figure 2."

Provenance: Lyndhurst Library Sale (660 or 662).

This drawing develops the rest of the rescue scene into a "Deposition" grouping.

—————— STUDY FOR OFFICER GROUP (verso of previous item [573]). Black and white chalk on gray-blue paper, 13¾″ x 22¹⁄₁₆″, 1788–89. Victoria and Albert Museum, London. [539]

Provenance: Same as previous item.

—————— STUDY FOR SIR ROGER CURTIS' LONGBOAT. Black, white, and red chalk on gray-blue paper, 19¾″ x 37″, 1788–89. Victoria and Albert Museum, London. [574]

Inscribed: Squared for enlargement.

Provenance: Lyndhurst Library Sale (660).

This is a final squared study for Curtis' longboat. In the finished painting minor changes are made in the position of the boat, the arms of Sir Roger and the figure in the bow, the head of the oarsman, and the rear figure between the two rescue groups who becomes hatless. The rescue group introduced in the front of the boat utilizes the earlier scheme, developed in the upper right of figs. 507 and 564.

Bibliography: Copley Exhib. '65, pp. 112, 141 (89).

—————— STUDY FOR FIGURE SCALING FLOATING BATTERY. Black and white chalk on blue-gray paper, 9⁵⁄₁₆″ x 6½″, 1788–89. Cleveland Museum of Art, Cleveland, Ohio (Norman O. Stone and Ella A. Stone Memorial Fund). [575]

Provenance: Lyndhurst Library Sale (661); Jupp-Amory; CDC-OPS.

—————— STUDY FOR FIGURES SCALING FLOATING BATTERY. Black and red chalk on gray-blue paper, 22½″ x 12¾″, 1788–89. Metropolitan Museum of Art, New York (Harris Brisbane Dick Fund, 1960). [576]

Inscribed: Squared for enlargement.

Provenance: Lyndhurst Library Sale (661); Jupp-Amory; CDC-OPS.

These two figures, studied to scale, hang from ropes attached to the battering ship behind and above Curtis in the painting.

—————— —————— Black, white, and red chalk on gray-green paper, 24¾″ x 20″, 1788–89. Victoria and Albert Museum, London. [577]

Inscribed: Victoria and Albert inscription, lower right, "No 613 2′ o ¾ x 1′ 8″ "; squared for enlargement.

Provenance: Lyndhurst Library Sale (660 or 662).

Rescuers and rescued cascade down the flank of the ship. In the lower right-hand corner of this drawing, figures reach up to receive the officer being lowered to them, again in what compositionally resembles a "Deposition." These figures stand in the British gunboat commanded by Captain Smith, which is behind that of Curtis and almost perpendicular to it.

—————— STUDY FOR FIGURES IN BOW OF CAPTAIN BRADFORD SMITH'S GUNBOAT. Black and white chalk on gray-blue paper, 9¾″ x 13¹⁵⁄₁₆″, 1788–89. British Museum, London. [578]

Provenance: Lyndhurst Library Sale (661, recorded as lots 661–64 in British Museum records).

Bibliography: Oskar Hagen, *The Birth of the American Tradition in Art* (New York, 1940), fig. 116.

An attempt is made here to clarify the relation between the two boats by superimposing a sketch of the prow of Curtis' boat with the figure hauling on a rope in front of a study of Smith's boat. In the final version the hauling figure handles a boat hook, a lineal descendant of the harpoonist in *Watson and the Shark*. Fig. 581 is an early drawing in which this figure also pulls on a rope instead of the hook. Unfortunately the relative positions of the gunboats are not clearly articulated even in the final painting.

—————— STUDY FOR FIGURE IN BOW OF CAPTAIN BRADFORD SMITH'S GUNBOAT PULLING ON ROPE. Black and white chalk on blue-gray paper, 15″ x 13½″, 1788–89. Munson-Williams-Proctor Institute, Utica, N.Y. [581]

Provenance: Lyndhurst Library Sale (661); Jupp-Amory; CDC-OPS.

Bibliography: *Panorama* (February 1949).

—————— STUDY FOR SEATED OARSMAN AND STANDING ROPE PULLER (recto of next item [580]). Pencil, black chalk heightened with white on blue-gray paper, 10¾″ x 9⅞″, 1788–89. Amherst College, Amherst, Mass. [579]

Inscribed: Center right, "Rowers"; scaled for enlargement.

Provenance: Lyndhurst Library Sale (661); Jupp-Amory; CDC-OPS.

—————— STUDY FOR ROPE PULLER (verso of previous item [579]). Black chalk heightened with white on blue-gray paper, 10¾″ x 9⅞″, 1788–89. Amherst College, Amherst, Mass. [580]

Provenance: Same as previous item.

—————— STUDY FOR HAULING FIGURES. Black and white chalk on gray-blue paper, 15¹⁄₁₆″ x 22⁹⁄₁₆″, 1788–89. Victoria and Albert Museum, London. [582]

Inscribed: Scaled.

Provenance: Lyndhurst Library Sale (660 or 662).

This drawing and the next one are additional studies of figures in Smith's boat, especially those tugging on a chain hooked to the battering ship in order to keep the gunboat in close while the injured are taken aboard.

—————— STUDY FOR CAPTAIN BRADFORD SMITH'S GUNBOAT AND BOW OF SIR ROGER CURTIS' LONGBOAT. Black, white and red chalk on gray-blue paper, 23½″ x 17⁹⁄₁₆″, 1788–89. Victoria and Albert Museum, London. [583]

Provenance: Lyndhurst Library Sale (660 or 662).

TRIBUTE MONEY, THE. Oil on canvas, 50½″ x 60½″, 1782. Royal Academy, London. [420]

Engraved: Valentine Green, mezzotint, published by Green, July 1, 1783.

Exhibited: British Institution, 1817 (42); Manchester Art Treasures, 1857 (108); Leeds, 1868 (1267).

Bibliography: Perkins, p. 127; Copley Exhib. '65, pp. 100, 140 (74).

———— STUDY FOR (recto of Study for *Elkanah Watson* [418]). Black and white chalk on blue-gray paper, 12¼" x 19¾", 1782. Metropolitan Museum of Art, New York (Harris Brisbane Dick Fund, 1960). [422]

Provenance: Lyndhurst Library Sale; CDC-OPS.

UNKNOWN SUBJECT, STUDIES FROM THE ANTIQUE [?] (verso of Study for *Daughters of George III* [471]). Black and white chalk on blue paper, 11" x 13⅜", 1774–75. Museum of Fine Arts, Boston (M. and M. Karolik Collection). [335]

Provenance: Probably Lyndhurst Library Sale; probably Jupp Sale, to Noseda; Weyhe Galleries, New York, c. 1929; Maxim Karolik.

Amory, p. 41, notes that, from the ancient reliefs and statues Copley studied in Rome, he "made studies in pencil, chalk, india ink, neutral tint, and color, many of which were destroyed in the great fire in Boston, November, 1872."

———— sometimes called ROMAN CONQUEST. Black and white chalk on blue-gray paper, 13½" x 30", 1774–75. Addison Gallery of American Art, Phillips Academy, Andover, Mass. [336]

Provenance: Probably Lyndhurst Library Sale (669 or 676); Albert Rosenthal, Philadelphia; Macbeth Gallery, New York, 1935.

Bibliography: Copley Exhib. '65, pp. 80, 139 (57).

———— STUDY FOR A HISTORY PAINTING. Black and white chalk on dark gray-blue paper, 11⅝" x 14¾", c. 1810. Metropolitan Museum of Art, New York (Harris Brisbane Dick Fund, 1960). [667]

Provenance: Lyndhurst Library Sale; CDC-OPS.

———— ———— Black, white, and red chalk on blue-gray paper, 23" x 27", c. 1810. Courtauld Institute of Art, London. [668]

Inscribed: Squared in red chalk.

Provenance: Probably Lyndhurst Library Sale; Sir Robert Witt.

Bibliography: BMFA '38, p. 34 (132).

———— ———— Black and white chalk on green-gray paper, 17" x 20¾", c. 1810. Courtauld Institute of Art, London. [669]

Provenance: Probably Lyndhurst Library Sale; D. Farr, Philadelphia, 1923; Sir Robert Witt.

Bibliography: BMFA '38, p. 32 (109).

———— ———— Black, white, and blue chalk on green-gray paper, 19" x 24", c. 1810. Courtauld Institute of Art, London. [670]

Provenance: Probably Lyndhurst Library Sale; D. Farr, Philadelphia, 1923; Sir Robert Witt.

Bibliography: BMFA '38, p. 32 (110).

It has been suggested that the above four subjects may have been studies for "The Death of Sir John More at Corunna."

VENUS AND CUPID. Oil on canvas, 24¾" x 20", c. 1779. Museum of Fine Arts, Boston. [386]

Provenance: Lyndhurst Sale (59), to Cox; Martha Babcock Amory; bequest of her daughter, Susan Greene Dexter, in memory of Charles and Martha Babcock Amory, 1925.

Bibliography: Perkins, pp. 128, 131; Bayley, pp. 34, 88.

VICTORY OF LORD DUNCAN, THE (SURRENDER OF THE DUTCH ADMIRAL DeWINTER TO ADMIRAL DUNCAN, OCT. 11, 1797). Oil on canvas, 111" x 147", 1798–99. The Camperdown Trustees, on permanent loan at Camperdown House and Estate to the Corporation of the City of Dundee. [621]

Provenance: Duncan family.

Engraved: James Ward, mezzotint engraving, 25⅝" x 31⅝", published by Copley, Aug. 1, 1800.

Bibliography: Perkins, p. 127; Bayley, pp. 236–37, 273.

Bayley incorrectly lists this painting as part of the Lyndhurst Sale.

———— STUDY FOR. Black and white chalk on blue-gray paper, 13" x 18⅜", 1798. Metropolitan Museum of Art, New York (Harris Brisbane Dick Fund, 1960). [623]

Provenance: Lyndhurst Library Sale (probably 667), to Graves; CDC-OPS.

———— ———— Black, white, and red chalk on gray-blue paper, 12⅜″ x 9″, 1798. Metropolitan Museum of Art, New York (Harris Brisbane Dick Fund, 1960). [624]

Provenance: Lyndhurst Library Sale (probably 667), to Graves; CDC-OPS.

Bibliography: Copley Exhib. '65, pp. 125, 142 (98).

———— ———— Black, white, and red chalk on dark gray-blue paper, 12⅛″ x 6¾″, 1798. Metropolitan Museum of Art, New York (Harris Brisbane Dick Fund, 1960). [625]

Provenance: Lyndhurst Library Sale (probably 667), to Graves; CDC-OPS.

———— ———— Black and white chalk on blue-gray paper, 11¼″ x 14¼″, 1798. Metropolitan Museum of Art, New York (Harris Brisbane Dick Fund, 1960). [626]

Provenance: Lyndhurst Library Sale (probably 667), to Graves; CDC-OPS.

VICTORY OF THE NILE, THE. Projected, but presumably never painted.

The brochure soliciting subscriptions for *The Victory of Duncan* noted, "*The Victory of the Nile* will be painted by Mr. Copley as a companion to the above work; and he has already collected the necessary information and materials for that purpose."

WATSON AND THE SHARK. Oil on canvas, 71¾″ x 90½″, 1778. National Gallery of Art, Washington, D.C. [371]

Inscribed: Signed center left in stern of boat, "J S Copley. P. 1778-"

Provenance: Brook Watson; bequeathed to Christ's Hospital, Horsham.

Engraved: Valentine Green, mezzotint (from original painting in possession of Brook Watson), published by Green, May 1, 1779.

Exhibited: Royal Academy, 1778 (65); Manchester Art Treasures, 1857 (112).

Bibliography: Amory, p. 74; Perkins, p. 128; Bayley, pp. 34, 36, 253–54; William Dunlap, *A History of the Rise and Progress of the Arts of Design in the United States*, I (New York, 1834), 132–34, 136–37; Copley Exhib. '65, pp. 94–96, 139 (68a).

Copies:

1. Oil on canvas, 20½″ x 24″. Metropolitan Museum of Art, New York. *Provenance*: Probably Lyndhurst Sale (61), to Cox; Amory-Dexter; gift of Mrs. Gordon Dexter, 1942. *Bibliography*: Amory, p. 74; Perkins, pp. 128, 132; Bayley, 253–54; Margaret Jeffery, "A Painting of Copley's English Period," *Metropolitan Museum of Art Bulletin*, I (Dec. 1942), 148–50; Albert TenEyck Gardner and Stuart P. Feld, *American Paintings: A Catalogue of the Collection of the Metropolitan Museum of Art*, I (New York, 1965), 49–51. This picture is apparently of eighteenth-century origin and differs from the engraving to such an extent that it is obviously not a copy after it; nor does it appear to be a later copy of the original picture. In fact it has a certain aura of originality (the absence of rigging on the boats in the distance; the rope below the coil, which is not included in the engraving). Moreover it did descend in the Copley family, having been bought at the Lyndhurst Sale by Martha Babcock Amory. One is tempted to speculate that the picture may in fact have been executed before the large painting by another artist, perhaps Henry Pelham. Pelham seems to have been Copley's sole pupil, and only for a short while. It was precisely at the period of *Watson and the Shark* that Pelham was living in Copley's house at Leicester Square and was exhibiting pieces at the Royal Academy. As Copley's pupil it would not be surprising to find Pelham sketching *Watson and the Shark* while that picture was in the process of creation.

2. Ink and sepia wash on white paper, 19¼″ x 23⅝″. The Art Museum, Princeton University, Princeton, N.J. *Provenance*: Leon Walker, Lexington, Mass.; M. Leon Walker Sale, Parke-Bernet, May 24, 1940 (11). *Bibliography*: Donald D. Egbert, in *Bulletin of the Department of Art and Archeology*, Princeton University (1943) p. 4; Charles E. Slatkin and Regina Shoolman, *Treasury of American Drawings*, plate 7; Museum of Modern Art, "Romantic Painting in America" (New York, November 17, 1943–February 6, 1944), p. 132 (56), by J. T. Soby and D. C. Miller. Like the oil copy at the Metropolitan Museum of Art, this drawing differs markedly from the engraving as well as from the finished pictures, yet does not

seem to be a preparatory study by Copley. Differences can be noted in the stern of the boat, the angle and size of the shark in relation to the boy, the position of the Negro's thumb, the single boat in the right distance, the angle of the merging oars on the left, the hair of the harpoonist, the waterspout of the shark, and the ribs in the boat.

3. Oil on canvas, 50″ x 68″. Formerly Copley Amory, Jr. *Provenance*: Baron Aberdare, London; Aberdare Sale, Christie, June 3, 1932. *Bibliography*: Bayley, p. 254 [as the original version].

4. Oil on copper, 19½″ x 23½″. Beaverbrook Art Gallery, Fredericton, New Brunswick. *Provenance*: Christie, Oct. 18, 1957 (36), to Clowes.

5. Oil on canvas, 35″ x 20½″. *Provenance*: Charles D. Childs, Boston.

6. Oil on metal, oval, 22″ x 27½″. *Bibliography: Antiques*, LXVII (Jan. 1955), 24. *Provenance*: Parnassus Gallery, New York, 1955.

7. Painted by Henry Sargent, oil on canvas, 23⅝ x 18¼. Museum of Fine Arts, Boston. *Provenance*: Mrs. Horace A. Lamb, Boston; gift of Mrs. Winthrop Sargent. *Bibliography: Catalogue of Paintings, Museum of Fine Arts, Boston* (Boston, 1921), p. 231 (779).

One of the most interesting copies, if it could be located, would be that made by William Dunlap, who copied *Watson and the Shark* and West's *Death of Wolfe*. When he sailed from New York to England in May 1784, Dunlap took along his copy of *Watson* as a credential picture to show to West, with whom he wished to study. He had made both of his copies on the basis of available engravings (Dunlap, p. 352).

———— Oil on canvas, 72⅛″ x 90¼″, 1778. Museum of Fine Arts, Boston. [372]

Inscribed: Signed and dated center left in stern of boat, "J. S. Copley. P. 1778."

Provenance: Lyndhurst Sale (61); Charles Hook Appleton; gift of his daughter, Mrs. George Von Lengerke Meyer, 1889.

Exhibited: British Institution, 1807 (110).

Bibliography: Amory, p. 74; Perkins, pp. 118–19; Bayley, pp. 253–54; BMFA '38 (80); Copley Exhib. '65, pp. 94–96, 140 (68b).

———— Oil on canvas, 36″ x 30½″, 1782. Detroit Institute of Arts, Detroit, Michigan. [373]

Inscribed: Signed and dated lower left, "Painted by J. S. Copley, R.A. London 1782."

Provenance: Property of Noel Desanfans, Christie, April 8, 1786 (396), "The well known subject of the shark," 44″ x 37″ [outside frame measurement]; property of W. Goddard, Christie, Feb. 5, 1791 (73), "The Shark," to Green; G. T. Anderson; from him in the middle of the nineteenth century to the family of W. P. Hunter; sold in London, c. 1946, from W. P. Hunter Collection; M. Knoedler & Co., New York.

Bibliography: E[dgar] P. Richardson, "Watson and the Shark by John Singleton Copley," *Art Quarterly*, X (Summer 1947), 213–18.

A replica or copy of *Watson and the Shark* was at one time owned by M. Allen, Brighton, Sussex, and the Witt Library records that this is the painting now owned by the Detroit Institute of Arts. But it could be the next item or one of the copies recorded above.

———— Oil on canvas, 35½″ x 30″. Bayou Bend Collection of Americana, Museum of Fine Arts, Houston, Texas.

Provenance: Perhaps the picture owned by M. Allen, Brighton, Sussex, noted in the previous entry; Charles D. Childs, Boston; Miss Ima Hogg, Houston, Texas.

The surface of this picture is so badly abraded that it is difficult to tell whether it is a replica of the Detroit picture or a contemporary copy. The stylistic evidence slightly favors the conclusion that it is a replica.

———— STUDY FOR HEAD OF BROOK WATSON [?] (verso of Study of Duke of Richmond for *Death of Chatham* [411]). Pencil and white chalk on gray-blue paper, 14³⁄₁₆″ x 22⁹⁄₁₆″, 1777–78. Museum of Fine Arts, Boston. [374]

Provenance: Probably Lyndhurst Library Sale (664); gift of Thomas Inglis, April 1883.

Bibliography: BMFA '38, p. 31 (99).

———— STUDY FOR HARPOONER AND OARSMAN. Black and white chalk on green-gray paper, 13½″ x 15⅝″, 1777–78. Detroit Institute of Arts, Detroit, Michigan. [375]

Inscribed: Center, "5ᶠ 3ᴵ [for left figure] / 1foot 11Inch [for right figure]."

Provenance: Lyndhurst Library Sale (probably 668); D. Farr, Philadelphia, 1923; Sir Robert Witt; M. Knoedler & Co., New York.

Bibliography: BMFA '38, p. 33 (124); John S. Newberry, Jr., "Four Drawings by Copley," *Detroit Institute of Arts Bulletin*, XXVIII, no. 2 (1949), 34–35.

———— STUDY OF FIGURE ON LEFT. Black and white chalk on green-gray paper, 12″ x 10″, 1777–78. Detroit Institute of Arts, Detroit, Michigan. [376]

Provenance: Lyndhurst Library Sale (probably 668); D. Farr, Philadelphia, 1923; Sir Robert Witt; M. Knoedler & Co., New York.

Bibliography: BMFA '38, p. 33 (123); John S. Newberry, Jr., "Four Drawings by Copley," *Detroit Institute of Arts Bulletin*, XXVIII, no. 2 (1949), 34.

———— STUDY FOR OARSMEN. Black and white chalk on green-gray paper, 9¾″ x 11⅞″, 1777–78. Detroit Institute of Arts, Detroit, Michigan. [377]

Provenance: Lyndhurst Library Sale (probably 668); D. Farr, Philadelphia, 1923; Sir Robert Witt; M. Knoedler & Co., New York.

Bibliography: BMFA '38, p. 33 (122); John S. Newberry, Jr., "Four Drawings by Copley," *Detroit Institute of Arts Bulletin*, XXVIII, no. 2 (1949), 34–35.

———— STUDY FOR RESCUE GROUP. Black and white chalk, squared and numbered in red chalk, on green-gray paper, 14½″ x 21⅞″, 1777–78. Detroit Institute of Arts, Detroit, Michigan. [378]

Inscribed: Upper right, "The length of the ship / is 2 feet 2 inches."

Provenance: Lyndhurst Library Sale (probably 668); D. Farr, Philadelphia, 1923; Sir Robert Witt; M. Knoedler & Co., New York.

Bibliography: BMFA '38, p. 33 (125); John S. Newberry, Jr., "Four Drawings by Copley," *Detroit Institute of Arts Bulletin*, XXVIII, no. 2 (1949), 34–35.

461

Bibliography

PRIMARY SOURCES

MANUSCRIPTS AND OTHER COLLECTIONS

The major documentary sources for Copley cover those periods when his family was separated and distances required letter writing. Our supply of information grows slim for those periods when the family dwelled together in Boston and London. There are two major collections of Copley manuscript material, both of which were comprehensively published many years ago. The "Copley-Pelham Letters, 1739–1776" at the Public Record Office, London, were apparently expropriated by the British from Henry Pelham when he arrived in England in mid-1776. It contains some early correspondence between the Pelhams in Boston and relatives in Ireland, but consists largely of letters exchanged by Copley and Pelham when the former was in New York in 1771 and on the continent in 1774–75. Other material in the collection suggests that Pelham, who more or less acted as Copley's agent in Boston, carried to England some of Copley's personal papers and old correspondence, which was commandeered along with his own. The Public Record Office material was carefully winnowed and edited by Guernsey Jones, *Letters and Papers of John Singleton Copley and Henry Pelham, 1739–1776*, LXXI, Massachusetts Historical Society Collections (Boston, 1914).

The "Copley Family Letters, 1800–1847," deposited at the Massachusetts Historical Society by Harcourt Amory in 1925, primarily contain correspondence between the Copleys in London and the artist's daughter Elizabeth, who married Gardiner Greene in 1800 and returned with him to Boston. Much of this material was used by Martha Babcock Amory (Elizabeth's daughter and Copley's granddaughter) in *The Domestic and Artistic Life of John Singleton Copley, R.A.* (Boston, 1882).

A related batch of Copley family papers was burned by a Copley descendant (see Flexner, *Copley*, p. 117), but some survive at the Library of Congress in Washington. Another reputed loss by fire was a Copley manuscript list of his pictures, burned in error by a family servant (Amory, p. 16). Much material of direct and indirect relevance still survives, however, although it is widely scattered.

At the Massachusetts Historical Society, in addition to the "Copley Family Letters," there is material in the Byles Papers, 1780, 1784 (Mather Brown letters); the Adams Papers, 1783–1815; the Paul Revere Day Books, 1763–1767; letters from Copley to Mercy Scollay, 1788–89 (about his mother); letters to Samuel Cabot and other Cabot correspondence, 1796–97 (about the sale of the Beacon Hill property); and correspondence between Michael and Benjamin Joy, 1810–11 (about relinquishment of claims to the Beacon Hill property). There is also a considerable amount of related material dealing with Copley's land entanglements at the Society for the Preservation of New England Antiquities, 1793–1810 (letters, depositions, maps).

The Boston Public Library has a varied collection of materials. Among the few Copley and Copley family letters is the particularly important letter from Mrs. Copley to her daughter, Mrs. Gardiner Greene, received June 23, 1821 (Ch.F.6.4), reviewing the contents of Copley's studio and giving valuations. Also in the collection is a fragment from Copley's diary kept during the trip through Belgium to Hanover in 1787 (Ch.I.3.12); an "Account of a possible case between Copley and the City of London" concerning *The Siege of Gibraltar* (Ch.I.3.10); the unique Copley poem, "Lines for a Garden-Seat at Stapleton" (Ch.J.5.72); and the long and informative letter from Edmund Malone to Copley, Jan. 4, 1782, regarding the projected *Charles I* picture (Ch.I.3.11)

The Clarke-Bromfield Papers at Yale contain family and business papers of Copley's in-laws, the most important item being Mrs. Copley's account for 1774–75 with the firm run by her father and brothers. There are bills and letters relating to Copley's dispute with John Trumbull (1756–1843) over an unpaid account, 1797–1799, in the Trumbull Papers. The John Hill Morgan (1870–1945) diaries and artists' file at the Yale University Art Gallery has also been occasionally useful.

Public and other records supplying factual data about Copley's life include the Early Court and Probate Records (1748–1772), Suffolk County Courthouse, Boston; Register of Baptisms, 1775–1791, St. Martins in the Fields, London; Tax Rate Books, New Street Ward, St. Martin's Parish (1773–1784), Westminster Public Library, London; the album of John Hunter (1728–1793) memorabilia, pp. 38–39, Royal College of Surgeons, London (plan and other information about the house at 28 Leicester Square); Tax Rate Books, Conduit Street Ward, St. George's, Hanover Square, Parish (1785–1806), Householder List, St. George's, Hanover Square (c. 1790), and Court Records, Middlesex County Record Office, London; a contemporaneous copy of the Croydon Parish Burial Records, 1785, Croydon Public Library; Fulham Poor Rate and Overseers' Acts, 1804, Fulham Public Library; and Probate Records, Principal Probate Office, Somerset House, London, Newcastle, foll. 372–73 (Richard Clarke) and Administration Acts, 1817 (Copley) and 1836 (Mrs. Copley).

It would seem logical to suppose that Copley and Henry Pelham corresponded after Pelham left London for Ireland, but efforts to locate Pelham manuscript material in Ireland were unsuccessful. Irish material is scanty in part because of the destruction of records fifty years ago. The problem is further complicated because Pelham's twin sons died unmarried, and there was no direct line of descent to preserve family papers. Searches in Dublin at the Genealogical Office, the Public Record Office, and the National Library were to no avail, but some material, including the record of Pelham's marriage to Catherine Butler (338.196.227133), was discovered at the Registry of Deeds. Brief visits to Quinville (the home of Copley's mother) and Cork (his father) uncovered no data. The fullest though not particularly relevant cache of Pelham material, relating to his tenure as agent for the Marquis of Lansdowne on his Kerry estates, is "Henry Pelham's Agency and Miscellaneous Letters, 1787–1798," Bowood Park, Calne, Wilts.

There was surprisingly little relevant material among the papers of Copley's son, Lord Lyndhurst, at Trinity College, Cambridge.

The rich collections of the British Museum yielded much primary information relevant to Copley, although there was little specific Copley manuscript material. There are a few letters, and scattered references, in the Cumberland Papers, "Diary of Elisha Hutchinson, 1774–1788," "Diary of Gov. Thomas Hutchinson, 1774–1780," "Letters of Elisha Hutchinson to His Wife, 1774–1777," and other loyalist letters. More fruitful were materials directly related to the arts. Copley's varnish recipes are found in the "Memo Book" of Ozias Humphry (1742–1810). An indispensable source of information is the Joseph Farington (1747–1821) "Diary," and the British Museum has a typescript copy of the original manuscript in the Royal Library, Windsor Castle. The cuttings and notes in the W. T. Whitley Papers are an invaluable source of material from contemporary newspapers, and this collection is reinforced by the "Cuttings from English Newspapers on Matters of Artistic Interest, 1686–1835" at the Victoria and Albert Museum. Also at the British Museum is a great deal of material brought together by the nineteenth-century arts antiquary, James Hughes Anderdon, including his "Collectanea Biographica," of which volume XXII is pertinent, and a collection of Royal Academy and Society of Artists exhibition catalogues interleaved with relevant cuttings and notations. Anderdon's "Scrapbooks" are at the Royal Academy itself, but the great storehouse of information at the academy consists of the "Minute Books" of the council and the general assembly, 1779–1811, in which Copley plays a prominent and often obstreperous role.

The "Sketch Books" of a knowledgeable observer of the arts, Sir George Scharf (1820–1895), are at the National Portrait Gallery, of which he was director. There are letters from Copley and his son to John Soane (1753–1837) at the Soane Museum, 1809–1816, relating to Copley's debts.

There is important material concerning *The Siege of Gibraltar* and *The Victory of Duncan* at the National Maritime Museum, Greenwich, notably John Drinkwater's (1762–1844) grangerized copy (32MS9777) of his *History of the Late Siege of Gibraltar* (4th ed., London, 1790); the Heathfield Papers; a letter to Copley from John Little, March 5, 1795, containing Benjamin Turner's sketch of the deck of the *Venerable*; and the "*Venerable* Log Book." The "*Venerable* Muster Book, March 1, 1797–March 14, 1798" is at the Public Record Office, along with the "*Kent* Muster Book, March 10– Aug. 30, 1799." Several manuscript volumes by John Drinkwater at the National Library of Scotland (Ms. 1836) shed further light on his connection with the planning of *The Siege of Gibraltar* —"Leading Incidents in the Life of Colonel Drinkwater" and "Recollections, Book I, Gibraltar, England, Toulon." Material directly relevant to *Gibraltar* is prominent in the "Committee Minutes" and the "Journals" of the Committee on General Purposes and the Court of Common Council of the Corporation of the City of London, 1783–1799, housed in the Corporation Record Office.

COPLEY EXHIBITION BROCHURES AND SUBSCRIPTIONS FOR ENGRAVINGS

[*Charles I Demanding.*] *Mr. Copley's Picture of King Charles the First, Demanding in the House of Commons the Five Impeached Members, A.D. MDCXLI–II. Now Exhibiting in Spring Gardens.* London, [1795]. British Museum.

[*Death of Chatham.*] *Proposals For Publishing, by Subscription, an Engraved Print, from the Original Picture, now Painting by John Singleton Copley, R.A. Elect, Representing The Death of the Late Earl of Chatham, to be Engraved by Mr. John Keyse Sherwin.* London, March 29, 1780. Tate Gallery.

[*Death of Peirson.*] *Proposals By Mr. Boydell, For Publishing by Subscription, an Engraved Print, from the Original Picture, Painted by John Singleton Copley, R.A., Representing the Death of the Late Major Peirson, and the Defeat of the French Troops in the Island of Jersey, 1781. To be Engraved by Mr. Heath.* London, May 22, 1784. Tate Gallery.

[*Siege of Gibraltar.*] *Proposals For Publishing by Subscription, an Engraving, from the Historical Picture of the Siege and Relief of Gibraltar, Painted by John Singleton Copley, R.A., Now Exhibiting in a Pavilion, erected by the gracious Permission of the King, for that Purpose, in the Green Park . . . To be Engraved by Francis Bartolozzi, R.A.* London, [1791]. British Museum; there are two editions of this brochure, one printed by B. McMillan, which simply describes the painting, and one printed by H. Reynall, which includes the subscription for the engraving.

[*Victory of Duncan.*] *Exhibition of An Historical Picture Painted by John Singleton Copley, R.A. Representing the Surrender of the Dutch Admiral De Winter and the Destruction and Dispersion of His Fleet, On the Memorable 11th of October, 1797; Containing the Portraits of Admiral Lord Duncan, Admiral De Winter, Capt. Sir W. Fairfax, and the Officers of His Majesty's Ship the Venerable, Pavilion, No. 24, Albemarle Street. Also Proposals for Publishing by Subscription an Engraved Print, From the above, Picture . . .* London, [1799]. British Museum.

SALES CATALOGUES

[Copley Print Sale.] *A Catalogue of the Genuine Collection of Prints and Copper Plates, the Property of the late John Singleton Copley, Esq., RA. & F.S.A.* Sotheby, Jan. 26–27, 1820 (Victoria and Albert Museum), or Feb. 15 and 17 (British Museum). The only difference between the two catalogues is the date.

[Davison Sale.] *A Catalogue of a Splendid Collection of Pictures, by British Artists, The Subjects taken from English History; Painted expressly for Alexander Davison, Esq., which will be Sold by Auction by Mr. Stanley.* June 28, 1823. Frick Art Reference Library.

[Jupp Sale.] *Catalogue of the Collection of Drawings and Engravings of Edward Basil Jupp, Esq., F.S.A.* Christie, Feb. 21, 1878. Christie, Manson & Woods.

[Lyndhurst Library Sale.] *Catalogue of the Valuable Library of the Rt. Hon. Lord Lyndhurst, Deceased: also, a few Engravings and Sketches by J. S. Copley, R.A.* Christie, Feb. 26–27, 1864. Christie, Manson & Woods.

[Lyndhurst Sale.] *Catalogue of the Very Valuable Collection of Pictures of the Rt. Hon. Lord*

BIBLIOGRAPHY

Lyndhurst. Deceased: Including Most of the Important Works of His Lordship's Father, That Distinguished Historical Painter, John Singleton Copley, R.A. Christie, March 5, 1864. Boston Athenaeum.

MODERN EXHIBITION CATALOGUES

An Exhibition of Paintings by John Singleton Copley. Metropolitan Museum of Art, New York, Dec. 22, 1936 — Feb. 14, 1937. Text by Harry B. Wehle.

John Singleton Copley, 1738–1815. Loan Exhibition, Museum of Fine Arts, Boston, Feb. 1–March 15, 1938.

John Singleton Copley, 1738–1815. National Gallery of Art (Washington), Metropolitan Museum of Art (New York), and Museum of Fine Arts (Boston), Sept. 18, 1965 — March 6, 1966. Text by Jules David Prown.

New England Miniatures, 1750–1850. Museum of Fine Arts, Boston, April 24–May 28, 1957. Compiled and edited by Barbara Neville Parker.

SECONDARY SOURCES

BOOKS

The first important monograph on Copley was Augustus Thorndike Perkins, *A Sketch of the Life and a List of the Works of John Singleton Copley* (1873). It contained some biographical information, but more important was its early list of Copley's paintings, mostly American portraits. The next two major publications on Copley, Martha Babcock Amory's biography (1882) and the *Copley-Pelham Letters* (1914), were based on large and important manuscript collections and are discussed above.

After a preliminary *Sketch* in 1910, Frank W. Bayley, proprietor of a Boston art gallery named for Copley, published *The Life and Works of John Singleton Copley* (1915), which indicated on the title page that it was based on the work of Perkins, and it does rely heavily on the earlier book. Bayley also incorporated exhibition records recently made available through the published compilations of Algernon Graves, and this added a considerable amount of information about Copley's English pictures. He further introduced a number of new attributions that are much less reliable than the data he took from Perkins and Graves, and the book must be used with caution.

All remained relatively quiet in the realm of Copley studies, with the exception of the only moderately useful checklist of paintings by Theodore Bolton and Harry Lorin Binsse published in *Antiquarian* in 1930, until 1937–38 when the bicentennial of Copley's birth was celebrated with exhibitions (and catalogues) at the Metropolitan Museum of Art, New York, and the Museum of Fine Arts, Boston, and the publication of a milestone in Copley studies, the book by Barbara Neville Parker and Anne Bolling Wheeler on Copley's American portraits (1938). Since that time the only book on Copley has been the study by James Thomas Flexner (1948), which blends scholarly insight and not so scholarly imagination into a readable account, enhanced by a very good bibliography.

BIBLIOGRAPHY

Those books particularly valuable in providing biographical information for Copley's American sitters are listed in Volume One.

Amory, Martha Babcock. *The Domestic and Artistic Life of John Singleton Copley, R.A.* Boston, 1882.

Angelo, Henry. *The Reminiscences of Henry Angelo.* Introduction by Lord Howard de Walden, notes and memoir by H. Lavers Smith. 2 vols. London, 1904.

Bayley, Frank W. *The Life and Works of John Singleton Copley.* Boston, 1915.

———— *Sketch of the Life and a List of Some of the Works of John Singleton Copley.* Boston, 1910.

Belknap, Waldron Phoenix, Jr. *American Colonial Painting: Materials for a History.* Cambridge, Mass., 1959.

Bemrose, William. *The Life and Work of Joseph Wright* [of Derby]. London, 1885.

Bromley, Rev. Robert Anthony. *History of the Fine Arts,* vol. I. London, 1793.

Bulfinch, Ellen Susan, ed. *The Life and Letters of Charles Bulfinch, Architect.* Boston and New York, 1896.

Burroughs, Alan. *John Greenwood in America 1745–1752.* Addison Gallery of American Art, Phillips Academy, Andover, Mass., 1943.

Camperdown, Earl of. *Admiral Duncan.* London, 1898.

Chamberlain, Allen. *Beacon Hill: Its Ancient Pastures and Early Mansions.* Boston and New York, 1925.

Chancellor, E. Beresford. *The History of the Squares of London.* London, 1907.

Chapman, John H., ed. *The Register Book of Marriages Belonging to the Parish of St. George, Hanover Square, in the County of Middlesex.* London, 1886.

Cholmondeley, R. H. *The Heber Letters, 1783–1832.* London, 1950.

Clarendon, Edward, Earl of. *The Lord Clarendon's History of the Grand Rebellion Compleated.* 2nd ed. London, 1717.

Codman, Martha C., ed. and arr. *The Journal of Mrs. John Amory, 1775–1777.* Boston, 1923.

Compton, William Bingham. *History of the Comptons of Compton Wynyates.* London, 1930.

A Concise Review of the Concise Vindication of the Conduct of the Five Suspended Members of the Council of the Royal Academy. London, 1804.

[Copley, John Singleton, Jr.]. *A Concise Vindication of the Conduct of the Five Suspended Members of the Council of the Royal Academy.* 2nd ed. contains "A Postscript" by John Soane. London, 1804.

Copley-Pelham Letters. See under Jones.

Cunningham, Allan. *The Cabinet Gallery of Pictures by the First Masters.* 2 vols. London, 1834.

———— *The Lives of the Most Eminent British Painters and Sculptors.* Vol. IV. New York, 1834.

Dibdin, Thomas Frognall. *Reminiscences of a Literary Life.* 2 vols. London, 1836.

Drinkwater, John. *A History of the Late Siege of Gibraltar.* 4th ed. (grangerized version in the National Maritime Museum). London, 1790.

Dunlap, William. *A History of the Rise and Progress of the Arts of Design in the United States.* 2 vols. New York, 1834.

Durell, E. *The Death of Major Frs. Peirson.* Illustrated by P. J. Ouless. Isle of Jersey, 1881.

Einstein, Lewis. *Divided Loyalties.* London, 1933.

Evans, Grose. *Benjamin West and the Taste of His Times.* Carbondale, Illinois, 1959.

Fèret, Charles James. *Fulham Old and New: Being an Exhaustive History of the Ancient Parish of Fulham.* 3 vols. London, 1900.

Flexner, James Thomas. *John Singleton Copley.* Boston, 1948.

Foote, Henry Wilder. *Robert Feke.* Cambridge, Mass., 1930.

———— *John Smibert.* Cambridge, Mass., 1950.

Gardner, Albert TenEyck, and Stuart P. Feld. *American Paintings: A Catalogue of the Collection of the Metropolitan Museum of Art,* vol. I. New York, 1965.

Garlick, Kenneth. *Sir Thomas Lawrence.* London, 1954.

BIBLIOGRAPHY

Graves, Algernon. *Art Sales.* 3 vols. London, 1918.

———— *The British Institution, 1806–1867.* London, 1908.

———— *A Century of Loan Exhibitions, 1813–1912.* 5 vols. London, 1913.

———— *The Royal Academy of Arts.* 8 vols. London, 1905–1906.

———— *The Society of Artists of Great Britain, 1760–1791: The Free Society of Artists, 1761–1783.* London, 1907.

———— and W. V. Cronin. *A History of the Works of Sir Joshua Reynolds.* London, 1899–1901.

Greenwood, Isaac John. *The Greenwood Family of Norwich, England, in America.* Edited by H. Minot Pitman and Mary M. Greenwood. Privately printed, 1934.

Hagen, Oskar. *The Birth of the American Tradition in Art.* New York, 1940.

Hayley, William. *The Life of George Romney.* London, 1809.

———— *Poems and Plays.* 6 vols. London, 1788.

Hilles, Frederick Whiley. *Letters of Sir Joshua Reynolds.* Cambridge, Eng., 1929.

———— and Philip B. Daghlian, eds. *Anecdotes of Painting in England (1760–1795) . . . Collected by Horace Walpole,* vol. V. New Haven, 1937.

Hipkiss, Edwin J. *Eighteenth Century American Arts: The M. and M. Karolik Collection.* Notes on drawings and prints by Henry P. Rossiter, comments on collection by Maxim Karolik. Boston, 1941.

Hodgson, J. E., and Fred A. Eaton. *The Royal Academy and Its Members.* London, 1905.

Jones, Guernsey, ed. *Letters and Papers of John Singleton Copley and Henry Pelham, 1739–1776.* Vol. LXXI, Massachusetts Historical Society Collections. Boston, 1914.

Marshall, John. *Royal Naval Biography: or Memoirs of the Services,* vol. IV, part 2. London, 1835.

Martin, Sir Theodore. *A Life of Lord Lyndhurst.* London, 1883.

Maxwell, Sir Herbert. *George Romney.* London and New York, 1902.

Mayo, Lawrence Shaw. *John Wentworth: Governor of New Hampshire, 1767–1775.* Cambridge, Mass., 1921.

Morgan, John Hill. *John Singleton Copley.* Walpole Society, 1939.

———— and Henry Wilder Foote. *An Extension of Lawrence Park's Descriptive List of the Work of Joseph Blackburn.* Worcester, Mass., 1937.

Morse, Edward L., ed. *Samuel F. B. Morse: His Letters and Journals.* 2 vols. Boston and New York, 1914.

Nicolle, Edmund Toulmin. *The Town of St. Helier.* Isle of Jersey, [1931].

O'Donoghue, Freeman. *Catalogue of Engraved British Portraits . . . in the British Museum.* 6 vols. London, 1908–25.

Oliver, Andrew, comp. *Faces of a Family.* Privately printed, 1960.

Oppé, A. P. *The Drawings of Paul and Thomas Sandby . . . at Windsor Castle.* London, 1947.

Park, Lawrence. *Joseph Badger and a Descriptive List of Some of His Works.* Boston, 1918.

———— *Joseph Blackburn: A Colonial Portrait Painter with a Descriptive List of His Work.* Worcester, Mass., 1923. Reprinted from *Proceedings of the American Antiquarian Society,* Oct. 1922.

Parker, Barbara Neville, and Anne Bolling Wheeler. *John Singleton Copley: American Portraits in Oil, Pastel, and Miniature, with Biographical Sketches.* Boston, 1938.

Parliamentary History of England, vol. XIX., London, 1814.

Pasquin, Anthony. *Memoirs of the Royal Academicians.* London, 1796.

Pellew, George, Dean of Norwich. *The Life and Correspondence of the Right Honble Henry Addington, First Viscount Sidmouth.* 3 vols. London, 1847.

Perkins, Augustus Thorndike. *A Sketch of the Life and a List of the Works of John Singleton Copley.* Boston, 1873.

———— *Supplementary List of Paintings by John Singleton Copley.* Boston, [1875].

Plumb, J. H. *Men and Places.* London, 1963.

Redford, George. *Art Sales.* 2 vols. London, 1888.

Sabine, Lorenzo. *Loyalists of the American Revolution.* Boston, 1864.

Sachse, William L. *The Colonial American in Britain.* Madison, Wisc., 1956.

Scherer, Margaret R. *Marvels of Ancient Rome.* New York and London, 1955.

[Simond, Louis]. *Journal of a Tour and Residence in Great Britain During the Years 1810 and 1811, by a French Traveller.* 2 vols. Edinburgh, 1815.

Sizer, Theodore, ed. *The Autobiography of Colonel John Trumbull.* New Haven, 1953.

Slatkin, Charles E., and Regina Shoolman. *Treasury of American Drawings.* New York, 1947.

Smart, Alastair. *The Life and Art of Allan Ramsay.* London, 1952.

Strickland, Walter G. *A Dictionary of Irish Artists.* 2 vols. Dublin and London, 1913.

Taylor, Basil. *Painting in England 1700–1850: Collection of Mr. and Mrs. Paul Mellon.* 2 vols. Virginia Museum of Fine Arts, Richmond, 1963.

Thane, J[ohn]. *British Autography.* 3 vols. London, [1793].

Vertue, George. *Medals, Coins, Great-Seals, Impressions, from the Elaborate Works of Thomas Simon . . .* London, 1753.

[Ward, Edward]. *The History of the Grand Rebellion.* 3 vols. London, 1713.

Ward, George Atkinson. *Journal and Letters of the Late Samuel Curwen.* New York and Boston, 1842.

Waterhouse, Ellis. *Painting in Britain, 1530–1790.* Baltimore, 1953.

Watson, Winslow C., ed. *Men and Times of the Revolution: or Memoirs of Elkanah Watson, 1777–1842.* New York, 1856.

Weis, Frederick L. *Checklist of the Portraits in the Library of the American Antiquarian Society.* Worcester, Mass., 1947. Reprinted from *Proceedings of the American Antiquarian Society,* April 1946.

Whitley, William T. *Art in England, 1800–1820.* New York and Cambridge, Eng., 1928.

———— *Artists and Their Friends in England, 1700–1799.* 2 vols. London, 1928.

———— *Gilbert Stuart.* Cambridge, Mass., 1932.

———— *Thomas Gainsborough.* London, 1915.

Williams, Clare, trans. *Sophie in London 1786, Being the Diary of Sophie v. la Roche.* London, 1933.

Williamson, George C. *Life and Works of Ozias Humphry, R.A.* London and New York, 1918.

ARTICLES

Allison, Anne. "Peter Pelham, Engraver in Mezzotinto," *Antiques,* LII (Dec. 1947), 441–43.

"Anecdotes of Artists of the Last Fifty Years," *Library of the Fine Arts,* IV (July 1832).

Bolton, Arthur T. "Hagley Park, Worcestershire, the Seat of Viscount Cobham," *Country Life,* XXXVIII (Oct. 16, 1915), 520–28.

Bolton, Theodore, and Harry Lorin Binsse. "John Singleton Copley," *Antiquarian,* XV (Dec. 1930), 76–83, 116, 118.

"The British School of Engraving," *The British Magazine,* II (July–Dec. 1800), 334–35.

Burroughs, Alan. "Young Copley," *Art in America,* XXXI (Oct. 1943), 161–71.

Comstock, Helen. "Drawings by John Singleton Copley," *Panorama,* Harry Shaw Newman Gallery, II (May 1947), 97–108.

———— "Drawings by J. S. Copley in the Karolik Collection," *The Connoisseur,* CIX (June 1942), 150–53.

"Copley's Picture," *The Living Age,* LXIII (Oct. 1, 1859), 119–21, from *Boston Daily Advertiser,* Aug. 12, 1859.

"The Copleys and Pelhams of New England," *Heraldic Journal,* IV (Boston, 1868), 175–82.

Dinsmoor, William B. "Early American Studies of Mediterranean Archaeology," *Proceedings of the American Philosophical Society,* LXXXVII (1943-44), 70–104.

Dresser, Louisa. "Copley's Receipt for Payment for the Portraits of Mr. and Mrs. Samuel Phillips

Savage, with a Note on Blackburn's Portrait of Hannah Babcock," *Worcester Art Museum Annual,* IX (1961), 32–38.

Foote, Henry Wilder. "When Was John Singleton Copley Born?" *New England Quarterly,* X (March 1937), 111–20.

Gardner, Albert TenEyck. "A Copley Primitive," *Metropolitan Museum of Art Bulletin,* XX (April 1962), 257–63.

Green, M. C. "The Invasion at La Rocque, 1781," *Bulletin of the Société Jersiaise* [Isle of Jersey], XVII (1957), 65–73.

Greifenhagen, Adolph. "Griechische Vasen auf Bildnessen der Zeit Winckelmanns und des Klassizismus," *Nachrichten von den Gesellschaften der Wissenschaften zu Göttingen,* n.s. III, no. 7 (1939), 217ff.

———— "Antiken als Beiwerk auf Porträts des 18. Jahrhunderts," *Pantheon,* XXVI (Dec. 1940), 292–93.

Grundy, C. Reginald. "British Military and Naval Prints," *The Connoisseur,* XL (Oct. 1914), 70, 72–73.

Howgego, James L. "Copley and the Corporation of London," *The Guildhall Miscellany,* IX (July 1958), 34–43.

[Jones, Thomas.] "Memoirs of Thomas Jones," *Walpole Society,* XXXII: 1946–1948 (1951).

Locquin, Jean. "Le Retour à l'antique dans l'école anglaise et dans l'école française avant David," *La Renaissance de l'art français et des industries de luxe,* V (1922), 473–81.

Mitchell, Charles. "Benjamin West's 'Death of General Wolfe' and the Popular History Piece," *Journal of the Warburg and Courtauld Institutes,* VII, no. 1–2 (1944), 20–33.

Mount, Charles Merrill. "A Hidden Treasure in Britain, Part II: John Singleton Copley," *Art Quarterly,* XXIV (Spring 1961), 33–51.

Murray, Edward Croft. "A Drawing of the Royal Academy by Henry Singleton," *British Museum Quarterly,* IX, no. 4 (1935), 106–08.

Newberry, John S., Jr. "Four Drawings by Copley," *Detroit Institute of Arts Bulletin,* XXVIII, no. 2 (1949), 32–35.

[Oxnard, Edward.] "Edward Oxnard's Journal," *New England Historical and Genealogical Register,* XXVI (1872), 3–10, 115–21, 254–59.

Parker, Barbara N. "Problems of Attribution in Early Portraits by Copley," *Bulletin of the Museum of Fine Arts* [Boston], XL (June 1942), 54–57.

Perkins, Augustus Thorndike. "Sketch of Some of the Losses to the Departments of Literature and the Fine Arts, Occasioned by the Great Fire in Boston of 1872," *New England Historical and Genealogical Register,* XXVII (1873), 370–71.

Prown, Jules David. "An 'Anatomy Book' by John Singleton Copley," *Art Quarterly,* XXVI (Spring 1963), 31–46.

———— "Copley's 'Victory of Duncan,'" *Art in America,* I (1962), 82–85.

[Quincy, Samuel.] "Diary of Samuel Quincy," *Massachusetts Historical Society Proceedings,* XIX (1881–82), 214–23.

Rogers, Alexander P. "Some Notes on Richard Clarke, of Boston, and the Copley Portraits of His Family," *Old-Time New England,* XI (April 1921), 160–62.

Rutledge, Anna Wells. "American Loyalists — A Drawing for a Noted Copley Group [*The Pepperrell Family*]," *Art Quarterly,* XX (Summer 1957), 195–203.

Salerno, Luigi. "Seventeenth-Century English Literature on Painting," *Journal of the Warburg and Courtauld Institutes,* XIV, no. 3–4 (1951), 234–58.

Sellers, Charles Coleman. "Mezzotint Prototypes of Colonial Portraiture: A Survey Based on the Research of Waldron Phoenix Belknap, Jr.," *Art Quarterly,* XX (Winter 1957), 407–68.

Sherman, Frederic Fairchild. "Recently Recovered Miniatures by John Singleton Copley," *Art in America,* XXIII (Dec. 1934), 34–38.

471

Slade, Daniel Denison. "The Bromfield Family," *New England Historical and Genealogical Register*, XXVI (1872), 37–43, 141–43.

Slade, Denison Rogers. "Henry Pelham, the Half-Brother of John Singleton Copley," *Publications of the Colonial Society of Massachusetts*, V, Transactions, Feb. 1898 (Boston, 1902), 193–211.

Soria, Regina. "Pittori americani nella Roma neoclassica," *Studi romani*, VI (July–Aug. 1958), 3–11.

Stokes, Hugh. "George Dance's 'Heads,'" *Print Collectors' Quarterly*, XVI (Jan. 1929), 8–32.

Sweet, Frederick A. "Mezzotint Sources of American Colonial Portraits," *Art Quarterly*, XIV (Summer 1951), 148–57.

Wind, Edgar. "The Revolution of History Painting," *Journal of the Warburg Institute*, II (1938–39), 116–27.

———— "Penny, West, and the 'Death of Wolfe,'" *Journal of the Warburg and Courtauld Institutes*, X, no. 3–4 (1947), 159–62.

Illustrations

(Figures 335-678)

335. Unknown Subject, studies from the antique [?] (verso of 471)   *1774–75*

336. Unknown Subject, sometimes called Roman Conquest   *1774–75*

337. The Ascension   *1775*

338. Study for The Ascension (verso of 361)   *1774–75*

339. Study for The Ascension   *1774–75*

340. Priam Beseeching Achilles for the Body of Hector, engraved by A. Fogg after Copley, published June 4, 1799

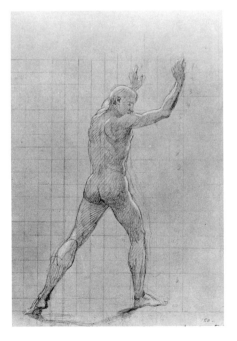

341. Study for Priam Beseeching
Achilles for the Body of Hector
1775 or 1797–99

342. Mr. and Mrs. Ralph Izard   *1775*

LEICESTER SQUARE

This Perspective VIEW of the South West Prospect ——— is most Humbly Inscrib'd to his Royal Highness the PRINCE of WALES.

by his most Obedient humble Servant to command ——— John Brindley.

343. The South Prospect of Leicester Square, engraved by Parr after Maurer   *1753*

344. The Copley Family   *1776–77*

345. Sketch for The Copley Family   *1776*

346. Sketch for The Copley Family   *1776*

347. The Nativity, mezzotint by Henry Kingsbury, published June 1, 1779

348. Study for The Nativity   *1776*

349. Study for The Nativity   *1776*

350. John Singleton Copley   *1776–80*

351. John Singleton Copley [?]   *1776–78*

352. Sir Francis Bernard, Bt.   *1776–79*

353. Squire Hyde of Hyde   *1777*

354. Robert Hyde, Squire of Hyde   *1778*

355. Mrs. Robert Hyde   *1778*

356. Sir William Pepperrell and His Family   *1778*

357. Study for Sir William Pepperrell and His Family   1777–78

358. Study for Sir William Pepperrell and His Family   1777–78

359. Study for Sir William Pepperrell and His Family
1777

360. Study for Sir William Pepperrell
and His Family *1777–78*

361. Study for Sir William Pepperrell
and His Family (recto of 338)
1777–78

362. Unidentified Subject, a Gentleman
1776–80

363. Mrs. Seymour Fort [?]   *c. 1778*

364. Mrs. Isaac Royall   *1769–80*

365. Benjamin West: Agrippina Landing at Brundisium with the Ashes of
Germanicus   *1768*

366. Benjamin West: The Death of General Wolfe   *1771*

367. Benjamin West: Penn's Treaty with the Indians
1772

369. "An Accurate Draught of the Old Straits of Bahama, made from Remarks taken in the year 1762," engraved by R. Bishop, published May 12, 1794

370. "A View of the Entrance to the Harbour of Havana, taken within the Wrecks," engraved by Peter Canot, drawn by Elias Durnford, published by Thomas Jefferys, August 1764

368. "Plano de la Ciudad y Puerto de la Havana," Don Tomas Lopez, Madrid, 1785

371. Watson and the Shark   1778

372. Watson and the Shark 1778

373. Watson and the Shark   *1782*

374. Study for Watson and the Shark, head of Brook Watson [?] (verso of 411) *1777–78*

376. Study for Watson and the Shark, figure on left *1777–78*

375. Study for Watson and the Shark, harpooner and oarsman *1777–78*

377. Study for Watson and the Shark, oarsmen   *1777–78*

378. Study for Watson and the Shark, rescue group   *1777–78*

379. The Gladiator in the Villa Borghese (as considered anatomically in Bernardino Genga, *Anatomia per uso* · · · [Rome, 1691], table 30), placed on side like figure of Watson

380. The Lion Hunt, engraved by Schelte à Bolswert, after Rubens

381. Unidentified Subject, Head of a Negro [study for Watson and the Shark?]   *1777–83*

382. Benjamin West   *1776–80*

383. Gilbert DeBlois   *1777–80*

384. Mrs. Clark Gayton   *1779*

385. Clark Gayton, Admiral of the Blue   *1779*

386. Venus and Cupid   *c. 1779*

387. Mrs. John Hay   *1780*

388. George Boone Roupell   *1780*

389. After Copley, Major Hugh Montgomerie, later
Twelfth Earl of Eglinton

390. Study for Major Hugh Montgomerie, later
Twelfth Earl of Eglinton   *1779–80*

390a. Study for Hugh Montgomerie, later Twelfth Earl of Eglinton

391. Samuel Relating to Eli the Judgements of God upon Eli's House   *1780*

392. The Death of the Earl of Chatham   *1779–81*

393. Key to The Death of the Earl of Chatham, 1794

1 Lord Cardiff
2 Late Earl of Ferrers, then Hon. Mr. Shirley
3 Late Lord Robert Bertie
4 Earl Faucenberg [sic]
5 Late Duke of Montague
6 Lord Viscount Mount Edgecumbe
7 Lord Viscount Valletort, then Hon. Mr. Edgecumbe
8 Late Earl Waldegrave
9 Lord Loughborough, then Solicitor-General
10 Lord Chancellor Thurlow, then Attorney-General
11 Late Lord George Germain
12 Earl of Guildford, then Lord North
13 Earl of Westmorland
14 Lord Onslow
15 Lord Westcote
16 Earl of Eglentoune
17 Dr. Hincheliffe, Bishop of Peter-borough
18 Dr. Shipley, Bishop of St. Asaph
19 Dr. Markham, Archbishop of York
20 Lord Chief Baron-Skinner
21 Earl of Mansfield
22 Earl Bathurst, then Lord Chancellor
23 Marquis of Stafford, then Earl Gower
24 Earl of Sandwich
25 Lord Amhurst
26 Earl of Dartmouth
27 Late Lord Viscount Dudley and Ward
28 Lord Scarsdale
29 Earl of Jersey
30 Earl of Harcourt
31 Earl Cholmondeley
32 Lord Camden
33 Richard Brocklerley, M.D. [sic]
34 Duke of Gordon
35 Late Duke of Manchester
36 Late Lord Viscount Courtenay
37 Earl of Coventry
38 Earl of Effingham
39 Right Hon. William Pitt
40 Earl of Stanhope, then Lord Viscount Mahon
41 Late Hon. Mr. James Pitt
42 Present Earl of Chatham
43 Duke of Devonshire
44 Duke of Portland
45 His late Royal Highness, the Duke of Cumberland
46 The late Earl of Chatham
47 Marquis of Lansdowne, then Earl of Shelbourne
48 Late Earl Temple
49 Earl of Radnor
50 Earl of Leinster, then Lord de Ferrers
51 Duke of Richmond
52 Late Marquis of Rockingham
53 Late Earl Spencer
54 Earl Fitzwilliam
55 Earl of Bessborough

394. The Death of the Earl of Chatham (detail)

395. The Death of the Earl of Chatham (detail)

396. The Death of the Earl of Chatham (detail)

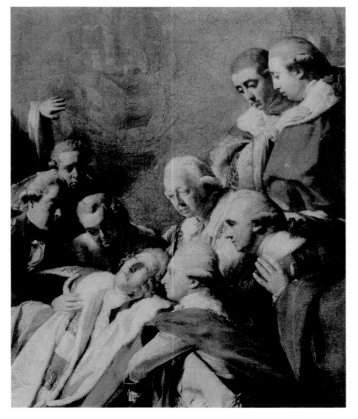

397. The Death of the Earl of Chatham (detail)

398. The Death of the Earl of Chatham (detail)

399. Study for The Death of the Earl of Chatham   *1779*

400. Study for The Death of the Earl of Chatham   1779

401. Study for The Death of the Earl of Chatham   1779

402.   Sketch for The Death of the Earl of Chatham   *1779*

403.   Sketch for The Death of the Earl of Chatham   *1779*

404. Sketch for The Death of the Earl of Chatham   *1779*

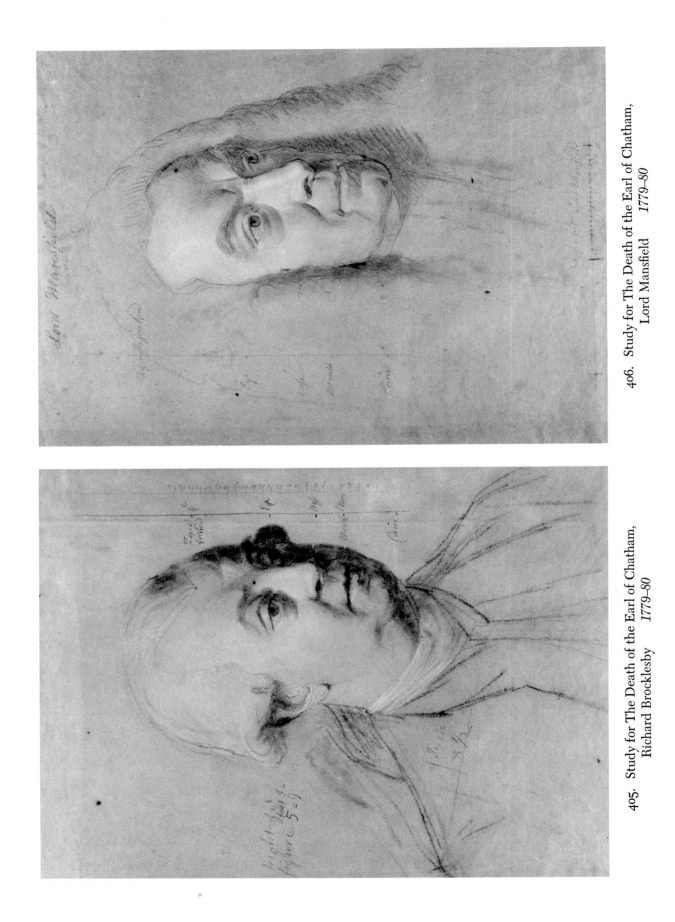

405. Study for The Death of the Earl of Chatham,
Richard Brocklesby   1779–80

406. Study for The Death of the Earl of Chatham,
Lord Mansfield   1779–80

409. Study for The Death of the Earl of Chatham, the Duke of Richmond   1779

408. Study for The Death of the Earl of Chatham, the Duke of Richmond   1779

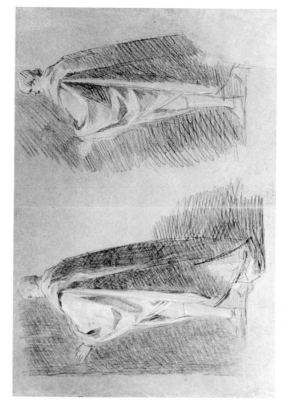

411. Study for The Death of the Earl of Chatham, the Duke of Richmond (recto of 374)   1779

407. Study for The Death of the Earl of Chatham, the Duke of Richmond (verso of 439)   1779

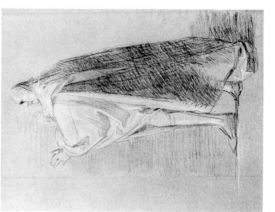

410. Study for The Death of the Earl of Chatham, the Duke of Richmond   1779

412. Study for The Death of the Earl of
Chatham, the Bishop of Peterborough
1779–80

413. Study for The Death of the Earl of
Chatham, Henry, Earl of Bathurst
1779

414. Study for The Death of the
Earl of Chatham, the Earl of
Stanhope   *1779–80*

415. Study for The Death of the Earl of
Chatham [?] (recto of 459)
c. 1779–80

416. Henry Laurens   *1782*

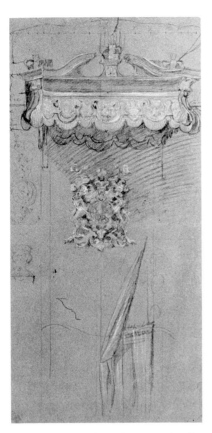

417. Study for The Death of
the Earl of Chatham, the
canopy   *1779–80*

418. Study for Elkanah Watson (verso of 422)
1782

419. Elkanah Watson   *1782*

420. The Tribute Money   *1782*

455. Study for The Death of Major Peirson, dying French officer
group and other figures   1782–83

453. Study for The Death of Major Peirson, central group
and fleeing woman and child   1782–83

454. Study for The Death of Major Peirson, officer and
wounded drummer   1782–83

451. Study for The Death of Major Peirson, central group
1782–83

452. Study for The Death of Major Peirson (verso of 448)
1782–83

450. Sketch for The Death of Major Peirson   1782–83

448. Study for The Death of Major Peirson, central group
(recto of 452)   1782–83

449. Study for The Death of Major Peirson (recto of 461)
1782–83

447. Study for The Death of Major Peirson, central group
1782–83

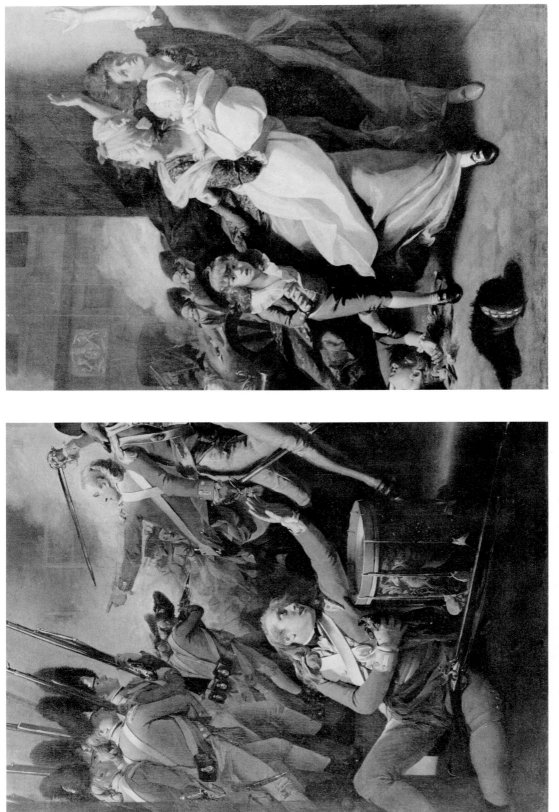

445. The Death of Major Peirson (detail)

446. The Death of Major Peirson (detail)

444. The Death of Major Peirson (detail)

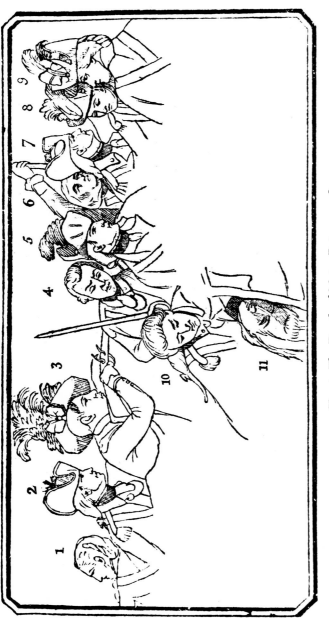

443. Key to The Death of Major Peirson, 1784

1. Captain Clephane
2. Captain Macneil
3. Major Peirson's black
Servant

4. Captain Corbett
5. Lieutenant Drysdale
6. Ensign Rowan
7. Ensign Smith

8. Captain Hemery
9. Lieutenant Buchanan
10. Adjutant Harrison
11. Major Peirson

442. The Death of Major Peirson   1782–84

440. Abigail Adams, engraved by H. S. Sadd

439. Study for John Adams (recto of 407) 1783

441. Unidentified Subject, a Cleric [?] 1780–85

438. John Adams   *1783*

436. Charles Callis Western (later Baron Western of Rivenhall) and His
Brother (later Rev.) Shirley Western   *1783*

437. View of Hanover Square, engraved by R. Pollard and F. Jukes,
drawn by E. Dayes, published by the engravers,
December 1, 1787

432. Study for William Murray, First Earl of
Mansfield   *1782–83*

433. Study for William Murray, First Earl of
Mansfield   *1782–83*

434. Study for William Murray, First Earl of
Mansfield   *1782–83*

435. Study for William Murray, First Earl of
Mansfield   *1782–83*

430.   Study for William Murray, First Earl of Mansfield   *1782–83*

431.   Study for William Murray, First Earl of Mansfield   *1782–83*

429. William Murray, First Earl of Mansfield   *1783*

428. Mrs. Daniel Denison Rogers   *c. 1784*

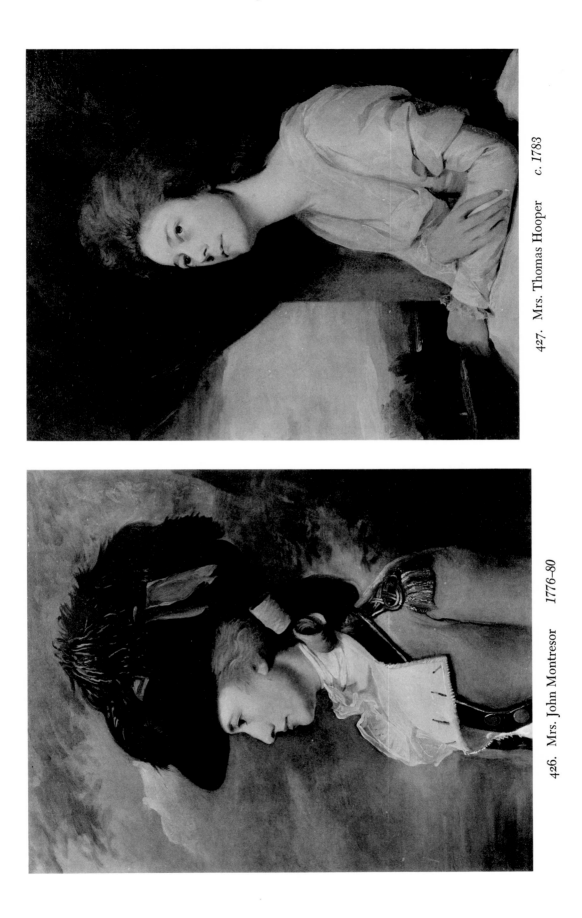

427. Mrs. Thomas Hooper   c. 1783

426. Mrs. John Montresor   1776–80

424. Richard Heber *1782*

425. Study for Richard Heber *1782*

423. Midshipman Augustus Brine   *1782–83*

TIBI DABO CLAVES REGNI CÆLORVM, ET QVODCVMQVE SOLVERIS SVPER TERRAM, ERIT SOLVTVM ET IN CÆLIS. Matth. 16

Celeberrimi excellentissimi in arte pictoria viri Ioannis Bernario, qui hanc tabulam in æternam patris sui q. Petri Bernarij pictoris clarissimi memoriam, admiranda Pet. Pauli Rubeni opera depictam ergo curauit. Ipsiusâ et benevolentia hoc Symbolum æri insculptum D.D. Petrus de Iode.

421. Christ Giving the Keys to St. Peter,
engraved by Pieter de Jode, the elder,
after Rubens

422. Study for The Tribute Money (recto of 418)   *1782*

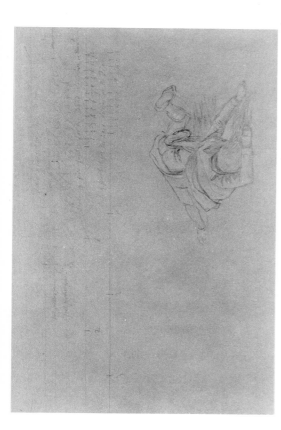

456. Study for The Death of Major Peirson, wounded soldier (verso of 462)   1782–83

457. Study for The Death of Major Peirson, dead figures (recto of 458)   1782–83

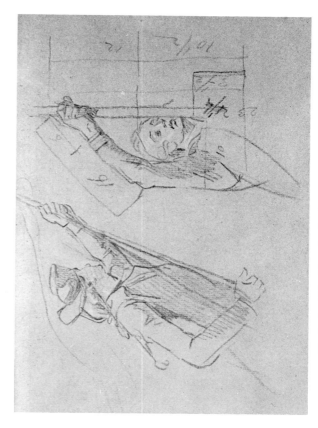

459. Study for The Death of Major Peirson, figure with flag (Ensign Rowan) (verso of 415)   1782–83

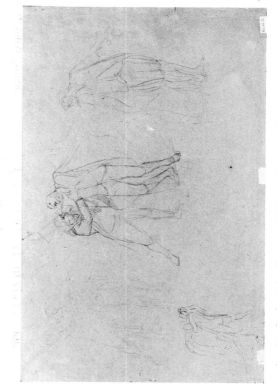

458. Study for The Death of Major Peirson, dying French officer group (verso of 457)   1782–83

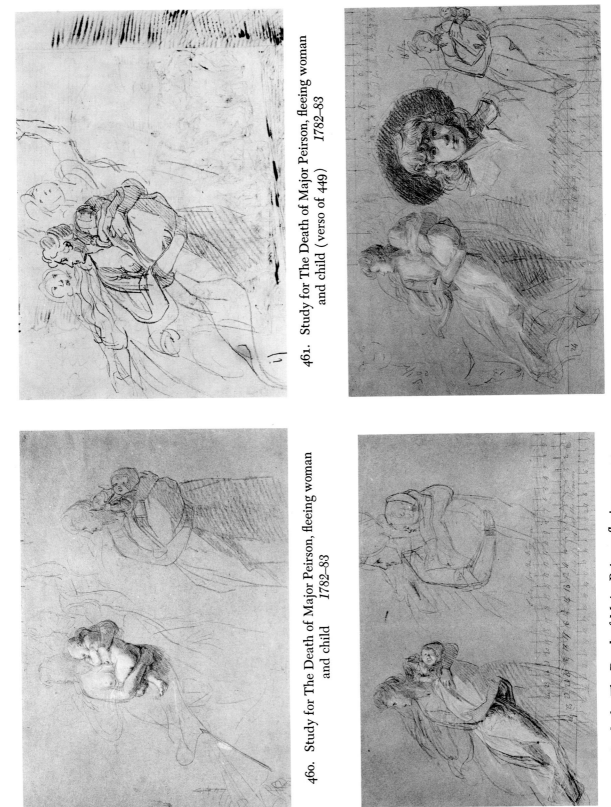

461. Study for The Death of Major Peirson, fleeing woman
and child (verso of 449)   1782–83

463. Study for The Death of Major Peirson, fleeing woman and
child and boy with hat (John Singleton Copley, Jr.)
1782–83

460. Study for The Death of Major Peirson, fleeing woman
and child   1782–83

462. Study for The Death of Major Peirson, fleeing woman
and child (recto of 456)   1782–83

464. "The Glorious Defeat of the French Invaders, on the Island of Jersey, Jany. 6, 1781 when the Valiant Major Francis Peirson was unfortunately Kill'd in the moment of Victory," etching published by Thos. Gram. Colley and E. Hedges, April 24, 1781

465. The Entombment, engraved by Pieter Soutman after a drawing by Rubens, after Caravaggio

466. The Massacre of the Innocents, engraved by Paulus Pontius,
after Rubens

467. Gilbert Stuart: John Singleton Copley *1783–84*

468. The Three Youngest Daughters of King George III
(Mary, Sophia, and Amelia)   *1785*

469. Study for The Three Youngest Daughters of
King George III   *1784–85*

470. Study for The Three Youngest
Daughters of King George III
1784–85

471. Study for The Three Youngest Daughters of
King George III (recto of 335)   *1784–85*

472. Study for The Three Youngest Daughters of
King George III   *1784–85*

474. Jonathan Jackson   c. 1785

473. Winslow Warren, Jr.   1785

476. Mrs. Charles Startin (Sarah Clarke)   c. 1783

475. Susanna Copley   1785

477. The Sitwell Family   *1786*

478. The Lyttelton Family   *1786–88*

479. Study for The Lyttleton Family   *1785–88*

480. Study for The Lyttelton Family   *1785–88*

481. Study for The Lyttelton Family [?]   *1785–88*

482. Study for The Lyttelton
Family [?]   *1785–88*

483. Unidentified Subject, Seated Boy and Girl in a Landscape *1783–88*

484. Thomas Lane and His Sister Harriot   *c. 1783–88*

485. Henry White *1782–86*

486. John Burgwyn *1788*

487. John Penn *c. 1782*

488. William Pitt, M.P., Son of the First Earl of Chatham, engraved by F. Bartolozzi from a drawing at Chevening, published by W. Dickinson, 1789

489. The Siege of Gibraltar   1783–91

SIR ROGER CURTIS,
Commanding Officer a-float

Captain BRADSHAW SMITH,
of the Navy.

ADMIRAL BARRINGTON.

EARL HOWE.

490.   Key to The Siege of Gibraltar, 1791

6 The Rt. Hon. Gen. Lord Heathfield, K. B. Governor
4 Lieut. Gen. Sir Robert Boyd, K. B. Lieut. Governor
5 Major General De la Motte, commanding the
   Hanoverian Brigade
7 Major General Sir William Green, Bart. Chief
   Engineer
9 Major General Picton
8 Col. Dachenhausen, Reden's Hanoverian Regiment
11 Col. Hugo, Sydow's, late Hardenberg's
10 Col. Schleppegrell, De la Motte's
21 Colonel Lewis, Commandant of Artillery

12 Col. Trigge, 12th Regiment
20 Lieut. Col. Vaughan, 39th Regt.
19 Col. Craig, 56th Regiment
16 Major Brown, 58th Regiment
17 Hon. Lieut. Col. Lindsay, late 2d Battalion, 73d
   Regiment
18 Lieut. Col. Hardy, Quarter Master General
22 Major Vallotton, Governor's first Aid-de-Camp
14 Lieut. Holloway, Aid-de-Camp to Chief Engineer
13 Major Perryn, 12th Regt.
15 Capt. Drinkwater, late 72d, Author of the History of the Siege of Gibraltar

491. George Carter: Sketch for The Siege of Gibraltar

492. Key to Carter's The Siege of Gibraltar

1 Col. Schrappenell
2 Col. Hugo.
3 Col. Hullet.
4 Maj.r Gen. de la Motte.
5 L.t Gen. S.r R. Boyd K.B. L.t Gov.r
6 Cap.t Wilson his Aid de Camp

7. Maj. Vallotton his de Camp
8 Gen.l Geo. Aug. Eliott K.B. Gov.r & Com.r in Chief in Gibraltar
9 Col. Cochrane.
10 Maj. Gen. Picton.
11 Maj. Gen. Green Chief Eng.r
12 L.t Holloway his Aid de Camp

13 Col. Trigge.
14 L.t Col. Phipps.
15 Col. J.c Craig.
16 Major Lloyd.
17 Major Grove.
18 Col. Gledstone.

19 L.t Col. Mackintosh.
20 Col. Dachenhausen.
21 Major Marton.
22 Major Cypre.
23 Lieut. Col. Lewis.
24 Col. Mackenzie.

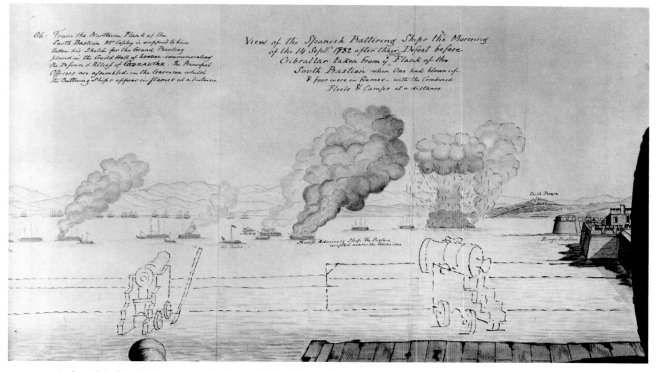

493. Colonel John Drinkwater: "View of the Spanish Battering Ships the Morning of the 14 Sept. 1782 after their Defeat before Gibraltar taken from ye North Flank of the South Bastion when one had blown up and four were in flames — with the Combined Fleets & Camps at a distance," watercolor

494. "General Eliott and his aide-de-camp, Lieutenant G. F. Koehler, in the King's Bastion during the action at Gibraltar," engraved after a drawing by Lieutenant G. F. Koehler

495. General George Augustus Eliott (later Lord Heathfield), Study for The Siege of Gibraltar   *1787*

496. Major General August de la Motte, sketch
for The Siege of Gibraltar   *1787*

497. Colonel Gustav Friedrich von Dachenhausen,
sketch for The Siege of Gibraltar   *1787*

498. Colonel Ernst August von Hugo and Lieut. Colonel
von Schlepegrell, sketch for The Siege of Gibraltar *1787*

499. Sketch for The Siege of Gibraltar   *1788*

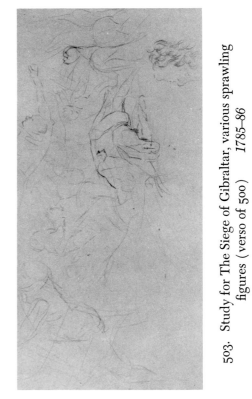

501. Study for The Siege of Gibraltar, figures in wrecked longboat *1785–86*

500. Study for The Siege of Gibraltar, the wrecked longboat (recto of 503) *1785–86*

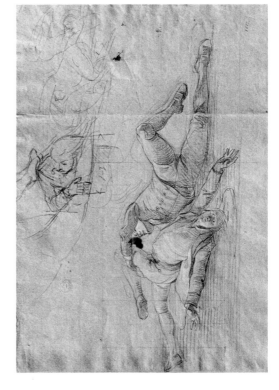

502. Study for The Siege of Gibraltar, sprawling figures in wrecked longboat *1785–86*

503. Study for The Siege of Gibraltar, various sprawling figures (verso of 500) *1785–86*

504. Study for The Siege of Gibraltar, figures on bowsprit of wrecked longboat   1785–86

506. Study for The Siege of Gibraltar, figures pulling on rope   1785–86

505. Study for The Siege of Gibraltar, figures pulling on rope   1785–86

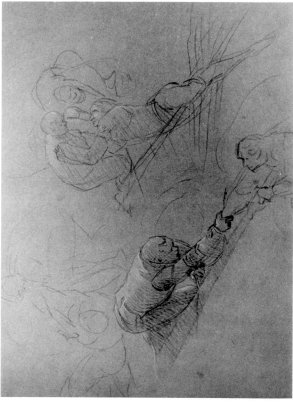

507. Study for The Siege of Gibraltar, English sailors in gunboat
pulling figures from water   1785–86

508. Study for The Siege of Gibraltar, kneeling figure and figure astride
cannon pulling down Spanish colors   1785–86

509. Study for The Siege of Gibraltar, figure
astride cannon pulling down Spanish
colors   1785–86

511. Study for The Siege of Gibraltar, figure on cannon in longboat
1785–86

510. Study for The Siege of Gibraltar, figure astride
cannon pulling down Spanish colors   *1785–86*

513. Study for *The Siege of Gibraltar*, three figures pulling on
Spanish colors   *1785–86*

514. Study for *The Siege of Gibraltar*, figure astride spar   *1785–86*

512. Study for *The Siege of Gibraltar*, figure on
cannon in longboat   *1785–86*

516. Study for The Siege of Gibraltar, three men
aloft on a spar   1785–86

515. Study for The Siege of Gibraltar, figure astride spar   1785–86

517. Study for The Siege of Gibraltar, figures clinging to wreckage
1785–86

519. Study for The Siege of Gibraltar, figures astride
spar   *1785–86*

518. Study for The Siege of Gibraltar, bowsprit groups (detail, verso of 527)
1785–86

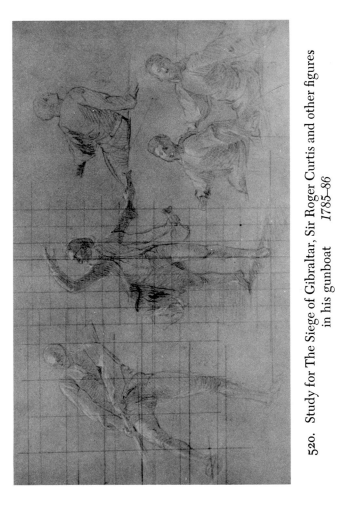

520. Study for The Siege of Gibraltar, Sir Roger Curtis and other figures
in his gunboat   *1785–86*

522. Study for The Siege of Gibraltar, figure astride cannon, sprawling figure, and cheering group   1785–86

524. Study for The Siege of Gibraltar, boat and wreckage groups (detail, verso of 527)   1785–86

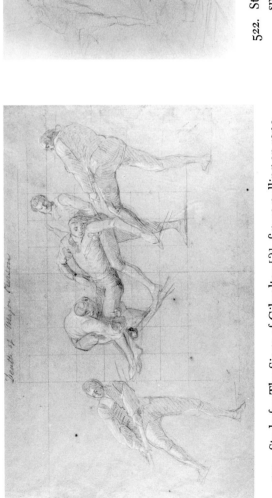

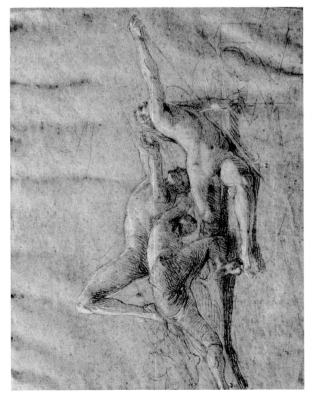

521. Study for The Siege of Gibraltar [?], figure pulling on rope and death group   1785–86

523. Study for The Siege of Gibraltar, sprawling group   1785–86

526. Study for The Siege of Gibraltar, figures on
sinking hulk   1785–86

525. Study for The Siege of Gibraltar, sprawling group   1785–86

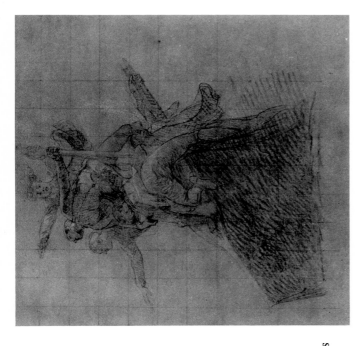

527. Study for The Siege of Gibraltar, figures on bowsprit and sinking hulk (recto of 518 and 524) *1785–86*

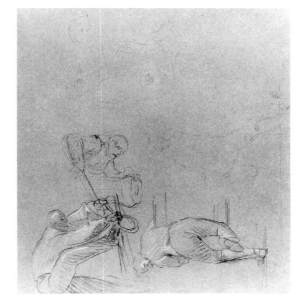

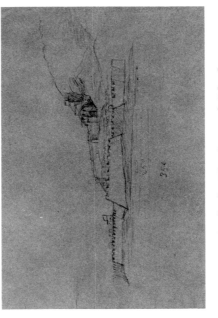

528. Study for The Siege of Gibraltar, figures on sinking hulk *1785–86*

529. Study for The Siege of Gibraltar, fortifications *1783–86*

530. Study for The Siege of Gibraltar, several figures *1785–86*

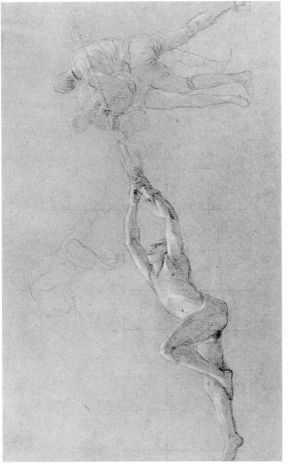

532. Study for The Siege of Gibraltar, rescued figure and two figures
pulling on oar   *1785–86*

531. Study for The Siege of Gibraltar, reaching figure
with leg raised   *1785–86*

533. Study for The Siege of Gibraltar,
officer group   *1786–87*

535. Study for The Siege of Gibraltar, figure for cannon group
1786–87

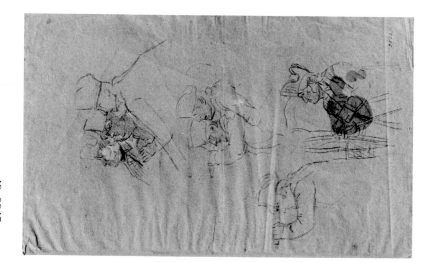

537. Study for
The Siege of Gibraltar,
officer group
1786–87

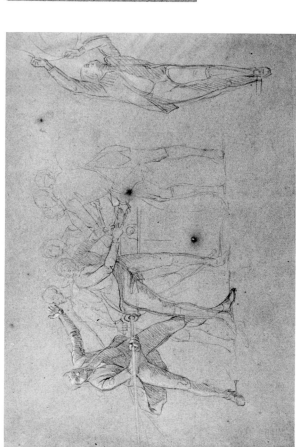

534. Study for The Siege of Gibraltar, figures loading cannon   *1786–87*

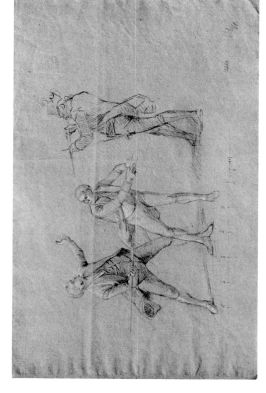

536. Study for The Siege of Gibraltar, cannon group and officer
1786–87

540. Study for The Siege of Gibraltar, officer group
1786–87

539. Study for The Siege of Gibraltar, officer group (verso of 573)
1788–89

538. Study for The Siege of Gibraltar, officer group (verso of 547)
1786–87

541. Study for The Siege of Gibraltar, officer group   *1786–89*

542. Study for The Siege of Gibraltar, officer group   *1786–87*

543. Study for The Siege of Gibraltar, officer group   *1786–87*

544. Study for The Siege of Gibraltar, officer group   *1786–87*

546. Study for The Siege of Gibraltar, officer group   1786–87

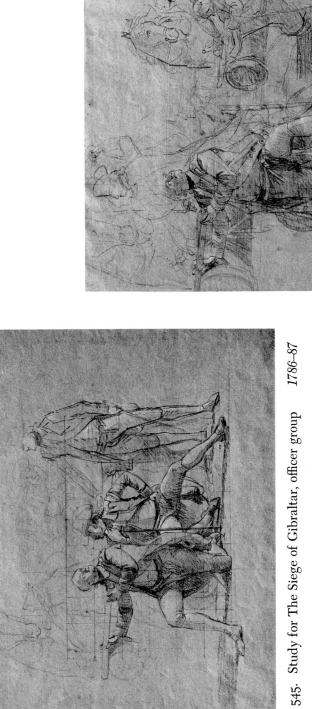

545. Study for The Siege of Gibraltar, officer group   1786–87

547. Study for The Siege of Gibraltar, officer group
(recto of 538)   1786–87

548. Study for The Siege of Gibraltar,
equestrian figure of General Eliott
1786–87

549. Study for The Siege of Gibraltar,
General Eliott *1786–87*

550. Study for The Siege of Gibraltar,
General Eliott *1786–87*

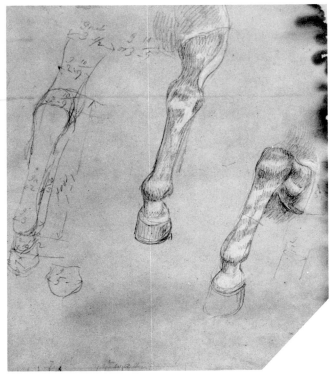

551. Study for The Siege of Gibraltar, General
Eliott's horse *1786–87*

552. Study for the Siege of Gibraltar, General Eliott's horse   *1786–87*

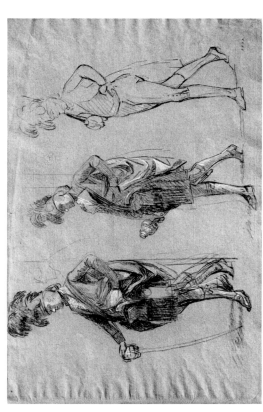

553. Study for The Siege of Gibraltar, Scottish officer and
figures pulling on rope   1786–87

554. Study for The Siege of Gibraltar, Scottish officer   1786–87

555. Study for The Siege of Gibraltar [?], cloaked figure
(recto of 556)   1786–87?

556. Study for The Siege of Gibraltar [?], cloaked figure
(verso of 555)   1786–87?

558. Study for The Siege of Gibraltar, bowsprit and falling figures in longboat, and drapery (verso of 561) 1788–89

560. Study for The Siege of Gibraltar, figures on bowsprit of longboat 1788–89

557. Study for The Siege of Gibraltar, figures clinging to mast of sinking longboat 1788–89

559. Study for The Siege of Gibraltar, figures on bowsprit of longboat 1788–89

561. Study for The Siege of Gibraltar, figures on bow-sprit of longboat (recto of 558) *1788–89*

562. Study for The Siege of Gibraltar, sprawling figures in longboat *1788–89*

563. Study for The Siege of Gibraltar, figure clinging to bowsprit of Spanish longboat *1788–89*

565. Study for The Siege of Gibraltar, various figures   1788–89

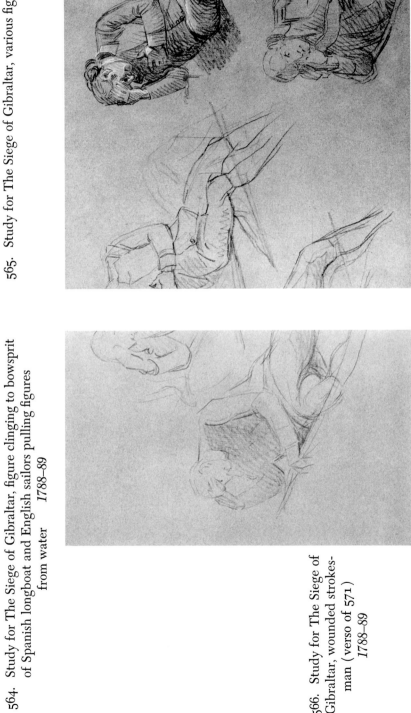

567. Study for
The Siege of Gibraltar,
wounded strokesman
(verso of 570)
1788–89

564. Study for The Siege of Gibraltar, figure clinging to bowsprit
of Spanish longboat and English sailors pulling figures
from water   1788–89

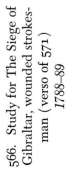

566. Study for The Siege of
Gibraltar, wounded strokesman (verso of 571)
1788–89

568. Study for The Siege of Gibraltar, wounded strokesman
and oarsman   1788–89

569. Study for The Siege of Gibraltar, helmsman and rescuing figure
1788–89

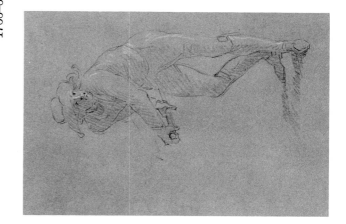

571. Study for The Siege of
Gibraltar, helmsman
(recto of 566)
1788–89

570. Study for The Siege
of Gibraltar, helmsman
(recto of 567)
1788–89

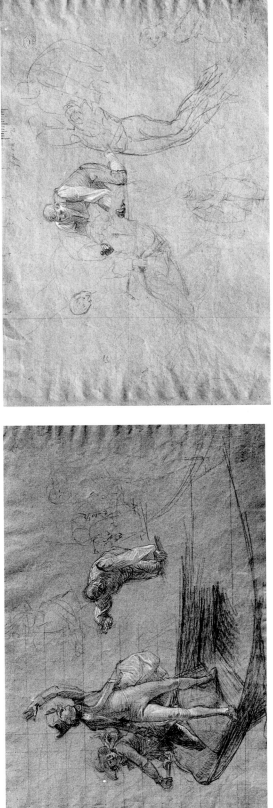

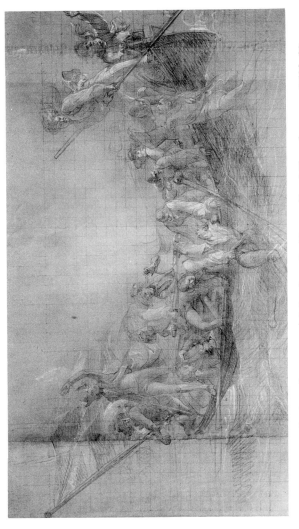

572. Study for The Siege of Gibraltar, Sir Roger Curtis in his longboat, the helmsman, the rescuing figure   1788–89

573. Study for The Siege of Gibraltar, sailors in Sir Roger Curtis' longboat pulling figures from water (recto of 539)   1788–89

574. Study for The Siege of Gibraltar, Sir Roger Curtis' longboat   1788–89

575. Study for The Siege of Gibraltar,
figure scaling floating battery
1788–89

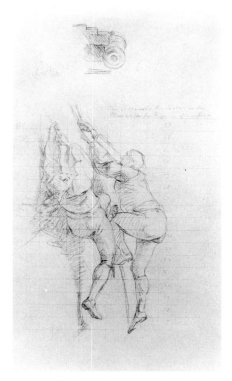

576. Study for The Siege of Gibraltar,
figures scaling floating battery
1788–89

577. Study for The Siege of Gibraltar,
figures scaling floating battery
1788–89

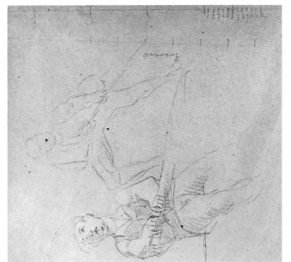

579. Study for The Siege of Gibraltar,
seated oarsman and standing rope
puller (recto of 580)   1788–89

581. Study for The Siege of Gibraltar, figure
in bow of Captain Bradford Smith's
gunboat pulling on rope
1788–89

578. Study for The Siege of Gibraltar, figures in bow of
Captain Bradford Smith's gunboat   1788–89

580. Study for The Siege of Gibraltar,
rope puller (verso of 579)
1788–89

583. Study for The Siege of Gibraltar, Captain Bradford Smith's gunboat and bow of Sir Roger Curtis' longboat   *1788–89*

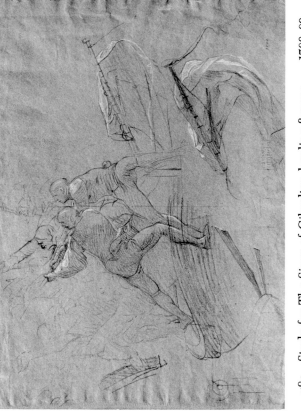

582. Study for The Siege of Gibraltar, hauling figures   *1788–89*

584.   Facsimile of ticket of admission to the 1791 exhibition of
The Siege of Gibraltar, engraved by F. Bartolozzi.

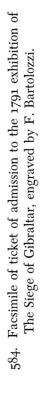

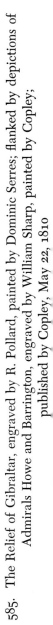

585.   The Relief of Gibraltar, engraved by R. Pollard, painted by Dominic Serres; flanked by depictions of
Admirals Howe and Barrington, engraved by William Sharp, painted by Copley;
published by Copley, May 22, 1810

586. Royal Academicians Gathered in Their Council Chambers, 1793, To Judge the Work
of the Students, engraved by C. Bestland, painted by Henry Singleton,
published by Bestland, May 1, 1802

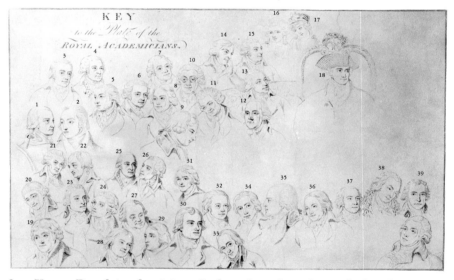

587. Key to Royal Academicians Gathered in Their Council Chambers, 1793,
published by Bestland, 1802

1. William Hodges. Late Landscape
   Painter to the Prince of Wales
2. Thomas Lawrence. Principal Painter
   in Ordinary to his Majesty
3. James Wyatt. Architect
4. William Tyler. Architect
5. George Dance. Professor in Architecture, & Auditor
6. Sir William Beechey. Portrait Painter
   to her Majesty
7. Charles Catton. Painter
8. Francis Wheatley. Painter
9. Thomas Sandby. Late Professor in
   Architecture
10. Joseph Wilton. Keeper, Sculptor
11. Edward Burch. Librarian & Medal-
    list to his Majesty
12. John Richards. Secretary, Painter
13. Ozias Humphry. Portrait Painter in
    Crayons to his Majesty

14. Thomas Stothard. Painter
15. Joseph Nollekens. Sculptor
16. Angelica Kauffmann. Painter
17. Mary Lloyd. Painter
18. Benjamin West. President & Histori-
    cal Painter to his Majesty
19. Sir William Chambers. Architect,
    late Treasurer
20. Francesco Bartolozzi. Engraver to
    his Majesty
21. Paul Sandby. Painter
22. John Zoffany. Painter
23. Philip James de Loutherbourg.
    Painter
24. Richard Cosway. Principal Painter to
    the Prince of Wales
25. Edmund Garvey. Painter
26. Henry Fuseli. Professor in Painting
27. John Francis Rigaud. Painter

28. James Barry. Late Professor in Paint-
    ing
29. Sir Francis Bourgeois. Landscape
    Painter to his Majesty & to the
    King of Poland
30. John Singleton Copley. Painter
31. Richard Westall. Painter
32. Robert Smirke. Painter
33. James Northcote. Painter
34. John Opie. Painter
35. Joseph Farington. Painter
36. William Hamilton. Painter
37. John Russell. Crayon Painter to his
    Majesty & to the Prince of Wales
38. Thomas Banks. Sculptor
39. John Hoppner. Portrait Painter to
    the Prince of Wales
40. John Bacon. Sculptor

589. John Singleton Copley, engraved after a drawing by Paul Sandby, published in 1798

588. John Singleton Copley, etched by
W. Daniell, drawn by George
Dance on March 30, 1793

590. William Ponsonby, Second Earl of
Bessborough   *1790*

591. Henry Belasyse, Second Earl of
Fauconberg   *before 1794*

592. The Red Cross Knight   *1793*

593. Sketch for The Red Cross Knight   *1792–93*

595. Admiral the Honorable Samuel
Barrington   1787–95

596. Richard Earl Howe. Admiral of the Fleet

594. Charles, Second Earl and First Marquis Cornwallis   before 1793

598. John Quincy Adams   1796

597. Admiral the Honorable Samuel
Barrington   1791–95

599. Charles I Demanding in the House of Commons the Five Impeached Members   1782–95

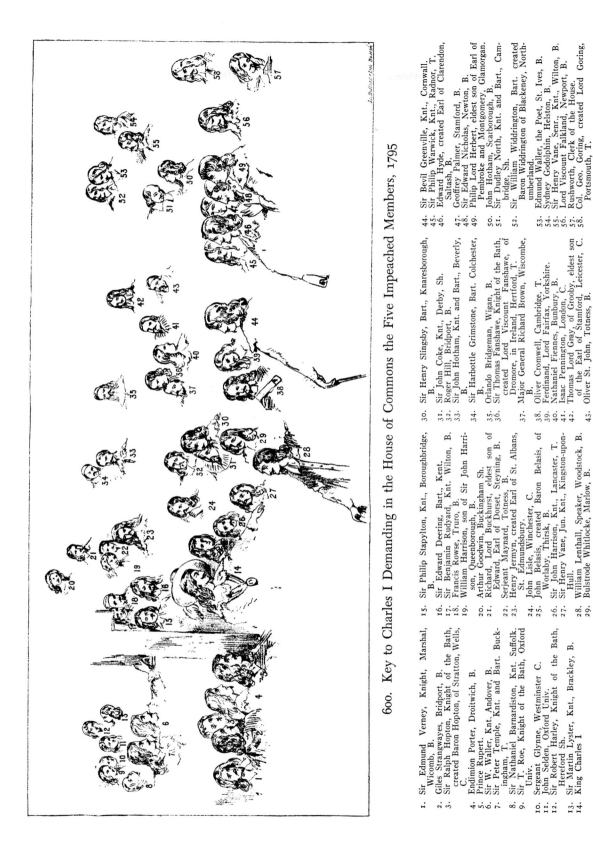

600. Key to Charles I Demanding in the House of Commons the Five Impeached Members, 1795

1. Sir Edmund Verney, Knight, Marshal, Wicomb, B.
2. Giles Strangwayes, Bridport, B.
3. Sir Ralph Hopton, Knight of the Bath, created Baron Hopton, of Stratton, Wells, C.
4. Endimion Porter, Droitwich, B.
5. Prince Rupert.
6. Sir W. Waller, Knt. Andover, B.
7. Sir Peter Temple, Knt. and Bart. Buckingham, T.
8. Sir Nathaniel Barnardiston, Knt. Suffolk.
9. Sir T. Roe, Knight of the Bath, Oxford Univ.
10. Sergeant Glynne, Westminster C.
11. John Selden, Oxford Univ.
12. Sir Robert Harley, Knight of the Bath, Hereford Sh.
13. Sir Martin Lyster, Knt., Brackley, B.
14. King Charles I

15. Sir Philip Stapylton, Knt., Boroughbridge, B.
16. Sir Edward Deering, Bart., Kent.
17. Sir Benjamin Rudyard, Knt. Wilton, B.
18. Francis Rowse, Truro, B.
19. William Harrison, son of Sir John Harrison, Queenborough, B.
20. Arthur Goodwin, Buckingham Sh.
21. Richard, Lord Buckhurst, eldest son of Edward, Earl of Dorset, Steyning, B.
22. Serjeant Maynard, Totness, B.
23. Henry Jermyn, created Earl of St. Albans, St. Edmundsbury.
24. John Lisle, Winchester, C.
25. John Belasis, created Baron Belasis, of Worlaby, Thirsk, B.
26. Sir John Harrison, Knt., Lancaster, T.
27. Sir Henry Vane, Jun. Knt., Kingston-upon-Hull.
28. William Lenthall, Speaker, Woodstock, B.
29. Bulstrode Whitlocke, Marlow, B.

30. Sir Henry Slingsby, Bart., Knaresborough, B.
31. Sir John Coke, Knt., Derby, Sh.
32. Roger Hill, Bridport, B.
33. Sir John Hotham, Knt. and Bart., Beverly, B.
34. Sir Harbottle Grimstone, Bart. Colchester, B.
35. Orlando Bridgeman, Wigan, B.
36. Sir Thomas Fanshawe, Knight of the Bath, created Lord Viscount Fanshawe, of Dromore, in Ireland, Hertford, T.
37. Major General Richard Richard Brown, Wiscombe, B.
38. Oliver Cromwell, Cambridge, T.
39. Ferdinand, Lord Fairfax, Yorkshire.
40. Nathaniel Fiennes, Bunbury, B.
41. Isaac Pennington, London, C.
42. Thomas Lord Gray, of Grooby, eldest son of the Earl of Stamford, Leicester, C.
43. Oliver St. John, Totness, B.

44. Sir Bevil Greenville, Knt., Cornwall.
45. Sir Philip Warwick, Knt., Radnor, T.
46. Edward Hyde, created Earl of Clarendon, Saltash, B.
47. Geoffrey Palmer, Stamford, B.
48. Sir Edward Nicholas, Newton, B.
49. Philip Lord Herbert, eldest son of Earl of Pembroke and Montgomery, Glamorgan.
50. John Hotham, Scarborough, B.
51. Sir Dudley North, Knt. and Bart., Cambridge, Sh.
52. Sir William Widdrington, Bart. created Baron Widdrington of Blackeney, Northumberland.
53. Edmund Waller, the Poet, St. Ives, B.
54. Sydney Godolphin, Helston, B.
55. Sir Henry Vane, Senr., Knt., Wilton, B.
56. Lord Viscount Falkland, Newport, B.
57. Rushworth, Clerk of the House.
58. Col. Geo. Goring, created Lord Goring, Portsmouth, T.

601. Sketch for Charles I Demanding in the House of Commons the Five Impeached Members   1782–94

605. Sketch for Monmouth Before James II Refusing To Give the Names of His Accomplices   1782–94

607. Sacrifice of Isaac, engraved by Schelte à Bolswert, after Theodore Rombouts

606. Abraham Offering Up His Son Isaac, mezzotint by Robert Dunkarton, published by Copley, Nov. 1, 1797

609. Hagar and Ishmael in the Wilderness, mezzotint by
R. Dunkarton, published by Copley, July 2, 1798

608. Study for Abraham Offering Up His Son Isaac   1791–96

610   Saul Renewed by Samuel for Not Obeying the Commandments of the Lord   1708

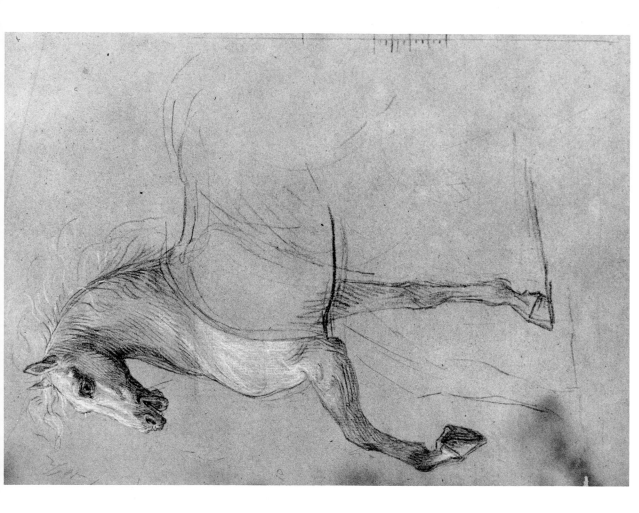

612. Study for Saul Reproved by Samuel for Not Obeying the Commandments
of the Lord   1797–98

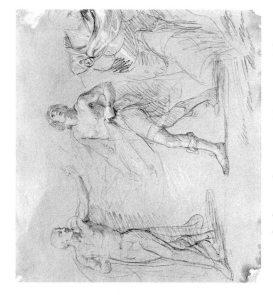

611. Study for Saul Reproved by Samuel for Not
Obeying the Commandments of the Lord
1797–98

613. Study for Saul Reproved by Samuel for Not
Obeying the Commandments of the Lord
1797–98

614. Henry Addington, First Viscount Sidmouth (as Speaker of the House)   *1797–98*

615. Henry Addington, First Viscount Sidmouth
c. 1797–98

616. Henry Addington, First Viscount Sidmouth
1809

617. John Andrew Graham   *1798*

Engraved by Ridley from an Original Picture by Copley

Richard Brocklesby, M.D. F.R.S.

Published by J. Sewell, Cornhill. June 1st 1798.

618. Richard Brocklesby, stipple
engraving by W. Ridley, painted
by Copley, published by J.
Sewell, plate in *European
Magazine*, 1798

619. Adam Viscount Duncan, Admiral of the White   *1797*

620. Adam Viscount Duncan, Admiral of the White   *1798*

621. The Victory of Lord Duncan (Surrender of the Dutch Admiral DeWinter to Admiral Duncan, Oct. 11, 1797)
1798. 00

622. Key to the Victory of Lord Duncan, 1799

5. Admiral Lord Duncan
3. Admiral De Winter
4. Captain Sir W. Fairfax
2. Captain Cleland
1. Mr. Porteous the Pilot
6. Mr. Burnet, Secretary to Lord Duncan

7. Lieutenant Little
8. Captain Trollope, of the Marines
11. Mr. Patterson the Master
9. Captain Oswald
10. Mr. Thompson, Midshipman
12. John Crawford, seaman

623. Study for The Victory of Lord Duncan   *1798*

624. Study for The Victory of Lord Duncan
1798

625. Study for The Victory of
Lord Duncan   *1798*

626. Study for The Victory of Lord Duncan   *1798*

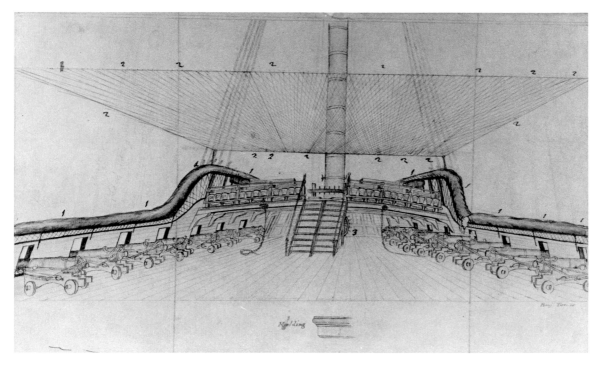

627. Benjamin Turner: "Quarter Deck & Poop of the Venerable," pen and watercolor on letter
from Lieutenant John Little to Copley, March 5, 1795

628. George John, Second Earl Spencer   *1799–1806*

630. John, Second Viscount Dudley and Ward   *before 1804*

629. George John, Second Earl Spencer   *1800*

631. William, Third Viscount Dudley and Ward   *1800*

632. Julia, Third Viscountess Dudley and Ward   *1800*

634. Mrs. Gardiner Greene (Elizabeth Copley)   *1800–03*

633.   Study for Julia, Third Viscountess Dudley and Ward
1799–1800

635. Colonel Fitch Saying Farewell to His Sisters, the Misses Fitch   1800–01

638. The Knatchbull Family, Sir Edward
Knatchbull, 8th Bt.   *1800–03*

637.   The Knatchbull Family,
Mary Knatchbull   *1800–03*

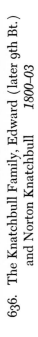

636.   The Knatchbull Family, Edward (later 9th Bt.)
and Norton Knatchbull   *1800–03*

639. Sketch for The Knatchbull Family   *1800–02*

640. Sketch for Norton Knatchbull
1800–03, probably 1800–01

641. Study for The Knatchbull Family, a Daughter
1801–02

642. Study for The Knatchbull Family,
Edward (9th Bt.) and Norton
Knatchbull *1800–02*

643. Study for The Knatchbull Family, Norton
Knatchbull *1800–02*

644. Study for The Knatchbull Family, Lady
Knatchbull and Children   *1800–02*

646. Study for The Knatchbull Family, Lady
Knatchbull and Child   *1800–02*

645. Study for The Knatchbull Family, Lady Knatchbull and Children
(verso of 647)   *1800–02*

647. Study for The Knatchbull Family, Lady Knatchbull and Children
(recto of 645)　　*1800–02*

648. Study for The Knatchbull Family, a Daughter
1800–02

649. Study for The Knatchbull Family, Sir
Edward Knatchbull, 8th Bt.　　*1800–02*

657. Richard Codman   *c. 1790*

658. John Codman (I)   *c. 1800*

659. John Codman (II)   *c. 1800*

660. Reverend John Codman   *1808*

661. George IV (as Prince of Wales)   *1804–10*

662. The Duke of Arenberg, engraved
by Pieter de Bailliu, after Van Dyck

663. Study for George IV (as Prince of Wales), head of George IV
1804–09

664. Study for George IV (as Prince of
Wales), George IV   *1804–06*

665. Study for George IV (as Prince of
Wales), Lord Heathfield
1804–06

666. Study for George IV (as Prince of Wales)   *1804–09*

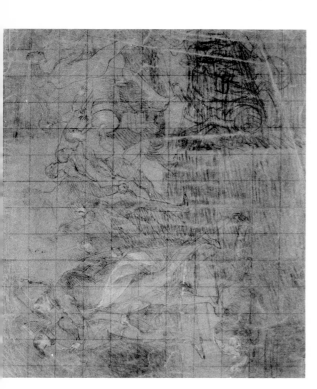

668. Unknown Subject, study for a history painting
c. 1810

670. Unknown Subject, study for a history painting   c. 1810

667. Unknown Subject, study for a history painting
c. 1810

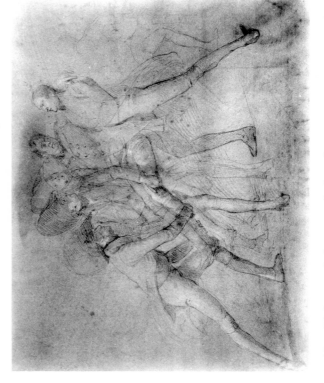

669. Unknown Subject, study for a history painting   c. 1810

671. Prince of Orange (later William VII,
King of Holland)   *c. 1812–13*

672. Prince of Orange (later William VII, King
of Holland)   *c. 1812–13*

673. Battle of the Pyrenees   *1812–15*

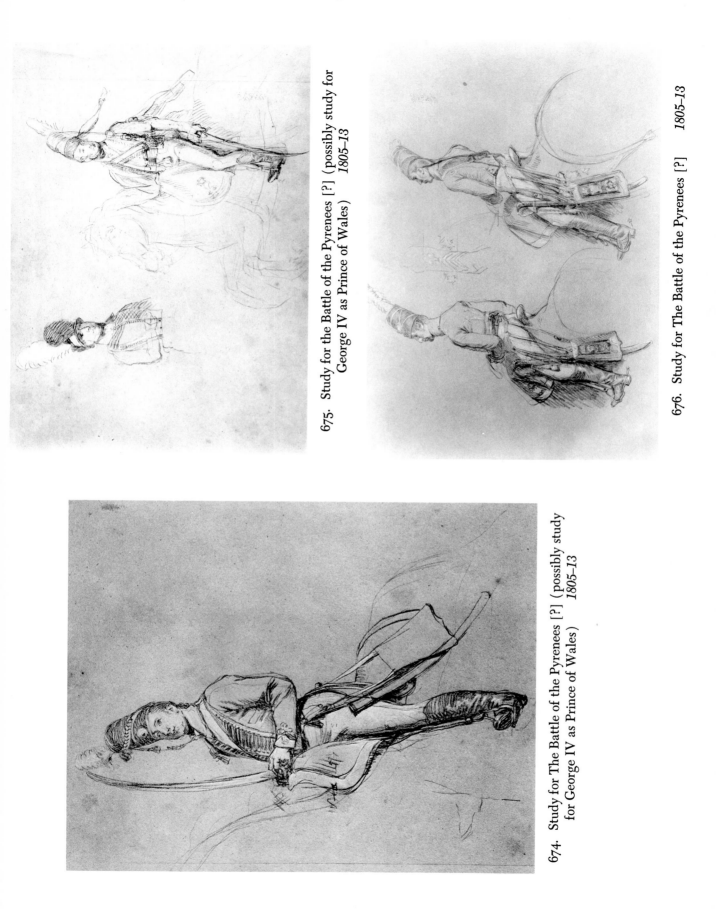

675. Study for the Battle of the Pyrenees [?] (possibly study for George IV as Prince of Wales) 1805–13

676. Study for The Battle of the Pyrenees [?] 1805–13

674. Study for The Battle of the Pyrenees [?] (possibly study for George IV as Prince of Wales) 1805–13

677. John Singleton Copley, Jr.   *c. 1813*

678. The Siege of Dunkirk   *1814–15*

Index

Index

This index covers the text and notes of both volumes, and selected parts of the appendices. The names of all Copley sitters are italicized. For biographical information on American sitters, see the appendices to vol. one, pp. 97–199. For data on specific works, see the American checklist, vol. one, pp. 205–44, and the English catalogue, vol. two, pp. 409–61.

INDEX

Winthrop, Mrs. John, 89, 98n. (Fig. 327)
Winthrop, Samuel, 89. (Fig. 329)
Wissing, William, *Princess Anne*, 19
Woburn, Mass., JSC sitter resident in, 118
Wollaston, John, 48
Woodforde, Samuel, 369n
Woodward, Joseph, 341
Woolett, E., 324n
Woolett, William, 325n
Worcester, Mass., 313
Worcester Art Museum, 14n, 25n, 35n
World, 288, 300n, 320, 327 and n, 328, 331n, 335n
Wrentham, Mass., JSC sitters resident in, 120
Wright, Joseph, of Derby, 34, 253, 314, 345n; *Children of Hugh and Sarah Wood*, 295n; *De-struction of the Spanish Floating Batteries off Gibraltar*, 325n
Wyatt, James, 366 and n, 367, 368, 369, 375

Yale University, 16n, 26n; JSC sitters attended, 123
Yale University Art Gallery, 30, 35n, 308, 309
Yale University Library, 92n, 296n, 310n
Yankee Doodle, parody on, 380n
Yarmouth, 353
Yenn, John, 366, 367, 368, 380n
York, Archbishop of, 286n
Young Lady with a Bird and Dog. See *Warner, Mary* [?]

Zoffany, Johann, 318